D1031827

What are the possibilities for democratic change in the United States? In *Goldbugs and Greenbacks,* Gretchen Ritter considers the great financial debate of the late nineteenth century in which farmers and workers fought to redirect economic policy. Ritter argues that both groups believed money and banking were key to continued economic opportunity for all.

Beyond the discussion about gold and silver was a broader dialogue about sectionalism, race relations, and the changing class structure. The farmer-labor groups that promoted antimonopolism contended that without a fair financial system the country would degenerate into a two-class society of very rich and very poor in which democracy would wither.

The antimonopolist movement failed, but the nature and fate of this distinctive and neglected political tradition, examined in depth in *Goldbugs and Greenbacks,* tells us a great deal about the possibilities for political change in America.

GOLDBUGS AND GREENBACKS

GOLDBUGS AND GREENBACKS

*The Antimonopoly Tradition
and the Politics of Finance in America*

GRETCHEN RITTER
University of Texas at Austin

CAMBRIDGE
UNIVERSITY PRESS

Published by the Press Syndicate of the University of Cambridge
The Pitt Building, Trumpington Street, Cambridge CB2 1RP
40 West 20th Street, New York, NY 10011-4211, USA
10 Stamford Road, Oakleigh, Melbourne 31566, Australia

First published 1997

Printed in the United States of America

Library of Congress Cataloging-in-Publication Data
Ritter, Gretchen.
Goldbugs and greenbacks : the antimonopoly tradition and the
politics of finance in America / Gretchen Ritter.
p.   cm.
Includes index.
ISBN 0-521-56167-1
1. Greenbacks.   2. Paper money – United States – History – 19th
century.   3. Gold standard – United States – History – 19th century.
4. Currency question – United States – History – 19th century.
5. Populism – United States – History – 19th century.   6. United
States – Politics and government – 1895–1900.   I. Title.
HG604.R57   1997
332.4'2 – DC20   96-25089
                                                                CIP

A catalog record for this book is available from the British Library.

ISBN 0-521-56167-1 hardback

For SK

Contents

Preface and acknowledgments

What are the possibilities for democratic change in the United States? This is the question that led me to write this book. To answer it, I examined efforts to regulate economic existence. I was interested in the political governance of the conditions of production, the distribution of wealth, the availability of economic opportunity, and the rights of workers. In these and other areas of economic life, the range of political options available to a society, and the extent to which those options provide for the autonomy and well-being of the population, are useful measures of democracy.

In the late nineteenth century, a series of farmer-labor parties promoted a political program that would change the governance of economic life. Their interest in economic issues stemmed from the belief that the preservation of economic opportunity was essential for meaningful democracy. These were the antimonopolists, and they included the Greenbackers, the Knights of Labor, and the Populists, among others. When I first became acquainted with the antimonopolists, I was struck by the depth and persistence of this tradition. These groups fielded candidates and participated in national debates on economic issues in every major election during the 1870s, 1880s, and 1890s.

Other scholars have noted the significance of the farmer-labor tradition in the late nineteenth century, when the United States was undergoing a transition from a primarily agrarian economy to a primarily industrial economy. What is less noted, however, and what is central to this book, is the prominence the antimonopolists gave to the financial question.

The financial question concerned what sort of monetary standard the country should have, how it should be regulated, and how the banking system should be structured. From the close of the Civil War until 1900, there was a great national debate over this issue, not unlike the debate over slavery that preceded the war. It was a debate that common citizens became involved in, that sold thousands of political pamphlets explaining the merits of silver or the necessity of gold, and that helped determine the outcome of one of the country's most important presidential contests – the election of 1896. Yet the extent and substance of this debate have not been widely considered.

Why were citizens in the late nineteenth century so interested in money? The debate was about more than the proper level of bank reserves or the benefits of gold versus silver. At the broadest level, the financial question concerned the direction of political and economic development. Other great political issues of the day – including sectional relations, changing class categories, nationalism versus internationalism, and racial and ethnic animosities – became intertwined with the debate over finance.

There were two main positions in the financial debate – financial conservatism and antimonopolism. The financial conservatives (mostly businessmen and financiers) were fervent in their defense of the gold standard, which they saw as providing a sound basis for the growth of the national economy. The antimonopolists (mostly farmers and laborers) saw the money and banking systems as central to their quest for economic opportunity for all classes and regions of the country. Without such opportunity, the Greenbackers and Populists believed that the nation would degenerate into a stratifed, two-class society in which real democratic community would wither. This book is about the antimonopolist tradition and what its failure tells us about the processes of political change in America.

One of the themes of the book is that history shapes politics. The failure of antimonopolism did not occur because its program was politically unpopular or economically naive. To understand the failure of the antimonopolists, one must see that political competition is historically contingent. Both the antimonopolists and their opponents used history to legitimate their cause or to vilify the opposition. Both sides were affected by their place in history – the Populists came to the fore just as organized labor was on the retreat; the Republicans took office just as the gold depression ended. Historical factors helped determine the winners and losers in this contest. History was also used by the political victors to shape the historical understanding with which later generations came to see the antimonopolists. It is perhaps for this reason that we know so little about them and the great debate in which they participated.

Many individuals have helped and influenced this work along the way. Thanks are due to my teachers – Suzanne Berger, Walter Dean Burnham, Joshua Cohen, Ira Katznelson, Michael Lipsky, and Charles Sabel – who encouraged, criticized, and provoked my thinking. They have all had a deep impact on my intellectual outlook. The mid-1980s was a wonderful time to be in the Political Science Department at MIT. In addition to having excellent teachers, I profited from the friendship and intellectual comraderie of my peers, including Stephen Amberg, Lawrence Aronovitch, Gerald Berk, Laura Hastings, Victoria Hattam, Christopher Heye, Roger Karapin, Richard Kazis, Anthony Levitas, Richard Locke, Cathie Jo Martin, Sharon Moran, and Simona Piattoni. I am especially grateful to Gerry Berk, whose intellectual depth and personal generosity I have benefitted from on many occasions.

I received able assistance from librarians and archivists at the Baker Library at Harvard University, the Boston Public Library, the Chicago Historical Society, the Duke University Libraries, the Houghton Library at Harvard University, the Illinois State Historical Library, the Manuscript Division of the Library of Congress, the Massachusetts Historical Society, the Newberry Library, the North Carolina Collection at the University of North Carolina in Chapel Hill, the North Carolina State Archives, the Southern History Collection, the State Historical Society of Wisconsin, and the University of Chicago Libraries.

I have also learned a great deal from my colleagues at the University of Texas at Austin, where I have been an assistant professor since 1992. My thanks go to Kirsten Belgum, Catherine Boone, David Braybrooke, Walter Dean Burnham, John Coleman (now at the University of Wisconsin at Madison), Ann Cvetkovich, James Fishkin, Michael Hanchard (now at Northwestern University), Barbara Harlow, Martha Merritt (now at Notre Dame), Anne Norton (now at the University of Pennsylvania), Lora Romero (now at Stanford University), Bartholomew Sparrow, Peter Trubowitz, Jeffrey Tulis, and Robert Vitalis (now at Clark University).

My deepest gratitude goes to Dean Burnham, Anne Norton, and Jeff Tulis, who each read and gave incisive comments on substantial portions of the text. The university supplied me with fellowship funds for one summer and part of one year away while I revised the manuscript. Suzanne Colwell of the Government Department at UT Austin assisted in preparing the manuscript. The university was also instrumental (special thanks to Dean Sheldon Ekland-Olson) in staging a conference on history and American political development held in Austin in 1994. That conference helped further my thinking on the issue of historical contingency.

I would like to thank all of the students from my "Topics in American Political Development" course for their feedback on some of the ideas developed in this book. Luis Guevara and Keith Abouchar provided me with able research assistance one summer.

Other people at other institutions have also helped with reading, suggestions, and sources. They include Richard Bensel, Sarah Deutsch, Leon Fink, Carlos Forment, Lawrence Goodwyn, Deborah Harrold, James Livingston, Eileen McDonagh, Uday Mehta, Karen Orren, Michael Rogin, Theda Skocpol, Richard Valelly, and Sean Wilentz. Richard Bensel, one of the readers of the manuscript for Cambridge University Press, is someone that I have come to greatly respect for the kindness and generosity with which he responded to my work. The Center for Domestic and Comparative Policy Studies at Princeton University provided me with a friendly and stimulating atmosphere while I finished the final version of the manuscript during the 1994–95 academic year. Paul DiMaggio, Kathleen McNamara, Sonya Michel, Sandy Paroly, Donald Stokes, and James Trussell were among those who made my year at Princeton enjoyable and productive. My editor at Cambridge University Press, Alex Holzman, has been encouraging throughout the preparation of this book. My manuscript editor, Ronald Cohen, made many suggestions that improved the book.

Finally, my thanks to my family. My parents, Sandra Herries and David Ritter, have always supported my academic pursuits. My partner, Sean Keel, has lived with this project since its inception. He has challenged, edited, encouraged, listened, and loved. This book is better because of him. Last, thanks to my daughter, Rose Hannah Ritter Keel, whose impending arrival motivated this book's completion.

1

The money debate
and American
political development

Here is the line of battle . . . If they tell us that the gold standard is the standard of civilization, we reply to them that this, the most enlightened of all
the nations on the earth, has never declared for a gold standard . . . More
than that; we can tell them that they will search the pages of history in vain
to find a single instance where the common people of any land have ever declared themselves in favor of the gold standard. They can find where the
holders of fixed investments have declared for a gold standard, but not where
the masses have.

William Jennings Bryan[1]

Thus began the presidential contest of 1896, a defining moment in American politics. It was a contest about money, pitting Republican William
McKinley against Democrat William Jennings Bryan. This election, referred to as the "Battle of the Standards," was the culmination of a debate between the supporters of financial reform (greenbackism and bimetallism) and the defenders of the gold standard. It was also a battle over
competing visions of America's political and economic future. In the three
decades prior to McKinley's victory, the money debate was central to
American politics. Half a dozen national third parties were formed, scores
of state-level parties organized and the two national parties were reorganized around this issue. Hundreds of books and pamphlets were released
in the argument over the nature of money and its role in regulating relations between classes and sections. At least one of these publications,
Coin's Financial School, reached a circulation of one million. Each of
these efforts contributed to the debate over finance. This book is about

---

1. This quote from Bryan's famous "Cross of Gold" speech given at the Democratic national convention in Chicago in 1896 can be found in William Jennings Bryan, *The First
Battle* (Chicago: W. B. Conkey, 1896), p. 205.

what was at stake in that contest and what can be learned from the anti-monopolists who fought for financial reform.[2]

The stakes were substantial. The nature of the national economy, the power of the sections, the relations between classes, the role of government, and the place of democratic citizens were all debated by the advocates of financial reform and financial orthodoxy. When the conflict concluded and the proponents of financial reform lost their position in national political competition, the country's political economy took on a new and distinctive shape. After a period of political possibility, the South retreated to an impoverished, extractive economy with little political competition and firm elite rule. This was the Solid South. The national party system that took shape after the critical election of 1896 was less participatory and competitive than what preceded or followed it. Likewise the federal government's role shifted from managing distributive issues to economic regulatory matters. This shift accompanied changes in the economy, from agriculture to industry, from firms to corporations, and from less integrated capital markets to a national capital market centered in New York and poised to fund large industrial investment projects. All of these changes have been carefully studied by scholars from numerous disciplines. This book addresses many of these issues through the lens of the money debate.

Goldbugs and Greenbacks has three themes. First is an exploration of the money debate as a dominant issue in American politics between 1865 and 1896. This wide-ranging national discussion about banks and money often dominated the political agenda during the three decades after the Civil War. I consider the ongoing character and significance of the contest over finance.

Second, *Goldbugs and Greenbacks* postulates the existence of two main programmatic alternatives in the money debate, and focuses attention on the failed alternative, financial antimonopolism. Antimonopolism addressed the economic and political changes of the late nineteenth century by calling for government regulation of the financial structure as a means of insuring economic opportunity and equal political rights for all classes and sections. Both the antimonopolists and the financial conservatives saw the financial system as central to economic and political development. I cover the vision of the antimonopolists again, and I argue for the intellectual coherence and political significance of their program

---

2. Much of the drama and language on money debate is captured in Bryan's *The First Battle*. The national parties formed included the Labor Reform party, the Greenback and Greenback Labor parties, the Antimonopolist party, the Union Labor party, the People's (Populist) party, and the National (Gold) Democratic party. For *Coin's* circulation figure, see Richard Hofstadter's introduction to William H. Harvey, *Coin's Financial School* (Cambridge, MA: Belknap Press, 1963), p. 5.

through an exploration of the pamphlet material that they and their opponents produced.

Third, *Goldbugs and Greenbacks* contributes to our understanding of the role of history in American political development. I call for both a reconsideration of the role of temporal order in shaping political opportunities and an analysis of the historical narratives that mediate our understanding of political change. Although the antimonopolists were politically defeated, I reinterpret the character of their failure and its significance for American political development.

This chapter introduces the money debate, its origins, and the programs and participants behind antimonopolism. Then it presents my theoretical approach, beginning with a discussion of history and political development, followed by shorter sections on the political economy of money and the political culture of money. The last section provides a brief summary of the rest of the book.

I. Antimonopolism and the money debate

The assertion that financial policy was a central political issue around which so much else revolved may seem curious to late twentieth-century observers of American politics. Yet the roots of the financial debate were both ideological and institutional. Ideologically, the importance of money dates back at least to the Jeffersonians and Hamiltonians, whose disputes over financial regulation were related to competing conceptions of republicanism. Institutionally, the conflict was more immediately rooted in the establishment of the National Banking System (NBS) and the distribution of government-issued paper currency (greenbacks) during the Civil War. From these sources, the financial debate grew to take up a broad space in the nation's political culture. Americans saw money as something that shaped the national political system. And in the panics, runs, depressions, and price falls of the 1860s to 1890s, they found good reason to keep their attention focused on finance.

Prior to the Civil War, republicanism was the language of resistance to centralized government, chartered corporations, federally sponsored banks, and the growth of a financial aristocracy associated with the increased fiscal capacities of the state. Banks and bondsmen were regarded as a danger to American society and the national government. Attacks on them were framed as part of a broader concern with corruption and the loss of citizen virtue. In the 1790s, John Taylor of Carolina opposed the Hamiltonian plan and its provision for a central bank. Taylor argued that this "dangerous monopoly" was designed "to make the rich, richer and the poor, poorer." In doing so, the Bank would succeed in corrupting the republic, for it demonstrated that a "design for erecting aristocracy and monarchy is subsisting, that a money impulse and not the public good is operating in Congress."[3]

Similar sentiments were expressed by William Leggett in an attack on the Second Bank of the United States during the Jacksonian era. He wrote, "First, we object to it as founded on a species of monopoly; and secondly, as supplying a circulating medium which rests on a basis liable to all the fluctuations and contingencies of commerce and trade," that is, on paper money. Having been given exclusive privileges by the state, chartered banks violated the equal rights doctrine, they held power as one group in society over others, which had implications for the preservation of republican virtue as well as for the maintenance of free competition. Leggett called for a laissez-faire system that would end economic speculation and tie economic growth to growth in production.[4]

Several elements of this outlook carried over to the postbellum antimonopoly movement, including concern with corruption and economic monopolies, the desire to preserve an independent and virtuous citizenry,

3. Lance Banning, *The Jeffersonian Persuasion* (Ithaca, NY: Cornell University Press, 1978), p.197. Major works on republicanism and the American political tradition include Joyce Appleby, *Liberalism and Republicanism in the Historical Imagination* (Cambridge, MA: Harvard University Press, 1992); Bernard Bailyn, *The Ideological Origins of the American Revolution* (Cambridge: Harvard University Press, 1967); Gordon Wood, *The Creation of the American Republic, 1776–1787* (NY: Norton, 1969); J. G. A. Pocock, *The Machiavellian Moment: Florentine Political Thought and the Atlantic Republican Tradition* (Princeton: Princeton University Press, 1975); Robert E. Shalhope, "Toward a Republican Synthesis: The Emergence of an Understanding of Republicanism in American Historiography," *William and Mary Quarterly*, 29 (1972): 49–80, and "Republicanism and Early American Historiography," *William and Mary Quarterly*, 39 (1982): 334–356; Isaac Kramnick, "Republican Revisionism Revisited," *American Historical Review*, 87 (1982): 629–654; and Lance Banning, "Jeffersonian Ideology Revisited: Liberal and Classical Ideas in the New American Republic," and Joyce Appleby, "Republicanism in Old and New Contexts," *William and Mary Quarterly*, 43 (1986): 3–34.
4. Lawrence H. White, ed., *Democratick Editorials: Essays in Jacksonian Political Economy by William Leggett* (Indianapolis, Liberty Press, 1984), p.74. On Jacksonian economics, see Bray Hammond, *Banks and Politics in America* (Princeton: Princeton University Press, 1957); Robert V. Remini, *Andrew Jackson and the Bank War* (New York: Norton, 1967); James R. Sharp, *The Jacksonians versus the Banks* (New York: Columbia University Press, 1970); and Peter Temin, *The Jacksonian Economy* (New York: Norton, 1970). On Jacksonian ideology, the classic work remains Marvin Meyers, *The Jacksonian Persuasion* (Stanford, CA: Stanford University Press, 1957). Concerning early labor republicanism, see Amy Bridges, "On Becoming American," in *Working Class Formation*, Ira Katznelson and Aristide Zolberg, eds. (Princeton: Princeton University Press, 1986); Sean Wilentz, *Chants Democratic: New York City and the Rise of the American Working Class, 1788–1850* (New York: Oxford University Press, 1984); and Alan Dawley, *Class and Community: The Industrial Revolution in Lynn* (Cambridge, MA: Harvard University Press, 1976). It should be noted that my reading of Leggett as a laissez-faire republican differs from the usual readings of him as a classical liberal.

and resistance to the extension of special privileges by the state. Yet, there were important differences as well. Later antimonopolists gave up anti-statism of the laissez-fairists, and many divorced themselves from the bullionism of the Jacksonians. The roots of this approach to monetary regulation may be found in the work of Edward Kellogg.

Although Kellogg was also part of the Jacksonian era, his work was decidedly different in tone and implications from the work of William Leggett. In *Labor and Other Capital: The Rights of Each Secured and the Wrongs of Both Eradicated,* (published in 1849), Kellogg laid out his legal tender theory of money and his theory of interest. These theories, which resembled the work of the French political economist Pierre Joseph Proudhon, delineated the roles of labor (that is, producers), capital, and government in economic development. Kellogg postulated that money was a legal creation whose value derived from government authority, and that interest was the means by which wealth was transferred from the producers of wealth to the holders of capital. The rate of interest and control of currency were crucial to economic expansion and the distribution of wealth between classes and regions. Kellogg argued that low interest rates and a flexible monetary system would provide the basis for a balanced economy and society, in which both labor and capital received their just rewards and extreme wealth or poverty was prevented. Unlike Leggett, then, Kellogg saw government as having a positive role in economic regulation, and saw the monetary system as a legally created entity rather than an element in a natural economy. The theory fit well with the political philosophy of labor republicanism. Kellogg's analysis of the role of the financial system became the basis for late nineteenth-century critiques of financial monopolies, the maldistribution of currency and credit, and the unbalanced nature of economic development in the growing corporate economy.[5]

Briefly, there were three central principles of financial antimonopolism in the post-Civil War period. The first concerned the distinction between independent and dependent citizens, or between producers and nonproducers. As a virtuous protector of the republic, an independent citizen was economically autonomous and concerned with the general interests of society. As labor leader William Sylvis said about working men, "A high degree of intelligence is necessary to enable us to discharge all the duties of

---

5. On Kellogg, see Chester MacArthur Destler, "The Influence of Edward Kellogg Upon American Radicalism, 1865–1896," in *American Radicalism, 1865–1901: Essays and Documents* (New London: Connecticut College, 1946), pp.50–77. Destler traces the use of Kellogg's ideas by the Knights of Labor, National Labor Union, greenbackers, and Populists, among others.

citizens. If we were sufficiently well paid for from six to eight hours work a day, to furnish ourselves with the means of cultivation, we would do better work and be more useful men." Dependent citizens fell into three categories: the poor and subservient (such as slaves, wives, and unskilled wage workers); wealthy nonproducers who depended on the labor of others (such as masters, bankers, and financiers); and permanent, self-interested government workers (such as career military men and tax collectors). For antimonopolists, the economic autonomy of producers and the political autonomy of independent citizens were interdependent.[6]

The second principle of antimonopolism was fear of political and economic corruption. Concern with corruption and the dangers of political instability are traditional republican issues. For the antimonopolists, corruption was represented in very distinct forms. Political corruption came mainly from the efforts of nonproducers to bend the government to their own interests, for example, when railroad lobbyists bribed legislators to pass laws favorable to their companies, or when foreign agents pressed for the demonetization of silver (the supposed "Crime of '73"). Economic corruption within society threatened the foundations of the republic. When nonproducers used special privileges granted by the government to exploit producers, they threatened to turn the country from a society of independent masses to one of dependent classes. Reflecting on this threat of corruption and the demands of independent citizenship, Knights of Labor (KOL) leader George McNeil wrote that there was "an inevitable and irresistible conflict between the wage system of labor and the republican system of government."[7]

Third, the antimonopolists were centrally concerned with the role of the financial system as the medium of corruption and exploitation. By distributing the nation's economic resources, the banking system was a powerful arbiter of economic opportunity. Further, government management

---

6. James C. Sylvis, *The Life, Speeches, Labors and Essays of William H. Sylvis* (Reprinted NY: Augustus M. Kelley Pubs, 1968 [orig. 1872]), p.113. Also see Victoria C. Hattam, *Labor Visions and State Power: The Origins of Business Unionism in the United States* (Princeton: Princeton University Press, 1993), pp. 97–109, for a discussion of antebellum labor republicanism and financial reform sentiment, and Chapter 4 on postwar producerism and the money debate. David Montgomery, *Citizen Worker: The Experience of Workers in the United States with the Democracy and Free Market during the Nineteenth Century* (NY: Cambridge University Press, 1993) discusses labor republicanism and citizenship throughout the nineteenth century. Chapter 1 of Montgomery deals with notions of slavery and wage slavery as defining aspects of labor ideology.
7. Quoted in Kim Voss, *The Making of American Exceptionalism: The Knights of Labor and Class Formation in the Nineteenth Century* (Ithaca: Cornell University Press, 1993), p.80.

of the money supply both indirectly (by determining the monetary standard) and directly (through Treasury operations) affected prices and incomes for producers and debtors more generally. Money could corrupt the government. A corrupted government might use its authority to further strengthen the position of financial managers and elites. The skewed operations of the financial system would then lead to increased inequality and political degeneration. As former Greenbacker James Weaver said at the 1896 Populist convention,

> We cannot be mistaken concerning the real issue involved in the struggle of the present year. It is between the gold standard, gold bonds, and bank currency on the one hand, and the bimetallic standard, no bonds, and government currency on the other. The people are asked to choose between enforced idleness, destitution, debt, bankruptcy and despair on the one hand, and an open door of opportunity under just laws and normal conditions on the other.

Finance was the key to the future economic and political development of the nation.[8]

Institutionally, the money debate addressed the new economic and political structures that emerged from the Civil War. The war destroyed much of the economic base of the South, spurred industrial development nationally, and afforded increasing economic transactions between the Northeast and Midwest. During the war, Congress established new national banking and currency systems. After the war, financial conservatives sought to shrink the money supply and reestablish the gold standard. They also defended the role of the NBS in managing credit and currency distributions. In contrast, the antimonopolists or financial reformers criticized both the gold standard and the NBS for skewing economic opportunities in favor of creditors, industry, and the Northeast. When antimonopolists and financial conservatives sought to promote their positions within the political arena, they discovered that the major parties avoided direct confrontation on monetary issues, and worked to maintain voter loyalty by rehearsing old Civil War antagonisms instead. Despite its breadth and duration, the financial debate was constrained by a party structure that made direct competition between opposing finan-

---

8. This speech was given by James Weaver, a former presidential candidate for both the Populists (1892) and the Greenback Labor party (1880). It is reprinted in Bryan, *The First Battle*, p.278. The centrality of financial reform for the Populists is the theme of Bruce Palmer's *"Man Over Money": The Southern Populist Critique of American Capitalism* (Chapel Hill: University of North Carolina Press, 1980). The importance of money to farmer-labor radicalism in the postwar period more generally is a theme of Chester McArthur Destler's *American Radicalism*. See especially chapters 1–4, 8, 9, and 11.

cial programs difficult. The financial debate both addressed and was affected by institutions that governed the economy and polity.[9]

Beginning with the second annual meeting of the National Labor Union (NLU) in 1866 and extending through the Populist campaigns of 1896, farmer and labor organizations gave prominent attention to their interest in financial reform. Small and medium-sized businessmen and manufacturers were also involved in antimonopolism, especially during the 1870s. Frustrated with the regular parties, the financial reformers established a series of third parties to promote their cause. For every presidential election (and most Congressional elections) between 1872 and 1896, there was a national third party competing that was committed to the cause of financial reform. These included small parties such as the Labor Reform party, the Antimonopolist party, and the Union Labor party. There were also larger parties, particularly the Greenback (and Greenback Labor) parties of the 1870s and the Populist party of the 1890s, which contributed to the realignment of the party system. Whether these parties were organized under the auspices of labor or farmer organizations, they consistently advocated currency expansion, banking reform, and democratic control of the financial system. Antimonopolism was a producers' movement rather than a farmer or labor effort.

The dispute over money spilled over from Congressional debates and the electoral arena to the wider political culture. A clear portrait of the rich cultural politics of money emerges from the books and pamphlets of the postbellum era. The nation was enthralled with the topic of money. Even L. Frank Baum, the author of the children's classic, *The Wonderful Wizard of Oz*, exhibited this fascination. Published in Chicago in 1900, the Oz tale contains numerous allegories about sectionalism, class, race, and gender relations. In the book, the people of the South are separated from their northern neighbors by hard-headed men (Hammerheads) who hold the sections apart. Among the central characters, the Scarecrow and

9. See Richard Bensel, *Yankee Leviathan: The Origins of Central State Authority in America, 1859–1877* (Cambridge: Cambridge University Press, 1990), for a discussion of the economic and institutional changes that emerge from the Civil War. Richard L. McCormick provides a fine review of the literature on party politics in the late nineteenth century in the first three chapters of his collected essays, *The Party Period and Public Policy: American Politics from the Age of Jackson to the Progressive Era* (NY: Oxford University Press, 1986). Other works that deal with labor or agrarian radicalism and the constraints of party politics include Richard Oestreicher, "Urban Working Class Political Behavior and Theories of American Electoral Politics, 1870–1940," *Journal of American History*, 74 (1988): 1257–1286; Sean Wilentz, "Class Consciousness and the American Labor Movement, 1790–1920," *International Labor and Working Class History*, no. 26 (Fall 1984) 1–24; and David Brody, "On the Failure of U.S. Radical Politics: A Farmer-Labor Analysis," *Industrial Relations*, 22 (1983): 141–63.

the Tin Woodman appear as class figures, the former as a senseless farmer and the latter as a hardened worker. The story's Flying Monkeys accord to contemporary images of Native Americans who were banished from the northern woods and placed under authoritarian rule in the West. Dorothy is the all-American girl from the heartland, with the big heart, independence, and daring, a fine example of the sort of woman that the suffragettes had in mind when they promoted their cause. The thread that weaves these themes together is money. Monetary allegories run throughout the book, from silver slippers to a golden cap, to a city the color of greenbacks. The discussion of the Wizard of Oz later in this chapter and throughout this work is a reminder of the broader meanings of monetary politics in the late nineteenth century, and of the ways that historical memory is shaped by political development.[10]

II. History, political development, and the financial debate

Within any work on political change there is an implicit or explicit conception of the role of history in shaping political alternatives and outcomes. Such conceptions have a broad effect on how past political contests and losing alternatives are understood and represented. Over the last couple of decades, as scholars in the social sciences and humanities return to history, their conceptions of history have changed. Recent works mark a break in the treatment of historical representation and historical development. The employment of contingent and interpretive theories of history opens up new possibilities for understanding American political development.[11]

Historical representation concerns the ways in which past events and experiences are depicted in historical accounts. Work on language and representation suggests that all depictions are partial and culturally bounded. Thus, historical accounts may never be said to objectively reproduce the past through the rational collection and ordering of facts and

10. L. Frank Baum, *The Wonderful Wizard of Oz* (Chicago, 1900). An overview of the interpretive literature on the Wizard of Oz appears later in this chapter.
11. The March 1989 issue of the *Journal of American History,* vol. 75, no. 4, is devoted to history and memory, with essays by David Thelen, Jackson Lears, and Leon Fink, among others. Other works that chronicle the shifting use of history in the humanities and social sciences include Hayden White's books, particularly his classic *Metahistory: The Historical Imagination in Nineteenth-century Europe* (Baltimore: Johns Hopkins University Press, 1973) and *Tropics of Discourse: Essays in Cultural Criticism* (Baltimore: Johns Hopkins University Press, 1978); Eric Monkkonen, ed., *Engaging the Past: The Uses of History Across the Social Sciences* (Durham: Duke University Press, 1994); and Brook Thomas, *The New Historicism and Other Old-Fashioned Topics* (Princeton: Princeton University Press, 1991).

artifacts that are opaque and separate (that is, not determined by their historical context) in their meaning. Rather, history, like memory, is understood as a matter of "construction rather than mere reproduction." Every history has a narrative structure and symbolic character that contributes to its argument and meaning.[12]

Students of development look to history to discover the laws of social change. From a modernist perspective, history is viewed as progressive and holistic – as time moves forward, humankind advances economically, politically, and socially. The pairing of industrial development with the spread of democratic rights exemplifies the comprehensive nature of historical progress. [13] Yet what was previously seen as progressive and whole is now often understood as fragmented, layered, and contingent. As social historians recover the experiences of the less powerful or publicly situated groups in society, they introduce competing historical narratives with different periodizations.[14] As political scientists contest the view of American history as a record of expanding liberal practices, politics as progress is displaced by a conflicting history of trends toward inequality and equality.[15] As pivotal political moments are treated as turning points in which real political choices are made, outcomes seem more contingent

12. The quote is drawn from an early study of memory by Frederick Bartlett – *Remembering: A Study of Experimental and Social Psychology* (1932) quoted in David Thelen's "Memory and American History," *Journal of American History,* 75, 4 (March 1989). See also Marshall Sahlins, *Culture and Practical Reason* (Chicago: University of Chicago Press, 1976) and *Islands of History* (Chicago: University of Chicago Press, 1985), and Paul Ricoeur, *A Ricoeur Reader: Reflection and Imagination* (Toronto: University of Toronto Press, 1991).

13. Karl Polanyi, *The Great Transformation* (Boston: Beacon Press, 1957, c1944); Alexander Gerschenkron, *Economic Backwardness in Historical Perspective, a Book of Essays* (New York, 1965); Friedrich A. Hayek, *The Road to Serfdom* (Chicago: University of Chicago Press, 1976, ©1944); Barrington Moore, *Social Origins of Dictatorship and Democracy: Lord and Peasant in the Making of the Modern World* (Boston: Beacon Press, 1967, ©1966); and Joseph Schumpeter, *Capitalism, Socialism and Democracy* (NY: Harper & Row, 1976).

14. Books that exemplify or discuss social history include Sean Wilentz, *Chants Democratic: New York City and the Rise of the American Working Class, 1788–1850* (Oxford: Oxford University Press, 1984); Joan Scott, *Gender and the Politics of History* (NY: Columbia University Press, 1988); and David Roediger, *The Wages of Whiteness: Race and the Making of the American Working Class* (New York: Verso, 1991).

15. Rogers Smith, "Beyond Tocqueville, Myrdal and Hartz: The Multiple Traditions in America," *American Political Science Review* 87 (Sept. 1993): 549–67; Carole Pateman, *The Sexual Contract* (Stanford: Stanford University Press, 1988); Anne Norton, *The Republic of Signs* (Chicago: University of Chicago Press, 1994); Michael Rogin, *Ronald Reagan the Movie and Other Episodes in Political Demonology* (Berkeley: University of California Press, 1987); and Mike Davis, *Prisoners of the American Dream* (London: Verso, 1986).

and less inevitable.[16] And as scholars of American politics examine the relation of the past to the present, they come to think of history as sedimented, layered, and indeterminate – the meaning of the Constitution and the traditions of the presidency are ever open to political reconstruction.[17]

This book uses two related conceptions of history – history as the sequence of time and history as political imagination. The first of these views history as structure, while the second considers history as narrative. The role of temporal sequencing emphasizes timing as a factor in political opportunities and choices. For example, for the Populists it mattered that their political challenge emerged in the wake of a realignment of the labor movement that left the farmers' most likely political allies alienated and unavailable for coalition formation. Likewise, developments in economic organization and the expansion in gold supplies from new mining discoveries at the end of the nineteenth century sustained and supplemented the Republican electoral victories of 1894 and 1896. All of this complicates our understanding of 1896 as a "critical moment," and makes the historical significance of that moment dependent on both prior and subsequent events. The temporal order of events – be they from the past, the present, or the future – affects the nature and significance of political opportunities and outcomes.[18]

Two sets of historical narratives matter for our understanding of the antimonopolists and the money debates. The first is from the post-Civil War period. During the late nineteenth century, various political actors interpreted historical events and experiences as they made claims for political loyalty or justified political goals. To counter the development of a class-based financial reform coalition, Democratic party leaders in North Carolina invoked the Civil War in demanding loyalty to the "party of the fathers" regardless of programmatic politics. Similarly, both parties to the financial debate of the 1890s offered their own interpretations of the lessons of the Greenback Era. For antimonopolists, the 1870s was a pe-

16. The paradigm of such an approach within American politics is critical realignment theory. See Walter Dean Burnham, *Critical Elections: The Mainsprings of American Politics* (New York: Norton, 1970).

17. Jeffrey Tulis, *The Rhetorical Presidency* (Princeton: Princeton University Press, 1987); Stephen Skowronek, *The Politics Presidents Make: Leadership from John Adams to George Bush* (Cambridge, MA: Harvard University Press, 1993); and William F. Harris, *The Interpretable Constitution* (Baltimore: Johns Hopkins University Press, 1993).

18. While I argue that ultimately these competing conceptions of history cannot be successfully separated, as a heuristic device they provide a useful starting point. My conception of the chronological structure of history appears to be similar to Reinhart Koselleck's idea of the prelinguistic or metahistorical aspects of human history. See "Linguistic Change and the History of Events," *Journal of Modern History*, 16, 4 (December 1989): 650–2.

riod in which economic and political elites worked together to create a monetary system that benefitted the few over the many – as exemplified by the "Crime of '73" in which silver was demonetized. For financial conservatives, the 1870s taught that consistent effort to educate the public and lobby national decision-makers worked in halting the schemes of financial heretics. Political leaders may use history to consolidate political identities by recalling common struggles, explain past injustices to demarcate current differences, and map the scope of the politically possible to exclude or legitimate present alternatives.

The second set of narratives are those written by twentieth-century historians and social scientists looking back at the late nineteenth century. There is an interesting dualism in the twentieth-century accounts of the money debate. For some, the 1890s was a critical moment when the political choices made by the American public shaped the future course of the polity. Others view the 1890s as a point in the progression toward modernity. The path was set, the trends clearly discernible. The political contests of the period were just noise surrounding the movement toward technological and social advance. Although these two historical readings of the 1890s seem theoretically opposed, they often coexist in accounts of the era. The drama and suspense of the depression, marches, and elections is remembered. But the outcome is understood as foreordained. This apparently contradictory mixture of historical understandings is itself an expression of the role of history in political development. One sense of historical understanding has been layered over another. Our view of history today gives us a sense of the destiny and legitimacy contained in the outcomes of the 1890s. But within that view remains some memory of the possibilities and political choices faced by the Populists.[19]

The outcome of the money debate has been read into the subsequent accounts of that contest. Irwin Unger's *The Greenback Era* is the definitive treatment of the money debate and antimonopolism (or "soft money" advocacy as he calls it) in the 1870s. There have been three major

---

19. One theoretical account of the problems of modernism in contemporary scholarship can be found in Anthony Giddens, *The Consequences of Modernity* (Stanford: Stanford University Press, 1990). Some of the general histories of the late nineteenth century include Robert D. Marcus, *Grand Old Party: Political Structure in the Gilded Age, 1880–1896* (New York: Oxford University Press, 1971); Samuel P. Hays, *The Response to Industrialism, 1885–1914* (Chicago: University of Chicago Press, 1957); Robert Wiebe, *The Search for Order, 1877–1920* (NY: Hill and Wang, 1967); Paul Kleppner, *The Cross of Culture: A Social Analysis of Midwestern Politics, 1850–1900* (New York: Free Press, 1970); Richard L. McCormick, *The Party System and Public Policy: American Politics from the Age of Jackson to the Progressive Era* (NY: Oxford University Press, 1986); and Richard Jensen, *The Winning of the Midwest: Social and Political Conflict, 1888–1896* (Chicago: University of Chicago Press, 1971).

treatments of Populism since the 1930s: John Hicks' *The Populist Revolt;* Richard Hofstadter's *The Age of Reform;* and Lawrence Goodwyn's *Democratic Promise.* The works of Unger, Hicks, and Hofstadter all display a modernist approach to historical development. I will treat these books together and then discuss the work of Lawrence Goodwyn.[20]

In his 1931 book, John Hicks presented agrarian protesters as rational, self-interested businessmen reacting to an economic downturn. For Hicks, protesting farmers were caught in the transition to a modern economy, and suffered from the fast development of the Western frontier that was fed by railroad expansion. Hicks concurs with the view of Lord Bryce "that perhaps the American West had grown too fast and that if development had been slower 'it might have moved upon better lines.'" Twenty-five years later, in his Pulitzer Prize-winning work, Richard Hofstadter portrayed the Populists as irrational reactionaries seeking to hold on to a romantic agrarian past and fighting against liberal modernism. In describing Populist ideology, he wrote, "The utopia of the Populists was in the past, not the future . . . What they meant – though they did not express themselves in such terms – was that they would like to restore the conditions prevailing before the development of industrialism and the commercialization of agriculture."[21]

Written in the 1960s, Irwin Unger's treatment of the greenbackers combines elements of the approaches by Hicks and Hofstadter. Like Hicks in his account of the Populists, Unger treats the economic hardships and hopes of the greenbackers seriously. The most obvious factor shaping the money debates was "the acquisitiveness normal to men in our society." Yet Unger also stresses political factors (for example, partisanship) and ideological factors as contributors to monetary thinking. Citing Hofstadter, Unger writes of the soft money advocates, "It is, however, in the 'Agrarian Myth,' possibly as much pagan as Christian, that the opponents of specie payment [the resumption of the gold standard] found inspiration and moral support." To varying degrees and in various ways, all three of these authors seem to share the liberal economic vision of the late nineteenth-century financial conservatives, in which good citizens are eco-

20. John D. Hicks, *The Populist Revolt: A History of the Farmers' Alliance and the People's Party* (Lincoln, Nebraska: Bison Books, 1961); Richard Hofstadter, *The Age of Reform: From Bryan to FDR* (New York: Vintage Books, 1955); Lawrence Goodwyn, *The Democratic Promise: The Populist Moment in America* (New York: Oxford University Press, 1976); and Irwin Unger, *The Greenback Era: A Social and Political History of American Finance, 1865–1879* (Princeton: Princeton University Press, 1964). For a broader review of the literature on Populism, see Robert C. McMath, Jr., *American Populism: A Social History, 1877–1898* (New York: Hill and Wang, 1993).
21. Hicks, *The Populist Revolt*, p. 2, Hofstadter, *The Age of Reform*, pp. 62–63.

nomically self-interested, rational actors, and progress comes through stable markets and minimal government regulation.[22]

With the publication of Lawrence Goodwyn's *Democratic Promise* in 1976 (and the shorter version, *The Populist Moment,* in 1978), the Populists were presented through a different historical lens. Goodwyn's Populists were the proponents of a coherent programmatic alternative that was politically imaginable. By recovering the political economy vision of the Populists, Goodwyn alters our understanding of historical development. In this account, history is more politically contested. There are different possible paths into the future, some that involve continued democracy and economic opportunity, and others that portend a loss of these things. Goodwyn echoes the Populists in arguing that citizens of the late nineteenth century faced real political choices about the future development of the American political economy. Yet by the end of the story, choice and possibility have vanished. Goodwyn writes that "The third party movement of the Populists became, within mainstream politics, the last substantial effort at structural alteration of hierarchical economic forms in modern America." For both Goodwyn and the Populists, democratic history ends in 1896.[23]

All four of these authors have implicit or explicit models of historical development. Goodwyn's work expresses a sense of history that includes contest, choice, and loss. Hicks, Hofstadter, and Unger, despite their differences, all tend to link the success of financial conservatism to natural economic forces and historical progress. Likewise for many twentieth-century historians and social scientists, industrial advance came to seem natural, while the victory of the antimonopolist alternative was historically unimaginable. These examples show not only the presence of models of historical development, but also the way these models reflect prior political outcomes, and subsequently shape our understanding of political contest and change.[24]

This is not to suggest that all models of historical development are the same, or that there is an inescapable historical relativism that derives from the narrative character of history. Goodwyn's account of the Populists is

---

22. Unger, *Greenback Era,* pp. 24 and 28–9.
23. Lawrence Goodwyn, *The Populist Moment: A Short History of the Agrarian Revolt in America* (Oxford: Oxford University Press, 1978), p.264.
24. I do not mean to diminish the contribution of the "modernist" historians that I discuss here, each of whom has much more nuance in his work than this brief review is able to suggest. Rather, I am interested in the models of historial development present in their work, and how these models are linked to the political struggles of the late nineteenth century.

distinguished by its attention to the political and historical imagination of Populism. In the other accounts of Populism and greenbackism discussed here, the intellectual world of these failed political alternatives is obscured by the apparent legitimacy of the winning historical alternatives. By undermining our assumptions about late nineteenth-century politics, Goodwyn calls into question our commonsense understandings of politics. He also moves us beyond a model of linear history, to one in which there are substantial political alternatives and the possibility of social choice. Thus there are things to learn about political development from failed alternatives that are less available in accounts that are animated by intellectual premises that legitimate and naturalize the ascent of historical winners.[25]

Still, the model of historical development and contingency presented in this book differs from Goodwyn's. The coherence and closure insisted on in *The Populist Moment*'s eloquent conclusion underscores what was at stake in the financial debate, and offers a valuable reminder of the hurdles faced by social movements. Yet it also creates a fixed history and a history that closely imitates the historical vision of the Populists Goodwyn studies. In his treatment of the Populists' opponents, and in his assertion that political history is complete in 1896, Goodwyn loses the contingent and complex quality found in the remainder of his narrative. The result is a return to a political singularity in which the political vision represented in a failed alternative paints over the political vision and efforts of the historical winners.[26]

This book emphasizes the role of history and historical narratives in political development and in the construction of past politics. All histories create a relationship between writers and readers of history and the subjects that they study. Narratives give history a purpose – be it progress, destiny, or demise. These purposes express and create the meanings that a present-day audience invests in the past. The terms of that creation are political in several ways. First, as present-day narratives relate themselves

---

25. This notion of historical contingency is similar to the one articulated by Roberto Unger in *Knowledge and Politics* (NY: Free Press, 1975).
26. For accounts of the financial conservatives that are more complex and contingent, see Richard Bensel, *Yankee Leviathan: The Origins of Central State Authority in American, 1859 – 1877* (Cambridge: Cambridge University Press, 1990) and James Livingston, *The Origins of the Federal Reserve System* (Ithaca: Cornell University Press, 1986). While I may disagree with some of the conclusions of these works, I am indebted to their careful appraisal of the financial conservatives (or financial capitalists and corporate liberals as Bensel and Livingston, respectively, call them). My book does not claim to treat the opponents of the antimonopolists as fully as these other works.

to past narratives and political outcomes, they may mimic, challenge, or otherwise represent the political imagination and understandings of past participants. Histories are political judgments. Second, whether this is done consciously or implicitly contributes to the critical awareness with which historical narratives are greeted. Some historical judgments are explicit, others reside in the assumptions or narrative structures of a text. History by assumption affords little critical space. Finally, by seeing history as narration or representation, we are reminded of the contingent, incomplete character of history even as we come to terms with the created coherence of historical accounts. All judgments are partial, and there can be no single, authoritative account of the past.

By viewing history as both structure and narrative, this book examines the tension between the institutional and cultural remnants of defeated political alternatives, and the political articulation of a created historical coherence. The Populists, their political program, and the political culture of money associated with that program, did not disappear on the day after the presidential election in 1896. Indeed, as L. Frank Baum's *Wonderful Wizard of Oz* suggests, the politics of money was still a part of the American cultural lexicon in 1900. The debates over the Federal Reserve Act in 1913 or the National Industrial Recovery Act of 1933 further attest to the fact that the language of antimonopolism was still politically employed well into the twentieth century. But as time went by and the human and cultural aspects of the Populist challenge faded, the liberal modernist view of history solidified, and these remnants were forgotten. The importance of 1896 as a political dividing line grew with time, as the post-1896 remnants were erased and the pre-1896 challengers were remembered through the eyes of their opponents.

III. Antimonopolism and economic development

Fundamental to the modernist historical view is the notion of a linear, progressive track of economic development. For scholars operating in both the Marxist and the classical economic traditions, technological innovation and industrial development are the engines of historical progress. As the economy develops and produces larger organizational structures such as the corporation, both the state and society replicate these changes with the development of government bureaucracies and regulatory structures, the growth of urban centers, and the integration of local communities into a national (and international) social and economic order. As Louis Galambos wrote in his classic statement of this view, the "important changes which have taken place in modern America have centered about a shift from small-scale, informal, locally or regionally oriented groups to large-scale, national, formal organizations . . . This shift in organization cuts across the traditional boundaries of political, economic, and social history." In the words of Samuel Hays, the "response to industrialism" is the lens through which many scholars have considered the changes in governmental structure and political organization that occurred between the nineteenth and twentieth centuries.[27]

A recent generation of historians and social scientists has begun to disentangle aspects of the modernist approach, looking more deeply at the institutional and political formations that shaped the struggles over the transition to a liberal corporate system. Instead of understanding the transition to a modern society as a natural and self-completing process, scholars such as Richard Bensel, Mike Davis, James Livingston, Martin Sklar, and Sean Wilentz have traced the struggles of labor organizations, the development of class identities among financiers and manufacturers, and the organization of government institutions as important factors in shaping the process of change. These works seek to complicate our understanding of the modernization process, stressing the influence of noneconomic factors, and even suggesting that more than one political path to modernity may be taken.[28]

Other challenges to the modernization thesis have come from students of economic development. These scholars explore the possibility that there are not just alternative political and social paths to modernity, but alternative economic routes as well. These are challenges that go to the roots of classical understanding of industrial capitalism. Some of these works are theoretical, others have studied competing patterns of economic development in other Western nations, and a few have focused on reinterpretations of regulation and business history in the United States. What these works have in common is the idea that there is no single, inherently superior path to economic development that emerges from market competition and technological innovation. As Gerald Berk argues in his work on Louis Brandeis, Brandeis's proposals for economic regulation in the early twentieth century remain difficult for many scholars to interpret because Brandeis set "aside the rigid distinctions between tradition and modernity, markets and administration, and state and economy to

27. Louis Galambos, "The Emerging Organizational Synthesis in American History," *Business History Review* 44 (1983); Hays, *The Response to Industrialism*.
28. Bensel, *Yankee Leviathan;* Davis, *Prisoners;* Livingston, *Origins;* Sklar, *Corporate Reconstruction;* and Sean Wilentz, "Against Exceptionalism: Class Consciousness and the American Labor Movement," *International Labor and Working Class History,* 26 (Fall 1984): 1–24.

give voice to the many practical experiments in industrial organization and self-regulation that populated the economy of his day."[29]

Assumptions about the nature of economic development affect our understanding of historical alternatives. In the case of the money debates, antimonopolists have often been understood by modernists as the advocates of limited economic interests or untenable programs for financial regulation. In the first view (Unger and Hicks), the greenbackers and Populists were self-interested economic men and women responding to high interest rates and low prices by calling for an expansion of the money supply. Rather than offering a coherent challenge to the long-term direction of economic development, financial reformers were motivated by a short-term defense of their standard of living. In the second view, that of the revisionists to modernization theory (Bensel, Livingston, and Sklar), there is a broader political account of the issues of class formation and the role of political institutions in economic development. The timing and shape of economic development depended on political compromises and coalitional formations on the part of financial conservatives. Further, antimonopolists' concerns over democracy and economic opportunity are treated seriously by the revisionists, while reform proposals for a dual monetary standard or an interconvertible bond scheme appear as unworkable schemes to reverse the concentration of capital, the integration of the national economy, and the advance of industrial production. In this view, the farmers and workers of the period clung to their memories of an era where there was greater local control and less competition. But their proposals were ultimately defeated by the financial conservatives, whose program offered superior efficiency and rewards of a modern manufacturing economy.[30]

29. Michael Piore and Charles F. Sabel, *The Second Industrial Divide: Possibilities for Prosperity* (NY: Basic Books, 1984); Charles F. Sabel and Jonathan Zeitlin, "Historical Alternatives to Mass Production," *Past and Present* (August 1985); Gerald Berk, "Constituting Corporations and Markets," *Studies in American Political Development*, 4 (1990): 130–168, and *Alternative Tracks* (Baltimore: Johns Hopkins University Press, 1993; and Philip Scranton, *Proprietary Capitalism: The Textile Manufacture of Philadelphia, 1880–1885* (Cambridge: Cambridge University Press, 1983).

30. C. B. MacPherson, *The Political Theory of Possessive Individualism*, offers a social theoretical account of the political culture of economic development. Following this approach, Bruce Palmer argues in *"Man Over Money"* that the Populists were mostly rural farmers still rooted in a simple market economy where they retained control over their labor and production. They resisted the emergence of an "advanced capitalist society. They lived at the fringes of it, where it seemed that if only things would go right, they could all become independent producers and maintain a just distribution of wealth while preserving a market economy, profit, and private property" (p.12). As will be seen in the pages that follow, the difference between Palmer's careful, nuanced reading of Populist political economy and my own lies in our assumptions about historical and

Yet as the mass production model of industrial capitalism has been called into question in the late twentieth century, the lost economic alternatives of the era in which that system emerged are being reconsidered. Gerald Berk reintroduces us to the proponents of regional railroad systems in the late nineteenth century whose fate was shaped as much by the courts as it was by market competition. Philip Scranton examines textile makers, machine toolers, and jewelry manufacturers to demonstrate the historic viability of custom and batch production. Both Kerry Odell and Naomi Lamoreaux carry the tale over to the banking sector, where they show regional financial networks in early nineteenth-century New England and in the late nineteenth-century Pacific region that efficiently benefited local economic development rather than feeding the national centralization of capital markets. These studies suggest that even in the land of Henry Ford, our assumptions about the inevitable historic supremacy of mass production should be questioned. This book contributes to that tale by arguing that the antimonopolists offered an intellectually coherent and politically imaginable program for financial regulation. It is an argument that calls into question our understanding of historical development and broadens our account of politics.[31]

IV. Goldbugs and greenbacks: The culture of money

When L. Frank Baum published *The Wonderful Wizard of Oz* in 1900, it was an immediate success. This children's tale was followed by a series of other Oz books, as well as theater and cinematic productions, including MGM's classic 1939 film "The Wizard of Oz," starring Judy Garland. Characters and phrases from the Wizard of Oz have become a part of America's cultural lexicon, and remain a vibrant part of our popular discourse even in the 1990s. Yet what few imagine or recall about Baum's original book is that it is filled with metaphors generated in the money debate of the late nineteenth century. The significance of these metaphors at the time that Baum wrote the book, and the loss of these meanings from twentieth-century representations of the Oz tale addresses the role of po-

economic development. Unlike Palmer, I do not regard the antimonopolists as representing an earlier stage of economic development that could not compete with the more advanced, and historically advantaged, system of industrial capitalism.

31. Berk, *Alternative Tracks*; Scranton, *Proprietary Capitalism*; Kerry A. Odell, *Capital Mobilization and Regional Financial Markets: The Pacific Coast States, 1850–1920* (NY: Garland Pub., 1992); and Naomi Lamoreaux, "Banks, Kinship and Economic Development: The New England Case," *Journal of Economic History*, 46 (1986): 649–667.

litical competition and outcomes in shaping our cultural and historical imaginations.[32]

The postbellum money debates were both formed by and formulated American political culture. As in the Oz tale, the discourse on money intersected other political discourses on sectionalism, race, class, and nationalism. The money debates provide an opportunity to outline some of the connections between these disparate pieces of American political culture in the late nineteenth century. There were hundreds of books and pamphlets from the period that explicitly or implicitly addressed financial issues. By using examples from the Oz tale, I will show how these connections might be mapped, and how they help us to think about issues of historical memory and political development.

In the thirteen years prior to the publication of *The Wonderful Wizard of Oz,* Frank Baum lived with his wife and children in Aberdeen, South Dakota (1887–1891), where he was a newspaper editor, and in Chicago, Illinois (1897–1900), where he was a writer and salesman. Historic events from these states provide clues about the characters and themes in the book. The Dakotas were still part of the frontier in the 1880s and 1890s. Indian politics, women's suffrage, the monetary question, and agrarian concerns all dominated the political agenda there. Discussions of these issues could be found in Baum's newspaper, *The Aberdeen Saturday Pioneer.* Illinois was the site of numerous political movements and nationally significant political events during the 1890s. The state's most significant contribution to the silver movement came from William H. Harvey, who published *Coin's Financial School,* a pro-silver booklet that reached a cir-

---

32. Other interpretive studies on L. Frank Baum and the Wizard of Oz include John Algeo, "Australia as the Land of Oz," *American Speech: A Quarterly of Linguistic Usage,* vol. 65, no. 1 (Spring 1990): 86–9; Stuart Culver, "What Manikins Want: *The Wonderful Wizard of Oz* and The Art of Decorating Dry Goods Windows," *Representations,* no. 21 (Winter 1988): 97–116; Peter Drier, "The True Story Behind the Wizard of Oz," *In These Times,* September 27, 1989; Fred Erisman, "L. Frank Baum and the Progressive Dilemma," *American Quarterly,* vol. 20, no. 3 (Fall 1968): 616–623; Edward W. Hudlin, "The Mythology of Oz : An Interpretation," *Papers on Language and Literature,* vol. 25, no. 4 (Fall 1989): 443–462; Nancy Tystad Koupal, "From the Land of Oz: L. Frank Baum's Satirical View of South Dakota's First Year of Statehood," *Montana: The Magazine of Western History* (1989): 46–57; William Leach, *Land of Desire: Merchants, Power and the Rise of a New American Culture* (NY: Pantheon, 1993); Henry M. Littlefield, "The Wizard of Oz: Parable on Populism," in Hennig Cohen, ed., *The American Culture: Approaches to the Study of the United States* (Boston: Houghton Mifflin Co., 1968): 370–382; Paul Nathanson, *Over the Rainbow: The Wizard of Oz As a Secular Myth of America* (NY: State University of New York Press, 1991); Hugh Rockoff, "The 'Wizard of Oz' as a Monetary Allegory," *Journal of Political Economy,* vol. 98, no. 4 (1990): 739–760; and S. J. Sackett, "The Utopia of Oz," *Georgia Review,* vol. 14, no. 3 (Fall 1960): 275–290.

culation of one million after its publication in Chicago in 1894. During these years, the Baum family was witness to the Pullman Strike, the division of the Democratic Party, and the "Cross of Gold" speech by William Jennings Bryan in 1896. Frank Baum is rumored to have marched for Bryan in Chicago. He was certainly aware of the great events going on around him.[33]

Baum may never have intended his book to be a political morality tale. There is no reason to doubt his assertion that he wrote his "modernized fairy tale . . . solely to pleasure children of today." Yet motive is not at issue. The argument here is that Baum lived in the midst of a highly charged political environment and that he borrowed from the cultural materials at hand as he wrote. As Richard Slotkin has written: "True myths are generated on a subliterary level by the historical experience of a people and thus constitute part of that inner reality which the work of the artist draws on, illuminates and explains." The content of Baum's book must be recovered at the "subliterary" level of the political and social experience in the 1890s. Or, as Roland Barthes argues, "it is human history which converts reality into speech, and it alone rules the life and death of mythical language." Just as history gave Oz its meaning in 1900, historical development and historical narrative unmade and remade those meanings in the twentieth century. Tracing the loss of the original political metaphors in the Oz tale reveals the linkages between political development and historical memory.[34]

Two brief examples will help to illustrate how the Oz tale reflects the political struggles of the late nineteenth century. The first concerns geography. When Dorothy arrives in Oz, she is greeted by the Munchkins and the Witch of the North. The Witch of the North tells Dorothy that Munchkins are "people who live in the land of the East." Since Dorothy remains wary of witches of any sort, the Witch of the North explains that

There were only four witches in all the Land of Oz, and two of them, those who live in the North and the South, are good witches . . . Those who dwelt

33. On South Dakota, see Herbert S. Schell, *History of South Dakota*, third edition (Lincoln: University of Nebraska Press, 1975), chap. 16. On Illinois, see Roy V. Scott, *The Agrarian Movement in Illinois, 1880–1896* (Urbana: University of Illinois Press, 1962), chaps. 2 and 3; John H. Keiser, *Building for the Centuries: Illinois, 1865 to 1898* (Urbana: University of Illinois Press, 1977), chap. 3; Chester M. Destler, "The People's Party in Illinois, 1888–1896: A Phase of the Populist Revolt" (unpub. diss., University of Chicago, 1932); and Harvey Wish, "John Peter Altgeld and the Background of the Campaign of 1896," *Mississippi Valley Historical Review*, 24 (1937–38): 506–510.
34. Baum, *New Wizard*, pp.5 and 98; Richard Slotkin, *Regeneration Through Violence: The Mythology of the American Frontier, 1600–1860* (Hanover, NH: Wesleyan University Press, 1973), p.4; and Roland Barthes, *Mythologies*, selected and translated by Annette Lavers (New York: Hill and Wang [1957] 1972), p.110.

in the East and the West were, indeed, wicked witches, but now you have killed one of them . . .

In this geography, the North and South are lands with good rulers, while in the East and West, the people may be good, but their leaders are oppressive. While the Witch of the North was a friend to the Munchkins, there was not much she could do for them. "I am not as powerful as the Wicked Witch who ruled here, or I should have set the people free myself." Thus, it was in the East that the greatest power resided until the cyclone that brought Dorothy's house down on the Wicked Witch.[35]

The geography of Oz recalls the cultural geography of the United States as seen by the Populists and their allies. William Jenning Bryan addressed the division between the East and other regions in his "Cross of Gold" speech:

> The gentleman who preceded me (ex-Governor Russell) spoke of the State of Massachusetts; let me assure him that not one present in all this convention entertains the least hostility to the people of Massachusetts, but we stand here representing people who are the equal, before the law, of the greatest citizens in the State of Massachusetts . . . We say to you that you have made the definition of a business man too limited . . . the merchant at the cross-roads store is as much a business man as the merchant of New York . . . we say not one word against those who live on the Atlantic Coast, but the hearty pioneers . . . are as deserving of consideration of our party as any people in this land.

The tensions here are both class tensions and sectional tensions. Bryan questions the dominance of the "greatest citizens" or prominent urban merchants of the Atlantic coast. Yet with "the people" of these places he has no quarrel. The North of Oz resembles the Old Northwest of the nineteenth century, while the East is like the Atlantic seaboard, the West resembles the frontier, and the South is like the old Confederacy. In the land of the Munchkins, the people, once freed from the Wicked Witch of the East, are kind and prosperous; they share their homes and food with Dorothy. All of the Munchkins dress in blue, "for in this country of the East blue was the favorite color," suggesting the color of the Union. It is these patriotic, independent white citizens that the Populists hoped to reach in uniting the productive classes of all sections.[36]

The second example concerns the monetary allegories of the Baum tale.

35. Baum, *New Wizard*, p. 23.
36. The Bryan speech appears in Bryan, *The First Battle*. Frank Baum lived in Chicago during the 1896 campaign, and was there when Bryan gave his famous speech at the Democratic convention. According to Nancy Tysdal Koupal of the South Dakota Historical Society, there is a family story that says Baum marched in the pro-Bryan parade during the campaign, although another family story suggests that as a travelling salesman in the state, Baum would express support for whichever candidate he thought was more popular in that community.

As Dorothy emerges from her fallen house, she discovers she is in the Land of Oz. "Oz" is an abbreviation for ounces, one measure of the worth of gold and silver bullion. In the land of Oz, gold and silver are often the arbiters of power. As Dorothy converses with the Witch of the North, the feet of the Witch of the East shrivel up, leaving nothing but her silver shoes. The Northern Witch gives the shoes to Dorothy.

> "The Witch of the East was proud of those silver shoes," said one the Munchkins; "and there is some charm connected with them; but what it is we never knew."

Indeed, the charm of the silver shoes is understood by none of the little people in the Land of Oz. Only the Witches understand it; particularly the Wicked Witch of the West.[37]

Later, when the Western Witch sees Dorothy in the silver slippers, she is alarmed.

> She looked down at Dorothy's feet and seeing the Silver Shoes began to tremble with fear, for she knew what a powerful charm belonged to them. At first the Witch was tempted to run away from Dorothy; but she happened to look into the child's eyes and saw how simple the soul behind them was, and that the little girl did not know of the wonderful power the Silver Shoes gave her.

Only after the Wicked Witch fools Dorothy and snatches one of her shoes does the Witch become more bold.

> The wicked woman was greatly pleased with the success of her trick, for as long as she had one of the shoes she owned half of their charm, and Dorothy could not use it against her, even had she known how to do so.

The Wicked Witch is melted before she can make use of her one silver slipper. Still, it is not until the end of the book that Glinda, the Good Witch of the South, reveals the secret of the silver slippers to Dorothy. "'The Silver Shoes,' said the Good Witch, 'have wonderful powers . . . they can carry you anyplace in the world in three steps.'" With this knowledge, Dorothy is finally able to return to Kansas. Unfortunately, she loses the slippers on her return trip.[38]

37. Baum, *New Wizard*, p. 25.
38. Baum, *New Wizard*, pp. 150, 153 and 257. Some interpreters of the Oz tale suggest that the Wicked Witch's death by water signifies her connection to nature and the brutality of droughts for western farmers, a view supported by reading the *Aberdeen Saturday Pioneer* where a lot of attention is given to droughts. See, for instance, Koupal, "The Wonderful Wizard," p. 212. It seems however, that the Witch signifies more than malign Nature. Her obsession with the silver slippers and exercise of power through the Golden Cap both suggest that the Witch is connected to mine owners or other financiers who exploited Western resources – such as gold, silver, timber, and coal – often with the assistance of oppressive labor practices. Even among Western Republicans such as Baum, there was often resentment expressed toward absentee owners in extractive industries.

After the Civil War and until 1896, Eastern financial elites tended to dominate financial policy formation in both major parties. The supremacy of the gold standard was established in the 1870s, first with the demonetization of silver coinage in 1873, and later with the official resumption of the gold standard (so that all national bank notes and government legal tender currency could be exchanged for gold) in 1879. Pleas for monetary expansion and a resumption of silver coinage from the political representatives of the North-central, Western, and Southern regions forced the government to purchase silver bullion (under the Bland-Allison Act in the 1880s and the Sherman Silver Purchase Act in the early 1890s). But even this gesture toward silver was abandoned when President Cleveland, a New Yorker committed to the gold standard, forced Congress to repeal the Sherman Silver Purchase Act in 1893. Thus, the "power of silver" remained under the control of Eastern elites and out of the reach of common citizens in the 1880s and 1890s. During those years, financial reformers sought to educate the public on the value of silver, a value that they believed would strengthen the producing classes and weaken the hold of Eastern financial elites (the "Money Power") over the rest of the country.[39]

When Dorothy goes off to find the Wizard of Oz, she is sent down the yellow brick road to the Emerald City. In the Land of Oz, it is a road the color of gold that leads to the political center. According to the Populists, Washington, D.C. was controlled by the "Money Power" and gold traders. After the Cleveland administration arranged some bond sales with the New York financial community to replenish the Treasury's gold stock during the 1890s depression, one Oklahoma editor wrote, "the United States today is completely under the control of the money power and the bondholders. Wrong doing, extraordinary oppression, and monopoly are so firmly entrenched that they will not yield, even to the plain laws of the country." The Populist senator from North Carolina, Marion Butler, expressed a similar sentiment when he accused the government of acting as if "they were agents for the gold combine instead of trusted servants of the people." The significance of the yellow brick road is altered,

---

39. In addition to the works cited here, see Allen Weinstein, *Prelude to Populism: Origins of the Silver Issue, 1867–1878* (New York: Yale University Press, 1970); Milton Friedman and Anna Jacobsen Schwartz, *A Monetary History of the United States, 1867–1960* (Princeton: Princeton University Press, 1963) chap. 3; Walter T. K. Nugent, *Money and American Society, 1865–1880* (New York, 1968); Cedric B. Cowing, *Populists, Plungers and Progressives: A Social History of Stock and Commodity Speculation, 1890–1936* (Princeton: Princeton University Press, 1965), pp. 3–24; and Richard E. Sylla, *The American Capital Market, 1846–1914: A Study of the Effects of Public Policy on Economic Development* (New York: Arno Press, 1975).

however, when Dorothy dons her silver slippers to travel along it. Here Baum's story provides a visible representation for bimetallism by combining silver with gold. For the Populists, the singular controlling power of gold was politically pernicious, but most financial reformers believed that the unity of gold and silver would provide greater monetary flexibility and abundance, making bimetallism superior to either a monometallic gold or silver standard.[40]

The cultural significance of the monetary debates appears to be largely lost in American politics after the early twentieth century. Gold and silver no longer helped to signify classes, sections, and races as they did in the late nineteenth century. Baum's use of monetary metaphors was by no means strictly Populist. Indeed, the text may be read as poking fun at believers in the mysterious power of silver, criticizing the false value of green paper currency, and celebrating the power of gold when properly used by wise rulers. Even so (and there is a more Populist reading), the prevalence and significance given to monetary metaphors in *The Wonderful Wizard of Oz* is hard to refute. That significance is lost when Oz takes to the screen as the silver slippers become ruby shoes and the Golden Cap is replaced by the Wicked Witch's crystal ball. With the establishment of the Federal Reserve System in the 1910s, the politics of monetary management was largely removed from the public realm. After World War II, the rising importance of the American dollar at home and abroad allowed the greenback to replace gold as the premier symbol of financial value. By the mid-twentieth century, financial issues no longer supplied the script by which other political debates were played.

How could the political content of a work that remains so vital and that is so well studied have been lost on Americans today? It is lost because the politics that sustained Baum's tale was lost after the rise of liberal pluralism and corporate capitalism in the early twentieth century. Americans today dimly recollect the Populists as rebellious farmers in search of better prices for their crops. The monetary debates, if remembered at all, are recalled as the pleas of economic amateurs against the sensible plans of business professionals and bureaucratic experts. These are memories seen from the world created by the corporate liberal victors who defeated the antimonopolist cause in the 1890s. They do not reveal the imagined political universe of the Populists and financial reformers. The loss of the Populist vision is not just empirical, it is also ideological, insofar as liberal pluralism guides our historical understanding of the Populist era.

40. The quote from Oklahoma appears in Gilbert C. Fite, "The Election of 1896," in Arthur Schlesinger, Jr., ed., *History of American Presidential Elections,* vol. II, p.178. Marion Butler, *To Stop the Further Issuance of Bonds* (Washington, 1896), p.4

V. Organization of the book

The chapters are organized both chronologically and topically. The first section concerns politics in the 1870s, when the financial debate took on renewed importance after the conclusion of the Civil War. Chapter 2 outlines the legislative history of the financial debate and discusses the constraints imposed by the party system on attempts to resolve the monetary issue during the period covered by this study. This establishes the role of national political institutions in the stalemate between financial conservatism and antimonopolism. Having demonstrated the importance of financial politics in Chapter 2, I use the next four chapters to deal with the antimonopolist alternative and the local significance of the money debate in three states.

Chapters 3 and 4 deal with the Greenback Era of the 1870s. Chapter 3 presents the competing programs and philosophies of the antimonopolists and the financial conservatives as revealed in pamphlets from the period. This chapter is divided into two parts. In the first part, I review the monetary debate, and in the second I examine the controversy over the NBS. Chapter 4 moves to the political struggles that demonstrated the greenbackers' appeal and the nature of the monetary contest in three regionally diverse states: North Carolina, where the weak antimonopolist movement was oriented toward state interests; Illinois, where farmers led the strong greenbacker coalition; and Massachusetts, where the labor reform movement was the center of antimonopolist politics in the 1870s, and where Benjamin Butler took control of the Greenback party in the 1880s. This summary of the Greenback Era shows the importance of politically geographical considerations in affecting the fate of the antimonopolists.

The historically contingent nature of the political outcomes of the 1890s is a prominent theme of the Populist section, Chapters 5 and 6. By the 1890s, the opportunity for a farm-labor coalition was diminished after the important political defeat suffered by the labor movement in the 1880s. Competing narratives of the financial debate of the 1870s were employed by the pamphleteers and theoreticians of the 1890s, as shown in Chapter 5 on the different financial programs of that period. The losses suffered by the greenbackers served to delegitimize and diminish elements of the antimonopolist analysis for the Populists, though in other ways the Populists built on the work of that earlier generation of financial reformers with new innovations such as the subtreasury plan. What Chapter 5 also reveals is the increased coherence and ideological authority of the financial conservatives. Chapter 6 returns to the three states to consider the politics of Populism and labor radicalism in three regional contexts. In North Carolina and Massachusetts, traditional sectional constructions of political interests were used to dissuade voters from anti-monopolism, while in Illinois, a more nationalist political appeal was used to counter the class and sectional messages of the labor radicals and their allies. The chapter ends with an analysis of the rise of the system of 1896.

The conclusion of this book considers the fate and historical relevance of the antimonopolist alternative. First, the coherence of the alternative is established. Next, antimonopolism's fate is explained in historically contingent and politically geographical terms. The antimonopolists made strategic mistakes and were constrained by established political and geographic alignments. Historical contingency increased the likelihood of defeat in the 1890s, when farmers were left isolated after the labor conflicts of the 1880s. History also affected future readings of the financial conservative victory in 1896, which was legitimized by subsequent economic and political events (for example, the influx of gold, the merger movement, and the national hegemony of the Republican party), and solidified by the historical self-understanding of Americans in the twentieth century, who imagined themselves as the carriers of modernity and progress. Finally, the question of reasonable plausibility is addressed, in an attempt to consider the possibilities for antimonopolism given the distribution of power and resources in the late nineteenth century. The instructive example of the Danish banking system, which supported the development of a mixed agrarian-industrial economy, is discussed. The book ends with a consideration of the ironies of the Federal Reserve System in light of the antimonopolist tradition.

2

Party politics and the financial debate, 1865–1896

We now come to the greatest question before the American people – a question of the very first importance to every producer in the land – a question in which is involved the freedom or slavery of every workingman in America – a question that must destroy the power of a monster moneyed aristocracy, or bind the whole labor of the nation, white and black, in fetters to gold – that question is one of finances.

> William H. Sylvis, 1868[1]

"That must be the Emerald City," said Dorothy . . . In front of them, at the end of the road of yellow brick, was a big gate, all studded with emeralds . . . Dorothy and her friends were at first dazzled by the brilliancy of the wonderful City . . . The window panes were of a green glass; even the sky above the City had a green tint, and the rays of the Sun were green.

> *The Wonderful Wizard of Oz*

For thirty years after the conclusion of the war, the Civil War party system organized political participation into a tight, highly competitive electoral market with high voter turnouts. Democrats and Republicans fought fiercely for control of the national government, and for many state and local governments. Five of the eight presidential elections in this period were decided by small margins. The structure of the party system influenced the articulation and competition of various political positions and programs. The regular parties mobilized voters primarily by relying on the loyal ties of partisan identity. Party leaders avoided taking clear stances on issues likely to divide the party membership. It was left to third parties and social movements to put forth clear programmatic alternatives. Understanding the significance of the financial debate in American politics requires a sense of the role of the party system in shaping and constraining the expression of political alternatives.

1. James C. Sylvis, *The Life, Speeches, Labors & Essays of William H. Sylvis* (NY: Augustus M. Kelley, Reprints of Economic Classics, 1968 [1872]), p. 236.

Within both major parties, the financial issue was regarded as a threat to their national electoral coalitions. When we look at presidential campaigns and congressional debates in this period, the financial debate is simultaneously everywhere and nowhere. National party leaders tried to suppress, subvert, and temporize on an issue that threatened the electoral base of both parties. Both Republican and Democratic presidents discovered the damage that could result from taking an ideologically committed stance on the money issue. When U. S. Grant vetoed the "Inflation Bill" in 1874, he alienated Western Republicans and set off a rebellion within his party. The Democrats were the beneficiaries. They took control of the House of Representatives in the next election. Similarly, in 1893, President Cleveland called Congress into special session to repeal the Sherman Silver Purchase Act. When Southern and Western Democrats resisted, Cleveland mustered his patronage power to punish the dissidents. The split within the party was never repaired, the Republicans retook control of the national government, and the Democrats repudiated Cleveland's leadership in the 1896 election. During most of this period, such riffs were avoided by short-term compromises in financial legislation (such as the Bland Allison Act and the Sherman Silver Purchase Act) and longer-term plays at partisan loyalty.[2]

The purpose of this chapter is to analyze the role of the party system in shaping and constraining political alternatives. The chapter also provides historical background on the party system, financial legislation, and financial politics between 1865 and 1896. The argument is that the party system distorted political opportunities, by suppressing issues that challenged the national bases of the major parties, and by structuring political interests around particular partisan identities and political geographies. For the financial issue, this meant that there was rarely a clear contest between the financial reform and financial conservative alternatives. The material comes mostly from secondary sources. The substantive story is developed through an analysis of the major parties and their relationship to the financial debate. Finally, the account shows some of the ways in which historical narratives and temporal order influenced political outcomes.

The controversy that shook the party system began with the passage of the first Legal Tender Act in February 1862. After the suspension of the gold standard in December 1861, the legal tender bill was passed to save the national economy and provide financing for the war. This bill, and

2. This is not to suggest that the outcomes of the 1874, 1894, and 1896 elections were based entirely on backlashes against Presidents Grant and Cleveland for their financial positions. Yet it is clear that within their own parties, the positions of Grant and Cleveland were undermined by their willingness to take committed stances on issues that divided both the membership and the elected officials of their parties.

two similar subsequent bills, created a new government-issued currency funded by federal bonds. This paper money was used to pay soldiers and handle other war-related expenses. Because of the color ink used to print the new bills, they became popularly known as "greenbacks." By war's end there were some $400 million worth of greenbacks in circulation.[3]

When the legal tender bill was first considered, two prominent arguments were made against it – that it was unconstitutional and that it was inflationary. Defenders argued that the new bills were a war necessity at a time when resources were needed to fund the military emergency. After the conflict concluded, questions about the greenbacks' legal validity reappeared, and were accompanied by other concerns about their redeemability in gold and the bonded debt contracted for their issuance.

By the late 1860s, the debate grew to include the role of the nation's banking system in economic development. In 1863, Congress passed the National Banking Act, creating a uniform national currency of national bank notes. Previously, notes from the various state banking systems were circulated, often at a discount. The national banks issued notes against bonds purchased from the government and left as security with the Treasury Department. Reserve requirements and other regulations provided a further guarantee of the worthiness of the new banks and their currency. Yet, despite the improvements contained in this new system, there were inequities within its structure that did particular harm to many debtors, agrarians, and rural residents.[4]

Throughout the late 1860s and the 1870s, financial issues were matters of popular politics. Third parties were formed on the issue. Pamphleteers and public figures gave their energies and attention to the debate. Labor, agrarian, and business organizations held long discussions and passed resolutions. Groups divided between supporters of the greenback standard, who were usually critics of the NBS, and opponents of greenbackism, who sought to reestablish the gold standard and protect the NBS. Superficially, the debate concerned declining prices, the maldistribution of credit, and short-term economic issues. Symbolically, the banking system and monetary standard were objects for the expression of sectional differences, war memories, and class identities. More broadly, the debate involved two competing visions of how the economic and political systems of the United States should develop and operate.

The remainder of this chapter is organized into five sections. Section I

---

3. On the legislative and economic history of the greenbacks, see Wesley Clair Mitchell, *A History of the Greenbacks, with Special Reference to the Economic Consequences of their Issue: 1862–65* (Chicago: University of Chicago Press, 1903). Various financial terms of the 1870s are defined in Appendix A.

4. Andrew McFarland Davis, *The Origins of the National Banking System* (Washington, DC: Government Printing Office, 1910).

places the argument in the context of the literature on party systems. That literature contains several dichotomies – between cultural and economic politics, workplace and homeplace politics, and local and national politics – which this book seeks to overcome. Sections II, III, and IV cover the Republican, Democratic, and antimonopolist parties and their participation in the financial debate. Section II shows that the Republican party was sectionally divided by the financial issue, which they sought to avoid or compromise on. The Democrats are covered in Section III. They were the party more often out of power, and therefore more given to political localism on the financial issue. The Northeastern elites who controlled the national party favored financial conservatism, but Southern and Western representatives often campaigned for financial reform. Section IV introduces the antimonopolists, who were the only political participants with a clear incentive to take a forceful stance on national finance. Yet they were constrained by a national party system that militated against the new political geographic alignment they sought to build. Section V discusses the birth of the System of 1896, and argues that it did not emerge from a clear contest between antimonopolism and financial conservatism.

I. Perspectives on nineteenth-century party politics

The literature on parties and politics in the late nineteenth century is organized around several divisions that obscure our understanding of the antimonopolists in a different way.[5]

Political scientists and historians working on the nineteenth century often assume a division between cultural or moral politics and economic or class politics. According to the new political historians, late nineteenth-century voters were motivated by ethnocultural concerns. Like the consensus historians of the previous generation, the ethnoculturalists help to preserve the theory of American exceptionalism by disclaiming the role of class division or economic conflict in American history. As Sean Wilentz has written, such an approach creates a false dichotomy between economic and cultural politics. Economic politics are presumed to be rational and unambiguous, and in America such politics are driven by a common interest in industrial prosperity. Economic change and technological progress remain exogenous to politics. From the other side, social historians proclaim the radicalism of the late nineteenth-century labor movement and the relevance of class consciousness. Yet they often fail to connect movement politics to programmatic party politics. The possibility

5. Richard L. McCormick provides a fine review of much of this literature up through the mid-1980s in the first three chapters of his collected essays, *The Party Period and Public Policy: American Politics from the Age of Jackson to the Progressive Era* (NY: Oxford University Press, 1986).

that competing paths to economic development were politically contested is largely unconsidered. This book seeks to mend this dichotomy by examining the way that economic and cultural visions are brought together in competing political programs.[6]

Similarly, Richard Oestreicher and Ira Katznelson have discussed the division between the politics of work and the politics of home, or the politics of labor radicalism and the politics of the election booth in the late nineteenth century. How is it, Oestreicher asks in an important article, that nineteenth-century voting is based on ethnoculturalism, while the politics of the workplace demonstrates labor solidarity and radicalism? Why did the class consciousness that produced so many violent strikes fail to produce a labor party? The answer to this is complex, but as Victoria Hattam demonstrates in her 1993 book, it is not that American workers had a bifurcated consciousness that made them, for example, workers in the workplace and Irish Catholics in the ballot booth. Rather, there were programmatic third parties of farmers and workers whose fortunes were frustrated by the political structure.[7]

Finally, nineteenth-century electoral politics is often described as local in character. The local character of American politics made the myriad diversity of ethnic and religious divisions politically manageable. Irish versus German animosity in one locale became immigrant versus Yankee conflict in another. This localism was reinforced by distributive politics, in which political machines and party institutions organized the allocation of economic resources from the government. In these accounts, na-

---

6. For overviews of the ethnocultural approach and the new political historians, see McCormick, *The Party Period and Public Policy,* introduction and chap. 1; and Peter H. Argersinger, *Structure, Process, and Party: Essays in American Political History* (Armonk, NY: M. E. Sharpe, 1992), chap. 1. Richard Oestreicher reviews both the ethnoculturalists and the social historians in "Urban Working Class Political Behavior and Theories of American Electoral Politics, 1870–1940," *Journal of American History,* 74 (1988): 1257–1286. See Wilentz's call for a bridge between identity and economic politics in "Class Consciousness and the American Labor Movement, 1790–1920," *International Labor and Working Class History,* no. 26 (Fall 1984): 1–24; and David Brody's attempt to forge such a bridge in "On the Failure of U.S. Radical Politics: A Farmer-Labor Analysis," *Industrial Relations,* 22 (1983): 141–63. The implications of the division between economic and cultural politics are discussed at length in Michael Rogin, "American Political Demonology: A Retrospective," in *Ronald Reagan, the Movie and Other Episodes in Political Demonology* (Berkeley: University of California Press, 1987). On the relevance of this division for how the Populists are constructed, see Michael Paul Rogin, *The Intellectuals and McCarthy: The Radical Specter* (Cambridge: MIT Press, 1967).

7. Ira Katznelson, *City Trenches: Urban Politics and the Patterning of Class in the United States* (Chicago: University of Chicago Press, 1981); Oestreicher, "Urban Working Class Political Behavior"; and Victoria Hattam, *Labor Visions and State Power: The Origins of Business Unionism in the United States* (Princeton: Princeton University Press, 1993).

tional political contests seem remote or insubstantial. The political particularism that infects the local level prevents the occurrence of genuinely programmatic politics at the national level.[8]

But as some recent works have argued, and this book confirms, the links between local and national politics were complex and substantial. For instance, in the 1890s, North Carolina farmers struggling to survive the crop lien had a great deal to say about what positions their congressional representatives should take on financial matters. Voters understood that the state played an important role in economic development, and they debated the character and direction of that role. Political identity claims were important, and while such claims at times frustrated the programmatic efforts of the antimonopolists (as with the use of race-baiting in North Carolina or Red-baiting in Illinois), such claims were not devoid of larger political meaning. Thus, as Chapter 5 shows, in the 1890s, gold was seen as the money of the Northeast and of British dominance, while silver was the money of honest farmers and workers of the West and South. The party system organized the links between economic and cultural politics, thereby affecting the prospects of political alternatives such as antimonopolism. The party system was neither devoid of economic politics, nor impervious to programmatic alternatives.

There are numerous intellectual reasons for the difficulty that both liberal and conservative scholars have in acknowledging the programmatic content of late nineteenth-century party politics, particularly among small third parties such as the antimonopolists. Like the progressive reformers of the early twentieth century, modern scholars are often convinced that the historical presence of machine politics or distributive networks was opposed to genuine programmatic efforts. Patronage systems were supposedly about managing popular sentiment and reaping economic rewards, not challenging the structure of government or the economy. Further, the new political historians note the prevalence of racism, ethnic hostility, anti-Semitism, and anti-Catholicism in the language of nineteenth-century partisans. That such sentiments helped to organize partisan identities is without question. But the further argument that ethnocultural politics excluded programmatic politics is suspect. Finally, two

8. The ethnoculturalists (see fn 6), such as Paul Kleppner in *Continuity and Change in Electoral Politics, 1893–1928* (NY: Greenwood Press, 1987), tend to view late nineteenth-century politics as local. Scholars on machine politics often argue that the electoral system is unprogrammatic. See, for instance, Martin Shefter, "Trade Unions and Political Machines: The Organization and Disorganization of the American Working Class in the Late Nineteenth-century," in Ira Katznelson and Aristide Zolberg, eds., *Working Class Formation: Nineteenth-century Patterns in Europe and the United States* (Princeton: Princeton University Press, 1986).

other factors help to explicitly blind scholars to the record of programmatic initiatives among the antimonopolists. The antimonopolists fail to
be taken seriously because they were against the "economic progress" of
corporate capitalism, and because they were the losers in the political contests of the late nineteenth century. These presumptions disguise the nature and significance of the antimonopoly tradition.[9]

II. The Republicans

The Republican party was divided by the financial issue. In Congressional debates, Republican representatives often voted along sectional lines.
Yet, after President Grant's veto of the Inflation Bill of 1874 nearly split
the party, Republican leaders renewed their commitment to compromise
on the financial issue. The Resumption Act of 1875 was designed to return the nation to the gold standard while minimizing currency contraction. Similarly, the Sherman Silver Purchase Act of 1890 was an effort to
placate silver inflationists without sacrificing the dominance of the gold
standard. Then, during the depression of the 1890s, as the Democrats
began to take a more decided stance on the monetary issue, Republicans
positioned themselves as the party of moderation and economic stability.
For the sake of party dominance, the Republicans compromised or avoided the financial issue through much of this period, yet they remained
ultimately committed to preserving the gold standard and maintaining
the NBS.[10]

The postwar period was one of adjustment for political partisans. The
war's end brought with it a difficult transition for the two major parties
that required them to shed their warrior roles and resume relations as
peaceful compatriots. The Republicans faced the problem of redefining
their party's primary goals after losing the antislavery issue. The Democrats had to overcome their association with national disloyalty. While the
major parties worked to determine their own agendas, minor parties
sprang up to address specific grievances such as prohibition, labor rela-

9. See, for instance, Richard Jensen's account of the 1896 campaign in the Midwest, in
   which the economic content of the battle of the standards is portrayed as emotional and
   millenarian. Richard Jensen, *The Winning of the Midwest: Social and Political Conflict,
   1888–1896* (Chicago: University of Chicago Press, 1971), chap. 10. In his writings on
   Massachusetts politics after the Civil War, Dale Baum provides a balanced account of
   the role of patronage discipline and programmatic politics. Dale Baum, *The Civil War
   Party System: The Case of Massachusetts, 1848–1876* (Chapel Hill: University of North
   Carolina Press, 1984), pp. 205–209.
10. On the Republican party after the Civil War, see James C. Mohr, ed., *Radical Republi-
    cans in the North: State Politics During Reconstruction* (Baltimore: Johns Hopkins Uni-
    versity Press, 1976).

tions, and financial issues that were often lost to the demands of major party redefinition.

In 1865, Hugh McCulloch was made Secretary of the Treasury. His views on monetary matters were quite conservative, and he pursued a severely contractionary monetary policy to retire greenback currency and return to the gold standard. The Secretary's views combined modified bullionism with religious moralism. In 1867, he wrote, "By common consent of all nations, gold and silver are the only true measure of value . . . I have myself no more doubt that these metals were prepared by the Almighty for this very purpose, than I have that iron and coal were prepared for the purposes for which they are being used." Such moral monetarism made McCulloch unresponsive to the economic slump that followed his contractionary policies in the late 1860s. But the less orthodox and more politically sensitive members of Congress were willing to question the prudence of contraction.[11]

Among the financial dissidents were the representatives of the mid-Atlantic region, an area where manufacturing was hard hit by the economic downturn of the postwar years. Many Pennsylvanians opposed contraction and supported continued use of the greenback standard. Representative William D. Kelley of Pennsylvania was a leading Republican greenbacker. Beginning with his opposition to contraction in the late 1860s, he went on to propose an interconvertible bond bill (a key greenback proposal) after the panic of 1873, and was one of the few Republicans from his region to oppose the Resumption Act in 1875. While early greenback interests in Pennsylvania may have arisen out of basic economic concerns, they were articulated and strengthened through the presence of reformers such as Kelley, political economist Henry Carey, and later, labor leader Terence Powderly. Amid this mixture of economic inclination, intellectual articulation, and political organization, Republican greenbackism flourished in Pennsylvania.[12]

In the mid-1860s, Reconstruction politics affected the financial debate. McCulloch was associated with the anti-Radical administration of Andrew Johnson, Lincoln's Southern Democratic successor. McCulloch's allegiance to Johnson made it easier for some Republicans in Congress to oppose contraction. In votes taken in 1866 and 1867, congressional Re-

---

11. Quoted in Robert P. Sharkey, *Money, Class, and Party: An Economic Study of Civil War and Reconstruction* (Baltimore: Johns Hopkins University Press, 1959), p. 60.
12. See Unger, *The Greenback Era*, on Kelley, throughout. On Kelley's Southern tour, see Montgomery, *Beyond Equality*, p. 436. Kelley's daughter, the famous social feminist Florence Kelley, was also allied with antimonopolist causes in Illinois in the 1890s. On Pennsylvania politics, see David Montgomery, "Pennsylvania, an Eclipse of Ideology," in *Radical Republicans in the North*, Mohr, ed.

publicans were less supportive of contraction than their Democratic opponents.[13]

The party reunited around the nomination of Ulysses S. Grant in 1868. After the election, the Radicals achieved their Reconstruction agenda with the passage of the Fifteenth Amendment. With this, the Radical wing of the party was increasingly fractured, and attention began to shift to other issues. Conservative Republicans, such as Civil War financier Jay Cooke, reconstituted the debt payment issue as a matter of morality (upholding the country's financial obligations) and patriotism (honoring the Union cause for which the debts were incurred). Those seeking to redeem legal tender bonds in cheaper greenbacks instead of more expensive gold (the initial enabling legislation had left the means of repaying the bonds' principal unspecified) were labeled repudiationists, whose loyalty to the Union cause was suspect. It mattered little that among the repudiationists were such staunch Unionists as Thaddeus Stevens. As Democrats became more identified with the greenback cause, soft-money advocates were often disparaged as "disloyalists." The Republicans voted in favor of resumption of the gold standard with the Public Credit Act of 1869.[14]

Early 1869 was perhaps the high point in coherent hard-money sentiment within the Republican party for the next decade. McCulloch left the Treasury Department in 1869 and was replaced by George Boutwell. Boutwell entered office with greater political than financial experience and set a course of practical moderation. His policy (and that of the administration through its first term) regarding resumption was one of "growing up to specie." The days of an actively contractionary approach were temporarily over. The new administration left the money supply stable, allowing economic growth to create "natural" contraction, in which a larger number of economic transactions were carried out with a fixed amount of currency. This approach was supported by the "stalwarts" – a newly formed group of Republican moderates.

Party crisis and resolution: The Inflation Bill and the Resumption Act

Republican solidarity ended with the panic of 1873. Under the stresses of administration corruption and economic depression, the stalwarts were eclipsed by the party factionalists. Crisis surrounded the passage and veto

---

13. On these shifts in party position and the congressional votes, see Sharkey, *Money, Class and Party*, pp. 75, 112, and 127–8.
14. Much of the analysis for this and the following paragraph is drawn from Montgomery's *Beyond Equality*, particularly chaps. 9 and 10.

of the Inflation Bill in 1874. The panic spurred increased public interest in soft-money propositions. Many blamed contraction and the inordinate power of gold dealers for the economy's woes. Reformers argued that there was insufficient currency to support the expanding economy, a shortage that was compounded by the rigidity of the NBS. Further, they contended that gold money made the country vulnerable to gold hoarders, whose pursuit of windfall profits might threaten the entire system with collapse. The shift in public sentiment led Western Republicans to withdraw their support from conservative financial policies.[15]

During the winter session of the Forty-third Congress (beginning December 1873), members offered a plethora of different financial remedies. After months of often hostile debate, the Republican-dominated House and Senate passed the Inflation Bill in April. It called for expansion of the money supply through an increase in national bank notes and greenback circulation. This moderate bill was immediately attacked by the Eastern hard-money forces who organized public and private appeals to President Grant calling for a veto. Grant did veto the bill, despite his allegiance to the stalwarts many of whom supported it. The veto created an internal conflict that threatened to divide the Republicans in half.

Having claimed the moral high ground, Grant held to his hard-money stance through the spring of 1874. With the upcoming elections, Western Republicans felt threatened by the President's position. They were reluctant to abandon their soft-money position, and only through the intervention of figures such as James Blaine was the party saved from disaster. Blaine garnered a compromise in which a moderate financial measure was passed and signed by the president. Again, the desire to retain party control overwhelmed attempts to articulate programmatic alternatives. Despite this action, the Republicans still suffered at the polls, and lost control of the House of Representatives. The political consequences of Grant's veto of the Inflation Bill showed Republicans that clear policy positions in this area were costly.[16]

During the lame-duck session of the Forty-third Congress, the Resumption Act was passed. This Act set the course for a return to the gold standard, and is often seen as an indication of the Republican party's return to the hard-money fold in 1875. However, as Irwin Unger writes, at the time it was regarded as a victory for the moderate stalwarts. It was

15. See, for instance, a pamphlet written by Massachusetts labor reformer E. H. Heywood entitled *Hard Cash: To Show that Financial Monopolies Hinder Enterprise and Defraud Both Labor and Capital; That Panics and Business Revulsions, Caused by Arbitrary Interference with Production and Exchange, will be Effectually Prevented Only Through Free Money* (Princeton, MA: Cooperative Publishing Co., 1874).
16. See Unger, *The Greenback Era*, chap. 7.

disliked by both soft-money advocates and hard-money orthodoxes. The act called for the retirement of eighty dollars in greenbacks for each one hundred dollars in new national bank notes issued, thereby providing a fairly painless path to resumption, without severe currency contraction. But the new Secretary of the Treasury, Benjamin Bristow, circumvented the Act's intent and shrank the supply of greenbacks without an offsetting increase in bank notes. Consequently, a compromise measure meant to end party division only renewed it. Only the political sensibility of party moderates such as Bristow's replacement, Treasury Secretary John Sherman, brought the party successfully through resumption in January 1879. The Greenback Era was over, and the financial controversy quieted down for several years.[17]

Renewed financial debate and Republican victories

The financial debate reopened in 1886, when the first of many "free silver" (see Appendix A) coinage bills came before Congress. (Silver had replaced greenbacks as the proposed instrument of currency inflation.) While the House Democrats split along sectional lines over the Bland Bill, the Republicans mustered the support needed to defeat free silver coinage on April 8, 1886. Similarly, the Republicans maintained party solidarity in passing the Interstate Commerce Act in 1887 and the Sherman Silver Purchase Act of 1890. These laws were designed to prevent party division over finance and railroad regulation. This capacity for compromise, along with the strength of the Republican political machines in New York and Pennsylvania, were indicative of the superior party organization which helped Benjamin Harrison win the Presidential election of 1888. In gestures to the party's Eastern and Western wings, Harrison's platform called for bimetallism, industrial regulation, and a strong tariff.[18]

But the Republican victories were short-lived. Resentment grew over the actions of the 51st, fiscally extravagant, "Billion Dollar" Congress. In the West, the growing storm of agrarian discontent threatened the party's

17. See Unger, *The Greenback Era*, chap. 8. The moderate position among the Republicans in the latter 1870s is identified with the stalwart faction, who often put party above policy. The "Half Breeds," a faction just forming at this time, were closer to the orthodox financial conservatives. See the Massachusetts section of Chapter 6 for more on this point.

18. On the silver vote of 1886, see James Sundquist, *Dynamics of the Party System* (Washington, DC: Brookings Institution, 1973), p.112. On the election of 1888, see R. Hal Williams, *Years of Decision: American Politics in the 1890s* (NY: Wiley, 1978), pp.2–3; and Robert F. Wesser, "Election of 1888," in Schlesinger et al., *History*, vol. II, pp. 1615–1650.

rule, and the addition of several new Western states added to the group of pro-silver Republicans in the Senate. The existing currency legislation was the Bland-Allison Act of 1878, which required the Treasury to purchase $2-4 million in silver bullion each month. Westerners helped to pass two free silver bills during the 1889–1890 session that were blocked by Speaker Thomas Reed in the House. Party managers then forwarded the Sherman Silver Purchase Act. It required the Treasury to purchase 4.5 million ounces of silver each month, funded with bonds redeemable (at the Treasury's discretion) in either gold or silver coin. For silverites the Act provided a customer for silver and an increase in the currency supply. For the Republican leadership, it assured the party peace needed to pass the McKinley tariff. Although the Sherman Act stopped immediate party division, it satisfied no one, and fostered contention almost immediately after its passage.[19]

Then a wave of labor conflict began – including the Haymarket incident of 1886, the Homestead strike of 1892, and the Pullman strike of 1894. These events dramatized the violent nature of industrial conflicts, the unwillingness of public authorities to mediate, and the abuses of privately licensed authorities such as the Pinkerton Agency. The timing of the Homestead strike helped undermine the Republican attempt to fashion an industrial politics of common interests with a strong tariff. By 1892, agrarians, Democrats, and Western dissidents were all opposed to the Republican President and his apparent favoritism to Easterners, industrialists, and gold men.[20]

While discontent favored the Democrats as the out party in 1890 and 1892, the situation was reversed in 1894 and 1896. After the 1892 elections, the Democrats had complete control of the national government for the first time since the Civil War. Then came the banking panic of 1893 and economic depression that lasted throughout Cleveland's term. The Republicans gained from voter discontent with the depression. The President's mishandling of the crisis magnified these gains just as it assured dissension within Democratic ranks. Third-party activity shifted from the Republican-ruled West to the Democratic-dominated South after 1892. By 1896, those Western Republicans who were unable to persuade the party councils of the importance of silver felt abandoned and alienated.[21]

19. Fred Wellborn, "The Influence of the Silver Republican Senators, 1889–1891," *Mississippi Valley Historical Review*, 14 (1928): 462–480.
20. John R. Commons et al., *History of Labour in the United States*, vol. II (NY: Macmillan, 1936), pp.495–497; and H. Wayne Morgan, "Election of 1892," in Schlesinger et al., *History*, vol. II, pp. 1703–1732.
21. Elmer Ellis, "The Silver Republicans in the Election of 1896," *Mississippi Valley Historical Review*, 18 (1932): 519–534.

President Cleveland blamed the Sherman Silver Purchase Act for the depression. He claimed the Act's operations drained the Treasury of gold and decreased business confidence. The President called a special session of Congress to repeal the Act in August 1893. After repeal was passed by the House, it dragged on in the Senate for months. There, it was the Republicans who finally ensured the success of repeal. The Republicans gained credit for helping to bring the matter to a close, acting in a bipartisan fashion in a time of national need, and promising to consider another coinage bill in the near future. Republican Senators voted 26–12 for repeal, whereas the Democrats split evenly, 22–22, and the three Populists voted against. Whereas the president based his monetary stance on economic principle, it was the Republicans who reaped the political benefits.[22]

The 1894 congressional elections swept the Republicans back into power. The President's attempt to safeguard the gold reserve failed, and forced the administration into a series of unfavorable bond deals with a group of New York investment bankers led by J. P. Morgan. While it was dealing with Wall Street, the administration reacted unsympathetically to industrial protests. When Coxey's Army, a group of unemployed men, marched to Washington to seek aid, they were beaten and arrested. At the request of Chicago business leaders, Cleveland sent federal troops to quell the Pullman strike in July 1894. Faced with this ongoing class conflict and economic depression, urban dwellers voted a Republican majority back into Congress.[23]

The elections of 1894 (and 1896) were not just anti-Cleveland elections. The Populists gained little relative to the Republicans from the anti-incumbency mood. In the West, the Republicans rebounded from their previous losses to the Populists. The party's 1894 victory reflected their strong party organization and the lure of patronage benefits likely to come to a new Republican president in 1896. This increased the value of party loyalty and the costs of third-party affiliation. Further, Western silverites no longer seemed crucial to the party's success, either electorally or within Congress, as demonstrated by the repeal vote. So while the Republican leadership did not actively alienate this faction, they no longer actively

22. Jeannette P. Nichols, "The Politics and Personalities of Silver Repeal in the United States Senate," *American Historical Review*, 41 (1935): 26–53; and H. Wayne Morgan, *From Hayes to McKinley: National Party Politics, 1877–1896* (Syracuse: Syracuse University Press, 1969), pp. 451–458.
23. Degler, "American Political Parties," p. 955; R. H. Williams, *Years of Decision*, p. 94; and J. Rogers Hollingsworth, "The Cuckoos Create a Storm," in Felice A. Bonadio, ed., *Political Parties in American History*, vol. II (NY: G. P. Putnam's Sons, 1974), pp. 923–924.

courted them. The demands of party no longer dictated compromise on the financial question.[24]

The Republican transition to financial conservatism and party domination

In sum, the Republican party underwent two important transitions during the 1865–1896 period. It changed its financial outlook from ambivalent moderation to financial conservatism, and they went from being one half of a competitive party system to being the dominant party in a new system. These transitions were linked, and both mattered for the defeat of the antimonopolist alternative. Republican leaders moderated their financial stance when they needed the cooperation of Western dissidents. But when the Democrats split on the issue and lost popular support, the Republicans responded by ignoring their Western insurgents. By 1896, the disgraced Democrats had realigned in favor of silver, thereby allowing the Republicans to associate a return to economic prosperity with financial conservatism. During the early part of this transition, the antimonopolists were disadvantaged because the party system worked to repress clear competition on economic issues. When the party stalemate broke and economic issues came to the foreground, the Democratic party's institutional, historical, and cultural disadvantages harmed the antimonopolist cause and helped the Republicans. The party system contained and conditioned this competition to the advantage of financial conservatism.

III. The Democrats

After the Civil War, the Democrats were the more conservative of the two national parties. They stood for constitutionalism, states' rights, government efficiency, and fiscal restraint. Although many Democrats from the South and West favored liberal economic policies, the national leadership was dominated by the party's Northeastern wing. Prior to the mid-1870s, the party was factionalized and unable to obtain power within the national government. Beginning in 1874, the Democrats became competitive with the Republicans in presidential and congressional elections. Although they always tended toward localism, in the later part of the Civil War party system, the Democrats tried to minimize divisive issues such as the financial controversy for the sake of party unity. Compromise and ob-

---

24. Ellis, "Silver Republicans," pp. 519–534; and John D. Hicks, *The Populist Revolt: A History of the Farmers' Alliance and the People's Party* (Lincoln, NE: Bison Books, 1961), chap. 12.

fuscation proved advantageous until President Cleveland felt compelled by the depression to take a strong stance in favor of gold in 1893. In the next two elections, the party lost control of both Congress and the Executive. The financial issue proved to be the unmaking of the Democratic party.

At first, the Democratic position on money matters was conservative. Postwar Democrats argued that the war debt was irresponsibly created, advantageous to a northeastern monied class, and placed an unfair burden on ordinary citizens. It was a bad Republican policy. Congressional Democrats made clear their support for a return to the gold standard and currency contraction. Voting on the Loan Bill in March 1866, House Democrats favored contraction 27–1, while the Republicans split 56–52 in favor. By the fall of 1867, public opinion was against Treasury Secretary McCulloch's contraction policy, which was blamed for falling prices and slower growth. Still, the Democrats remained closer to the Secretary's conservative financial policies than the Republicans. On the Anti-contraction bill of December 1867, the House Republicans voted 103–18 for, while the Democrats split 24–18 in favor of the measure.[25]

The following year, Western Democrats began responding to public disaffection with monetary contraction. George Pendleton of Ohio put forth a financial program that became known as the Pendleton Plan. The plan contained many early greenback ideas. It criticized the NBS, supported the continued use of greenback currency, called for ending contraction, and proposed an interconvertible bond scheme. Yet neither the plan nor the election succeeded in bringing a united Democratic party to national prominence. Although the Pendleton Plan (also known as the Ohio Idea) had captured the support of many Westerners, it failed to win the backing of Eastern Democrats. Financial contraction was a less pressing issue in the East, where there were more banks and a larger per capita currency supply. The resulting division was illustrated by the 1868 national ticket, headed by conservative New York banker Horatio Seymour, who ran on a platform that contained the Pendleton Plan. Democratic support for soft-money proposals helped to unify the Republican party in opposition to the "disloyal" Democratic financial policies.[26]

From the 1860s through the 1890s, a faction of Eastern conservatives fought to retain the party's commitment to the gold standard, and were often involved in efforts to promote free trade and patronage reform. Their positions were based on a combination of economic interest (their

25. Sharkey, *Money, Class and Party*, tables on p. 75 and p. 112.
26. On the Pendleton Plan, see Chester McArthur Destler, "The Origins and Character of the Pendleton Plan," *American Radicalism, 1865–1905: Essays and Documents* (New London: Connecticut College, 1946), pp. 32–41. Mitchell, *A History of the Greenbacks*, pp. 53 & 59n.

industries were typically railroads, textiles, and international finance), political tradition (Jacksonian bullionism), and intellectual orthodoxy (represented by such Ivy League academics as Amasa Walker, William Graham Sumner, and Francis Bowen). Elite proponents of Democratic financial conservatism in the late 1860s included August Belmont, the international financier and national party chairman; Horatio Seymour, the New York banker and 1868 presidential candidate; and Samuel Tilden, a railroad lawyer, future New York state governor, and the 1876 presidential candidate for the party. The persistent strength of this element within the party was more institutional than political in nature. While these elites sought to impose a hard-money position on the Democrats, their efforts were moderated by the growing importance of financial reformism within the party.[27]

On both sides of the party, the Jacksonian tradition was being reinterpreted. In the West and among some Eastern labor elements, Jacksonian producerism was reshaped into an advocacy of paper money. This change is exemplified by the transformation of George Pendleton from a bullionist to the author of the Ohio Idea. What remained intact was the Jacksonian condemnation of bankers, speculators, and government-granted special privileges. Western Democrats condemned Eastern financial elites, and saw the greenback standard as a means of reclaiming equal economic rights and preventing the upward redistribution of wealth. The Western wing of the Democratic party participated in the intellectual creation of an antimonopolist alternative to financial and corporate concentration.[28]

Meanwhile, Eastern Democrats held firm to bullionism and the notion of limited government, demanding a return to the gold standard and the withdrawal of greenbacks. At the 1868 New York Democratic convention, Horatio Seymour characterized greenbacks as inflationary and destabilizing, the NBS as sectionally biased, and each as being part of an overly expansionary and strong central state. Small government, states'

27. Unger refers to this New York group of Democrats as the descendants of the Hunkers, who in the late 1860s were associated with the Albany Regency. The newspaper most closely associated with the powerful group was the New York *World*. See Unger, *The Greenback Era,* pp. 84–85. On the economic interest, see Sharkey, *Money, Class and Party,* pp. 282–4; and Montgomery, *Beyond Equality,* pp. 71 and 350. On the political tradition, see Sharkey, *Money, Class and Party,* pp. 283–4. On the intellectual orthodoxy, see Robert Green McCloskey, *American Conservatism in the Age of Enterprise, 1865–1910* (New York: Harper Torchbooks, 1964), esp. chap. 3. Note that in contrast to other notions of the politics of sectionalism (for example, the more economistic views of Elizabeth Sanders and Richard Bensel) sectionalism here is understood as a political and social construct into which economic differences were strongly bound.

28. On Jacksonian ideology, see Marvin Meyers, *The Jacksonian Persuasion: Politics and Beliefs* (Stanford, CA: Stanford University Press, 1957).

rights, and hard currency were key elements of Democratic financial conservatism.[29]

The rise of the Democrats

After the panic of 1873, Republican financial policy came under attack, and Democratic political fortunes improved. The Democrats won House majorities in both the 1874 and 1876 elections. Yet, the party's choice of national leaders demonstrated the continued dominance of the Eastern hard-money interests. After the 1874 election, the new Democratic House majority elected Michael Kerr as Speaker. Kerr appointed other like-minded hard-money men as the chairmen of the essential House committees. In the 1876 campaign, Samuel Tilden, a longtime gold advocate, was selected as the party's presidential candidate.

Even with the prospect of a Democratic administration in the offing, divisions over the financial issue took their toll. With Speaker Kerr's blockage of soft-money proposals, and the apparent contribution of eastern hard-money Democrats to the demise of the western soft-money candidates in 1875, the party split was open to public view. For the remainder of the decade there was a wrangle over the party's financial position, and the issue remained unresolved, leaving Democrats to develop locally oriented positions instead. Not until the election of a Democratic president, would the benefits of unity clearly outweigh the costs of compromise.

Former New York Governor Grover Cleveland led the party through the 1880s and 1890s. As Northeastern financiers understood, Cleveland was fundamentally a financial conservative. Further, his reputation as a principled reformer made him attractive to the political independents such as the Mugwumps. For the sake of party unity, Cleveland signalled a superficial willingness to compromise on the finance issue until the depression of 1893. Then his determination to pursue "sound" financial policy polarized his party and led to the overthrow of the Northeastern wing and its replacement by silverites behind William Jennings Bryan.[30]

Grover Cleveland was his party's presidential nominee in 1884, 1888, and 1892. He won the first and last of these elections. His 1884 victory

---

29. George T. McJimsey, *Genteel Partisan: Manton Marble, 1834–1917* (Ames, IA: Iowa State University Press, 1971), p. 123.

30. "Mugwumps" was the derisive nickname given to political reformers who were said to be partisan fence sitters, with their "mugs" on one side and their "wumps" on the other. On the Mugwumps and their role in politics in the 1880s and 1890s, see John G. Sproat, *"The Best Men:" Liberal Reformers in the Gilded Age* (NY: Oxford University Press, 1968); and Gerald W. McFarland, *Mugwumps, Morals and Politics, 1884–1920* (Amherst: University of Massachusetts Press, 1975).

against James Blaine is attributed by historians more to the latter's blunders and shady reputation than to the former's strengths. Besides his reform record, Cleveland's greatest campaign assets were his managers. As Robert Wesser writes, these were "'Bourbon' leaders who symbolized the inherently conservative character of the national Democratic party." They also had access to money. While uttering the old themes of states' rights and constitutionalism, the Democratic candidate also stressed civil service and tax reform. The New York Mugwumps claimed credit for Cleveland's narrow victory.[31]

After early skirmishes against pro-silverites such as Richard Bland in 1888, Cleveland appealed to monetary expansionists through the tariff issue. Tariff reform would release the Treasury surplus that had grown from import duties. The president argued that when the Treasury "idly holds money uselessly subtracted from the channels of trade," then it may cause "a condition of financial distress." The solution, however, was neither to increase public expenditures ("unnecessary and extravagant appropriations") nor to deposit the surplus in private banks ("fostering an unnatural reliance in private business upon public funds"), but to reduce the surplus by reforming the tariff. Thus, Cleveland promoted conservative economic policies (tariff reform and fiscal conservatism) while using traditional Democratic language designed to appeal to Southerners and Westerners. Concerned about currency contraction and financial panics, Democratic voters were told to support tariff reform.[32]

The Democrats lost the presidential election of 1888 in a tightly competitive race. The 1890 contest broke this national electoral stalemate. The Republicans lost seventy-eight seats in the House. Even staunchly Republican Massachusetts elected a Democratic governor – William Russell was another conservative, reform-minded Democrat. Jubilation over victory, opposition to Harrison, continued economic hardship in the West, and dissatisfaction over the Sherman silver compromise held the party together through the 1892 elections. With a bimetallist plank and Vice-Presidential nominee (Adlai Stevenson of Illinois), Cleveland was reelected.[33]

The depression of 1893 and Democratic decline

The depression of 1893 shattered the fragile party unity. The depression was triggered by the third banking panic of the post-Civil War period. By

31. On Cleveland's political career, see Allan Nevins's *Grover Cleveland: A Study in Courage* (New York: Dodd, Mead & Co., 1934); Wesser, "Election of 1888," p. 1615.
32. The quotes are from Cleveland's annual message of December 3, 1887, reprinted in Schlesinger et al., *History*, vol. II, pp. 1664–1665.
33. R. H. Williams, *Years of Decision*, pp. 46–51.

the early 1890s, there was an excess of railroad and industrial capacity (resulting from overinvestment encouraged by the National Banking System's pyramid reserve structure), making it difficult for financiers to recoup on their investments. The agricultural slump contributed further to the nation's debt load. When a series of international bank crises occurred, foreign investment and exports both declined. This created the conditions for the stock-market crash of 1893. By the end of that year, some 500 banks and 1600 businesses had closed. Cleveland blamed silver, and sought to protect the gold standard.[34]

The long drive to repeal the Sherman Silver Purchase Act may have sealed the fortunes of the Democratic party after 1893. Many Democrats felt betrayed by the President's actions. By now Cleveland made no effort to disguise his determination to maintain the gold standard. Senate Democrats offered the President a compromise that would end silver purchases in October 1894. Cleveland would have none of it. By the end of the battle, silver Democrats had hardened their positions as well. "I have done with all compromises . . . Free coinage or nothing," said Richard Bland. The Populists exclaimed that the President's behavior revealed his allegiance to Northeastern financial concerns. By focusing on the contentious currency issue, Cleveland undercut the likelihood that the party would support his policies in other areas. For Cleveland, matters of principle came before the party.[35]

Instead of economic salvation, repeal was followed by continued economic hardship. In early 1895, the administration turned to the Morgan banking syndicate. For a handsome fee, it agreed to handle a European bond offering to purchase gold and "save the gold standard." While the bonds were an economic success, they were politically disastrous. One Oklahoma editor wrote, "the United States today is completely under the control of the money power and the bondholders. Wrong doing, extraordinary oppression, and monopoly are so firmly entrenched that they will not yield, even to the plain laws of the country." By the next election, Cleveland was left without any political organization behind him.[36]

From the mid-1870s until the mid-1890s, the Democrats were a strong national party. But their political strength had little to do with positive policies on issues related to economic change. While tariff reduction ap-

---

34. On the "long depression" view, see Kirkland, *Industry Comes of Age*, pp. 7–10. On the depression and Cleveland's response, see, in addition to Kirkland, Hollingsworth, "Cuckoos," pp. 918–920; Nichols, "Politics and Personalities," pp. 26–53; and James Livingston, *The Origins of the Federal Reserve System: Money, Class and Corporate Capitalism, 1890–1913* (Ithaca: Cornell University Press, 1986), pp. 84–86.
35. Morgan, *Hayes to McKinley*, pp. 456–458.
36. Gilbert C. Fite, "Election of 1896," in Schlesinger et al., *History*, vol. II, p. 1788.

pealed to the sectional interests of Southerners and Westerners, it did not address clashing economic interests within sections or the dominance of Northeastern industrialists and financiers in other areas. Party diversity on labor relations and monetary policy emerged forcefully after the onset of the 1890s depression. President Cleveland's actions polarized the party factions, which led to the ousting of the conservative Northeastern Democrats from control of the national organization in 1896.

Neither of the two major parties supported financial reform before the mid-1890s. Despite the presence of many reformers, the dominance of the Northeastern conservatives prevented the Democratic party from shifting toward antimonopolism until the depression of 1893. The depression and the political blunders of Grover Cleveland made the transition to financial reform possible. But these same factors limited the vehicle that the producers' coalition inherited. The party that William Jennings Bryan laid claim to was associated with economic decline and political mismanagement.

IV. The antimonopolists

In post-Civil War politics, finance was at the center of debates over economic change. Five national antimonopolist parties competed between 1872 and 1896. They were the Labor Reform, Greenback, Antimonopolist, Union Labor, and Populist parties. Each pursued an agenda of financial reform. All represented farmer-labor coalitions, and signalled the importance of financial antimonopolism as an alternative to the rise of corporate liberalism. The two most successful and significant of these were the Greenbackers and the Populists. The Greenbackers appeared during the economic crisis of the 1870s and contributed to the midterm adjustment of the Civil War party system. The Populists arose during the economic and political crisis of the 1890s and were part of the critical realignment that ended the Civil War party system and led to the emergence of the System of 1896.

The Labor Reform party was the first national antimonopolist party. It was organized by the National Labor Union (NLU), which was established shortly after the Civil War to provide a forum for the country's labor organizations to address issues of common concern. Beginning with its second national convention in 1867, the NLU asserted that upholding democratic rights and preserving the republic depended on reforming the financial system. Its Declaration of Principles (modelled on the Declaration of Independence), which was approved by the convention, explains the significance of financial reform. It begins by recalling the role of government in preserving natural rights and the duty of citizens to correct governmental injustices. The document goes on to protest unjust laws that favor the nonproducers at the expense of the producers. At the center of these injustices is the monetary system – the vehicle by which wealth is redistributed. The authors assert that it is government's responsibility to regulate money, a responsibility that was forfeited with the passage of the National Banking Act, which gave governmental sovereignty over to private hands. This created the money monopoly, the parent of all monopolies, and an offense to the principles of equality and democracy. Only by returning to a just financial system can cooperation between labor and capital be achieved and democracy restored. For the NLU, financial antimonopolism provided the basis for both analysis of current problems and for programmatic reform proposals.[37]

By the time of the national Labor Reform party's appearance in 1872, the reform labor movement was in disarray. The NLU was weakened by the loss of its president, William Sylvis, who died in 1869. Many national unions had withdrawn from the NLU, to focus on trade union action in a period of general economic prosperity. Those who remained, such as the Knights of St. Crispin, proposed the creation of a separate political entity to compete in electoral campaigns. The new party held an early convention in the hopes of capturing the reform political agenda from critics of Republican rule. Its platform drew from the Declaration of Principles and included other planks meant to appeal to a wider constituency. In its transformation from a movement to a third party, the NLU carried its financial reform agenda along with it.[38]

Despite its efforts to unify reformers, the party was itself used by more experienced politicians. After gaining the Labor Reform nomination, David Davis sought the endorsement of the Liberal Republicans as well. Failing at this, he withdrew from the race entirely, leaving the Labor Reformers without a candidate. This disaster ended the short life of the party. Ironically, labor reform greenbackism was dispersed on the eve of the great greenback insurgence in the wake of the panic of 1873.[39]

The Greenback party

In the mid-1870s, after a decade of agitation on Civil War financial issues, the national Greenback party was formed. This sectionally broad and socially diverse political organization did well during its brief electoral ca-

---

37. On the history of the NLU, see John R. Commons et al., *History of Labour in the United States*, vol. II (NY: Macmillan Co., 1936), chap. 4. Commons et al., eds., *Documentary History*, vol. IX, pp. 176–181.
38. McKee, *National Conventions and Platforms*, pp. 154–56.
39. See Haynes, *Third Party*, p. 99, for Davis's declination letter.

reer, obtaining 13.8 percent of the national vote in 1878. (The party's electoral returns in New England, the West North-Central region, and the West all exceeded this national average.) The historical significance of the party comes both from its electoral success and from its representative character in the financial antimonopolist tradition. The record of the National Greenback Labor party shows that there was substantial support for a fundamentally different course in economic development.[40]

In November 1874, laborers, farmers, and businessmen in Indiana called a national convention to unite the strands of antimonopolist electoral insurgency that had appeared during the previous two years. This gathering was the starting point for political greenbackism. National interest in financial reform grew substantially after the panic of 1873. In the fall elections of 1874, the Republicans were routed, resulting in Democratic control of the House of Representatives for the first time since the Civil War. In the Midwest, several small independent parties were formed to protest railroad practices and other monopolistic activities. Between 1874 and 1876, three more conventions were held before the first nominating convention of the National Independent (or Greenback) party in May 1876.[41]

The platform of this new party was short and direct. Repeal of the Resumption Act passed in January 1875 was the first plank. The second plank endorsed the interconvertible bond (a plan to automatically adjust the volume of currency in proportion to economic growth), thus rooting the party in the tradition of Edward Kellogg. A further plank expressed a producers' vision of economic development: "It is the paramount duty of government, in all its legislation, to keep in full view the full development of all legitimate business – agricultural, mining, manufacturing, and commercial." The last planks protested government bond policies, including the sale of gold bonds to foreigners, and bonds designated for silver purchase. The convention nominated Peter Cooper, an old Jacksonian and wealthy New York businessman, for president, and Newton Booth of California for vice president. Booth declined, and Samuel F. Cary of Ohio replaced him.[42]

---

40. On the national and regional vote share of the Greenback party and how it compared with the Populists, see Kleppner, *The Third Electoral System*, table 7.5, p. 260.
41. Haynes, *Third Party*, pp. 105–119; Unger, *Greenback Era*, pp. 293–302; and Commons, *History of Labour*, vol. II, pp. 167–171, all provide accounts of the origins of the Greenback party. Note that the party is known variously as the Independent, Greenback, and Greenback Labor party. In 1884, the Anti-Monopoly party endorsed the same ticket as the Greenback party – Benjamin F. Butler and Alanson M. West. Their platforms differed slightly. See McKee, *National Conventions and Platforms*, pp. 214–215, 223–225.
42. McKee, *National Conventions and Platforms*, pp. 174–175.

Recent analyses of the labor movement suggest that there was a great deal of mainstream support for greenbackism. Support for financial reform existed from the mid-1860s through the 1880s, and even into the 1890s, among the segments of the labor movement committed to producerism. The continuity of labor greenbackism from the NLU through the Greenback party is readily observed both in personnel and programmatic positions. Most early labor reformers (such as Andrew Cameron, Alexander Campbell, and Wendell Phillips) were sympathetic to greenbackism. Miners, shoemakers, ironmolders, shipbuilders, and printers were among the unions whose leaders were represented in the antimonopoly financial reform ranks. Ideological continuity was expressed in belief in the labor theory of value, a producerist vision of class harmony, and a focus on the financial system as the source of class disequilibrium. Growing inequality, labor greenbackers argued, could be corrected by a fair financial system, typically including a greenback standard and an interconvertible bond scheme.[43]

Another important segment of the greenback movement came from the business world. The business component of greenbackism presents difficulties to scholars who view the movement as a reaction to industrial development. Such scholars see greenbackism as an agrarian reaction to economic decline and changes in the social structure resulting from industrialization and urbanization. Since businessmen are presumed to act in their own economic self-interest, and to be the agents of economic progress, their presence within the greenback movement raises questions about traditional notions of what constitutes economic progress. Where business greenbackism is considered, as in Irwin Unger's work, it is often treated as a short-term inflationary impulse rather than a challenge to the direction of development of the economic structure.[44]

Yet the diversity of the business greenbackers belies simplistic explanations of their political sympathies. For instance, some Northeastern business greenbackers, such as Peter Cooper, came to the party through the

43. David Montgomery, *Beyond Equality;* and Victoria Hattam, "Economic Visions and Political Strategies: American Labor and the State, 1865–1896" *Studies in American Political Development*, vol. 4 (June 1990): 82–129. On the continuity of labor reformers in the greenback tradition, see appendix D of *Beyond Equality*, where a dozen such labor careers are readily identified out of a sample of 95.

44. Unger, *The Greenback Era,* chap. 9. Thomas Cochran and William Miller, *The Age of Enterprise: A Social History of Industrial America,* rev. ed. (NY: Harper & Row, 1961), pp.164–5; Richard Hofstadter, *The Age of Reform* (NY: Vintage, 1955), pp. 4–5, 74–75, and fn p. 100; Charles Edward Merriam, *American Political Ideas: Studies in the Development of American Political Thought, 1865–1917* (NY: Augustus M. Kelley, 1969 [1920]), pp. 39–40; and Robert H. Wiebe, *The Search for Order, 1877–1920* (NY: Hill and Wang, 1967), pp. 7–9, characterizes 1870s economic protest politics as a desire to return to a fundamental morality.

Jacksonian locofoco tradition. Others, such as those associated with the New York Board of Trade (organized in dissent from the New York Chamber of Commerce's monetary position in the mid-1870s), reproduced the mercantilist connection to antimonopolism begun with Edward Kellogg. Pennsylvania's iron industry also contained many greenback sympathizers concerned with the geographic inequities of the financial system. Many of these business greenback leaders were brought together by Moses Field for a Detroit convention in August 1875 in preparation for the national convention held several months later.[45]

Finally, there were the farmers. Western farmers began their antimonopolist politics with resistance to high railroad rates and perceived inequalities in the treatment of small and large shippers. That movement started with the National Antimonopoly Cheap Transportation League in the 1860s. By the early 1870s, the upper Mississippi Valley was the center of the railroad regulatory movement. By then, the Grangers (an agrarian self-help group) were established throughout the region. When their attempts to seek legislative relief from high and discriminatory shipping rates were frustrated, partisan organization resulted. A series of antimonopoly, reform, and independent parties were formed in Illinois, Indiana, Wisconsin, Missouri, Iowa, Kansas, Nebraska, Minnesota, Michigan, California, and Oregon. Through independent victories, or fusion with one of the old parties (typically the Democrats), these independent parties functioned as an effective political force for regulatory reform. But with the exception of Illinois, where the influence of Alexander Campbell and the labor greenbackers was decisive, these parties were conservative on monetary matters. They typically went on record in favor of resumption and fiscal frugality.[46]

The South was slower in developing a Granger movement and in moving toward independent political action. The region that would witness a

45. The locofocos were a Jacksonian antimonopolist group in New York concerned with financial reform and equal rights. See Carl Degler, "The Loco-focos: Urban 'Agrarians,'" *Journal of Economic History,* 16, 3 (1956): 322–53. On the other roots of business Greenbackism, see Unger, *Greenback Era,* pp. 288–289, 300; Chester McArthur Destler, "The Influence of Edward Kellogg Upon American Radicalism, 1865–1896," *American Radicalism,* pp. 50–77; Haynes, *Third Party,* chaps. 9 and 11; Gerald Berk, *Alternative Tracks: The Constitution of American Industrial Order, 1865–1917* (Baltimore: Johns Hopkins University Press, 1993); and Ellis Usher, *The Greenback Movement of 1875–84, and Wisconsin's Part in It* (Milwaukee: Meisenheimer Printing Co., 1911).

46. For the 1860s antimonopoly history, see Lee Benson, *Merchants, Farmers and Railroads: Railroad Regulation and New York Politics, 1850–1887* (Cambridge, MA: Harvard University Press, 1955). On the independent parties, see Haynes, *Third Party,* chap. 6; Solon Buck, *The Granger Movement: A Study of Agricultural Organization, Its Political Economic and Social Manifestations, 1870–1880* (Cambridge, MA: Harvard University Press, 1913), chap. 3; and Nathan Fine, *Labor and Farmer Parties in the United States, 1828–1928* (New York: Russell & Russell, 1961), chap. 3. On Mid-

firestorm of independent farmer politics in the 1890s was still struggling to regain its political and economic status. Southerners were receptive to critical analysis of the financial system. Given their experiences with the crop lien system and the absence of banks, currency, or credit in the region, southern farm and business interests were willing proponents of alternatives to the NBS and currency contraction. Financial reform sentiment was expressed through nonpartisan activities, such as Granger-built cooperative marketing groups, or through the Democratic party. But in 1878 and again in 1880, the Greenback party made a strong showing in Alabama, Arkansas, Kentucky, and Texas. (Greenback fusion slates also made gains in other states, such as North Carolina.) By its own paths and in its own forms, greenbackism took hold among many farmers in the South and West in the late 1870s.[47]

The Greenback party gained momentum in 1877 and 1878. In its national election in 1876, the party was frustrated by a lack of resources, organization, and credibility. Peter Cooper was over eighty years old and few viewed him as a serious presidential candidate. But after the great railroad strike of 1877, and with the continued economic depression, the party's position improved. Greenback candidates received 187,095 votes in 1877, more than double their 1876 vote of 82,640. The next year's tally rose to over a million votes (estimates vary between 1 and 1.2 million). The party won fourteen congressional seats and looked to the future with great enthusiasm. But, despite the energetic campaign of James Baird Weaver in 1880, the party's tally was cut to 308,578 votes. The economy was recovering, the gold standard was reestablished, and the party was troubled by internal divisions. While the Greenback party continued to exist well into the 1880s, it had ceased to be an important political force.[48]

Labor reform in the 1880s

When the antimonopoly alternative reemerged on the national scene in the mid-1880s, it was under the auspices of labor reform. The hope for labor in the 1880s lay in uniting farmers and laborers around political

western Copperheads and antimonopolism, see Frank L. Klement, "Middle Western Copperheadism and the Genesis of the Granger Movement," *Mississippi Valley Historical Review*, v. 38, n. 4 (March 1952); Martin Ridge, "Ignatius Donnelly and the Greenback Movement," *Mid-America*, v. 39, n. 3 (July 1957), pp. 156–168; R. C. McCrane, "Ohio and the Greenback Movement," *Mississippi Valley Historical Review*, v. 11, n. 4 (March 1925); and John D. Hicks, "The Political Career of Ignatius Donnelly," *Mississippi Valley Historical Review*, v. 8, n. 1–2 (June-Sept. 1921), esp. pp. 92–100.

47. Theodore Saloutos, *Farmer Movements in the South, 1865–1933* (Lincoln, NE: Bison Books, University of Nebraska Press, 1960); and Buck, *Granger Movement*, pp. 51–59 and chap. 3.

48. The voting statistics come from Haynes, *Third Party*, pp. 124 and 141.

and economic action. Twenty years of American progressive politics laid the foundation for such a union on the basis of antimonopolism and producerism. Hundreds of local efforts in the Midwest, Northeast, and South had pressed for antimonopolist reform. The experiences of the NLU (1865–1872), the Labor Reform party (1872), the Greenbackers (1876–1880), and the Antimonopolists (1884) provided the context for a national effort. Financial reform was used by these groups to critique the role of monopoly capitalism and express common bonds among producers. During the middle 1880s, when the Knights of Labor (KOL), the largest labor organization of the nineteenth century, sought to unite the productive classes around a common political economy agenda, the moment for a producers' alliance seemed ripe.

The outlook for labor politics in the mid-1880s was optimistic. Between 1885 and 1888, labor tickets appeared in 38 states and 189 localities. These tickets went by many titles, including United Labor, Union Labor, KOL (despite the KOL's official ban on political activity), Workingmen, and Independents. Every section of the country was represented – Washington to Vermont, Alabama to Iowa. The labor reform movement was fed by other reform movements of the 1880s, including agrarianism, Bellamy Nationalism, the single-tax movement, and socialism. The dramatic expansion of the KOL in 1885–86 inspired many toward third-party activism. The Knights' new recruits included unskilled workers less likely to succeed through economic activism alone. Finally, the eight-hour movement further politicized many labor men and women, as they turned to the state for specific legislative enactments.[49]

Inevitably, some tried to channel this enthusiasm into a national organization. A convention was held in Cincinnati on February 22, 1887. Some 450 delegates attended, representing all of the major reform groups. They voted to form the National Union Labor party. A. J. Streeter (former Greenback and Antimonopolist candidate in Illinois and longtime agrarian progressive) was named the new party's presidential candidate. Robert Schilling, the Milwaukee KOL leader and longtime advocate of labor-farmer cooperation, also played a prominent role. Nonetheless, labor organizations and Easterners were underrepresented at the convention. It was primarily a Western, agrarian gathering. The votes this party received in 1888 came predominantly from Western rural areas. The Union Labor party was a weak forerunner of the Populists.[49a]

As the Union Laborites prepared to compete nationally, many labor groups were withdrawing from politics locally. Following their dramatic

49. Leon Fink, *Workingman's Democracy: The Knights of Labor and American Politics* (Urbana: University of Illinois Press, 1983), table 1, pp. 28–29.
49a. Fine, *Labor and Farmer Parties*, p. 72.

rise in 1885–86, the KOL suffered severe reversals beginning with the Southwest strike and Haymarket Riot of 1886. By the end of the decade, the Knights were eclipsed by the newly founded American Federation of Labor (AF of L). The philosophy of the AF of L differed from that of the KOL in several respects. Whereas the KOL advocated a vision of shared interest between workers, farmers, and small businessmen (the producers), the leaders of the AF of L argued that the working class had distinct and separate interests. Producerism held that the course of economic development was not inevitably set and advocated decentralized development that preserved economic autonomy and republican citizenship. In contrast, AF of L leaders accepted mass production and corporate concentration, although they resisted the loss of worker autonomy on the shop floor. Finally, there was the question of political action. KOL members had greater faith in their democratic rights and ability to affect the course of government. Business unionists distrusted politics, which they regarded as divisive and unrewarding. Sometimes, trade unionists turned to legislatures to defend workers against a hostile judiciary, but primarily they relied on economic militance to win gains for labor. As trade unionism came to dominate the labor movement, the possibilities for farmer-labor politics declined.[50]

Ironically, just as labor withdrew from politics in the late 1880s and early 1890s, farmers entered the electoral arena and sought out labor groups to join them. Some did join. In states such as Illinois, labor was a strong partner in the Populist movement. Many former Labor Reformers, Greenbackers, and Antimonopolists (as well as those from the anarchist and socialist movements) joined the People's party campaigns. At the agrarian conventions of the late 1880s and early 1890s, there were labor groups in attendance and labor planks were added to the platform. Eighty-five representatives from the KOL attended the Populist convention in St. Louis in 1892. But this was not enough. As agrarian mobilization increased in the early 1890s, workers' organizations, particularly from the Northeast, were notably absent from the Populist coalition.[51]

Ultimately, the strain of government repression (for example, the Haymarket Riot, the Homestead Strike, and the Pullman Strike) and economic hardship thwarted the labor reform effort. In frustration, some workers turned to defending themselves through political neutrality and private bargaining. Others became socialists and sought to democratically recapture the state from capitalist control. By the latter 1890s, Terence Powderly of the KOL was supplanted by Samuel Gompers of the AF of L and

50. The terms "producerism" and "trade unionism" are used by Hattam in her excellent essay "Economic Visions and Political Strategies: 82–129. See also Nick Salvatore's introduction to *Seventy Years of Life and Labor: An Autobiography,* by Samuel Gompers (Ithaca, NY: ILR Press, 1984), pp. xi–xli.

51. Fine, *Labor and Farmer Parties,* p. 75; and Destler, *American Radicalism,* pp. 14–31.

Eugene Debs of the Socialist party as national labor leaders. Neither Gompers nor Debs lent their active support to Populism, and the people's crusade lost in the battle to gain the cities.[52]

The People's party

The Populists were the last of a long line of nineteenth-century antimonopolist groups. Antimonopolists were the true purveyors of America's progressive alternative to corporate capitalism. The efforts of earlier antimonopolists established the context in which the Populists' political efforts took place. The vision of a broad producers' coalition was harmed by the political events of the late 1880s and early 1890s, which deprived the farmers of their needed labor partners. While earlier antimonopolist efforts attested to the political possibilities of a farmer-labor alliance, the disillusionment and disorganization that followed Haymarket, Homestead and Pullman had resounding consequences for the Populists.[53]

The first Farmers' Alliance began in Texas in 1880 as an economic self-

52. On the history of labor organizations and politics, see Irwin Yellowitz, *Position of the Worker in American Society, 1865–1896* (Englewoods Cliffs, NJ: Prentice-Hall, 1969); Dubofsky, *Industrialism;* David Montgomery, *The Fall of the House of Labor: The Workplace, the State, and American Labor Activism, 1865–1925* (Cambridge: Cambridge University Press, 1987); Fink, *Workingmen's Democracy;* and Commons et al., *History of Labour in the United States,* vol. II.

53. The most thorough account of the People's party's involvement in national politics is still Hicks' *Populist Revolt.* But Hicks fails, as Goodwyn has noted, to effectively distinguish Populism from the silver movement. The reactionary Populists resemble Unger's idealistic and fanatical Greenbackers in Unger, *The Greenback Era.* Also see Richard Hofstadter, *The Age of Reform* (NY: Vintage Books, 1955), where Populism is equated with the thought and career of William Jennings Bryan. On the mass society theorists, see Michael Paul Rogin, *The Intellectuals and McCarthyism: The Radical Specter* (Cambridge, MA: M.I.T. Press, 1967). Historians who view the Populists in the socialist tradition include Norman Pollack, *The Populists Response to Industrial America* (Cambridge: Harvard University Press, 1962); and James Green, *Grass-Roots Socialism: Radical Movements in the Southwest, 1895–1943* (Baton Rouge: Louisiana State University Press, 1978). The interest group view of the Populists can be found in Fred A. Shannon's *The Farmer's Last Frontier: Agriculture, 1860–1897* (Armonk, NY: ME Sharpe, 1989); and Theodore Saloutos, *Farmer Movements in the South, 1865–1933* (Berkeley: University of California Press, 1960). The view of the Populists as grassroots democrats appears in Lawrence Goodwyn, *Democratic Promise;* and the later, shorter version, *The Populist Moment: A Short History of the Agrarian Revolt in America* (Oxford: Oxford University Press, 1978). Recent studies in the Goodwyn tradition include Steven Hahn, *The Roots of Southern Populism: Yeoman Farmers and the Transformation of the Georgia Upcountry, 1850–1890* (NY: Oxford University Press, 1983); Palmer, *"Man Over Money";* and Barton C. Shaw, *The Wool-Hat Boys: A History of the Populist Party in Georgia* (Baton Rouge: Louisiana State University Press, 1984). Also see Robert McMath, Jr., *American Populism: A Social History, 1877–1899* (NY: Hill and Wang, 1993), which offers a mostly social and cultural overview of the movement.

help group in the style of the Grange. The Alliance quickly surpassed the Grange in articulating farmers' common problems and formulating co-operative responses. The Southern and Northern Alliances spread rapidly in the late 1880s and early 1890s. Agricultural cooperatives of various types were tried, and had some success, but ultimately failed due to hostility from local economic elites and a lack of credit. The Alliances then became political. Beginning in 1890, in both the Midwest and the South, Alliancemen competed for office, either through independent third parties (as in Kansas and Colorado) or though the Democratic party (as in Georgia and South Carolina). Their victories were heartening for those interested in national economic reform. This led to the creation of the People's party in 1892.[54]

Populism as a political movement emerged in two stages. First, it swept through the Midwest and West, where in states such as Kansas, Colorado, and the Dakotas, Populists displaced the Democrats as the alternative to the Republicans. In the early 1890s, Populist senators, representatives, and governors were elected from this region. Third-party activity was slower to emerge in the South where the burden of partisan identity was greater. During Populism's second stage (1893–1896), Southerners fought against the yoke of Democratic loyalty to join the People's party. Their efforts were met with race baiting and accusations of treason. Where this did not work, conservatives used disenfranchisement measures to remove the dissidents from the voting rolls. As the Populists fought political institutions and cultural norms in the South, the national party competed in federal elections.[55]

From 1892 through 1896, the People's party was a significant electoral force. It obtained 8.5 percent of the vote for its presidential candidate James Weaver in 1892. In 1894, during the congressional elections, the vote tally increased 42 percent over the 1892 total. Seven representatives and six senators were elected. But the regional limitations of the party were apparent. This prompted a debate over whether to remain independent or fuse with one of the major parties. In 1896, the party divided, with the convention nomination going to Democrat William Jennings Bryan for president and Populist Thomas Watson for vice president. The confusion, defeat, and disillusion that followed effectively ended the career of the party.[56]

54. McMath, *American Populism*, chap. 5.
55. Gene Clanton, "'Hayseed Socialism' on the Hill: Congressional Populism, 1891–1895," *Western Historical Quarterly*, 15 (1984), p. 139–162; and Kousser, *Shaping of Southern Politics*, p. 7
56. The 1892 vote tally comes from Kleppner, *Continuity & Change*, p. 60. The figures for 1894 come from Haynes, *Third Party Movements*, p. 281.

Despite their electoral strength between 1890 and 1896 (they obtained 25–45 percent of the vote in several regions), the Populists never penetrated the Northeast. This political-geographic failure had three major causes. First, there was the cultural barrier. The Southern, pietistic, agrarian appearance of the party alienated urban immigrants. Second, they were harmed by the dominance of orthodox liberalism in the Northeast, where opposition to free silver was widespread. Finally, the People's party failed to find continuity with previous antimonopoly reform organizations from that region. The absence of a Populist base in the Northeast made the turn to the Democrats in 1896 a more politically appealing choice.[57]

Ironically, the movement that sought to transcend sectionalism helped to expose the sectional divisions within the party system. Southern and Western representatives from the major parties responded to the regional rather than class dimensions of the Populist message. Silver became the perfect vehicle for such a strategy. It promised relief to the hinterlands through currency expansion while providing a market for a major Western industry. As financial matters became more prominent with the bank failures, gold standard crisis, and depression of the mid–1890s, silver became the rallying cry for Populists concerned with the dominance of Northeastern financial interests, Southerners desiring monetary relief, and Westerners wanting buyers for their products. The crisis of the 1890s narrowed financial antimonopolism to silver versus gold, and made it a sectional matter. As a result, the parties divided, not as producers versus nonproducers, as the antimonopolist Populists had hoped, but as Northern Republicans versus Southern Democrats.

Wherever Populism emerged, it altered the course of normal politics. In the West, the Populists challenged Republican rule and ended that party's dominance of Congress in the early 1890s. Populist disruption in the South was suppressed by race-baiting, violence, and disenfranchisement. The forces unleashed by Populism removed the Democratic conservatives from power nationally and realigned the party internally. But this last great antimonopolist movement failed to control or direct the political realignment they helped inspire. There was no clear confrontation between the producers and the nonproducers, the antimonopolists and the corporate liberals. Populism's overlap with the Democratic party allowed for the identification of the Republican party with corporate liberalism and industrial prosperity, but prevented the clear emergence of a national, antimonopolist alternative.

57. Hicks deals extensively with the electoral history of the party. See Hicks, *Populist Revolt*, chaps. 6, 8, 9, and 12–14.

There are many ironies in the history of Populism. It was the last in a long line of antimonopolist farmer-labor groups, but it failed to obtain substantial labor support. Its economic program was at once far-reaching and regionally diverse, yet sectionally biased and intellectually narrow. It was a movement that sought to transcend sectional prejudices to form a national producers' alliance, yet its presence helped prompt the emergence of a sectionally skewed party system. The trajectory of Populism was distorted by the political system in which it operated. This complexity belies simplistic explanations of Populism's fate.

V. The election of 1896 as a critical moment in American politics

William Jennings Bryan was a candidate on whom many pinned their hopes for the final success of a producers' alliance in America. After rising quickly to national prominence as a congressman from Nebraska, Bryan gathered many of the diverse strands of third-party radicalism within his political coalition. Besides being the Democratic party standard bearer in 1896, he gained the endorsement of the People's party. Yet, despite the addition of agrarian progressives and their allies in the South, Midwest, and West, Bryan lost the election to William McKinley, who swept the Northeast, Midatlantic, and Northcentral regions. This election marks the end of the Civil War competitive party system and the start of a long era of Republican hegemony on a platform of industrial expansion.[58]

Supporting Bryan was a critical error for the Populist movement. By the time the People's party joined forces with the Democrats in 1896, the electoral tide was turning, with the Republicans holding a majority of the seats in the Congress. The decision to endorse the Democrat cost the Populists dearly. Particularly in the South, supporters who had sacrificed heavily to join the Populists felt betrayed by fusion. Paul Kleppner estimates that half of the 1894 Populist voters (mostly former Democrats) in the ex-Confederacy voted Republican in 1896. There was also a sacrifice of principle involved, both economic and political. In fusion, the breath and promise of the Omaha platform was narrowed to the immediate lift of silver inflation. The political vision of transcending petty partisan machinations was also lost in the union with the Democrats. Even on their

58. Bryan is often depicted as the Cowardly Lion in the Oz tales (in some accounts Bryan is identified as the Wizard, though I find this reading less plausible). The lion, uncertain of his role as a leader, usually gets by with a loud roar. When the lion attempts to challenge the Wizard in the Emerald City, he is confronted by a giant ball of flame that singes his whiskers. These images parallel Bryan's history as someone who rose on the strength of his oratory, and was burned in his attempt to confront the powers of Washington.

own terms the fusionists lost; their broad compromises of principle and support did not bring electoral victory.[59]

Several factors must be considered in explaining the outcome of the election of 1896. These include the economic and cultural appeals of the candidates, the partisan identities of the voters, and the historical possibilities for constructing a producerist coalition. Finally, it must be remembered that the Democrats were the party in power when the depression of 1893–1897 took hold. There was, therefore, an element of negative backlash against the party of governance, just as there would be against Herbert Hoover and the Republicans in 1932. While none of these elements alone convincingly accounts for McKinley's victory, together they offer a solid explanation. Nor can this one election elucidate the reasons for decades of Republican hegemony. The institutional entrenchment of Republican government and the solidified cleavages among Democrats under Bryan in the decades that followed make that history comprehensible. The meaning of the 1896 electoral moment was compounded by both past and future events.[60]

There were two sorts of economic messages being sent by both candidates in the 1896 election. One concerned monetary economics. The other was broader. It related to beliefs about what type of economic structure contributed most to the general welfare. The first issue – "the battle of the standards" – was the conflict between gold and bimetallism or free silver. Bryan's opponents portrayed him as a free silver doctrinaire, thus alienating many potential supporters in the industrial states where "sound money" organizations had popularized support for gold. McKinley supported the gold standard but softened this position by calling for an international conference on bimetallism after his election. He also campaigned on the general message of economic prosperity through protectionism and industrial growth. Bryan's attempt to create an image for himself as the champion of a producerist coalition of labor, small busi-

59. Paul Kleppner, *Continuity and Change in Electoral Politics, 1893–1928* (Westport, CT: Greenwood Press, 1987), p. 81. On the difficulties faced by fusion efforts in this era, see Peter Argersinger, "'A Place on the Ballot': Fusion Politics and Antifusion Laws," *Structure, Process and Party*, pp. 150–171. Analyses of the 1896 election include Argersinger, "'A Place on the Ballot,'" pp. 159–64; Walter Dean Burnham, "The System of 1896: An Analysis," in *The Evolution of American Electoral Systems*, Paul Kleppner et al. (Westport, CT: Greenwood Press, 1981), esp. pp. 158–65; Jensen, *Winning of the Midwest*, chap. 10; Morton Keller, *Affairs of State: Public Life in the late Nineteenth Century* (Cambridge, MA: Belknap Press, 1977), pp. 580–87; Kleppner, *Continuity and Change*, esp. chaps. 2 and 3; and Samuel McSeveney, *The Politics of Depression: Political Behavior in the Northeast, 1893–96* (NY: Oxford University Press, 1972), chap. 6.

60. For Bryan's own account of the election of 1896, see William Jennings Bryan, *The First Battle* (Chicago: W. B. Conkey Co., 1896).

ness, and farmers was never successful, especially among industrial workers. He remained to many a Midwestern preacher's son who spoke the
language of rural, Protestant America.

The silver campaign obscured the deeper economic message of producerism. There were too many conflicting interests within the silver
coalition for the broader message of antimonopolism to get through.
Western mine owners were unsympathetic to labor appeals, nor were
many Southern inflationists understanding about the plight of landless
farmers. Northeastern workers may have heard correctly when they listened to the sectional message of free silver rather than the quieter national message of producerism, for this was the message that many of
Bryan's backers, if not Bryan himself, intended to deliver. Corporate liberals were less discriminating, and both the antimonopolist and the silver
movements were defeated by the election's outcome.[61]

Manufacturing workers were repulsed by Bryan's cultural image as
well. Bryan's Midwestern pietism, while firmly based in the Yankee political reform tradition, alienated immigrant Catholics who made up an
increasingly large proportion of the industrial workforce. This conflict became forcefully clear years later when Bryan prosecuted the Scopes trial
– an example of moral intervention by a Protestant state authority, a
threatening symbol to the Catholic religious minority. Cultural symbol-
ism also imbued the party labels. In the South, the Democrats were the
"the party of the fathers," and the party of white supremacy. In the North,
Republicanism meant economic progress and union loyalty. In both regions, third parties sometimes succeeded where culturally constrained
second parties failed. Bryan lost not only as a pietist among ritualists, but
also as a Democrat among the children of Union loyalists.[62]

Finally, the Bryan campaign occurred at a moment when the possibilities for a farmer-labor alliance had declined. Producerism was being
eclipsed by business unionism and socialism. The 1896 election came after Haymarket, Homestead, and Pullman. Craft workers in the AF of L
sought shelter in their skill and in their distance from the state. The in-
clusive ideology of the KOL had been shattered by lockouts and dis-
missals. The dream of industrial unionism and democratic socialism had
yet to come strongly to the foreground. In the mid-1890s, political strategies were separate from economic ones, as one segment of the labor move-

61. Burnham, "System of 1896," pp. 160–1; McSeveney, p. 178.
62. See J. Rogers Hollingsworth, *The Whirligig of Politics* (Chicago: University of Chicago
    Press, 1963); Jensen, *Winning of the Midwest*, chap. 10. Kleppner's analysis suggests
    that Bryan's appeal briefly halted the drift of rural Protestant Yankees in the Metropole
    to the Republicans. Among urban immigrants such as the Germans, on the other hand,
    there was a loss of Democratic support. Kleppner, *Continuity and Change*, p. 76.

ment moved toward party politics and socialism, and the other moved toward business unionism and voluntarism. The farmer-labor coalition was missing its labor component in the mid-1890s.

Having inspired the regime shift of the 1890s, the Populists were unable to manage it. They were limited by the party system in which they operated. That system obscured the financial debate, and cast it in politically and economically limited terms during the realignment process. A movement that attempted to pit a national coalition of producers against nonproducers instead was trapped into a competition of sectionally aligned and economically distorted blocks. The Populists also made mistakes. Fusion reinforced the reign of a conservative Democratic party in the South, thus limiting the opportunity for progressive politics in the future. By limiting the main economic appeal of the campaign to free silver, potential labor allies in the Northeast were alienated. Finally, they were hurt by timing. Either an earlier or later Populist movement might have found an available labor partner for its campaign against corporate liberalism. But as it was, the antimonopolists' loss in the 1890s proved decisive.

William Jennings Bryan remained the steward of his party's fortunes until the 1910s. For nearly two decades, the Democratic party remained divided, Bryan continued to champion limited economic reform, and the economy exploded under the reign of the Republicans. The period from 1898 to 1907 was the second highest growth decade in the history of American capitalism. The corporate economy was triumphant, and the cooperative commonwealth was lost. Meanwhile, Republican hegemony at the turn of the century became institutionalized through government patronage in much of the North. After a short break in Republican rule in the 1910s, faith in unfettered capitalism and the Republican party continued until the 1930s. Subsequent events expanded the significance of the 1896 election.

The regime shifts of the 1890s represented the decisive defeat of the antimonopolist alternative. Before that decade, the antimonopolist program was both coherent and potentially plausible in the United States. By the early twentieth century, the corporate liberal system was firmly established. There were still antimonopolist advocates hoping to modify corporate capitalism until the New Deal (and even later), but the vision of a mixed agrarian-industrial economy, regionally organized and dominated by small and medium-sized producers, was no longer politically viable at the end of the 1890s. The reasons for this failure are complex. Strategic errors, the effects of historical timing, and structural constraints all contributed to this outcome. This was not the inevitable rise of a modern corporate liberal society but the historically contingent defeat of another alternative.

3

Greenbacks versus gold: The contest over finance in the 1870s

> There was, in her cupboard, a Golden Cap, with a circle of diamonds and rubies running round it. This Golden Cap had a charm . . . Twice already the Wicked Witch had used the charm of the Cap. Once was when she had made the Winkies her slaves, and set herself up as ruler of their country.
>
> *The Wonderful Wizard of Oz*

According to the greenbackers, finance was at the heart of the nation's economic and political problems. Their analysis of the country's woes and their prescriptions for correcting them centered on money and banking. This obsession with finance was shared by the financial conservatives. Both the defenders of gold and the NBS, and the promoters of a government-managed flexible currency system, saw themselves as the protectors of the republic. How did finance become the defining issue for these competing visions of the national good? The answer lies in an examination of the philosophies and programs of the greenbackers and financial conservatives.

Both parties to the financial debate drew from earlier American political philosophies in responding to the economic crisis of the 1870s. Moreover, both were concerned with larger issues of economic and political development. Greenbackism provided a coherent way of understanding the economic changes of the 1870s, and offered political correctives to the problems of economic concentration. Financial conservatism, in the name of market liberalism, advocated a stable, strong money supply as the basis for economic growth and international prestige. This chapter shows that each of these programs had intellectual coherence, political depth, and broad cultural resonance.

Many later histories present the two sides of the financial debate in a dichotomous fashion. The defenders of the gold standard and the NBS appear as economistic and sensible, while the proponents of greenbackism are seen as economically short-sighted and self-interested, or as culturally motivated by fear, hardship, and prejudice. The understanding of the pamphlet material offered here is quite different. No separation is made between economic reasoning and cultural meaning. Participants in the financial debate commonly combined intelligent economic analyses with cultural readings of race, class, sectionalist, and nationalist issues. Such readings are quite important since they help to situate the financial debate in broader political concerns that often underlay conflicts over exchange rates and reserve requirements.[1]

This chapter has three purposes. First, it establishes that there were two main positions in the debate over finance in the 1870s. Although diverse proposals and critiques were offered on the subjects of money and banking, out of these can be discerned distinct greenback and financial conservative positions. Second, the chapter establishes the economic, political, and cultural depth of these programs. Explication reveals that each program contained an economically coherent (though flawed) analysis. These analyses were informed by broader political concerns and imbued by cultural meanings that reflected some of the primary conflicts of late nineteenth-century American society. Finally, having argued for the intellectual parity of these programs, the chapter explores the normative and political differences between them. While the financial conservatives sought to shield financial institutions from the intrusions of an uninformed public, the greenbackers believed that a democratically controlled government was needed to guarantee the availability of equal financial resources and services to all classes and sections.

The 1870s was a time of tremendous intellectual creativity. There were myriad proposals for reducing the debt, establishing strong banking, and securing the monetary standard. These schemes inspired debate at party and reform conventions, academic meetings, in the halls of government, and among the general public – debates that fill the pages of the period's journals, legislative records, and, above all, pamphlets. There are hundreds of pamphlets from this decade devoted to expositions on financial and monetary matters. Continuing a tradition begun in colonial times, speeches and essays were reproduced in this cheap, easily circulated form.[2]

---

1. Irwin Unger, *The Greenback Era: A Social and Political History of American Finance, 1865–1879* (Princeton: Princeton University Press, 1964); Richard Hofstadter, *The Age of Reform: From Bryan to FDR* (New York: Vintage Books, 1955); Robert H. Wiebe, *The Search for Order, 1877–1920* (NY: Hill and Wang, 1967); Fred A. Shannon, *The Farmer's Last Frontier: Agriculture, 1860–1897* (Armonk, NY: M. E. Sharpe, 1945), pp. 186–187; and Richard Franklin Bensel, *Yankee Leviathan: The Origins of Central State Authority in America, 1859–1877* (Cambridge: Cambridge University Press, 1990).
2. On the American pamphleteer tradition, see Bernard Bailyn, *The Ideological Origins of the American Revolution* (Cambridge, MA: Harvard University Press, 1967).

Some pamphleteers argued that there should be no banks, or no banks of issue, while others sought to "democratize" access to the banking system by instituting free banking.[3] Alongside the NBS, some sought to revive the state banks or expand savings banks. Many felt that the NBS should be made more financially accountable and sectionally balanced, while others argued it ought to be protected and given a preferential position. Critiques of the NBS combined a Jacksonian hostility to banking with contemporary analysis of banking's role in the skewed structure of economic development.

Diversity also reigned in the debate over the monetary standard. Many believed that economic stability depended on the nation's returning to a gold standard. Others claimed that money was a purely legal creation, thus deeming the cheaper and more portable greenbacks superior to gold. Orthodox thinkers contended that gold-backed national bank notes were better suited to the demands of a fluctuating economy, and opposed the interconvertible bond scheme, which would tie the currency volume to the level of economic growth. These were the main alternatives in the financial conflict of the 1870s. Among the ideas discussed, the greenback and financial conservative positions were popularly recognized, conscious attempts to create comprehensive plans for financial regulation.[4]

The greenback position (the name given by paper currency advocates to themselves) was antimonopolist in character. It posited the labor theory of value and assumed the mantle of the equal rights tradition. To greenbackers, the financial system was central to economic development and income distribution and had major effects on the social and political systems. Financial conservatism (the term used here for the supporters of financial orthodoxy) called for a clearer division between the economy and polity, in which the economy was an autonomous system regulated by the forces of supply and demand. Yet most financial conservatives supported government aid for industrial development. The presentation of these two sets of positions is meant as a broad generalization of each.[5]

Two events sparked the financial debate of the 1870s. One was the Civil War. The other was the panic of 1873. The war left the government with

3. Free banking refers to systems in which banks are organized by general incorporation principles, with few or no barriers to bank entry, or where there are no limits on note issuance. See Appendix A for financial terms.
4. Two issues that are not addressed in this chapter are the bonded debt and the silver standard. The debt was developmentally important but politically less salient. See Jeffrey G. Williamson, "Watersheds and Turning Points: Conjectures on the Long-Term Impact of Civil War Financing," *Journal of Economic History,* 34 (1974): 636–661. The silver dispute is discussed in Chapters 5 and 6.
5. The opponents of the greenbackers were generally orthodox liberals with broad philosophical views on the role of money in the economy and government in society.

a debt of over three billion dollars, and left the nation with a new banking system and monetary standard. These three factors were intimately connected. The suspension of gold and implementation of the greenback standard were both consequences of war financing (greenbacks were a form of government debt). Further, the NBS was instituted partly to provide a market for government bonds (these bonds were required to secure national bank notes). Finally, greenbacks and national bank notes both constituted forms of paper currency. They were sometimes viewed as competing to meet the nation's monetary needs. Discussion of any one of these issues – the burden of the national debt, the role of the national banks in supplying credit and currency, and the merit of an unsecured, government-issued paper currency – logically led to the other two.[6]

The financial debate accelerated after the panic of 1873 and subsequent depression of 1873–1878. The initial panic was centered in the financial sector. Banks collapsed and highly financed businesses (for example, railroads) went bankrupt. The peak came with the downfall of Jay Cooke's brokerage firm in Philadelphia. Cooke had led the wartime drive to finance the greenback issues. So his firm's bankruptcy set off renewed questions about the war debt and the currency standard. The 1870s depression was the worst of the late nineteenth-century economic downturns. Responding to these events, each side in the financial debate felt confirmed in its views. Greenbackers contended that the contraction of the money supply and the structure of the NBS had caused the panic. The financial conservatives argued the opposite – that the speculative bubble created by a redundant and unsecured currency had finally burst. Their prescriptions for economic renewal also differed. Greenbackers called for the abolition of the NBS and an extension of greenbacks. Financial conservatives sought to speed the path back to the gold standard and protect the NBS. From 1873 until the resumption of the gold standard in 1879, the public debate over national financial policy was intense.[7]

What follows is an explication of two different political economy visions – visions that begin with a distinct understanding of the relationship between the economy and polity, proceed with a coherent analysis of the role of the financial system in economic development, and argue for different financial regulatory measures. Much was at stake for the participants in this debate. The great abolitionist leader, Wendell Phillips, con-

6. In addition to the Williamson article cited here, see Richard E. Sylla, *The American Capital Market, 1846–1914: A Study of the Effects of Public Policy on Economic Development* (New York: Arno Press, 1975), especially chap. 5, "The Mature Capital Market: Federal Debt Policy and Postbellum Open Market Credit Conditions," pp. 163–203.
7. Edward Chase Kirkland, *Industry Comes of Age: Business, Labor and Public Policy, 1860–1897* (Chicago: Quadrangle Books, 1967), pp. 7–10.

sidered the battle against the "money monopoly" to be more profoundly revolutionary than the fight against slavery. This was not a struggle to recapture some romantic past but an effort to determine the nation's future. The greenback crusade was the first skirmish in a long conflict between the antimonopolists and the financial conservatives over the direction of American political development.[8]

The remainder of this chapter proceeds as follows. The discussion is broken into seven sections. Sections I and II provide historical background on the issues involved in the debates over the banking system (Section I) and the monetary standard (Section II). Sections III and IV present the financial conservatives' position on banking and money. Sections V and VI do the same for the financial reformers. Finally, Section VII concludes with reflections on the role of the financial debate in American political development.

I. The National Banking System

Between 1836, when the Second Bank of the United States was discontinued, and 1863, when the National Banking Act was passed, the country's finances were managed primarily by state banks. Under this system, the laws governing capital and reserve requirements, note distribution, loan management, and the like differed from state to state. The result was a chaotic jumble of banks and bank notes, which earned the period its designation as the "wildcat" banking era. Some state bank systems, such as those of New York and Louisiana, were quite sound. But others, particularly those along the Western frontier, were unstable and poorly managed. Since bank notes were often of uncertain value, they were heavily discounted by Eastern banks. The nation's prewar banking system hindered interstate commerce and encouraged panics, such as the panic of 1857.[9]

The National Banking System (NBS) was designed to correct these problems. Established in 1863, the NBS was the primary manager of the nation's finances until the Federal Reserve Act was passed in 1913. The original laws governing the NBS reflected the war emergency during

---

8. Wendell Phillips, *Who Shall Rule Us? Money, or the People?* (Boston: Franklin Press, 1878).

9. For a general history of the banking and finance system, see Margaret G. Myers, *A Financial History of the United States* (NY: Columbia University Press, 1970). The relationship between the banking system and panics is discussed later. Recently, many scholars have concluded that antebellum state banking systems with general incorporation laws and branch banking (including several Southern states) operated quite well. See Larry Schweikart, "U. S. Commercial Banking: A Historiographical Survey," *Business History Review*, 65 (1991): 606–661.

which the system was born. In approving the legislation, Congress intended for the national banks to eventually replace the state banks, so that there would be but one banking system in the entire country. With the passage of a 10 percent tax on state bank notes in 1864, it appeared that this goal would be realized. The state banks declined precipitously in the late 1860s, but by the 1870s they began to recover. By 1900, the number of state banks exceeded the number of national banks. Their recovery reflected the deficiencies of the NBS and the ongoing financial crisis.

Although the NBS was defective in its design and operations, there was great resistance to dismantling it. Southerners and Westerners complained that poor note distribution and high interest rates left their regions with little currency and few credit services. Farmers complained that the banks were not oriented to the needs of agriculture, and businessmen complained that the pyramid reserve structure (PRS) made the economy vulnerable to financial panics. Yet many financial conservatives defended the original design because they feared a return to state banking or a move toward greater governmental control. Although the inadequacies of the NBS were widely apparent, the system was maintained until the antimonopolist threat receded.

The legislative provisions of the NBS

The problems that developed under the NBS were contained in its initial legislation. The features of the National Currency Act (later known as the National Banking Act) included specifications regarding capital requirements, note issuance and distribution, loan restrictions, redemption provisions, and reserves. A brief review of the early history of the NBS provides much of the information needed to understand the financial debates of the 1870s.

With the original act, Congress sought to create a uniform national currency guaranteed by public credit and limited in overall volume. Each new national bank would deposit federal bonds with the Treasury Department. The banks were permitted to issue currency notes worth up to 90 percent of the value of the bonds. Should a bank fail, the Treasury would redeem its bonds to settle the notes. Otherwise, the banks received the interest that accrued on the bonds. These bond profits were characterized by critics as an unfair privilege to the banks. These basic provisions regarding note issuance remained in place during the late nineteenth century.[10]

10. For the National Bank Acts, see Herman E. Krooss, *Documentary History of Banking and Currency in the United States,* vol. 2 (New York: Chelsea House Pub., 1983), pp. 297–327.

The overall limit and distribution of national bank notes changed during the 1870s. The limit was initially set at $300 million, but due to public pressure rose another $54 million in 1870. Then the note limit was abolished altogether. Yet this move toward "free banking" did little to change the volume of national bank notes. When the price of U.S. bonds was high, it became unprofitable for the banks to deposit bonds in order to issue more currency notes. After the note limit was lifted in 1877, the overall volume of national bank notes remained stagnant until 1881, and from 1882 to 1891, actually declined.[11]

Under the NBS, there was a perpetual controversy over the sectional distribution of banks and bank notes. The 1863 act provided that note circulation be geographically apportioned according to previously existing banking institutions and population share. But as large banks joined the system in the mid-1860s, circulation became concentrated in the Northeast. Historian Fritz Redlich writes:

> In fact, circulation was allocated to the various parts of the country in reverse proportion to their needs. Because of the survival of traditional business methods in the back country this unfortunate maldistribution alone was bound to impede in the less advanced sections the establishment of banking, because banking there was still identical with note issue as it once had been throughout the land.[12]

The new notes allotted in 1870 were intended for the South and West, where there was less bank currency per capita. But the law had little practical effect. In the South, where banking was devastated by the war, financial services lagged behind the rest of the nation. As of 1880, the amount of national bank capital in the South was $30.8 million compared with $165.7 million for New England, while the national bank deposits in the two regions were $41.9 million and $140.8 million, respectively. Although the South and Southwest had more than a quarter of the na-

11. On the volume of the note issue, see John James, *Money and Capital Markets in Post-bellum America* (Princeton: Princeton University Press, 1978), p. 77. There is a debate over why the national bank note circulation remained stagnant in the 1870s and declined in the 1880s – see, for instance, Bruce W. Hetherington, "Bank Entry and the Low Issue of National Bank Notes: A Reexamination," *Journal of Economic History*, 50 (1990): 669–675 – but no disagreement over the existence of this stagnation and decline.
12. The currency estimates and quote come from Fritz Redlich, *The Molding of American Banking: Men and Ideas*, part II (NY: Johnson Reprint Corp, 1968), p. 118. This may overestimate the South's per capita circulation, since it underestimates the region's population relative to circulation (population figures were taken from Roger Ransom and Richard Sutch's "Debt Peonage in the Cotton South After the Civil War," *Journal of Economic History*, 32 (1972): 645, with twelve state regional estimates, as opposed to Redlich's fourteen state currency estimates).

tion's population as of 1874, they held just over a tenth of its currency resources.[13]

The capital requirements and loan provisions of the NBS further impeded the entrance of Western and Southern banks. As of 1864, the capital requirements were $100,000 for country banks and $200,000 for city banks (with populations over 50,000). Further, the national banks were forbidden from making loans on real estate. This made the NBS unsuited to meet the needs of the agricultural sector where land was the greatest asset. The problem of farm credit remained unresolved until the passage of the Federal Reserve Act. The provisions of the National Banking Act were oriented toward the needs of commerce and urban areas rather than those of the national economy as a whole.[14]

The most significant provision of the National Bank Act involved its reserve structure. Banks were required to hold a substantial reserve from their total notes and deposits. A portion of these reserves could be placed in national banks in central reserve cities. As later modified, the reserve structure involved three tiers: the country banks, the reserve city banks, and the New York City national banks. The country banks kept a 15 percent reserve, three-fifths of which could be held in a reserve city. The reserve city banks held a 25 percent reserve, one-half of which could be placed with national banks in New York. Since the larger banks paid interest on these funds, this resulted in a tremendous outflow of funds to the New York banks.

This was the PRS. It skewed the distribution of the nation's financial capital, concentrating it in New York City, and affecting the course of economic development during the late nineteenth century. As banking historian Rondo Cameron summarizes:

> . . . the banking system promoted industrialization and thus encouraged the
> growth of the northeastern states generally, . . . at the expense (in terms of

13. These figures come from Sylla, *American Capital Market,* p. 57. See also Sylla, pp. 47–82; and Redlich, *Molding,* part II, p. 118.

14. Sylla, *American Capital Market,* pp. 51–52; Ransom and Sutch, "Debt Peonage," p. 646; James, *Money and Capital,* pp. 66–7; and Eugene Nelson White, "The Political Economy of Banking Regulation, 1864–1933," *Journal of Economic History,* 42 (1982): 33–42. The importance and effect of capital requirements on bank entry has been challenged, particularly where state and private banks were forming as alternatives to the national banks. See John J. Binder and David T. Brown, "Bank Rates of Return and Entry Restrictions, 1869–1914," *Journal of Economic History,* 51 (1991): 47–66. Yet even these works suggest that capital requirements may have affected bank entry. The significance of the real estate loaning prohibition is reaffirmed in Richard H. Keehn and Gene Smiley, "Mortgage Lending by National Banks," *Business History Review,* 51 (1977): 474–491, which finds that some national banks found ways to provide land loans in agricultural areas, but that the percentage of such loans was small.

slower growth than might otherwise have occurred) of agriculture, and of the South and West generally . . . The superimposition of various devices that mobilized capital for employment in industry must be credited with a large share of the impressive growth rates of American manufacturing when, on grounds of comparative advantage, one might have expected more rapid growth in agriculture and the extractive industries.

Whether by institutional design or market measures of productive opportunity, the NBS encouraged Northeastern industrial development at the expense of economic growth in the South and West.[15]

The interest rates set by banks in the NBS and other financial intermediaries (particularly mortgage companies) were also skewed. Economic historians have found that the New York national banks were more competitive and had lower interest rates than the banks of the interior. National banks in the South and Far West achieved higher earnings than those in the other regions, although the rate discrepancies narrowed as the century wore on. The cause of these interest rate discrepancies is debated. Some scholars argue that risk factors were responsible, while others point to institutional features of the NBS and capital markets more generally to account for these differences. If the cause was institutional, then the greenbackers were right in concluding that the hinterland was financially disadvantaged by a biased banking structure.[16]

Finally, we may consider the relationship of the NBS to other banks. The NBS was intended to be the primary source of financial services for the nation. Since most major banks were state banks in the early 1860s, advocates of national banking hoped that the NBS would absorb these voluntarily. But the state banks were reluctant to join. Many did so only under the pressure of the 10 percent tax on their notes. In the South, there were few state banks left to join the NBS on any terms. Yet, as the use of

15. On the PRS see James, *Money and Capital*, chap. 4; Margaret G. Myers, *The New York Money Market, Volume I: Origins and Development* (NY: Columbia University Press, 1931); Redlich, *Molding*, part II, pp. 115–117; and Sylla, *American Capital Market*, pp. 90–92. Cameron is quoted in James T. Campen and Anne Mayhew, "The National Banking System and Southern Economic Growth: Evidence from One Southern City, 1870–1900," *Journal of Economic History*, 48 (1988): 128.

16. James, *Money and Capital*, chapter 6 and appendix A; Richard Sylla, "Federal Policy, Banking Market Structure, and Capital Mobilization in the United States, 1863–1913," *Journal of Economic History*, v. 29 (December 1969), pp. 657–686, and *American Capital Market*; and Lance Davis, "The Investment Market, 1870–1914: The Evolution of a National Market," *Journal of Economic History*, v. 25 (September 1965), pp. 355–399, all argue that institutional impediments created regionally segmented capital markets. Other scholars contest this view. See, especially, Binder and Brown, "Bank Rates": 47–66. For a summary of this debate and the debate over mortgage rate differentials, see Schweikart, "US Commercial Banking": 628–629, who concludes that the local studies all "have generally supported the Sylla-James view or modified it only slightly" (p. 629).

demand deposits expanded, the note issue privilege mattered less. State banks were better suited to agricultural regions where they could organize with less capital and provide mortgages to farmers. Indeed, the strengths that led to the resurgence of the state banks reflected many of the weaknesses of the NBS.[17]

National and regional capital market development

The structure of the NBS had important consequences for capital market development. After the Civil War, the level of capital formation increased dramatically. Gross capital formation jumped from 14 percent relative to GNP in the antebellum period (1849–1858) to 22 percent in the postbellum period (1869–1878). As Richard Bensel and Jeffrey Williamson have argued, this change was due largely to the government's war and postwar debt-management policies. A new class of financial capitalists emerged from the war experience with new resources to expend on economic development. Two features of this market that mattered for the financial debate of the 1870s were segmentation and concentration.[18]

The national capital market was segmented into regions. Before the war, the South saw the beginnings of an integrated regional network of banks. After the war, there were fewer banks, with weaker links to one another. This raised the cost of capital and slowed the spread of financial innovation. In the West, the absence of financial networks meant that money was not internally circulated within these new boom regions. Instead, funds were funnelled in from the East, which raised the cost of capital and slowed the spread of financial innovation. While in the South, the absence of funding may have meant that economic opportunities remained untaken, in the West, the form of funding lowered chances for economic success. An integrated national market, built on regional financial networks, could have changed the flow of funding and investment opportunities in the United States.[19]

17. Roger L. Ransom and Richard Sutch, *One Kind of Freedom: The Economic Consequences of Emancipation* (Cambridge: Cambridge University Press, 1977), chap. 6. Also see Redlich, *Molding*, vol. II, chap. 16.

18. Figures on capital formation come from Sylla, *American Capital Market*, p. 4. Similar figures appear in Williamson, "Watersheds": 638–40. On the new financial capitalist class, see Bensel, *Yankee Leviathan*, pp. 252, 281–285.

19. On evidence of capital market segmentation, see William Clark and Charlie Turner, "International Trade and the Evolution of the American Capital Market, 1888–1911," *Journal of Economic History*, 45 (1985): 405–410; Stephen H. Haber "Industrial Concentration and Capital Markets: A Comparative Study of Brazil, Mexico and the United States, 1830–1930," *Journal of Economic History*, 51 (1991): 559–80; Ransom and Sutch, "Debt Peonage": 641–669; James, *Money*, throughout; and Sylla, *American Capital Market*, throughout.

Further, capital was concentrated in the Northeast through PRS. New capital went to New York, where through the call loan market it funded speculation on the stock exchange. The dearth of financial opportunities in the hinterlands was mirrored by the excess of investment funding in New York. There it funded railroads and manufacturing, often to the point of excess capacity. To most historians, this boom was the natural outcome of technological advance and economic modernization. The money went where the opportunities were. The alternative view is that government policies and political choices played a much greater role in the cost and location of capital. Policies that shaped the banking system and capital markets may have "unnaturally" (that is, politically) altered the path of economic development.[20]

The importance of the shape and development of the American capital market in the late nineteenth century depends on its relationship to economic development. This is a question that scholars have long debated, particularly in the context of comparative patterns of industrialization. This book does not directly address the question, but simply raises doubts about the accepted understanding of the role of capital markets in American industrial development. Even scholars who allow for institutional constraints in capital flows between regions during the late nineteenth century praise the system's ability to mobilize capital for industrial investment.[21]

Instead, this interpretation stresses the discrepancies in economic development in the South and West versus the Northeast and Northcentral regions. While recognizing the role of capital markets in mobilizing funds for industrial development, it may still be argued that the market was segmented, monopolistic, and slow to spread innovation in particular areas. Further, different financial institutions and practices, such as branch banking, regional financial networks, and recyclings of local savings

---

20. On regional capital markets, see Kerry A. Odell, "The Integration of Regional and Interregional Capital Markets: Evidence from the Pacific Coast, 1883–1913," *Journal of Economic History*, 49 (1989): 297–310; Kerry A. Odell, *Capital Mobilization and Regional Financial Markets: The Pacific Coast States, 1850–1920* (NY: Garland Pub., 1992); Naomi Lamoreaux, "Banks, Kinship and Economic Development: The New England Case," *Journal of Economic History*, 46 (1986): 649–667. Regional networks seem to develop out of merchant-banker relations. Such relations were also important to the nascent banking networks in the antebellum South where they grew from the cotton factoring system. See Larry Schweikart, *Banking in the American South from the Age of Jackson to Reconstruction* (Baton Rouge: University of Louisiana Press, 1987).
21. Scholars who have theorized about the relationship between capital markets and industrial development include Joseph Schumpeter, *The Theory of Economic Development*; Alexander Gershenkron, *Economic Backwardness in Historical Perspective: A Book of Essays* (New York, 1965); and Karl Polanyi, *The Great Transformation* (New York : Farrar & Rinehart, 1944).

through merchant-banker ties, might have made for a pattern of development in which industrialization was less regionally centralized and slower growing. Under these alternative institutions, the agricultural and extractive industries might have remained more important to the national economy. Would such a development pattern represent a less efficient use of capital? If the determinates are risk and profits, then this institutional perspective suggests that the risk and profit levels would have been positive under either arrangement. If the determinates are instead social and political factors, then we enter into a different debate, of the sort that was held between the greenbackers and financial conservatives.

II. The financial standard: Greenbacks or gold?

The debate over the monetary standard was about more than mere money. At issue were competing visions of economic development and political change. The choice between greenbacks and gold was a choice between a democratically controlled, national monetary standard and a market-oriented, international monetary standard. Concern with inflation and contraction went beyond prices to matters of class and sectional relations. Beliefs about the value of money and who should control it went to fundamental differences over the relationship between economic and political life. For antimonopolists, money was social and political, while for the financial conservatives, it was natural and objective. Eventually, the orthodox liberals won the debate – not necessarily on its merits, as this book reveals – but on the basis of politics.[22]

Prior to the Civil War, the nation's currency consisted primarily of coin and specie-backed state bank notes. Except for periods of panic (see Appendix A), when the banks temporarily suspended the payment of gold coin for bank notes on demand, the nation was primarily on the gold standard. This ended in 1862. The demands of war financing depleted the gold reserves of the large banks and forced them to suspend gold payments. Greenbacks filled the gap created by the gold shortfall. At the time of their issue, greenbacks were irredeemable; they could not be exchanged for gold. However, most people assumed that the nation would return to the gold standard eventually and that the greenbacks would be paid out in their coin equivalent. When resumption occurred on January 2, 1879, greenback dollars became gold-backed, or redeemable, currency.

Between 1865 and 1879 there was $300-$400 million in irredeemable

---

22. On the history of the American monetary system, see Milton Friedman and Anna Schwartz, *A Monetary History of the United States, 1867–1960* (Princeton: Princeton University Press, 1963), pp. 15–88.

greenback notes in circulation. There was also $200-$300 million in national bank notes in circulation. National bank notes were the approximate economic equivalent of greenbacks. They were an irredeemable paper currency, which could be exchanged for gold on resumption. Prior to resumption, the value of the national bank notes was tied to the value of the greenbacks, since greenbacks were used in the reserve funds of banks. When one currency was made redeemable in gold, the other would follow. Thus, the banks and their notes were intimately involved in the move toward resumption.[23]

Besides greenbacks and national bank notes, there was gold specie. Gold was used for foreign exchange and to pay the interest (and later the principal) on federal bonds issued during the war. Gold was treated as a commodity in the United States during the 1870s. Many banks held separate currency accounts for greenback and gold deposits. Although little used in domestic transactions, gold was an important force in the United States monetary system, since the price of gold relative to greenbacks (or the "gold premium") was the main barometer of the nation's progress toward resumption. When gold and greenbacks reached par value in prewar dollars (when one greenback dollar equaled the value of the bullion in one gold dollar), then the gold standard could be resumed.

Currency volume

The following discussion is organized around four topics: volume, value, currency interrelations, and monetary control. The financial debate of the 1870s is remembered for its concern with the currency volume. For the financial conservatives, there was an excess of currency that created inflation, while the greenbackers complained that a money shortage was resulting in economic hardship. The currency expanded greatly during the Civil War, the total outside the Treasury rising from $435 million in 1860 to $859 million in 1867. Under Treasury Secretary Hugh McCulloch, the currency volume shrank over $45 million between 1865 and 1868, and remained fairly steady over the next decade, until the period just before resumption, when the volume of greenbacks declined again. But currency only constitutes one factor of the money supply, the other major portion consisting of demand deposits. Deposits rose (1865–1873), dropped, rose (mid-1870s), then dropped again as the public closed accounts after

---

23. There were some functional differences between greenbacks and national bank notes. Greenbacks held a greater legal tender status and could be used as national bank reserves. Occasionally, greenbacks were valued at a small premium over national bank notes. Further, the greenbacks were issued and controlled by the federal government, while the bank notes were issued and controlled through the national banks. See Bensel, *Yankee Leviathan*, chap. 4.

a series of bank failures in 1877 and 1878. Given the high rate of economic growth, the overall money stock grew very little, rising 17 percent in the twelve years between 1867 and 1879. The per capita money stock shrank over the greenback period.[24]

Currency value

Contraction raised the value of money – dollars could buy more goods. Wholesale prices declined, and the differential between greenbacks and gold narrowed. From 1865 to 1879, the general price level declined by half as the money supply remaining stable while output rose. Not all areas of the economy changed at the same rate, and those sectors where growth in output was especially high, such as agriculture, showed greater downward movement in prices. With the settling of the Civil War and the passage of the Homestead Act, westward expansion accelerated and agricultural productivity rose. As the South shifted from a plantation economy to a tenant and small farming economy, production intensified. All of this contributed to higher output and declining prices. But the greatest factor affecting prices was the quantity of money. The magnitude of the deflation required to achieve parity between greenbacks and gold was a consequence of the government's desire to return to the prewar price level. The option of declaring the currency devalued and resuming at the new price level was never seriously considered.[25]

24. Myers, *Financial History*, table 4, p. 177; Robert P. Sharkey, *Money, Class, and Party: An Economic Study of Civil War and Reconstruction* (Baltimore: Johns Hopkins University Press, 1959), table, p. 81; and Friedman and Schwartz, *Monetary History*, chart 4, p. 55. See also Williamson, "Watersheds," table 2, p. 642. As Friedman and Schwartz point out, one of the unusual things about this period is its simultaneous price deflation and economic growth. Despite the expansion in output and wages, the period between 1873 and 1879 is remembered as one of the nation's worst depressions. These contradictory images of prosperity and depression are discussed in the conclusion.
25. On the overall price decline, see Friedman and Schwartz, *Monetary History*, p. 41. For the debate over its causes, see Michael D. Bordo and Anna J. Schwartz, "Money and Prices in the Nineteenth Century: An Old Debate Rejoined," *Journal of Economic History*, 40 (1980): 61–72, and commentaries by Michael Edelstein, pp. 68–69, and Richard Sylla, pp. 70–72. On the Western agricultural economy, see Chester M. Destler, "The People's Party in Illinois, 1888–1896: A Phase of the Populist Revolt" (unpublished Ph.D. dissertation, University of Chicago, 1932), pp. 9–10. On the South, see Ransom and Sutch, *One Kind of Freedom*. For the 1864 gold premium, see Wesley Clair Mitchell, *A History of the Greenbacks, with Special Reference to the Economic Consequences of their Issue: 1862–65* (Chicago: University of Chicago Press, 1903), appendix A, table 1, p. 424, where he states that the gold price for $100 in paper currency was $38.70 for the month of July 1864. Friedman and Schwartz also note the government's unwillingness to consider devaluation (*Monetary History*, p. 82, footnote 95). In my reading of the pamphlets, I found only one writer who suggested such a move. See F. R. Chandler, *A Strike for the Revival of Business* (Chicago: 1877), pp. 5–7.

The view that monetary value was created through legal authority was still unique in the 1860s and 1870s. The predecessors to the financial antimonopolists, including the Jacksonians, were hard-money advocates. On money (as with labor), the Jacksonians distinguished between a "real" or "natural" economy and an "unnatural" or "speculative" economy. They regarded specie-based currency as a tangible good that had intrinsic worth. The shift among the greenbackers to a soft-money (irredeemable paper currency) stance was therefore a dramatic innovation in beliefs about how money obtained its value.

Less radical was the advocacy of silver currency. In the late 1870s, as resumption appeared certain and the difficulties associated with monetary contraction persisted, expansionists turned to silver. Currency inflationists could concede the need for a specie standard and still expand the money supply by remonetizing silver along with gold. The passage of the Bland-Allison Act in 1878, which required that the Treasury purchase silver bullion each month for coinage, was the outcome of the political stalemate between greenbackers and financial conservatives. Silver expansion was a monetary half-breed. It demonstrated the intellectual victory of financial conservatives in its accession to specie, while providing a practical victory to currency expansionists in the form of a new money supply. While the financial conservatives won the war against government-regulated paper currency, they still had to fight against currency inflation.[26]

Support for the gold standard grew with the expansion of international trade. Hard-money advocates emphasized the global shift toward the gold standard. Great Britain adopted the gold standard in 1821, while most other European nations did so in the 1870s. As the United States expanded production and began seeking overseas markets (a process that intensified with imperialist expansion in the 1890s), the attractiveness of gold as the standard of international exchange increased. Nationalism and internationalism influenced the analyses of both the greenbackers and the financial conservatives about the value of money.[27]

Interrelationship of currencies

Analysis of the relationship between different currencies pivoted around the issue of resumption. Politically, greenback supporters opposed national bank notes, while gold standard advocates sought to limit the use

26. On the strategic role that silver played in the congressional debates, see Richard H. Timberlake, "Ideological Factors in Specie Resumption and Treasury Policy," *Journal of Economic History,* 24 (1964): 29–52.
27. Robert A. Degen, *The American Monetary System: A Concise Survey of Its Evolution Since 1896* (Lexington, MA: Lexington Books, 1987), p. 8.

of greenbacks. Theoretically, there was little reason for this distinction. Both greenbacks and national bank notes were forms of irredeemable paper currency. Proponents of a legal tender standard could readily use national bank notes, just as the greenbacks could serve on a gold standard basis. But the broader outlooks of financial conservatives and greenbackers made them reluctant to use both currencies. Greenbackers believed in democratizing the financial system and desired publicly created and controlled money, while the financial conservatives wanted to limit the role of the government and base the financial system on market forces and private bank notes.

As monetary policy was debated and decided over the 1870s, each side saw its positions reinforced by the course of events. Both groups recognized the power of the federal government as the most immediate instrument for affecting the money supply. The financial conservatives sought to use this power to contract the currency, resume the gold standard, and secure the dominant position of the national bank notes. This is precisely what Treasury Secretary Sherman did under the Resumption Act. Greenbackers tried to expand the currency with the Inflation Bill of 1874, efforts to repeal the Resumption Act of 1875, and sporadic attempts to pass an interconvertible bond bill. For both groups, their pursuit of monetary policy and views on the relationship between different currency standards were tied to their positions on resumption.

Financial authority

While the financial conservatives were principally laissez-fairists who celebrated the rule of the market, they had greater influence over national financial policy than their opponents. Greenbackers were never more than a minority force in the government, either as third party representatives or as a coalition of greenback sympathizers from different parties. Opposition to the NBS, support for the interconvertible bond, and belief in a legal tender standard, distinguished true greenbackers from mere inflationists. Greenbackers sought public, democratic control over finance. But none of these goals was achieved in the 1870s, a period in which the nation moved toward an orthodox liberal rather than an antimonopolist system of finance.

Although the financial conservatives were the ultimate victors in the financial debates, they did not clearly dominate the party system or the government. The Northeastern financial community initially resisted the formation of the NBS, and was often at odds with the Treasury Department or the Congress. Within Congress, clear financial policy choices were often avoided, and the legislative acts passed were regarded as compromises. This left it to the Treasury Department to complete resumption, which it did over a fourteen-year period. The party system and the government were not the clear conveyors of economic interests or policy preferences for any one group. The major parties avoided sharp divisions on financial matters, although the government aligned itself more closely with the financial conservatives than with the antimonopolists challengers.[28]

In sum, along with Reconstruction, money was the central political issue of the 1870s. The volume of the currency remained steady while the economy grew, contracting the per capita money supply. This resulted in price deflation and raised the value of greenbacks and national bank notes as measured by gold. The federal government's strategy for "growing up to specie," brought the country back to the gold standard in 1879. The pursuit of resumption also governed the use of the different currencies in the economy, favoring national bank notes over legal tenders. While the monetary conservatives dominated government financial policies, congressional decisions often represented compromises between the opposing parties in the financial debate.

III. The financial conservative position on banking

The financial conservatives supported the NBS because it was privately based and structured to facilitate national financial transactions. They argued that the superiority of the NBS derived from the combined attributes of government regulation, which provided for uniformity of standards, and market regulation, which made the NBS responsive to the needs of a changing economy. Further, they supported the note issue provisions of the National Banking Act, which allowed for a private, gold-backed currency. Private banks and bank notes fit with the conservatives' desired return to the gold standard. The NBS was promoted as the system that was most responsive to market laws, while providing the resources needed for economic development and industrial expansion.

Whatever its problems, conservatives found the NBS to be infinitely superior to the previous system of state banking. The defenders of national banking were often classical economists or liberal statesman who com-

---

28. My view of the party system and government contrasts with that of Richard Bensel in *Yankee Leviathan*, chap. 4. Bensel detects greater antagonism between the financial community and the federal government (which comes as a reaction to the government's partisan character), and more affinity between the government and agrarian and manufacturing interests. My view is consistent with Richard Timberlake's, who found that congressional opinion was not sharply polarized and that resumption proceeded despite the public's neutral or negative attitudes toward contraction. See Timberlake, "Ideological Factors," pp. 29–30.

bined a laissez-fairist vision with interest in the advance of industrialization. From their writings, we can discern the views of financial conservatives on the desirability of a private rather than a public system, the need for uniformity in banking, the reasonableness of national bank profits, the need for a limit on the bank note issue, and concerns over resumption and panics.

Private banking

For reasons of principle, practicality, and law, the financial conservatives preferred a privatized system of banking and currency. Principally, supporters felt that the NBS was subject to the laws of supply and demand, and therefore economically superior. Practically, they contended that bankers were better suited to regulate currency and credit flows than the Congress or the Treasury Department. Legally, they argued that government-issued paper currency was unconstitutional.

James Garfield believed that a private banking system offered superior currency regulation, "because the higher law above legislation – the law of supply and demand – pervading and covering all, settles that great question far above the wisdom of one man, or a thousand men to determine it [the proper amount of currency]." Market signals provided the best means for performing regular currency adjustments. As former bank commissioner George Walker stated, "Now it is impossible for the Government, which is not also a banker, to accomplish anything like this steady adjustment of the currency to the wants of business." National banks were the instrument of the market, which expanded or contracted the credit and currency supplies as it became more profitable to do so. The government was not suited to perform the same function.[29]

Financial conservatives invoked a deep distrust of the government as having neither the integrity nor the capacity to accomplish economic tasks well. As Garfield said in a stump speech, "No men are wise enough to do it [regulate currency], and if they were, dare you trust so delicate a thing as that to the partisan votes in Senate and House? If you have so much faith as that in Congress, your faith exceeds mine. [Laughter.]" The greenbackers also invoked this distrust in government, but they still adhered to the possibility and necessity for democratic reform.[30]

---

29. James Garfield, *Honest Money*, speech delivered at Fanueil Hall, September 10, 1878 (Boston, 1878); George Walker, *Considerations Touching Mr. Randall's Bill for the Suppression of the National Banks, and for a Further Inflation of the Currency* (Springfield, MA: Samuel Bowles & Co., 1867), p. 24.
30. Garfield, *Honest Money*.

Defenders of the NBS invoked the nation's legal obligations as reason not to cancel the national banks' note-issue privilege, and interpreted the Constitution as limiting the government to dealing in coin, except in national emergencies. As Representative Samuel Hooper said, "No one can doubt that it was the intention of those who framed the Constitution to make gold and silver the standard of money in this country . . ." He argued that the government should withdraw its irredeemable greenbacks, and leave the NBS to manage a specie-backed currency supply.[31]

Uniformity

Financial conservatives advocated both a uniform currency and institutional uniformity throughout the banking system. Uniformity made the NBS superior to the previous state banking system. Reviewing a proposal for a new type of bank, Amasa Walker condemned this further complication of the financial system. He called for a single-currency system based on the national banks. Walker compared the new banks to the old state banks, which offered a fluctuating currency with little capital base. Likewise, James Garfield argued that the NBS was superior. "I do not hesitate to affirm that while it may not be a perfect system, the present National banking system is the most perfect this country ever knew, and to abolish it is to go back to the wretched old system that prevailed before the war." Recalling the First and Second Banks of the United States, Henry Poor suggested that centralized banking regulation was needed to avoid speculation and panics. Most financial conservatives believed that uniformity could be achieved under the NBS without more extensive government involvement.[32]

Critics argued that the NBS was not uniform, that it provided uneven note distribution, and unfairly high interest rates in some regions. Financial conservatives rejected this view. As George Boutwell testified in 1874, "In the absence of general active business the capital of the country, as far as it is represented by the currency, flows to the places where it belongs. Therefore, it naturally accumulates in the city of New York." The market determined the flow of notes and rates of interest. The greater demands of commerce in the Northeast attracted larger amounts of currency. The

31. Samuel Hooper, *Necessity of Resuming Specie Payments*, speech delivered in the House of Representatives, February 5, 1869 (Washington: F. & J. Rives & Geo. A. Bailey, 1869), p. 6; Walker, *Considerations*, p. 5.
32. Amasa Walker, *Expansion or Contraction?* [reprinted from *Lippincott's Magazine*, December, 1870]; Garfield, *Honest Money*, pp. 10–11; and Henry V. Poor, *The Currency and Finances of the United States* [reprinted from the *North American Review* for January, 1874].

higher risk factors associated with business on the frontier raised the cost of loans in those regions. Conservatives made it clear that uniformity of standards did not imply equality of results.[33]

Profits and patriotism

Critics charged that the national banks received unreasonably high profits, and claimed that national bankers had immorally benefitted from the war crisis. NBS defenders denied these charges. As Representative John Wentworth of Illinois said, "Now, the managers of our national banks are among the shrewdest business men in the country; and, with scarce the number of exceptions that invariably attend general rules, proved themselves, in the late war, among the most patriotic." Others went further. "Banks and bankers go into business to make money . . . The old system was more profitable to the bankers generally . . . The national system . . . has raised the standard of banking generally." Within the financial world, national banking was seen as beneficial to the public and justifiably profitable for the bankers.[34]

National bank notes

Most national bankers opposed unlimited note issuance and free banking. But the views of NBS supporters varied and changed over time. The term "free banking" comes from the New York State Free Banking law of 1838. This general incorporation law allowed any adequately capitalized bank to issue as many notes as it could properly secure. Citing English precedent, financial conservatives initially supported a note limit for the NBS. After the war, they favored continuing the note limit for fear of inflation. With an eye toward resumption, many financial conservatives opposed all currency expansions.[35]

Yet two factors softened the financial conservatives' position on free banking. First, Republicans were concerned with party unity. To assuage the demands of Western party members, Easterners were willing to consider either note redistributions or note increases in non-Eastern areas. Second, many realized that there were regional disparities in currency dis-

33. George S. Boutwell, *The Currency–Specie Payments,* Speech in the United States Senate, January 22, 1874 (Washington: Government Printing Office, 1874), p. 5.
34. John Wentworth, *Loan Bill,* Speech in the House of Representatives, March 15, 1866 (Washington: Congressional Globe Office, 1866), p. 7; *The Advantages of the National Banking System* (1880?).
35. See Boutwell, *The Currency,* and Amasa Walker, *Expansion or Contraction?,* for examples of the opposition to free banking.

tribution. In principle, orthodox liberals found the ideal of free banking to be unobjectionable. Hard-money advocates, such as Carl Schurz and Edward Atkinson, felt that under some circumstances free banking ought to be allowed. As the nation approached resumption, more financial conservatives acceded to demands for free banking. In the conflict between principle and interest, principle was not always the foremost consideration.[36]

Financial panics

Financial panics occurred regularly in the nineteenth century. When they did, they caused economic loss, bankruptcy, and human distress. The demands of the harvest season strained the nation's inflexible and overextended banking system, sometimes leading to a systemwide collapse. Against accusations that the NBS contributed to panics, financial conservatives defended the system as a stabilizing force. They argued instead that panics were caused by inflation and speculation. As David Wells wrote, "And the cause of our present financial and industrial depression is due, in no small degree, to the uncertainty in the future respecting the rights of property and of creditors."[37]

Yet there was also partial acknowledgment of the problems caused by the PRS. George Boutwell (former Secretary of the Treasury) attributed "the panic to the inflation of the currency" but recognized that inflation, centered in New York, was caused in part by "unnatural processes" – namely, the "general practice of banks of that city, of paying interest on deposits" from other banks. This "evil practice" inflated the value of stocks on the New York market, increasing the likelihood of panics. Despite this flaw, the desire to protect the NBS kept financial conservatives from calling for any changes.[38]

Resumption

Finally, the financial conservatives believed that the NBS aided in the move toward resumption. "The national banks will be ready for specie payments as soon as the Secretary of the Treasury is," wrote one banker. Two steps were involved in preparing for resumption. First, greenbacks must be brought to par with gold. Second, gold reserves must be obtained

36. For the views of Schurz and Atkinson, see the Edward Atkinson Papers, Massachusetts Historical Society.
37. David A. Wells, *Contraction of Legal Tender Notes vs. Repudiation and Disloyalty* (New York, 1876).
38. Boutwell, *The Currency*, pp. 4–5.

to meet public demand for gold after resumption. To build the gold reserves, the cooperation of the banks seemed necessary, since the government was unlikely to obtain sufficient gold on its own. Although the national banks were often reluctant to assist the government, their publicly stated support for resumption led many to believe that cooperation was taking place.[39]

Support for the NBS

For its defenders, the NBS provided the best blend of government and market regulation. Government regulation gave the NBS uniformity, which facilitated financial relations between different sections of the country. Beyond this, government involvement was not welcome. Financial conservatives believed democratic oversight of banking was inferior to regulation by market-oriented banks. As a result of market demands, the NBS accumulated more capital and provided lower interest rates in some regions than others. Likewise, the market dictated bank profits and limited currency expansion. Most financial conservatives defended the NBS against charges that it contributed to financial panics, and claimed that member banks were cooperating with the federal government to achieve resumption. For conservatives, the great merit of the NBS was that as a legally designated, market-based system, it unified the national economy and sped economic development.

IV. The financial conservatives' defense of the gold standard

The monetary philosophy of the financial conservatives was founded on their commitment to gold. To the faithful, belief in the value and stability of gold made any other position a heresy. For those who thought that gold represented true value, the proposition that money be created out of mere paper was senseless. Gold offered market-managed stability, rather than the inflationary temptations of a government-managed currency. At the end of the war, financial conservatives thought the currency volume was too high. They favored contraction, which shrank the currency volume and raised the value of greenbacks. Conservatives argued that the market value of greenbacks derived from the expectation that they would be redeemable in gold. Although convenience and the size of the econo-

---

39. The quote appears in Wentworth, *Loan Bill,* p. 7; Unger discusses the reluctance of the national bankers to help Sherman obtain gold for resumption, pp. 366–370; and see Chandler, *A Strike for the Revival* (Chicago, 1877), on the popular perception that the cooperation of the national banks was an important route toward resumption.

my dictated the need for some (specie-based) paper currency, bank notes were preferable to greenbacks, since they were more subject to market discipline and less liable to popular whims for inflation.

Currency volume

The most clearly remembered aspect of the money debates concerns the currency volume. Financial conservatives are remembered as anti-inflationists, while greenbackers are recalled as expansionists. But such differences mislead as much as they inform our understanding of these two groups. The concerns of financial conservatives and antimonopolists over currency volume were enmeshed in their broader views about business ethics, the role of the monetary system in the economy, and the place of the market and government in American society.

After 1865, specie resumption was the predominant financial concern of Congress. Financial conservatives disagreed on how quickly to resume and by what method, but they agreed that excessive currency was a barrier to resumption. Comparing prewar to postwar per capita circulation, Joseph Ropes argued, "We have no reason to think that the general conditions of the question have changed, so as to render a larger proportion of currency to the population necessary than before." Considering a proposal for currency expansion Amasa Walker asked,

> Does any reasonable man suppose that with a circulation of two hundred and seven millions previous to the war, and a present circulation of seven hundred millions, it would be of the best interests of the nation that a fresh amount of irredeemable currency should be issued, still further to disturb the standard of value and postpone to a more distant future the resumption of specie payments?

Excessive currency demonstrated the inflationary tendencies of an unsecured money supply.[40]

According to conservatives, without the discipline of gold there was nothing to guard against monetary inflation. As one Midwestern banker argued:

> Redeemability in coin is mainly important, not because of any hidden virtue in coin or any taint in paper, but because it offers the only means of keeping the quantity of the circulating medium in its proper relation to the business of the community . . . So when paper is redeemable and too much is out for

40. Joseph S. Ropes, *Restoration and Reform of the Currency*, American Social Science Association (Cambridge, MA: Riverside Press, 1874), p. 52; A. Walker, *Expansion or Contraction?*, p. 648.

the work it has to do, it goes back from whence it came, and the people retain control of the quantity; when it is irredeemable the Secretary of the Treasury, or a committee of ignorant and needy congressmen may decide how much of it shall circulate.

Only privately managed currency would shrink and expand according to the needs of the economy.[41]

Financial conservatives argued that excessive currency and speculation caused the panic of 1873. "The real cause of the panic was the abuse of individual and corporate credit, and the speculations caused by an inflated currency," wrote the Secretary of the Honest Money League of the Northwest. This was true not just for the panic of 1873, but for panics in general. Many conservatives blamed the overextension of bank credit for panics, a situation induced by sudden expansion in the currency supply. Yet conservatives did not consider that currency contraction might still be accompanied by fund expansion in some places, as occurred under the PRS of the NBS.[42]

After inflation and instability, the third count in the indictment against greenbacks was immorality. When paper money was abundant, debts had less meaning, investments were more lightly made, and financial responsibility was lacking. "Every scheme which adds to the volume of currency has in it the element of immorality and the quality of injustice." This was particularly evident during panics. As one old Jacksonian said, "whenever more paper money circulates than is wanted . . . the market is excited, speculation is encouraged, a panic follows, banks suspend, and gamblers revel in the calamities of the people who have lost every standard of value." The bubble of artificial growth burst in the disaster of banking collapses.[43]

If pursued gradually, contraction restored financial responsibility. Joseph Ropes wrote that "It still remains true however, that nothing but contraction can save us from continued inconvertibility, depreciation, and ultimate repudiation . . . It must be so definite and direct, but so gradual and cautious, that not a single legitimate business interest of the community shall be imperiled by it; yet so sure and irrevocable in its action that all the influences and stock gamblers shall be unable to interfere with it." On the eve of resumption, conservatives such as James Garfield claimed

41. John Johnston, *An Address on the Currency* (Chicago: Honest Money League of the Northwest, 1878), pp. 15–16.
42. Thomas Nichols, *Honest Money: An Argument in Favor of a Redeemable Currency* (Chicago: Honest Money League of the Northwest, 1878), p. 41; Poor, *Currency and Finances,* passim.
43. Boutwell, *The Currency,* p. 13; Wentworth, *Loan Bill,* p. 3.

that Ropes' vision had been fulfilled. The best means of avoiding excessive currency was to maintain a gold standard.[44]

Monetary value

It was on the subject of value that the theoretical opposition between the greenbackers and the financial conservatives was most pronounced. According to conservatives, there were two types of money – real money based on intrinsic value, and fiat money based on government declaration. The first type was commodity money, money that contained worth in itself, as best exemplified by gold and silver. The second type, which included the greenbacks, contained only a legal obligation that it be accepted for debts and taxes. Gold was a constant currency whose value remained steady and provided stability to the entire economy. Greenbacks were legislated money, subject to the whims of partisan politics and the uncertainties of the public. Greenbacks had no real value, since the law could not create value. The remedy for financial uncertainty was to discontinue irredeemable paper currency and restore the gold standard.[45]

To financial conservatives, history confirmed the value of specie. "It cannot be denied that gold and silver have been longer and more successfully used as money than any other commodities. The universal estimation in which they are held for this purpose among civilized nations after many centuries of trial, justifies the assertion that such estimation rests on their inherent fitness for this purpose." There were also rare attempts, such as that made by Nathan Appleton, to combine an intrinsic theory of value with the labor theory of value.

> The great thinker . . . Adam Smith . . . has forcibly stated that the only possible standard of value is the direct product or result of human labor. [For monetary standards] it was necessary that the amount of labor to produce them should be subject to slight and not irregular variations, and next that it should be easy to put them in a certain shape and size, and afix marks to them which would show what the amount of this labor was, or in other words, what was their value. Of these substances, it is hardly necessary to say that the most important have been gold and silver . . .

This mixture of liberalism and producerism suggests a political culture that contained competing understandings of political economy. Various

---

44. Ropes, *Restoration and Reform,* p. 64; and Garfield, *Honest Money,* p. 11–12.
45. For an intelligent and insightful discussion of the view of specie money as a natural commodity, see Walter Benn Michaels, "The Gold Standard and the Logic of Naturalism," in Michaels, *The Gold Standard and the Logic of Naturalism: American Literature at the Turn of the Century* (Berkeley: University of California Press, 1987), pp.137–180.

justifications of gold's value were given by financial conservatives, but all relied on a notion of natural value.[46]

Conservatives asserted that the value of gold or silver was unaffected by government action. "The form of coins in which these metals circulate as money, and the government stamp which certifies their genuineness, are adopted for the convenience and protection of the public, but do not add to their intrinsic value." Money was seen not as a social product, but as a commodity valuable in its own right, apart from governmental recognition.[47]

To explain monetary value, financial conservatives distinguished between exchange and measurement. A measure, such as length, volume, or weight, had its monetary equivalent in the notion of the dollar. But for an exchange to occur, for the measure to obtain meaning, it had to be backed by actual value:

> Money, technically defined, is the measure of exchangeable value, as a yard is a measure of length, or a gallon of capacity. The form and material of all these measures may be various, but the one condition indispensable to each of them is, that they possess, in a fixed and definite degree, the quality which they profess to measure . . . So money must possess a definite exchangeable value of its own, or it cannot measure other values.

Another pamphleteer explained that paper – the mere measure of money – would not represent any value loss were it destroyed, but that the destruction of gold would mean the loss of real wealth. The notion of intrinsic value was fundamental to financial conservatism's understanding of money.[48]

Conservatives argued that unlike gold, fiat currency could not provide a uniform standard. Referring to gold-based Treasury notes, Amasa Walker wrote, "They constitute an inflexible standard of value and a reliable instrument of exchange, without which justice between man and man in pecuniary transactions is impossible." Although some financial conservatives acknowledged that gold was also subject to market influences, they believed that its value was so stable as to make it essentially unchanging.[49]

Greenback currency was viewed by critics as a mere promise to pay real money. Until resumption, conservatives claimed that greenbacks constituted a "forced loan" from the public to the government. The value of greenbacks derived from the public's belief that they would be made redeemable. Uncertainty about resumption created fluctuations in their

---

46. Nichols, *Honest Money*, p. 10; Nathan Appleton, *Coinage* (Boston, 1876), pp. 1–2.
47. Ropes, *Restoration and Reform*, p. 46.
48. Ropes, *Restoration and Reform*, p. 46; Nichols, *Honest Money*, p. 8.
49. A. Walker, *Expansion or Contraction?*, p. 649.

value. "What is paper money, so called? Is it money? It is a title to money, a deed for money, but it is not money." On the front of each greenback dollar was written, "The United States will pay the bearer one dollar." Gold advocates felt that failure to fulfill this promise to pay violated the national honor.[50]

Currency interrelationships and resumption

There were many forms of money in the 1870s. There were gold and silver coins, currency notes from both national and state banks, gold and silver certificates, and various interest and noninterest-bearing Treasury notes, including greenbacks. All of these forms of money had different economic roles and political meanings. For financial conservatives, the role of each form of money was judged according to its relationship to resumption. Gold-based money facilitated American participation in the international economy and brought stability to the domestic economy. The use of notes, coins, and certificates that promoted resumption was viewed positively, while unsecured greenbacks were regarded as an impediment.[51]

Although silver was specie-based currency, financial conservatives declared that silver money was inferior to gold, as indicated by the nations that used it. As F. R. Chandler wrote, "The true policy seems then to retain the gold the better instrument, the most valuable, the cheapest in the end, and export the silver to China, India, and other nations who still adhere to the wooden plows and old fashioned spinning wheels of our less enterprising ancestors." In making links between currency types and the people who used them, advocates on both sides of this debate often employed racist or nationalist sentiments to indicate the inferiority of a particular type of money. For a growing economic power such as the United States, a gold standard was needed. "We want a currency that can walk like an American all over the world," declared James Garfield. Financial conservatives saw gold as the nationally and internationally superior standard.[52]

Some conservatives granted that a positive shift in the balance of trade was necessary before a specie standard could be successfully maintained. Otherwise, American gold holdings would flow abroad and the nation

---

50. Garfield, *Honest Money,* p. 7; Johnston, *An Address,* p. 12.
51. Note that the list of money types does not include such things as demand deposits, which economists today regard as an essential component of the money supply. The omission is made to reflect the contemporary nineteenth-century understanding of what was money.
52. Hooper, *Necessity of Resuming,* p. 7; Johnston, *An Address,* p. 10; Chandler, *A Strike for the Revival,* p. 2; and Garfield, *Honest Money,* p. 9.

would be forced to suspend gold payments. But others argued that by going back on the gold standard, the United States would find a natural financial elasticity within the international system. "So, when a nation has more money than is needed to measure and exchange its other commodities, it will lend the surplus to other nations, as Great Britain is continually doing, or it will use it for the purchase of foreign commodities ... This is the true elasticity of a currency based on specie, i.e., on actual value, the only elasticity that deserves the name; all pretense to any other elasticity is a mere figment of the imagination." Gold provided the best basis for international financial exchanges, particularly for a growing industrial economy such as the United States.[53]

Greenbacks were not an exportable currency and tended to encourage an autarkic development of the economy. Financial conservatives associated greenbackism with isolationism. This was not the role that they envisioned for the United States. That "the nation most zealous of commercial supremacy should abandon the field, destroy her shipping, overthrow her commerce, and become voluntarily dependent for capital and credit on her European rivals" was an immoral rejection of economic potential and national strength.[54]

Domestically, the financial conservatives favored national bank notes over greenbacks. That preference reflected broader political factors, such as the desire to limit governmental oversight and to resume the gold standard. Further, national bank notes were supposedly free from partisan influences. According to George Walker, these notes constituted "a single national currency, amply secured, watched over and controlled by the government, limited in amount, of equal value everywhere, and possessing the confidence of the people." Financial conservatives distinguished between currency types according to their political affiliations, market orientation, and relation to resumption.[55]

Financial conservatives were sometimes divided over the proper path to resumption. Secretary McCulloch's pursuit of a rigorous contractionary policy in the late 1860s created dissension within the Republican party. McCulloch's replacement, George Boutwell, instituted the milder "growing up to specie" strategy. Rather than contracting the currency that brought unemployment and economic hardship, Boutwell had relied on an expanding economy to bring the nation's currency back up to par

---

53. Boutwell, *The Currency*, pp. 16–17, on the necessity of a positive balance of trade for resumption; and Ropes, *Restoration and Reform*, p. 53, on the international elasticity afforded by a specie standard.
54. Wentworth, *Loan Bill*, p. 1; Ropes, *Restoration and Reform*, p. 70.
55. G. Walker, *Considerations*, p. 26.

with gold. This strategy for achieving resumption was supported by financial conservative opinion and policy for the remainder of the decade.[56]

When resumption was imminent in the late 1870s, its advocates hailed its arrival. During the resurgence of greenbackism in 1878, voters were asked to be patient. The price of contraction had been paid, and only the benefits of a gold standard remained to be received. Others exclaimed that it was time to "STOP TINKERING AT THE CURRENCY LAWS AND LET THEM BE ADMINISTERED AS THEY NOW STAND." Financial conservatives again asserted that resumption was a matter of moral obligation and national honor. With resumption, the subjugation of greenbacks to a less significant role in the monetary system was complete, and the position of gold-backed bank notes was secured.[57]

Currency control

Finally, there was the question of control over the money supply. This issue may serve as a summary of the financial conservatives' position. Given a choice between control by the market and control by the government, the financial conservatives always favored control by the market. The volume of the currency was naturally regulated under a gold standard, which supplied the necessary elasticity for a growing economy. In contrast, government-created irredeemable paper currency led to inflation and panics. The value of specie-based currency was the highly stable, market-based value of gold and silver. Precious metals derived their value from their usefulness to consumers and gained nothing from government involvement. Even the interrelationship between currencies was governed by the market, a mechanism that demonstrated the depreciated and highly fluctuating value of greenbacks while attesting to the superiority of gold. The most popular path toward resumption relied least on government intervention and instead made use of natural economic growth. It was gold rather than the government that the financial conservatives put their faith in, since the yellow metal was the international medium of economic transactions.

V. The Greenback critique of the NBS

Greenbackers believed that the NBS threatened the foundations of America's democratic republic. They saw the NBS as an abuse of public au-

---

56. Boutwell, *The Currency*, passim, especially pp. 3, 13–14.
57. Garfield, *Honest Money*, pp. 8–9; David A. Wells, *Contraction of Legal Tender Notes vs. Repudiation and Disloyalty* (New York, 1876), passim; and Nichols, *Honest Money*, p. 53.

thority, a false delegation by Congress of its responsibility to manage the currency and interest rates, and a license to private interests for the exploitation of producers. Financial antimonopolists argued that the national bankers were extracting wealth from workers, farmers, and businessmen, thereby impoverishing many citizens. The critique of the NBS was fundamentally concerned with justice and economic survival. Greenbacker views on banking included advocacy of public versus private finance, concern over interest rates, and complaints against the role of monopoly. This section will also discuss briefly the greenbackers' views on panics and resumption.

Public versus private finance

In creating the NBS, Greenbackers argued, Congress had unjustly delegated its own authority to private interests. Citing the Constitution and early American history, financial reformers contended that it was the government's responsibility to control the currency. By allowing private banks to issue notes and profit from them, Congress had forfeited that responsibility. As Alexander Campbell wrote:

> The Constitution of the United States expressly delegates to the Congress power to coin money and regulate the value thereof . . . The States, or people, granted these powers to Congress for the public good, and not for the benefit of any privileged class of individuals or corporations.

Further, the value of the national bank notes was based on public credit. As Representative Townshend of Illinois stated, "The note is good everywhere in the Union because the Treasury of the United States is the guarantor for the redemption of the national-bank note." Antimonopolists argued that these benefits should be returned to the public.[58]

Greenbackers saw the NBS as providing a small class the privilege to make and profit from money. This violated the Jeffersonian motto of "equal rights for all and special privileges for none," which appeared in reformer pamphlets and on the mastheads of greenback newspapers. Special privileges were corrupting. They created particular interests for the few against the common interests of the many. In contrast, government-managed greenback currency was a neutral medium that favored no par-

---

58. Alexander Campbell, *The True American System of Finance: The Rights of Labor and Capital; and the Common Sense Way of Doing Justice to the Soldiers and Their Families* (Chicago: Evening Journal Book and Job Print, 1864), p. 28; and Richard W. Townshend, *National Bank Circulation*, Speech in the House of Representatives, January 21, 1880 (Washington: 1880), p. 7.

ticular class. Reformers referred to the National Banking Act as "class legislation."[59]

Financial reformers sought to expand the role of government in finance. Some argued that there should be no banks of issue, but only a government-issued paper currency. Citing the tradition of Jefferson and Jackson, Townshend opposed "any kind of bank paper, State or national." Others suggested that banks of issue should operate under a free banking system. Then financial privileges would be equalized and the right of note issuance made available to all qualified citizens. At the National Commercial Convention of 1868, Moses Field "Resolved, that the national banking act should be amended as to make it a Free banking law instead of a monopoly." In either case, government regulation would supersede private control.[60]

As regulators, Greenbackers preferred Congress to the bankers. "The question is not what the money shall be made of: the question *today* is, WHO SHALL MAKE THE MONEY, BANKS OR THE GOVERNMENT? *money-kings* or the *people?*" asked Wendell Phillips during the Massachusetts gubernatorial campaign of 1878. Similarly, William Goudy explained that *"The question of the amount of paper currency must be decided by someone* . . . Which is safest? Is it wiser to trust the Senators elected by States and representatives, one chosen by the voters in every district, or the bankers?" For financial reformers, bankers and the banking system represented a private interest in conflict with the public good.[61]

Greenbackers argued that the profits of the national banks were unreasonably high and unfairly gotten. The banks profited from the public credit and from the federal bonds held as collateral for their notes. Reformers contended that this expense would be avoided if the government issued notes directly. The banks also profited from the use of government deposits, yet they paid few taxes. Reformers sought to abolish the NBS.[62]

59. Townshend, *National Bank Circulation;* William Goudy, *Issues of the Campaign of 1878,* Speech at Farwell Hall, Chicago, September 14, 1878 (Chicago: J. S. Thompson & Co., 1878); Campbell, *True American System.*

60. Townshend, *National Bank Circulation,* p. 8; and Moses Field, *A Plea for Greenbacks,* Remarks in the National Commercial Convention held at Boston, February 1868 (Detroit: The Daily Post Book and Job Printing Est., 1868), p. 12. Calls for free banking appear in William B. Greene, *Mutual Banking: Showing the Radical Deficiency of the Present Circulating Medium, and the Advantages of a Free Currency* (Worcester: New England Labor Reform League, 1870), p. iii; and John A. Logan, untitled, speech before the US Senate, 1874 (Washington: 1874), p. 30.

61. Phillips, *Who Shall Rule,* emphasis in original, p. 5; Goudy, *Campaign of 1878,* emphasis in original, p. 14.

62. See, for instance, Townshend, *National Bank Circulation,* pp. 4–10; Goudy, *Campaign of 1878,* pp. 11–15; and Campbell, *True American System,* pp. 19–26.

Interest rates

According to the greenbackers, interest was the instrument by which productive wealth was redistributed:

> The rate of interest on money governs the rent or use of all property, and consequently the reward of labor. The centralization of the property of the nation into the large cities and the pockets of a few capitalists, is in proportion to the rate of interest maintained on loans of money above the average rate of increase in the national wealth.

Interest was a powerful tool in the arsenal of financial capitalists. The cost of capital affected the wages of labor and the profits extracted from production. Higher interest rates enabled bankers to gather a larger portion of the wealth produced. Greenbackers measured financial exploitation by the number of points that interest ran above the rate of economic growth. The natural rate of interest was economically neutral between classes, and rose or fell with the economy.[63]

Greenbackers criticized the NBS for setting high interest rates, particularly in the South and West. They rejected the view that interest rates varied because of local risk factors, and posited that high rates were associated with the monopolistic position of the national bankers. Further, greenbackers did not discern that the interest-rate differentials between regions reflected more on the behavior of local bankers and the bank structure than on the behavior of bankers in New York City.

Monopoly

To financial reformers, the NBS was a "money monopoly." Many different things were meant by this term. Here I will consider the institutional and economic rather than the political uses of the phrase. Financial reformers argued that the NBS monopolized the money and credit supplies. The money supply was regarded as a means for redistributing wealth. Credit affected opportunities for investment and competition. Financial capital was needed to secure the means of production, and cheaper capital offered its users a competitive advantage. Thus, if the national banks determined the flow of money and credit in the economy, they then had a profound effect in selecting economic winners and losers.

Greenbackers were concerned that national bank notes might become the exclusive currency of the country, thereby empowering the national bankers. As Thomas Ewing said during the campaign of 1878, the policy of financial conservatives was "designed to increase and multiply the National Banks, and give them complete and perpetual control of the issue

---

63. Campbell, *True American System*, p. 9

of currency and the consequent aggrandizement in wealth and political power." According to E. M. Davis, that was why the national bankers hoped "to get the greenbacks out of the way that they may fill their place with national bank notes, and thus enable them to not only supply all the paper currency needed, but monopolize the money issue of the land." Monopolistic control of the currency would place the national bankers in a position that threatened democracy.[64]

Greenbackers also believed that the national bankers favored resumption for self-interested reasons. Currency contraction increased the value of notes, including the national bank notes. Further, government efforts to create reserves for resumption offered profitable opportunities to national bankers. Once resumption occurred, having gold-based notes was advantageous. Gold was fairly rare and easily hoarded, making for a highly valued and readily controlled currency. The presumption was that the bankers would be protected from gold hoarders in case of a panic. But in an apparent contradiction, the Greenbackers also believed that the national bankers had supported the two-class currency system, with depreciated greenbacks for the public and more valued gold for the bondholders. Greenbackers did not acknowledge the classic liberal philosophy that led many conservatives to support the gold standard. Financial reformers presumed that conservative policy positions were determined by self-interest rather than ideology.

Greenbackers argued that monopoly control allowed the NBS to concentrate banking resources sectionally. The note distribution system, the commercial (and therefore Northeastern) bias, and the PRS of the NBS were all indicative of this sectional skew. In 1864, Alexander Campbell commented that the National Bank Act would "give a few of the eastern cities and villages the control of the currency of the nation," and that "the Wall Street gamblers will, as heretofore, have the controlling influence in the regulation of the currency of the whole nation." Five years later, Benjamin Butler concluded that this had occurred. "In many sections of the southern States . . . money cannot be obtained at any price, on any security, and if got at all the average rates are twenty-four percent." Southerners were particularly incredulous at the claim that the nation was suffering from an excess of currency.[65]

---

64. Ewing's speech appears in *The Great Campaign*, July 25, 1876; E. M. Davis, *To the Friends of a Greenback Currency* (Shoemakertown: 1880).

65. Campbell, *True American System*, p. 21; Benjamin F. Butler, *Speech of Honorable Benjamin F. Butler upon His Bill to Authorize the Issue of a National Currency, to Assure Its Stability and Elasticity, Lessen the Interest on the Public Debt, and Reduce the Rate of Interest* (January 1869), p. 3; and various editions of the *Great Campaign* and *Workingmen's Advocate*, January 16, 1869 and May 8, 1869.

Sectional differences were compounded by sectoral differences that favored industry over agriculture. Greenbackers criticized the PRS, which funnelled money from the country banks to the New York City national banks. "The whole course of such [banking] legislation was calculated to transfer the money of the country to the North and the East, and leave the South and West as dry as a 'remainder biscuit.'" Or, as the president of the New England Labor Reform League, E. H. Heywood, said, the NBS "subjected the whole material interests of the people to the plundering instincts of the stock exchange." In *A Financial System for the "Granger,"* John G. Deshler wrote that this arrangement put the reserves of the country banks in danger and increased the potential for a panic. In sum, the PRS created a money drain from the less developed areas, jeopardized the reserves of the entire NBS, contributed to the overbuilding of industry, and furthered the likelihood of panics. Behind the phrase "money monopoly" there was a detailed analysis of the role of the financial system in economic development.[66]

Greenbackers asserted that the NBS was detrimental to democracy. Through special privileges granted by a corrupt government, national bankers were gaining a monopoly over credit and currency. It was a monopoly used to pursue self-interest and high profits rather than to promote the common interest. Equal access to financial resources was essential to the preservation of equal economic opportunity, without which political democracy would suffer. The orientation of the banking system to commercial, industrial, and Northeastern interests was the consequence of institutional structures created at the behest of a powerful money monopoly. The South and West were deprived of the opportunity to compete and their citizens were being reduced to dependent lower-class subjects. The greenbackers saw in the NBS a threat to the republic itself.

The greenbacker alternative to the NBS was the interconvertible bond scheme, a concept that originated with Edward Kellogg in the 1840s and popularized by Alexander Campbell in the early 1860s. This scheme would have established a self-regulatory system of finance in which the money supply kept pace with economic demand. The interconvertible bond scheme would return currency control to the public, through its direct participation in the buying and selling of bonds, or through its elected representatives in Congress. It would also lower interest rates and halt

---

66. The quote from the Southerner appears as a letter by R. M. T. Hunter in the *Courier-Journal*, October 1, 1878, in the Daniel L. Russell Scrapbooks, vol. 1, North Carolina Collection, University of North Carolina, Chapel Hill; E. H. Heywood's comment appears in the foreword to Greene, *Mutual Banking*, p. iv.; John G. Deshler, *A Financial System for the "Granger"* (Columbus: Ohio State Journal Book and Job Rooms, 1874), pp. 12–13.

the redistribution of wealth to nonproducers. The sectional maldistribution of currency and credit would end, and the system's tendency to produce panics would stop with the creation of a highly elastic money supply. In short, economic democracy would be restored. A fuller analysis of this plan follows Section VI.[67]

VI. Greenbacks: A monetary alternative

The greenbackers' philosophy was concerned with the democratic promise of American life. Their interest in money was an interest in regulating the distribution of productive wealth and preserving equal economic opportunity. They promoted a plan for self-regulated currency growth – the interconvertible bond scheme – whereby the volume of money grew with economic expansion. Financial reformers believed that currency value was based on public authority rather than intrinsic worth. The greenback standard was seen as national in character, unlike gold, which was controlled by international trade and prone to manipulation by foreign economic powers. Greenbackers fought for a democratically controlled system of finance against the perceived encroachment of a money monopoly.[68]

Currency volume

Critics claimed the greenbackers simply wanted more money. Indeed, the greenbackers did oppose contraction and advocate currency expansion. In their view, the postwar economic prosperity was associated with a high currency volume. Then, when monetary contraction was implemented, economic depression followed. Further, greenbackers opposed the use of specie-based currency, contending that gold and silver money was insufficient for a dynamic economy and made the banking system vulnerable to panics. Instead, the greenbackers proposed a currency standard that grew with economic expansion, like the interconvertible bond plan. Al-

---

67. On Kellogg's interconvertible bond scheme and its importance to the antimonopolist tradition, see Chester M. Destler, "The Influence of Edward Kellogg on American Radicalism, 1865–1896," *American Radicalism, 1865–1901: Essays and Documents* (New London, CT: Connecticut College, 1946), pp. 50–78. Also see Redlich's discussion of early support among bankers for interconvertible bond proposals, *Molding*, vol. II, p. 124.

68. My own reading reveals wider diversity in the monetary philosophies of professed greenbackers than among the financial conservatives. Here, I seek to outline the main tenets of greenbackism. In the next chapter, the differences among financial reformers are explored.

though they were concerned about currency contraction, the greenbackers had a longer-term interest in reforming the national financial system. The experience of the immediate postwar years led financial reformers to associate plentiful currency with economic prosperity. "History shows that the periods of the world's highest prosperity have been precisely those when the volume of money was the greatest, and that every reduction in the volume of money has been followed by an increase of misery." The 1870s offered a different lesson. Greenbackers blamed monetary contraction for economic depression. Contraction brought high interest rates, bankruptcy, unemployment, greater sectional tension, economic centralization, and higher tax burdens. Greenbackers called for a currency volume that met the needs of the economy. "Money being indispensably necessary to represent, measure and exchange values, it should only be limited by the amount of property and products to be exchanged." As the economy grew, so, too, should the money supply.[69]

Greenbackers argued that there was not enough gold and silver in the world to supply the needs of commerce. "The production of gold is limited, and confined to a small scope of the country . . . As a [monetary] basis it would fail in quantity – also in elasticity." To compensate, gold standard advocates were forced to supplement gold coin with paper currency. "It has been established by experience that gold and silver coin cannot alone effect all the objects of money. It must be aided by notes or bills which also circulate as money." This supplemental currency created problems of its own. In times of high demand, there was too little gold to redeem all of the specie-based paper notes. The gold standard created either an insufficient specie currency or an insecure paper currency based on specie.[70]

Without a secure and sufficient currency, the gold standard system was prone to panics. One Midwesterner recalled the history of the old specie-based state banking system as one of "expansion, contraction, and ruin." Sudden changes in demand often led to financial crises. Benjamin Butler summarized the problem:

> It will be readily seen that the fluctuations in the amount and value of the currency caused by the banks being obliged to contract to meet every considerable demand in specie were destructive . . . since once in every ten years and a large part of the time much oftener, the banks were obliged to refuse to redeem their notes in specie, . . . Every few years panics ensued, and whole

69. John Mathers, Untitled, Speech at Jacksonville, IL, September 19, 1878, p. 12; on the evils of contraction, see Thomas Ewing and Peter Cooper in *The Great Campaign*, July 15 and July 25, 1876; and Campbell, *True American System*, p. 15.
70. Deshler, *A Financial System*, p. 18; Goudy, *Campaign of 1878*, p. 7; and Mathers, untitled, p. 3.

classes of solvent, prudent, enterprising men were involved in ruin from causes which it was impossible for them to foresee or control.[71]

As an alternative, the greenbackers proposed the interconvertible bond
plan. The plan, though imperfect, was a creative and intelligent response
to the problems of the financial system. The features of the plan were simple. Legal tender notes (greenbacks) would be issued by the Treasury Department. Concurrently, the government would issue 3.65 percent (annual) bonds. The bonds could be converted into greenbacks, or vice versa,
on demand. These bonds would regulate the money supply. When the
economy expanded, then the demand for money rose, making it profitable
for bondholders to exchange their bonds for currency. Once the supply
increased, the demand for money would fall and the conversion process
halted. Likewise, with an inflated currency, the price of money fell, making it more profitable to hold bonds, thereby inducing contraction. The
interest rate on the bonds would be set to conform to the expected year-
ly growth rate in the economy. If the plan operated correctly, interest rates
would be low, and there would be greater elasticity of supply.[72]

According to Alexander Campbell, the interconvertible bond scheme
had broad political advantages, including public control of the money
supply, creation of a uniform currency standard, lower taxes (cheaper
bonds making for a cheaper federal debt), respect for the economic interests of every class and section (thereby encouraging national unity), and
an end to the corrupting influence of money monopolists. Although proposed by several Congressmen (Cary, Butler, Kelley, and Kuyenkall among
them) in different bills, the interconvertible bond scheme was never adopted. Conflict over the plan developed in the late 1870s. But the idea behind
it – of "a circulating medium that will meet the wants of the people . . .
that need not of necessity become inflated, nor yet so scarce as to cripple
industry" – remained intact among financial reformers throughout the
period.[73]

71. Mathers, untitled, p. 4; Butler, *Speech*, p. 13.
72. Destler, "Influence of Edward Kellogg," passim.
73. Campbell, *True American System*, pp. 25–27; and *The Great Campaign*, August 22,
    1876. Campbell discusses the dispute over the interconvertible bond scheme in *To the
    Voters of the Seventh Congressional District of Illinois* (Chicago: Blakely, Brown and
    Marsh's, 1878), pp. 23–25. Besides the major Greenback and Greenback-related con-
    ventions (for instance, the NLU), which endorsed the interconvertible bond scheme,
    many pamphleteers did as well, including R. M. T. Hunter (Russell Scrapbook, NCC);
    Peter Cooper, Thomas Ewing, and Samuel Cary (*The Great Campaign*); Benjamin But-
    ler; Moses Field; John Deshler; Henry Carey Baird; An American Citizen; Sydney My-
    ers; John Magwire; and, of course, Alexander Campbell. Opinion was divided con-
    cerning the amount of Congressional oversight involved in the use of coin, and use of
    the bond issue for federal debt management and bank regulation.

Currency value

Greenbackers took the sophisticated position that money was the legal representative of value. Rather than constituting a value in exchanges, money was the medium of exchange. This position represented a radical break from the monetary philosophy of the Jacksonians, who were committed to a specie standard. Greenbackers argued that the value of money was affected by politics and criticized the monopolistic privileges used to elevate the value of gold. The depreciated market value of greenbacks relative to gold was attributed to the absence of full legal tender status for the paper currency. Those greenbackers who spoke of paper money as the representative of actual value were referring to the value of productive labor or the national economy. Sophisticated greenback thinkers argued that it was the national economy that undergirded the government's legal issue of paper currency.

Greenbackers criticized both the commodity and legal value of specie-based currency. As a commodity, specie value was too variable. "Gold and silver are natural products of the earth, whose absolute amounts cannot be controlled by the necessities of trade or the action of legislative bodies; a fact which the advocates of specie payments appear wholly to ignore . . . What, then, becomes of the assumed idea of 'fixedness' and 'invariableness' of this unit of value, so far as these facts show?" Others argued that gold was overpriced because of its scarcity. Further, high-priced gold brought high interest rates, according to labor reformer Richard Trevellick. As a commodity, specie was easily hoarded, making it easy for financiers to raise monetary values. In sum, specie was scarce, overpriced, and easily monopolized.[74]

Legally, specie money was protected and elevated by the government. Some asserted that specie's only monetary value came from its legal tender status, while others argued that specie currency mixed legal and intrinsic value. Legal tender theorists thought that paper currency was equally worthy. "Gold is not money until coined, and made money according to the law; and paper is equally money, when conditioned and issued according to the same law." Or, according to labor reformer William Greene, "Now, money, so far forth as it is mere money, ought to have NO VALUE; and the objection to the use of the precious metals as currency is, that, as soon as they are adopted by society as a legal tender, there is superadded to their natural value this new, artificial and unnatural value." Citing Edward Kellogg's distinction between legal and actual value,

---

74. Logan, untitled, pp. 4–5; *Workingmen's Advocate,* May 22, 1869; Goudy, *Campaign of 1878,* p. 4.

Greene argued that money should have a purely representative function, with its value residing strictly in its legal tender status. The intrusion of other commodity values created economic distortions that were conducive to speculation. For both specie and nonspecie currency, reformers contended that legal tender status was a primary basis of monetary value.[75]

Finally, there were those who argued that specie-based currency was inflated. "This paper currency promising specie currency in redemption is almost invariably an 'inflated' currency . . . with an issue of two, ten, twenty and even fifty promises of dollars to every one dollar, in specie, on deposit to redeem with." For whatever value specie might hold as a commodity, the paper dollars legally issued on a specie base held far less. The criticism was not of legal tender value, but of attaching legal tender authority to specie, thereby robbing paper currency of its economic neutrality and ability to fairly represent the value of other goods.[76]

In contrast, the security and uniformity of greenbacks was guaranteed. For paper currency advocates, the credit-worthiness of the government was at least as valuable as the promise to pay specie. Greenbacks "would have security and fixedness of value, equally good with notes based on specie. They would be as sure to be paid as the government is to exist, for the government cannot exist without levying taxes." The stability of the government provided greenbacks with stable value.

Within a greenback system, the interconvertible bond system would maintain currency value. "We must have steadiness in value, and in order to have steadiness in the value of the currency, we must have elasticity in its volume, and that is effected by the interconvertible certificate." To the greenbackers, financial conservatives confused currency elasticity with currency fluctuation. "Elasticity increases or lessens the volume determined by the necessities of its use. Elasticity is by no means synonymous with fluctuation, the latter being the increase or diminution of the currency at one time as compared to another." By providing for changes in the volume of the currency, the value of the currency would be maintained.[77]

Financial reformers attributed the pre-resumption discrepancy between gold and greenback values to the incomplete legal tender status of greenbacks. Greenbacks could not legally be used for customs duties or certain taxes. The few financial reformers who supported a return to the gold standard argued that par value between greenbacks and gold could be

75. Timothy H. Carter, *The Financial Problem* (1874), p.13; and Greene, *Mutual Banking*, emphasis in original, pp. 17 and 46.
76. Edward D. Linton, *Specific Payments Better Than Specie Payments: The Question of Money Divested of Verbiage and Technicalities* (Boston, 1876), p. 4.
77. Myers, *Financial History*, p. 12; Butler, *Speech*, p. 2.

reached through the extension of *full* legal tender status for greenbacks. As Peter Cooper explained, "This return to specie payments may be made without such injury, by honoring the currency in every way: by making it exclusively the money as well as the legal tender of the country; by receiving it for all forms of taxes, duties and debts to the government, as well as payment of all private debts . . ." Greenbacks were generally accepted and greatly valued by the public. When they depreciated, it was due to constraints placed on the greenback standard by the government. According to the financial reformers, the value of money was social and political in nature.[78]

Currency interrelationships and resumption

The greenbackers' perception of currency interrelationships was governed by their commitment to national currency. Financial reformers associated gold with internationalism and British dominance. Specie currency brought with it detrimental foreign influences such as classism and monarchy. National bank notes were regarded as proxies for a gold standard system. Greenbackers resisted strengthening bank notes at the expense of the legal tenders. In contrast to greenbacks, financial reformers saw other currencies as a political threat that symbolized the advance of elite rule and foreign influence.

Benjamin Butler, a longtime antagonist of the British, associated paper currency with national strength.

> I propose a paper currency . . . its value based not only upon the gold in the country but upon every other source and element of the national prosperity . . . It is the currency for a free people, strong enough to maintain every other of their institutions against the world, whose Governments they have antagonized; strong enough to sustain the measure of their business transactions with each other independent of kings, the least, or bankers, now the most potent sovereigns in the world.

For Butler, greenbacks were better precisely because they were a national rather than an international monetary standard. They promoted internal economic relations and discouraged relations with foreign economic powers. Just as American citizens must remain autonomous for the republic to be preserved, so too the nation's producers and productive capacity needed to remain national for republicanism to prosper.[79]

The desire to elevate the national economy over international trade did not imply a desire for autarky. Most greenbackers recognized that gold

---

78. Peter Cooper, in letter published in *The Great Campaign*, August 1, 1876.
79. Butler, *Speech* (1869), pp. 14–15.

was necessary for trade. They proposed a bifurcated monetary system in which gold remained the standard for international relations, while domestic transactions were carried on in greenbacks. A strong greenback currency would increase domestic production and turn the balance of trade back in favor of the United States. Accumulated gold would pay the interest on the nation's foreign debts, thereby decreasing foreign dependency.

> At the present time it requires more than one hundred millions in gold annually to pay interest on our national and state bonds, held in foreign countries; besides which, the balance of trade, to be paid in gold, is steadily and largely against us, and will long continue so. It is not possible, therefore, to meet these heavy and steady drains upon the gold in the country, without keeping it at a high premium, and making it nonsense to entertain the thought of putting upon the face of our currency that it shall be payable in gold . . .

Domestic economic needs were better served by legal tender currency, while gold could be reserved for use in international economic relations.[80]

The price differential between gold and greenbacks was taken by financial conservatives as evidence of the superiority of gold. Greenbackers disagreed. They attributed this differential to manipulations by money monopolists. Monopolists hoarded gold, making it more valuable, and denied greenbacks full legal tender status, making them less valuable. When bonds were issued to fund the new greenback notes during the Civil War, greenback currency inflation benefitted bondholders due to be repaid in gold. Samuel Cary argued that "For every disaster of the war, every time our boys were driven back from the field, it only added to the gains of the Moneyed Power." Wartime greenback inflation was taken as evidence of political corruption.[81]

For the reformers, the difference between national bank notes and greenbacks was between monopolistic and democratic money. The issue was not whether paper currency should exist, but who should control it.

> The only enquiry is, therefore, What is the best system for supplying the necessary paper money? . . . In other words, is the creation of paper money a proper function of government? . . . It is a remarkable fact that the advocates of hard money all urge the redemption of greenbacks and their retirement, yet they have no word of opposition to the circulation of bank notes; on the contrary, every effort is made to inflate the bank paper. This proves that the hard money men are not, in good faith, the advocates of a metallic currency, but are in favor of the control of money by bankers.

80. Carter, *Financial Problem*, pp. 9–10.
81. *The Great Campaign*, September 5, 1876, p. 23.

Reformers were concerned with the accumulation of economic power by financiers through the monopolization of paper currency.[82]

Opposition to resumption also affected the reformers' views. The elevation of some currencies over others shifted economic power between groups. Gold-backed currency created opportunity for speculation. Stability resulted not from a currency's reliance on a single commodity such as gold, but from being based on the entire productive economy. The proper form of redemption was redemption in goods, not gold.[83]

Democratic control of finance

Greenbackers favored a public system of finance. Equal economic opportunity depended on the broad availability of money and credit for all producers. Financial reformers sought to preserve a middle-class society of independent producers vigilantly protecting the republic. Without a fair monetary system, financial control accumulated among the nonproducers who directed economic development toward a more centralized system of production in which labor was subjugated. In such a society, the polity was corrupted by the concentration of economic power and the loss of democratic vigilance. Greenbackers believed that they saw evidence of this process in policies that sanctioned a two-class monetary system profitable to the bondholders, privatized control over currency through the NBS, shrank the currency supply, thereby putting farmers and workers into economic crisis, and reestablished the gold standard, making the economy subject to international business interests and domestic financial turbulence.

Democratic control of the financial system meant a government-issued paper currency standard whose volume was regulated by interconvertible bonds. Such a currency system would be neither inflationary nor contractionary and favored neither debtors nor creditors. The self-regulated currency system would maintain parity between geographic sections instead of concentrating economic resources in New York. The value of these legal tender dollars would be based on the productive resources of the country and the public's faith in the national government, rather than on the narrow base of specie. Greenback money was all-American money. Free of the threat of displacement by national bank notes and the gold

---

82. Goudy, *Issues of the Campaign*, pp. 9 and 11.
83. On conversion, see Greene, *Mutual Banking*, p. 46. For the notion of a legal tender standard redeemable in goods, see Henry Carey Baird, *Argument of Henry Carey Baird Before the Committee on Ways and Means, March 9, 1876, In Opposition to the Issue of $500,000 30-year Goldbonds for the Refunding of an Equal Amount of 5–20 Bonds* (1876), p. 6.

standard, legal tender would represent and preserve the republican system of government.

VII. Financial philosophies as competing visions
of the public good

These are the specifics of the financial programs of the greenbackers and the financial conservatives. For each group, its views on banking and money were situated within a broader political economy philosophy. In summarizing this philosophical conflict, several points of difference bear illuminating. Both conservatives and reformers believed in the notion of a natural economy, but meant different things by it. Greenbackers believed a natural economy must remain competitive and oriented toward production, while financial conservatives praised the efficiency of economic concentration and saw financial functions as essential to economic advance. Both groups favored economic development, yet had distinct visions of the political economy which ought to result from such a process. Socially, each side opposed class divisions, and criticized its opponents for contributing to class differences. Finally, the financial reformers' primary goal was to promote economic and political democracy, while the financial conservatives sought to expand the realm of market authority. These four areas of philosophical difference will be considered in turn.

For greenbackers, the idea of a natural economy was based on the labor theory of value. As Edward Linton argued, the two sources of wealth in the world were natural resources and labor power. Real economic expansion occurred when labor was applied to nature. Productive activity was activity that resulted in the creation of new goods, a view often employed to argue for policies favoring manufacturing over finance.

> Trade and commerce are the [out]growth of, and are subordinate to, production; . . . commerce can never fail to flourish when the hands and machinery of production are in full work. This condition is produced and sustained only by an abundant circulating medium; and a high state of prosperity can be produced and maintained in no other way.

The function of finance was to serve the needs of the real, productive economy. To do so, finance must remain competitive and financial resources abundant.[84]

Financial antimonopolists saw the natural economy as socially embedded, and judged economic outcomes by social standards. The elevation of labor power not only increased economic wealth, it also preserved re-

---

84. Linton, *Specific Payments Better Than Specie Payments,* p. 4

publican society. For early nineteenth-century financial republicans, the natural economy could be preserved without government involvement. Democracy guarded against the misuse of the state by special economic interests. But by the late nineteenth century, antimonopolists contended that accumulations of power within the public and private realms had altered the terms of economic competition to such an extent that an activist state was needed to maintain a democratic economic order. Thus, greenbackers placed the role of issuing and adjusting the amount of currency in the domain of the federal government.

The financial conservative notion of a natural economy implied a marked division between the economic and the social or political realms. For orthodox liberals, the economy was ruled by the market laws of supply and demand. Market mechanisms made the most efficient use of the nation's natural resources, resulting in economic progress. The proper role for financial institutions was to respond to market signals by supplying credit and currency to competing entrepreneurs. Rather than be disturbed by the accumulation of financial capital in New York, the financial conservatives saw this as the natural outcome of market signals. Concentrated control of financial capital was the logical outcome of large-scale efficiencies. Investment demands made capital markets an essential component of the natural economy. Many of the things that greenbackers viewed as undemocratic or immoral, such as interest above cost or the PRS, orthodox liberals saw as functionally necessary to a modern economy.[85]

Greenbackers were neither economically naive nor politically reactionary. This was not a stubborn agrarian attempt to preserve a simple market economy against the advance of industrialism. Both financial reformers and financial conservatives believed in economic development. Yet they sought to guide development down different paths. Greenbackers rejected the conservatives' development trajectory because they foresaw in it a two-class system of the unworthy rich and the dependent poor. Instead, they envisioned economic development that maintained a growing, democratic society. Antimonopolists advocated growth based on a decentralized, regionally organized, and sectionally balanced economy. Pennsylvania economists Henry Carey and Henry Carey Baird eloquently articulated this view during the middle decades of the nineteenth century. They argued that low-cost credit and abundant currency were necessary for the success of small and medium-sized producers nationally. Moreover, they contended that financial monopolies should be prevented

85. On the link between the conservative financial system and investment, see Wells, *Contraction*, pp. 8–9. On liberalism's acceptance of economic concentration, see Robert Green McCloskey, *American Conservatism in the Age of Enterprise, 1865–1910* (NY: Harper, 1964), chap. 3.

in order to avoid investments that favored large-scale system building over equally viable small-scale productive networks. This was the development path which reformers believed would preserve democratic republicanism.[86]

Financial conservatives were content with development that resulted in Northern dominance and economic centralization. Republican conservatives believed that Northern society was superior to Southern society. The North was more progressive and open to economic innovation and therefore more successful financially. Conservative Republicans envisioned a unified economy that included national currency and banking systems. Unity was necessary for the full development and integration of the American economy. National markets would engender increased competition and use of natural resources. Yet, as many Republicans became disillusioned with state activism and democracy after the war, they found solace in the teachings of Manchester liberalism, which urged laissez-fairist solutions to the problems of economic development. Having established national banking and monetary systems, the federal government ought to leave financial matters to the marketplace.[87]

Both greenbackers and financial conservatives detected disturbing changes in the class structure of American society. While reformers perceived the development of a powerful money aristocracy, conservatives became alarmed by the appearance of a radical working class. Neither greenbackers nor financial orthodoxes accepted the idea of a class-based society. Reformers argued that the producers – farmers, laborers, and small businessmen – were the "real society." They discounted the legitimacy of nonproducers such as bankers and bondholders. A fair financial system would reduce the class of nonproducers. Growth in the ranks of speculators and financiers was a development that alarmed greenbackers for it implied economic distortions and political corruption.

Financial conservatives also advocated social harmony. Conservatives saw the harmony between workers and managers disrupted by the labor radicalism, which swelled the ranks of the Greenback Labor party in 1878. Opponents of financial reform attacked greenbackism as communistic and class-based. At times, this argument was even given in a republican, antimonopolist tone:

> The state of the currency has rendered almost unavoidable an elaborate system of class legislation and wide-spread monopoly, most unjust and injuri-

86. An extensive list of the pamphlets of Henry Carey Baird and Henry Carey is provided in Unger, *Greenback Era*, pp. 421–422.
87. On the North as a progressive and therefore economically dominant society, see Poor, *Currency and Finances*. See James Garfield on national and financial unity, *Honest Money*. On radical disillusionment and the growth of Liberal Republicanism, see the Massachusetts section in the next chapter, and Eric Foner, *Reconstruction: America's Unfinished Revolution, 1863–1877* (New York: Harper & Row, 1988), chap. 10.

ous to the people, and dangerous to our republican institutions . . . When the government sets the example of breaking its most positive, solemn, and reiterated promises . . . what can we expect but what we see . . . a few flourishing at the expense of the many . . . [and] speculation, gambling, defalcations, and dishonesty of every kind.

Few conservatives used such antimonopolist language, but many did consider themselves to be republicans committed to social harmony.[88]

There was one class distinction both groups were willing to make – that between debtors and creditors. Financial reformers identified debtors with the producers, who were morally superior to the nonproductive creditors. Greenbackers argued that contraction hurt the honest producers.

Look at the effect of contraction in the relation of debtor and creditor; two-thirds of the nation to the other third . . . While the lender gets more than his due, it does not diminish his mortgage; it only diminishes the poor man's ability to pay, tending fearfully against the borrower and in favor of the lender.

Hard-money advocates took the opposite view – that creditors were responsible savers and debtors were reckless speculators. Moral societies had fewer debtors. Financial conservatives equated inflation with disrespect for property rights. "And our present financial and industrial depression is due, in no small degree to the uncertainty in the future respecting the rights of property and of creditors." The distinctions between creditors and debtors reveal some of the social and political reasoning that underlay the financial debate.[89]

The differences between the greenback and the financial conservative programs may be summarized as differences in their orientation toward democracy and the market. Philosophically, reformers were more deeply rooted in republicanism, while conservatives moved steadily toward market liberalism. Antimonopolists called on the equal rights tradition in the fight against special privilege and political corruption. To them, economic and political issues were inseparable. The money power arose with the aid of government favors and its reshaping of the American economy threatened democratic continuity. But to orthodox liberals, there was no money power. Economic forces were not social but universal. The value of money came not from man or law but from nature, from the inherent worth of precious metals such as gold. Economic difficulties and financial distortions were the result of political interference and human mismanagement. Their distrust of social regulation led liberals to advocate mar-

88. Ropes, *Restoration and Reform*, pp. 59–60.
89. Carter, *The Currency Question: A Plan for Permanent Relief* (Boston, 1875), p. 8; Wells, *Contraction*, pp. 8–9.

ket regulation instead. For one side, political engagement was the solution, for the other, this was the problem.

Greenbackers and financial conservatives understood that the United States was undergoing a period of tremendous change that was reshaping the class structure, the economy, and the state. Each group sought to mediate and direct these changes to preserve a good society. Financial conservatives, disillusioned with democratic excesses and government activism, sought to insulate the financial system from popular demands for easy access to credit and currency. Greenbackers saw the same insulation as a betrayal of their republican heritage that could only be corrected through democratic reform. Centralization and hierarchy diminished economic opportunity and tore at the fabric of democratic republicanism. In this battle over financial regulation, the stakes were high indeed.

Which of these two groups offered a better analysis of the economy and financial systems of the society in which they lived? As this chapter argues, that is a difficult question to answer. Each group's program had its strengths and weaknesses. Conservatives were right to claim that the bankers of the NBS were not defending a monopolistic structure for reasons of personal greed. The profits of the national banks were relatively low, and the New York bankers in particular were part of a highly competitive commercial banking market. Yet, its defenders were unwilling to acknowledge the institutional biases that existed within the NBS that favored the Northeast at the expense of the South and West. Likewise, they often failed to acknowledge that the PRS contributed to financial instability and the likelihood of panics. For their part, the greenbackers tended to fault financiers for personal avarice when they should have criticized the institutional structures of the banking system instead. Farmers and workers in the South and West knew that the financial system was biased, but they did not always correctly analyze how or why. However, their arguments concerning the NBS's use of the public credit for private gain and of the problems of the PRS were valid. In the political stalemate between greenbackers and financial conservatives, the banking system would wait decades before being substantially reformed.

On the subject of money, the greenbackers may have held an intellectual advantage. Their views on the nature of monetary value conform to modern understandings. Their belief in the ability of governments to print and regulate paper currency is confirmed by modern practice. Greenbackers also understood the need for a flexible currency standard that would grow or shrink with the productive economy, and offered a creative (though flawed) proposal for achieving it. In many ways, the greenbackers were ahead of their time. But in the late nineteenth century, when most citizens believed in the value of gold and the government was still inexperienced in managing a paper currency standard, financial conservatives may have been right to argue that the gold standard was necessary for monetary stability. They were also right in detecting the tendency of popular governments to inflate the currency. Popular legitimacy and the lack of government sophistication helped give the financial conservatives the advantage in the monetary debate.

The political and economic understanding of the greenbackers stands in sharp contrast to their lack of political success. In some ways, the economic analysis of the greenbackers was superior to that of the financial conservatives. This is not to say that the views of the financial conservatives lacked merit or force, but it is to suggest that the financial reform program was both intellectually coherent and analytically admirable. Whether or not it was workable given the economic and political realities of late nineteenth-century America is another matter. To approach this question, we must consider the financial antimonopolists, not through the lens of the financial conservatives who delegitimized them but as dispassionate observers willing to consider the historical possibilities of another age.

4

The "people's money": Greenbackism in North Carolina, Illinois, and Massachusetts

"I thought I had beaten the wicked Witch [of the East] then, and I worked harder than ever; but I little knew how cruel my enemy could be. She thought of a new way to kill my love for the beautiful Munchkin maiden, and made my axe slip again, so that it cut right thought my body, splitting me in two halves. Once more the tinner came and fashioned me a body of tin . . . But alas! I had now no heart . . . "

The Tin Woodman, *The Wonderful Wizard of Oz*

After a decade of political ferment, the Greenback party emerged as the vehicle for grassroots interest in financial reform. Although the party's focus was national, the roots of greenbackism were local. Around the country, the effects of contraction, the devastation of war, the consequences of railroad expansion, and the growth of manufacturing impelled different communities to contend with the processes of economic change. Their concerns and responses differed depending on the particular political and economic conditions of their states. Yet producers from various states and political backgrounds found common cause in the fight against financial monopoly.

Greenbackism was the most geographically diverse of the antimonopoly movements of the late nineteenth century. It was also politically particular in different states, where local issues drove and shaped the movement. This chapter analyzes the financial debate in three states. What follows is an interpretive analysis of the writings, convention records, and speeches of politically active citizens in the financial debate. The account is supplemented with the findings of secondary literature. Whereas the previous chapter analyzed the competing intellectual programs of the greenbackers and financial conservatives nationally, this chapter looks at the financial debate locally. There, it examines the way that financial politics were expressed within popular politics, and how different political structures (such as political geography and the party system) shaped the financial contest.[1]

In North Carolina, widespread financial antimonopolist sentiment failed to translate into an organized Greenback party. State Democrats succeeded in containing and channelling the financial reform impulse into sectional demands that supported the party's local supremacy. In Illinois, greenbackism built on the broader antimonopolist sentiments of farmer and labor organizations. There, organizational lethargy and regular party loyalty depleted an otherwise vital movement. The greenback impulse in Massachusetts arose from the labor reform movement and evolved into support for that maverick political figure, Benjamin Butler. But Butler's leadership personalized greenbackism, confusing it with other political causes, thereby diluting the party's economic message. These three cases demonstrate how the intersection of local, sectional, and national politics shaped the political sentiments of those involved in the financial debate.

Political geography, as used here, is an approach that treats geography as a set of institutional and social constructs over which political actors and groups strategize. Within late nineteenth-century American politics, there were several relevant geographical units bound up with political identities and institutions. The major geographical units were local, state, sectional (or regional), and national. International geography also played a role in this political universe. Many institutions mapped the relations between these political locations. For instance, the national and state constitutions charted the relationship between the federal, state, and municipal governments. Similarly, the National Banking System (NBS) included a pyramid reserve structure (PRS) in which New York formed the core and the South and West were the peripheries. Alternative forms of regional financial circulation were discouraged by this arrangement. Particularly relevant in this chapter is the way in which the political parties helped to construct geographical politics. Parties helped to organize geographical coalitions within and between the state, sectional, and national systems. At times, this political geography discouraged the expression of programmatic alternatives within the money debate, while at other times it limited or manipulated the form in which such expressions occurred.[2]

---

1. By politically active citizens, I am referring to those who expressed themselves publicly on this issue. That group is broader than the political elite, since it includes not just elected officials and organizational leaders, but also those who spoke out at conventions, wrote to their local newspaper, signed petitions, or wrote to their congressmen.

2. For a more typical use of the term political geography, see Peter J. Taylor, *Political Geography: World-Economy, Nation-State and Locality* (London: Longman, 1985). Taylor is also the editor of the journal *Political Geography Quarterly*. Traditional political ge-

In the nineteenth century, sectional geography was a primary component of political identity. Southerners were distinct from Westerners, who
in turn differed from Northerners or Easterners. The political identity of
geography was variously mixed with class and party identity. In class
terms, producerism was often associated with the South and West, while
the nonproducers were thought to dominate in the Northeast. The geography of the party system was aligned differently. In terms left over from
the Civil War, the North (represented by the Republican party) remained
opposed to the South (represented by the Democratic party). Although
each state had its share of both Democrats and Republicans, this was how
the parties were geographically identified nationally. Local and sectional
geographies were also associated with national and international identities, as in the Midwestern heartland, or the supposed affiliation of the
Northeast with England. The geographies of political institutions and
identities were debated as political actors attempted to create new meanings and coalitions in the money debate.[3]

The three states in this analysis not only had different political geographies, but different political economies as well. North Carolina, a Southern Democratic state, was agrarian and depressed after the war. Illinois,
which was Midwestern and politically competitive, had a mixed agrarian-
industrial base and a fast-growing economy. Massachusetts, in the heart of
Republican New England, was an early manufacturing state with a strong
financial center. Their economies, party systems, political cultures, and po-

ography has been criticized for economic determinism. See Aristide R. Zolberg, "Origins
of the Modern World System: A Missing Link," *World Politics*, 33 (1981): 253–81. In
American politics, my approach resembles that of E. E. Schattscheider in *The Semisov-
ereign People* (NY: Holt, Rinehart and Winston, 1960), who believed that every form of
political orgainization represented a mobilization of bias and that "what happens in politics depends on the way in which people are divided into factions, parties, groups, classes, etc." (p. 62). I have extended Schattscheider's approach by adding geography as a factor in political organization.

3. Many social geographers, working in the tradition of French philosopher Henri Lefebvre, regard geography as the construction of social space. In the United States, Edward
Soja and Neil Smith are leading scholars of this new "postmodern critical human geography," as Soja has called it. While this approach has much to offer, it frequently neglects
organized politics and political and economic institutions. See Henri Lefebvre, *The Production of Space*, trans. by Donald Nicholson-Smith (Oxford: Blackwell, 1991); Edward
W. Soja, *Postmodern Geographies: The Reassertion of Space in Critical Social Theory*
(London: Verso, 1989); Neil Smith, *Uneven Development: Nature, Capital and the Production of Space* (Oxford: Blackwell, 1990); Ann R. Markusen, *Regions: The Economics and Politics of Territory* (Totowa, NJ: Rowman and Littlefield, 1987); Rob Shields,
Places on the Margin: Alternative Geographies of Modernity (London: Routledge, 1991);
and David Harvey, *The Condition of Postmodernity: An Inquiry into the Origins of Cultural Change* (NY: Oxford, 1989).

litical geographies all varied. But all three witnessed the rise of financial reformism and conservative responses to greenbackism. This diversity expresses the myriad ways in which institutions, identities, and economic interests can be brought together around particular political programs.

Greenbackism had diverse origins in the three states. In North Carolina, it was a state-led movement, in Illinois it was farmer and labor-led, and in Massachusetts it was labor-led. In each of these cases, the nature of the Civil War party system and the structures of political geography hindered the organization of greenbackism. In these states, those who became involved with the Greenback party were contending with the consequences of economic change, and trying to affect the direction of that change. In so doing, they adhered to a program rooted in antimonopolism and republicanism, which proposed reforms to the financial system that would create a less concentrated and more regionally based form of economic development. The movement's failure resulted from structural contraints, strategic errors, and the exigencies of historical timing. Failure was not an indication of the popularity of greenbackism. Elements of the greenback program would reappear in various farm, labor, and third-party movements over the next fifty years as alternatives to the development of a corporate capitalist economy.

The remainder of the chapter is divided into four sections. The first three sections cover the financial debates in North Carolina, Illinois, and Massachusetts, respectively. The fourth section summarizes the discussion, with some reflections on the role of political geography and historical contingency in political development.

I. North Carolina: Financial reform but little greenbackism

The political geography and party system of North Carolina both fostered and constrained the expression of financial reformism there. Geographically, North Carolina faced financial shortages in money and banking that were common to ex-Confederate states. Further, the state's Democratic party, representing itself as the proponent of sectional interests, often pushed for reform of the national banking and monetary systems. But within the state, class interests cut across sectional concerns and intersected in complex ways with both political geography alignments and the party structure. Thus, efforts to develop a clear financial reform alternative were cut short by the political liabilities of the Republican party and the upper-class allegiances of the state's Democratic elite. Even the small Greenback party failed to gain much support in a system where the tides of sectional identity and party loyalty washed over efforts to promote programmatic economic alternatives.

At the close of the Civil War, North Carolina was economically devastated. Besides such problems as making the transition to a new labor system, reestablishing the agricultural sector, renewing trade relationships, and repairing the damage of war destruction, the state had to completely rebuild its banking industry. Much of the capital held by North Carolina banks in the early 1860s was invested in the Confederacy, and became worthless with the South's defeat. All of the state's banks were closed after the war ended. The attempt to reorganize state-chartered banks was thwarted by the 10 percent tax on state bank notes. The effort to establish national banks was also limited by the high capital requirements, loan restrictions, and note issue limitations of the NBS. Six years after the war, there were still only seventeen banks in the entire state – nine national, two state, and six private. Throughout the 1870s, financial resources remained scarce.[4]

Without traditional financial resources, Southern states were forced to rebuild their economies with imaginative credit practices. Among the most odious was the crop lien system. The old cotton plantations were broken up into sharecropping plots that were intensively cultivated by former slave families and poor whites. Each year, sharecroppers and tenant farmers were obliged to return one-third to one-half of their harvest to their landlords. Between harvests, sharecroppers lived on credit from store merchants who typically charged exorbitant rates for often inferior goods. If a poor farmer failed to pay out his or her debt to the store merchant at the end of a harvest season, then the merchant obtained a lien on the next year's crop. This reduced a class of Southern farmers to a form of debt peonage. In the early 1870s, the North Carolina General Assembly revised the Landlord and Tenant Act, as historian Eric Anderson writes, to "give the landlord a crop lien that was virtually ironclad." In an editorial on the subject in the 1880s, *The Progressive Farmer* concluded, "It [the crop lien] has proved a worse curse to North Carolina than drouths, floods, cyclones, storms, rust, caterpillars, and every other evil that attends a farmer."[5]

4. H. H. Mitchell, "A Forgotten Institution – Private Banks in North Carolina," *North Carolina Historical Review*, v. 35, n. 1 (January 1958): 34–49; and, George Anderson, "The South and Problems of Post-Civil War Finance," *Journal of Southern History*, v. 9, n. 2 (May 1943): 181–195.
5. Eric Anderson, *Race and Politics in North Carolina, 1872–1901: The Black Second* (Baton Rouge: Louisiana State University Press, 1981), p. 20. *The Progressive Farmer* quote appears in Hugh Lefler and Albert Newsome, *North Carolina*, second edition (Chapel Hill: University of North Carolina Press, 1963), p.494. Roger L. Ransom and Richard Sutch, *One Kind of Freedom: The Economic Consequences of Emancipation* (Cambridge: Cambridge University Press, 1977), esp. chaps. 6 and 8. For a discussion of North Carolina's economic development in this period, see Dwight B. Billings, Jr., *Planters and*

Politically, the state took several years to emerge from the effects of Reconstruction. At war's end, Republicans replaced the traditional Bourbon Democrats in controlling the state government. Many Republicans were former Whigs or Unionists, and most were white men. In the state's traditional division between its poorer mountain western region and its wealthier plantation eastern region, the Republicans found support among white yeomen in the west and black freedmen in the east, while the Democrats' base of support remained white voters in eastern and central (or Piedmont) regions. During the late 1860s, the Republicans dominated the governor's office (for three years out of five) and the General Assembly. The state government approved a new Reconstruction constitution in 1868, and underwent an ambitious program of economic development. The Republicans appealed to the state's producers to resist returning to the old, aristocratically ruled plantation system, and to join the larger nation as an economically dynamic state. They also appealed to black voters with promises to protect civil rights.[6]

No matter the authenticity of the Republicans' appeal, their political tenure was short-lived. In 1868, Republican William Holden was elected governor under Congressional Reconstruction. Holden had previously been appointed governor by President Andrew Johnson. During Holden's second term, the General Assembly approved special tax bonds to help refund the antebellum state debt and to provide new funds for railroad development. Funds from these bonds went to corrupt developers, and the Holden administration was implicated in the scandal. During the 1870s, the "Swepson-Littlefield fraud" served as the Democrats' prime example of Republican corruption. The national politics of Reconstruction and local politics of scandal both limited the success of the Republican party.[7]

The governor's final downfall came after an upsurge of Ku Klux Klan activity. As Klan violence against black and Republican voters became more widespread, Holden called out the state militia in early 1870. After violating the habeus corpus rights of the prisoners taken in, Holden was impeached by the new Democratic General Assembly. This marked the

the Making of the "New South": Class Politics, and Development in North Carolina, 1865–1900 (Chapel Hill: University of North Carolina Press, 1979).

6. See Table 2 of Terry L. Seip, *The South Returns to Congress: Men, Economic Measures and Intersectional Relationships, 1868–1879* (Baton Rouge: Louisiana State University Press, 1983), p. 15, on the demographics of the Republicans in North Carolina's congressional delegation.

7. On the Swepson-Littlefield case, see Eric Foner, *Reconstruction: America's Unfinished Revolution, 1863–1877* (New York: Harper & Row, 1988), pp. 386–392. On the politics of the late 1860s and early 1870s, see Douglass C. Dailey, "The Elections of 1872 in North Carolina," *North Carolina Historical Review*, v. 40, n. 3 (Summer 1963).

beginning of Democratic ascendancy on a platform of white supremacy, home rule, and Republican cupidity. It was an effective platform, which allowed the Democrats to neglect the concerns of economically troubled farmers under the cover of white solidarity. The consolidation of conservative rule came in 1876 with the return of former Confederate Governor Zebulon Vance to the gubernatorial mansion. From then until the rise of the Farmer's Alliance in the late 1880s and early 1890s, the Democrats controlled North Carolina state politics.[8]

Yet the Republicans remained an important political force. Indeed, the state retained a competitive electoral system throughout the 1870s, with most statewide and congressional elections decided by small margins. To retain their political advantage, the Democrats attempted to merge party identity with Southern identity, while accusing local Republicans of constituting a foreign interest and national Republicans of representing the force of repression. Democratic leaders were able to assert a soft-money position within the context of national politics, and a party (and racial) loyalty position within the context of state politics. The Republicans faced a more difficult task in constructing their party identity. For while party partisans could lay claim to the free labor and abolitionist traditions, it was harder to square the financial interests of Southerners with the national party's hard-money position. Southern Republicans (the North Carolina delegation included) generally voted with their section of the country on monetary and banking issues, which put them at odds with President Grant on the Inflation Act of 1874. So, while there was sympathy with greenbackism among North Carolinians, it tended to be obscured by the dynamics of the party system, or to be expressed as a sectional interest by Democrats.[9]

Financial reform sentiment develops

Articulations of greenback sentiment appear throughout the discussions of financial issues by North Carolinians in the 1870s. During this decade, resolution of the state's debt problems was a prominent political issue.

8. Southern Democrats were often referred to as the Conservatives in the postwar years. On the KKK and North Carolina politics, see Edward Hobson McGee, *North Carolina Conservatives and Reconstruction* (unpub. PhD dissertation, University of North Carolina at Chapel Hill, 1972), esp. chap. 6.

9. Paul Escott, *Many Excellent People: Power and Privilege in North Carolina, 1850–1900* (Chapel Hill: University of North Carolina Press, 1985), p.181. Seip, *The South Returns*, chap. 6, demonstrates that for most votes, region mattered far more than party on banking and monetary issues in the 1870s. An important exception concerned the Resumption Act of 1875, which was presented as a Republican compromise bill.

The Democrats addressed the issue in terms of Republican malfeasance and resistance to domination by Northern financial elites. The Democratic platform of 1872 stated:

> *Resolved,* That the general tendency, both at Washington and in our own State, of radical action is entirely in the interest of monopolists and the wealthy classes, and for the oppression of the masses of our countrymen, and that, instead of such conduct, it is the duty of the Government to aid, elevate, and dignify, the laborer, to whose efforts, mainly, we may look to our prosperity.[10]

The term "radical" refers to Northern radical Republicans, the authors of the more severe provisions of Reconstruction rule. Thus, class, party, and sectionalism were brought together in a formulation that pitted Northern Republican monopolists (and their local representatives) against the Southern Democratic masses.

Sensitive to the way the debt issue was being presented in North Carolina, and seeking to recover its investment, a committee of New York bondholders published a pamphlet in North Carolina that attempted to defuse negative perceptions of the bondholders' interest:

> Many savings institutions in the City of New York, and elsewhere in the Northern states, then became purchasers of these bonds and still hold them. It is also known to the gentlemen of this Committee, that many individuals who invested in them the savings of years, have been reduced to the most straightening circumstances . . . The Committee are in a position to state, that a large percentage of these bonds is still in the hands of original purchasers, or holders. Having great faith in the future of the "old North State," many holders of the ante-war and funding bonds, also invested in several issues made since the war.

The authors sought to present themselves not as ruthless, self-interested bondholders, but as smallholders – original investors with much at stake, who are being rewarded for their faith in North Carolina's future with the threat of repudiation. Despite the tremendous harm done to the state's credit rating, the logic of sectional politics and partisanship led North Carolina to join with many of its Southern neighbors in partially repudiating their Reconstruction debts.[11]

10. *The American Annual Cyclopaedia and Register of Important Events of the Year 1872,* v. 12 (New York: D. Appleton and Co., 1873), p. 598.
11. *Argument of the Executive Committee of Bond-holders of the State of North Carolina* (Raleigh: Raleigh News, Public Printer and Binder, 1877), pp. 4–5; Elgiva D. Watson, "The Election Campaign of Governor Jarvis, 1880: A Study of Issues," *North Carolina Historical Review,* v. 48 , n. 3 (1971): 286–289; and James Tice Moore, "Origins of the Solid South: Redeemer Democrats and the Popular Will, 1870–1900," *Southern Studies: An Interdisciplinary Journal of the South,* v. 22 , n. 3 (Fall 1983): 292–293.

Democrats were not the only ones in North Carolina to demonstrate financial reform tendencies. Members of the state Grange (including L. L. Polk and S. B. Alexander, future Farmers' Alliance leaders) also favored reform. At its first statewide convention in 1874, the North Carolina Grange called for the establishment of banks "owned, officered and directed by farmers with reduced rates of interest, so that farmers who are compelled to borrow money can do so at living rates . . . " The Grange began promoting cooperative efforts to deal with the credit problem, and turned their attention to national financial policy as well. Combining sectionalism with greenbackism, the state Grange called for an abolition of the 10 percent tax on state banks, and the establishment of banks whose notes would be redeemable in national treasury notes (greenbacks), to be loaned at a maximum interest rate of 8 percent. The call for monetary inflation was widespread in the South, while the stipulation of greenback redemption and the anti-usury provision were unusual, suggesting some direct familiarity with greenback principles.[12]

In 1878, the state Grange called for repeal of the Resumption Act and the remonetization of silver. Its resolution stated: "The effect of the Resumption Act so far has been such contraction of the currency as to cause a shrinkage of values in property and labor, so as to bring bankruptcy, ruin, and, in many cases, crime and starvation to many portions of our country." Under the crop lien system, North Carolina farmers were obligated to raise cash crops. As the state's ability to provide for food self-sufficiency declined, production of cotton and tobacco grew. Yet the prices for these crops fell even as more farmers turned to cash crop production. Along with the high costs of credit and transportation, falling prices forced more small farmers into tenancy. Under these circumstances, the effects of monetary contraction were widely unpopular.[13]

Generally, North Carolinians of all political persuasions favored monetary expansion and were suspicious of financial interests. In 1869, the General Assembly called on the state's Congressional delegation to secure more banking facilities for North Carolina. Around the same time, Republican Representatives Joseph Abbott and John Pool spoke in the House of Representatives about the cost and scarcity of money in the

12. *Constitution, By-Laws, and Proceedings of the First Annual Meeting of the North Carolina State Grange, Patrons of Husbandry* (February 1874); Summary from the North Carolina State Grange Proceedings for the Second Annual Session, 1875, State Historical Society of Wisconsin.
13. The resolutions are enclosed with a letter written in 1878 by J. E. Porter, Secretary of the North Carolina State Grange, to Senator Matthew Ransom, Matthew Ransom Papers, Southern Historical Collection. On North Carolina agriculture, see Lefler and Newsome, *North Carolina,* chap. 36.

South, and protested the Northeast's unwillingness to engage in currency redistribution. Citing "a scarcity of money that is hardly endurable," Democratic Senator A. S. Merrimon led in the fight to increase the amount of national bank notes in 1874. The following year, Samuel Hughes of Stokes County wrote to former governor William A. Graham that "The greatest danger now menacing the liberties of the masses, had its origins, if I have any correct comprehension of its nature, in 'the love of money,' and the consequent encroachments of *capital,* representing the concentrated *power of money* . . . "[14]

There were many more expressions of concern about the power of finance and the need for additional monetary resources in 1878 and 1879, as the Greenback movement reached its peak and the nation moved toward resumption. In a letter to the editor in the *Raleigh News,* one citizen wrote, "there is money enough in the country for all reasonable purposes, if it were only put into circulation . . . It is holed up in the banks and hidden in the rat holes. It is where those who need it can't get it; and those who want it to speculate in the necessities of the people can; the very ones who ought not to have it . . . " Anger at high interest rates led the General Assembly to pass a usury law capping the interest rates charged by state banks. Summing up the attitude of many Southerners toward resumption, one constituent wrote to Senator Matthew Ransom, "I'm all for silver, gold, greenbacks, and plenty of it." In his first session of Congress, Democratic Representative William H. Kitchin offered this view of the money question and the parties:

> The hard money wing of our side, I fear, will split us asunder – Every thing on the money side tends to consolidation & the curtailing of the rights of the people. And besides this, if we do not capture the Greenbackers so called we are gone in 80 – They hold the balance of power in the country – and in my opinion the only salvation of this country is in the fusion of affiliation of these elements . . . [15]

For North Carolinians, the monetary issue had several dimensions. Many shared Samuel Hughes's suspicion of money interests generally.

14. Seip, *The South Returns,* pp. 178–9, 185 and 189. *The Papers of William A. Graham,* vol. VIII, 1869–1875, p.452.
15. *Raleigh News,* March 22, 1878, and January 3, 1878. Seip, *The South Returns,* p. 213. Aubrey Lee Brooks and Hugh Talmage Lefler, eds., *The Papers of Walter Clark,* vol. 1, 1857–1901 (Chapel Hill: University of North Carolina Press, 1948), p. 204. For additional examples of the financial views of North Carolinians, see A. S. Merrimon, *Silver Money,* speech in the United States Senate, February 13, 1878 (no date or publisher listed); *The Raleigh News,* January 8, 1878, for Representative J. J. Davis's position; and Walter R. Steele to Samuel A. Ashe, August 14, 1878, Samuel A'Court Ashe Papers, North Carolina State Archives.

Nearly all agreed that there was not enough currency or bullion to meet the needs of the state's economy. As a result, local financiers were able to exploit producers and, nationally, the Northeast benefitted from plentiful capital and currency while the South went without. In party terms, both Republicans and Democrats sympathetic to financial reform felt constrained by national party interests favoring contraction. Given the weakness of the greenbackers in North Carolina and their short career in national politics, there was little hope of finding a clear, effective advocate for financial reform.

Finally, among these Representatives, editors, Grangers, and newspaper readers, there was a sense that the nation's financial policies were being directed by a Northeastern or European money power. They believed that contraction and resumption allowed the privileged few to profit from the woes of the many. Praising a letter from Representative J. J. Davis, the *Raleigh News* warned, "It is right that the people should be put on their guard against the New York press. If not actually subsidized by the Bond-holders, yet it is so clearly in their pecuniary interest to stand in absolute sympathy with the money powers of the North in all financial matters, that none of them dare take sides with the people in the pending silver contest. The Democrats as well as the Republican journals of that city are in league with the Resumptionists." More ominous still, the corrupting influence of the money power threatened republican government itself, as alluded to by Senator Merrimon:

> It is a well-known fact that in Europe and in some of the eastern countries capitalists in large degree control the policies of nations and direct their fortunes . . . I am not an alarmist, but I do not deem it out of place here to say that the great rising public danger in this country at this time is the ever-increasing power and influence of capital as concentrated and organized through great and multiplied corporations.

Likewise, in favorable front-page coverage of a speech by Indiana Senator Daniel Voorhees, the *Raleigh News* reported that "He referred to the continued agitation of the financial question and said it would never cease until the people are satisfied . . . or until on the other hand they are subjugated into silent submission and the government itself becomes changed in spirit and form into a moneyed aristocracy." To the North Carolinians, as to greenbackers elsewhere, the struggle over the finance question was a struggle between the people and the money power.[16]

---

16. *Raleigh News,* January 8, 1878; Merrimon, *Silver Money,* p. 6; *Raleigh News,* January 16, 1878.

Greenbackism

In 1876, Greenbacker William M. Coleman published *The Independent Party to the People of North Carolina*. This pamphlet addresses the monetary debate within the context of North Carolina's political traditions and problems. It begins with a quote from the North Carolina Constitution on the evils of monopolies and perpetuities as "contrary to the genius of a free state." Coleman goes on to excoriate the depression of the 1870s, adding that Congress had become the instrument of the money power, the "bankers, bullionists and bondholders," who "reap the benefits of Government while sharing none of its burdens." The real monetary choice was not between gold and paper, but between "one *kind* of paper against another *kind* of paper money"; between national bank notes and greenbacks. Without quick action, "Corporation money and the specie basis swindle will take the place of government money. The subjugation of the people will be complete." Coleman argued that the national financial debate was a struggle against political and economic domination.[17]

How Coleman's pamphlet was received is unknown. No state Greenback ticket was fielded in North Carolina. Yet it is clear that the state's Grangers were influenced by greenback doctrines. It is also evident that many of the state's Representatives spoke the language of financial antimonopolism. Beyond this, North Carolinians were sympathetic to greenback critiques of the NBS and the gold standard, and inclined to believe in the existence of a Northeastern financial elite, whose control of currency and credit hampered economic development in the South. But they were less willing to accept a purely paper currency under the control of the federal government. The old Jacksonian faith in hard money held firm, as did their distrust of a national government during Reconstruction. Whether or not Southerners' sympathies for greenbackism outweighed their preference for hard money and states' rights is difficult to judge since clear choices were rarely offered.[18]

In the one case where a Greenback candidate ran in North Carolina, he was elected. Although Daniel Russell ran for Congress on both the Greenback and Republican tickets in 1878, his biographers and his campaign broadside make it clear that he was running primarily as a Greenbacker.

17. William M. Coleman, *The Independent Party to the People of North Carolina* (pub. unknown, 1876), pp. 1–8.
18. Eric Anderson, *Race and Politics in North Carolina, 1872–1901: The Black Second* (Baton Rouge: Louisiana State University Press, 1981) also discusses instances where local candidates ran as Greenbackers or national candidates (for example, William H. Kitchin) used the language of greenbackism, pp. 67, and 75–76.

Further, the Republican endorsement for Russell's candidacy did not come until a few days before the election. Like Coleman, Russell called for a greenback standard instead of national bank notes, and repeal of the Resumption Act. Russell also predicted that under current policy, the money and bondholders would "eventually become the owners and masters of the country." These were the convictions that the future Populist-Republican fusion governor presented to the voters in the late 1870s. Still, Russell may have been perceived by voters as a Republican, since he had previously been elected a judge on that party's ticket. Further information about Russell's greenbackism is not available. But his election is suggestive. Beyond the constraints of the party system, there was broad potential appeal for greenbackism in North Carolina.[19]

Most scholars conclude that there was little support for greenbackism among Southerners. They argue that until the late 1870s, the South was taken up with the issues of Reconstruction. By the time that region's citizens turned their attention to the financial debate, the nation was on the verge of specie resumption. Further, while the call for reforms in the financial system appealed to Southerners suffering from a shortage of credit and currency, the call for a permanent paper currency issued by the federal government offended Southern preferences for hard-money and states' rights. This traditional view suggests that Southerners rejected the third-party alternative because the Southern wing of the Democratic party fought for currency expansion and restoration of the state banking system, and resisted returning to a narrowly gold-based currency standard. Although inflationist sentiments found broad appeal in North Carolina and elsewhere, true greenbackism obtained no purchase.[20]

The history of North Carolina suggests that this account is, at best, insufficient. Although there was little organized greenbackism, it was not for lack of sympathy with financial reform. The breadth of North Carolinians' financial reform beliefs and the logic of their economic circumstances suggests there was strong potential support for greenbackism there. No area of the country was more deprived of banking services by the NBS. Nor did any other region have a greater need for (or a lesser supply of) currency than the former Confederate states. The price depression

19. Daniel L. Russell, "To the Voters of the Third Congressional District of North Carolina," North Carolina Collection, University of North Carolina, Chapel Hill; Jeffrey J. Crow and Robert F. Durden, *Maverick Republican in the Old North State: A Political Biography of Daniel L. Russell* (Baton Rouge: Louisiana State University Press, 1977), esp. pp. 34–42.
20. See, for instance, Unger, *The Greenback Era*, pp. 341–2; and C. Vann Woodward, *The Origins of the New South, 1877–1913* (Baton Rouge: Louisiana State University, 1951), pp. 82–86.

in agriculture, the crop lien system's debt peonage, and the manufacturing sector's unanswered need for infrastructure and capital to rebuild and invest were all related to the course of national financial policy. Further, there was a rich antimonopoly and antibank heritage on which the greenbackers could build. This legacy is evident in the early writings of John Taylor of Caroline, the later support for Andrew Jackson in the bank wars, the pamphleteering of a North Carolina citizen proposing financial reform in 1861, and the 1870s speeches, letters, and public utterances of citizens from all around the state. Surely, hard-money and states' rights sentiments were obstacles to the development of a broader greenback outlook. But the same or similar sentiments were confronted and overcome by farmers and laborers in both the Midwest and the Northeast. The ground was fertile and it was a movement that should have grown, yet it did not.

The failure of greenbackism to emerge as a strong third party in North Carolina owed much to the structure of the party system. In the early Reconstruction years, there was potential for programmatic competition as the yeomen masses confronted the Bourbon elites in competitive elections. Instead, North Carolina became a state under the rule of a Democratic hegemony. The dominance of the Democratic party, its defense of sectional interests in the national context, and its subjugation of local economic concerns to party and racial loyalty hindered the formation of a financial reform alternative. Nonetheless, financial reformers were appearing all around the South among the Grangers, Independent Democrats, Readjusters, and Greenbackers. That the Bourbon Democrats met such challenges with Klan violence, white supremacy campaigns, and appeals to sectional identity argues that they were not a satisfactory vehicle for the expression of economic concerns. Through an astute combination of representation of state interests in the national arena, and financial reform interests where they were politically profitable in the local arena (as with the debt issue), the Democrats maintained their dominance and contained the development of greenbackism in North Carolina.[21]

II. Illinois: A center for farmer-labor radicalism

Party and economy conflicted in the political geography of Illinois. Politically, the state was associated with the North, the Union, and the Re-

21. C. Vann Woodward speaks of a similar manipulation of party, race, and regional loyalties in suppressing third-party financial reformers. See *Reunion & Reaction: The Compromise of 1877 and the End of Reconstruction* (Garden City, NY: Doubleday Anchor Books, 1956), pp. 257–260. On the economic interests represented by the Redeemer Democrats, see J. Moore, "Origins": 285–301.

publican party. But economically, emerging class tensions, a fast-growing agrarian-industrial economy, and an underdeveloped banking system led many Illinoians to identify with the South and producerism. The fluidity and contradictions of these competing political identities contributed to a dynamic antimonopolist tradition there. Antimonopolist efforts to regulate railroads, destroy the warehouse monopoly, halt land speculation, and above all, reform the financial system, emerged repeatedly in the decades after the war only to recede as quickly as they began. The inability of these efforts to gain institutional strength and stability owed much to the way that political alignments were already set.

At the close of the Civil War, Illinois was in transition from prairie state to corporate state, from a sparsely populated, agricultural frontier to the financial and industrial center of the Midwest. Southern Illinois was poor, agrarian, and Democratic. Its residents tended to sympathize with the South. The region had a strong Jacksonian tradition and was given to periodic expressions of economic radicalism and states' rights. In contrast, northern Illinois included wealthy farm communities, new industrial towns, and the burgeoning commercial metropolis of Chicago. The north's political allegiance was Republican and Northeastern. Northern Illinois had both economic barons interested in industrial advance, and union organizers promoting labor reform. Thus, Illinois' politics in the late nineteenth-century was a politics of competing possibilities – of agrarian radicalism, labor reform, corporate capitalism, and Western regionalism. In the late 1800s, Illinois was a state with the potential to form a successful farm-labor alliance, and ultimately it was a place where corporate liberalism was victorious.

In Illinois, partisanship followed class and geography. The south was primarily Democratic and the north was primarily Republican. Laborers around the state often voted Democratic or Socialist. Despite southern Illinois' sympathy with the Confederacy, the state fought with the Union, and afterward war prejudices and flag waving were manifest in politics. Yet the state retained a fairly competitive party system. While the Republicans dominated the governorship during the late 1860s and 1870s, the state legislature was divided with third-party reformers holding important minority positions. The Republicans were also troubled by dissension within their own ranks. Leaders such as Governor John Palmer, Senator Lyman Trumbull, Representative John Wentworth, and Judge David Davis all defected to the Liberal Republicans in 1872. Many former Democrats who had turned Republican became disillusioned in the 1870s and drifted back to their old party or to a third-party alternative. It was a dynamic period, in which the politics of old war identities were infused with newer concerns over economic development, and a partial realignment occurred.[22]

Unlike North Carolina, whose antebellum banking system was destroyed by war, Illinois failed to establish a strong financial system before 1860. While the war crisis destroyed what banks there were, this was just the latest in a series of financial catastrophes that closed the banks. In the 1820s, 1840s, and 1850s, similar disasters occurred in which most or all of the state's banks were forced to shut their doors. The new banking legislation of 1861 came too late to save banks whose capital was invested in Southern bonds. Fred R. Marckhoff estimates that as of 1860, two-thirds of Illinois' bank note circulation was secured by Southern state bonds. By May 1862, 93 of the state's 110 banks had liquidated, and by war's end the free banking system had collapsed. As a result, Illinois's bankers were eager supporters of the new NBS, authorized in 1863. Greenbacks and national bank notes were quickly taken up to replace the notes of the old state banks. Desperately in need of financial resources, and with few investments in the old state banking structure, the Illinois financial community turned to the new national financial system during and after the Civil War.[23]

While the financial sector struggled to find a firm foundation, the industrial and commercial sectors rapidly expanded. Between 1870 and 1880, the value of manufacturing products produced in Illinois grew by 102 percent, while the number of people employed in manufacturing and mechanical work grew by 159 percent in the same period. This growth occurred despite the depression of the 1870s. The relation between the agricultural and industrial population changed more gradually. In 1870, the proportion of the population engaged in agricultural work (50.8 percent) was more than twice as large as that engaged in manufacturing and mechanical work (23.1 percent). Not until 1900 did census statistics show that Illinois had a larger population of factory workers than farmers (32.2 percent versus 25.7 percent). By that year, Illinois was the third largest industrial state in the nation, following New York and Pennsylvania.[24]

22. For an overview of Illinois politics, see John H. Keiser, *Building for the Centuries: Illinois, 1865–1898* (Urbana: University of Illinois Press, 1977), chap. 3; Charles A. Church, *History of the Republican Party in Illinois, 1854–1912* (Rockford, IL: Wilson Brothers Co., 1912); and Ernest L. Bogart and Charles M. Thompson, *The Industrial State, 1870–1883: Centennial History of Illinois, III* (Springfield, IL: Illinois Historical Commission, 1920).
23. Fred R. Marckhoff, "Currency and Banking in Illinois Before 1865," *Journal of Illinois State Historical Society,* v. 52, n. 3 (Autumn 1959), p. 397; Joseph William Charlton, "The History of Banking in Illinois since 1863," (unpub. PhD dissertation, University of Chicago, 1938), p. 14; and Fritz Redlich, *The Molding of American Banking: Men and Ideas,* Part II (New York: Johnson Reprint Corporation, 1968), p. 109.
24. Keiser, *Building,* p. 180 and appendix, tables C and E, pp. 336–337, 340–341.

The Civil War, as Barrington Moore has noted, confirmed a shift in the balance of trading relations within the country from a North-South axis to an East-West one. With the cessation of trading ties to the Confederacy, the Northeast turned to the West to supply its needs for industrial raw materials and agricultural goods. By the 1870s, Chicago was the marketing center of the Midwest and the transit point for shipments heading east. Railroad mileage in Illinois nearly doubled between 1865 and 1873, and after a brief pause with the onset of the panic of 1873 resumed growth. During the late nineteenth century, Illinois consistently had more miles of track than any other state in the nation. It was a building process assisted by the government at all levels. The federal government made its first land grant to the Illinois Central Railroad in the 1850s, and during the late 1860s and 1870s, local communities took out millions in bonded debt to finance railroads. The growth of national markets and the shift to East-West commercial ties made Illinois a center of activity in the nationalizing economy.[25]

Early political unrest: Labor reform, liberal Republicans,
and the Illinois State Farmers' Association

Rapid economic development provoked political responses. Workers responded to the appearance of the wage system, the loss of shop floor control, and the segmentation of communities that accompanied the advance of the corporation. There was a resurgence of the union movement at the end of the 1860s around a labor reform agenda that emphasized the financial question. Several nationally known labor reform figures lived in Illinois, including Alexander Campbell and Andrew Cameron. Cameron was the editor of *The Workingmen's Advocate*, the official newspaper of the National Labor Union (NLU), and Campbell was the author of *The True American System of Finance*, a widely read pamphlet published in 1864, which was the most important single articulation of the greenback philosophy.

Illinois miners from both the northern and southern parts of the state became interested in financial reform in the late 1860s, when the recession caused wage cutbacks, layoffs, and strikes. The views of reformers such as Alexander Campbell and Edward Daniels were well received by

25. Barrington Moore, Jr., *Social Origins of Dictatorship and Democracy: Lord and Peasant in the Making of the Modern World* (Boston: Beacon Press, 1966), chap. 3; Keiser, *Building*, chap. 5; Edward Chase Kirkland, *Industry Comes of Age: Business, Labor and Public Policy, 1860–1897* (Chicago: Quadrangle Books, 1967), chap. 3; and Jonathan Lurie, *The Chicago Board of Trade, 1859–1905: The Dynamics of Self-Regulation* (Urbana: University of Illinois Press, 1979), chap. 2.

workers, and given further advocacy by labor leaders such as John Hinch-cliffe (editor of the *Weekly Miner*) and John Bingham (president of the American Miners Association).[26] After 1867, political organizations were formed and independent candidates were elected from mining towns in both northern and southern Illinois on platforms of financial reform and antimonopolism.[27]

Campbell, Cameron, and Hinchcliffe all played prominent roles at the NLU conventions of the mid-1860s. The NLU was the first national la-bor association in the nineteenth century. At the 1867 convention in Chicago, these Illinois reformers participated in the discussions of anti-monopolism and financial reform. From this came the NLU's Declaration of Principles, which stated that the "money monopoly is the parent of all monopolies." The financial section of the document echoed the analysis of Alexander Campbell:

> [Resolved] That . . . it is the imperative duty of Congress to institute it [mon-ey] upon such a wise and just basis that it shall be directly under the control of the sovereign people who produce the value it is designed to represent, measure and exchange, that it may be a correct and uniform standard of val-ue, and distribute the products of labor equitably between capital and labor according to the service or labor performed in their production.

From 1867 on, the NLU's platform was devoted to financial reform. La-bor reformers believed that the monetary system was crucial to the abili-ty of producers to control the productive process and to receive their just rewards. To them, money was the representative of value, and government regulation of the money supply was an essential condition of democracy. Illinois labor reformers led both the state and national movements in pur-suing financial reform.[28]

The early 1870s was a time of widespread political dissension. In 1872, the leadership of the Illinois Republican party was split by the Liberal Re-

26. For Alexander Campbell's views, see his pamphlets, including *The True American Sys-tem of Finance: The Rights of Labor and Capital, and the Common Sense Way of Do-ing Justice to the Soldiers and Their Families* (Chicago: Evening Journal Book and Job Print, 1864) and *To the Voters of the Seventh Congressional District of Illinois* (Chica-go: Blakely, Brown and Marsh's, 1878).

27. On the miners and financial reform, see David Montgomery, *Beyond Equality: Labor and the Radical Republicans, 1862–1872* (Urbana: University of Illinois Press, 1981), pp.435–440.

28. John R. Commons et al., eds., *A Documentary History of American Industrial Society*, vol. IX (Cleveland, OH: Arthur H. Clark Co., 1910), pp. 126–179. Andrew Kuykendall was also present at the 1867 NLU convention. Kuykendall was a greenback represen-tative elected from a southern mining district. See Fred E. Haynes, *Third Party Move-ments Since the Civil War, with Special Reference to Iowa* (Iowa City, IA: State Histor-ical Society of Iowa, 1916), pp. 95–102 on the Labor Reform Party.

publican movement. The state's governor, one of their U.S. senators, and a prominent national representative all left the party to join the liberal movement. In addition to John Palmer, Lyman Trumbull, and John Wentworth, Horace White, the editor of the *Chicago Tribune,* joined the liberals, as did Supreme Court Justice David Davis, another Illinois native with broad political ambitions. After the Civil War, the Republican party was no longer united by the fight to end slavery and preserve the union. In its search for new principles, party divisions became apparent in conflicts over Reconstruction, civil service reform, and economic policy. Trumbull, Palmer, and Wentworth were all former Democrats who believed in states' rights and limited national government. Many liberals were advocates of tariff reform. All were disturbed by the allegations of corruption within the Grant administration. These men entered the liberal fold often on their way back to the Democratic party.[29]

Farmers were also restless. In 1869–70, a constitutional convention was held to correct problems with the old state constitution and address issues that earlier constitutional designers had not anticipated. One of the topics addressed by the assembly was the need for railroad and warehouse regulation. The delegates agreed with Reuben Benjamin that the railroads were created for the public good, and should be regulated by the state legislature (the General Assembly) in the public interest. Having received this constitutional mandate, the Legislative Farmers Club proposed a bill in 1871 that created the Railroad and Warehouse Commission. Over the next several years, this law was repeatedly modified and challenged in the state and federal courts. The federal cases concerning these "Granger laws" (most famously, *Munn v. Illinois*) helped to establish the national principle of economic regulation. In Illinois, disputes over these laws led to the first significant antimonopolist electoral challenge.

In the early 1870s, Illinois farmers from the Grange protested the abuse of concentrated economic power by large railroad corporations that set "discriminatory" rates against small rural shippers. When the state supreme court overturned the first Granger law, agrarian activists re-

29. On the Liberal Republicans, see Earle Dudley Ross, *The Liberal Republican Movement* (NY: Henry Holt and Co., 1919). On Illinois and the Liberal Republicans, see Mario DiNunzio, "Lyman Trumball, the States' Rights Issue, and the Liberal Republican Revolt," *Journal of Illinois State Historical Society,* v. 66 , n. 4 (Winter 1973): 364–375; Harris L. Dante, "Western Attitudes and Reconstruction Politics in Illinois, 1865–1872," *Journal of Illinois State Historical Society,* v. 49, n. 2 (Summer 1956): 149–162; and Joseph Logsdon, *Horace White, Nineteenth Century Liberal* (Westport, CT: Greenwood, 1971), chap. 9. On the divisions within the Illinois Republican party, see Philip D. Swenson, "Illinois: Disillusionment with State Activism," in James C. Mohr, ed., *Radical Republicans in the North: State Politics During Reconstruction* (Baltimore: Johns Hopkins University Press, 1976), pp. 104–118.

sponded by forming the Illinois State Farmers Association (ISFA) in January 1873. At its convention, it resolved that "cheap transportation is of vital interest to the west, and that every combination to increase the price above what is just and legitimate is a conspiracy against the rights of the people, and a robbery which we loudly protest against." Later that spring, the ISFA decided to enter the electoral arena, and called on "the anti-monopolists of this state to nominate such candidates for the Supreme and Circuit Judges as are pledged to sustain the constitution, and laws of this state in accordance therewith." Chief Justice Charles Lawrence, who wrote the opinion striking down the 1871 law, was defeated in the subsequent election.[30]

Indeed, agrarian candidates around the state were successful. Independent slates were put forward in 66 of the state's 102 counties. Where they ran, the farmers' candidates received over one-half of the total – 94,188 of 176,263 votes. At an enthusiastic convention held a month later, the ISFA convened with representatives of Granges and clubs from 97 counties and approved a broad agenda for political reform. The platform exclaimed that the nation's troubles resulted from the acquiescence of the producing classes to economic monopolies that were corrupting the government. Among the correctives called for was the cessation of "loans of the public credit" to corporations and abolition of the NBS. Like the labor reformers, the farmers expressed their belief in the unity of the producing classes, and identified the threat to the economy and the government as the concentration of economic power. They also expressed their faith in democracy and their desire to renew republican vigilance through independent political action. It was a call that agrarians, financial reformers, and labor agitators clearly heard as they united to address the money question.[31]

30. On the Western radical tradition, see Chester McArthur Destler, "Western Radicalism, 1865–1901: Concepts and Origins," in *American Radicalism, 1865–1901: Essays and Documents* (New London, CT: Connecticut College, 1946), pp. 1–31; Joe L. Norris, "The Land Reform Movement," *Papers in Illinois History and Transactions for the Year 1937* (Springfield, IL: Illinois State Historical Society, 1938), pp. 73–81; James A. Woodburn, "Western Radicalism in American Politics," *Mississippi Valley Historical Review*, v. 13, n. 2 (September 1926): 143–168; Frank L. Klement, "Middle Western Copperheadism and the Genesis of the Granger Movement, *Mississippi Valley Historical Review*, v. 38 , n. 4 (March 1952), pp. 679–694; and Stanley Jones, "Agrarian Radicalism in Illinois's Constitutional Convention of 1862," *Journal Of Illinois State Historical Society*, v. 48, n. 3 (Autumn 1955), pp. 271–282. Commons et. al., eds., *Documentary History*, vol. X, pp. 49 and 60; and Solon Justus Buck, *The Granger Movement: A Study of Agricultural Organization and its Political, Economic and Social Manifestations, 1870–1880* (Cambridge: Harvard University Press, 1913), pp. 74–77, and 82–85.
31. *The American Annual Cyclopaedia and Register of Important Events of the Year 1873*, vol. 13 (New York: D. Appleton and Co., 1874), p. 369.

130 Goldbugs and greenbacks

Most of the ISFA meeting of December 1873 was devoted to the money issue, a pressing question in the aftermath of the panic of 1873. Around the country political assemblies debated the causes of the collapse and the effects of the banking system and monetary standard on the economy. Both the farm and manufacturing communities of Illinois were sharply affected by the panic. Several national banks failed in 1873–74, and then an even larger number of state savings banks defaulted in 1877. Afterward, credit was tightened, as capital became more scarce, and the remaining banks became more cautious. The national monetary contraction was felt sharply in the West, where currency scarcity was a greater problem. Contraction caused a price deflation, particularly of agricultural goods, adversely affecting Illinois's farmers. The effects of the panic made producers receptive to the arguments of financial reformers.[32]

At first, farmers were reluctant to adopt the fiat currency views of the greenbackers. Jacksonian faith in hard money remained powerful among agrarians. As president W. C. Flagg of the Farmers' Association stated, "I will only say that I believe the resumption of specie payment . . . to be for the best interests of the laboring, honest and nonspeculative masses of the country, because the simplest systems are the best for the great body of the people." While Flagg agreed that there was a danger posed by the "moneyed monopolies," he believed that financial speculators were given greater opportunities for profits by the price gap between greenbacks and gold. Further, since farmers exported their crops to nations on a gold standard, an inflated domestic currency lowered their returns, and raised the price of goods purchased at home. The resilience of Jacksonian beliefs and the logic of their trading position made many agrarians support a return to the gold standard.[33]

Labor reformers helped to change these views. Horace Day came from New York to deliver a long oration on greenbackism in December 1873. Day focused on the role of money in the distribution of wealth and the need for a government-controlled paper currency standard that would be neither expansionary or contractionary. This flamboyant political figure went further, adding his own beliefs about the existence of a money power conspiracy to exploit and subjugate producers. Registering his faith in the spread of the financial reform movement, Day concluded that "the light which broke in the East, among the toiling masses there, is now shining upon the farmers in the West." M. M. Hooton, a vice-president of the

32. R. G. Thomas, "Bank Failures in Chicago Before 1925," *Journal of the Illinois State Historical Society*, v. 28, n. 3 (October 1935), pp. 190–194; Milton Friedman and Anna Schwartz, *A Monetary History of the United States, 1867–1960* (Princeton: Princeton University Press, 1963), pp. 15–88, on the monetary history of the late 1860s and 1870s.

33. W. C. Flagg, *Aim and Scope of the Farmers' Movement*, Speech at Riggs' Grove, Winchester, Scott County, August 7, 1873 (Chicago: Prairie Farmer Co., 1873).

Farmers' Association, was more subdued, but equally committed to educating farmers on the merits of financial reform. By the end of the convention, the farmers had endorsed a fiat standard with full legal tender value, the interconvertible bond scheme, and the repeal of the national banking law.[34]

The emergence of greenbackism

As the agrarian reform movement evolved into greenbackism, the independents became a successful third-party force in Illinois. The 1874 Illinois elections followed the national pattern – the Republicans lost their majorities in both houses of the state legislature. The lost Republican seats were split between the Democrats and the independents. The independents also elected S. M. Etter (running as a fusion candidate with the Democrats) as the state's Superintendent of Public Instruction. Illinois's congressional elections also produced Republican losses. Of nineteen seats, eight went to Republicans, nine to Democrats, and two to independents, including one to Alexander Campbell. Many Illinoisians expressed their dissatisfaction with Republican rule and economic decline by supporting greenbackers.[35]

Two years later, the Republicans rebounded, though more weakly in Illinois than nationally. The congressional elections returned a slight Republican majority of eleven seats versus eight for the Democrats. In the state legislature, the reformers again held a pivotal position between the Democrats and Republicans. There was also an extremely close gubernatorial election between Shelby Cullom, a moderate Republican with sympathies toward the regulatory movement, and Lewis Steward, the fusion candidate of the Democrats and the Greenback party. Of the more than half a million votes cast in the contest, Cullom won by fewer than seven thousand. Despite the national Republican comeback, the greenback movement remained strong in Illinois.[36]

---

34. *Proceedings of the Second Annual Meeting of the Illinois State Farmers' Association,* held at Decatur, Illinois, December 16–18, 1873 (Chicago: E. Southard, 1874), p. 50 for Day's quote; Irwin Unger, *The Greenback Era: A Social and Political History of American Finance, 1865–1879* (Princeton: Princeton University Press, 1964), p. 233; and *America's Annual Cyclopaedia and Register of Important Events for the Year 1874* (New York: D. Appleton and Co., 1875), p. 403.
35. *America's Annual . . . 1874,* p. 404; Church, *History,* p. 124.
36. Church, *History,* p. 129; Keiser, *Building,* pp. 88–89. The continuity between the agrarians and the greenbackers is pointed out by Buck, Montgomery, and Unger. Montgomery is also correct in noting the dual labor and agrarian roots of greenbackism, although I think he understates the agrarian contribution. See Buck, *Granger Movement,* pp. 100–102; Montgomery, *Beyond Equality,* pp. 433–444; and Unger, *Greenback Era,* pp. 229–233.

Eighteen seventy-six was the first year in which the official Greenback party competed in Illinois. It was also its strongest year electorally. The new Greenback party received support from agrarians, labor reformers, and some small businessmen around the state. Greenbackism began earlier in Illinois than elsewhere, and had more diverse origins. Greenbacker Andrew Kuykendall was elected to Congress from a southern mining district in the late 1860s, and two more financial reformers were sent to the House of Representatives as part of the agrarian uprising in 1874. At its height, the Greenback party was a substantial force in the state, electing statewide officials, nearly electing the governor, and forcing the selection of reformer David Davis as United States Senator in 1877. But by 1878, the statewide Greenback candidates trailed far behind their Republican and Democratic opponents, and Greenbacker A. J. Streeter received less than 5 percent of the vote in the 1880 gubernatorial election. The party declined with the resurgence of Republican hegemony in the state and the successful resumption of the gold standard in 1879. Although the party faded, antimonopolism and financial reform remained part of Illinois political culture, appearing again in the Knights of Labor (KOL) campaigns of the 1880s and the Populist movement of the 1890s.[37]

In the mid-1870s, the Republicans were vulnerable, the Democrats gained strength, and the Greenbackers held the balance of power between the two. Within both major parties there was broad support for financial reform. But this support was outweighed by hard-money sentiment. Despite its flirtation with the Liberal Republican movement, the normally Republican *Chicago Tribune* was unequivocal in its condemnation of greenbackism and paper currency. "Can the Commune devise a more effective means for a redistribution of wealth than depreciated legal-tender units?" On the 1876 nominees for the Greenback-Democratic ticket, the paper commented, "[they] are about as intelligent as horseblocks, but all of them are inflationists and dilutionists of the most crazy description." After their strong showing in 1876, the Democrats decided to run independently, at which point they joined the chorus of antigreenbackism. The state's leading Democratic newspaper, the *Illinois State Register,* described the Greenbackers as "Inflationists and Lunatics" and warned that greenbacks were "the invention of the devil."[38]

The severity of the depression of 1873–79 caused a defensive attitude on the part of unionists whose primary concerns were to maintain em-

---

37. Church, *History,* p. 132–133; and Keiser, *Building,* pp. 88–89.
38. *Chicago Tribune,* Jan 6, 1874; Feb. 17, 1876; and *The Illinois State Register,* March 1878. Quoted in Joseph Logsdon, *Horace White,* p.266; Bogart and Thompson, *The Industrial State,* pp. 111 and 123, respectively.

ployment and union membership. Nonetheless, the old leaders of the labor reform movement such as Campbell, Cameron, and Hinchcliffe continued to be politically active, and local political action among laborers was evident, especially in the state's mining communities. In Joliet, Illinois, where there were unions among the steel, quarry, and mine workers, the Greenback party had a large following among laborers, merchants, and small manufacturers. After the great railroad strikes of 1877, the labor reform movement expanded nationally. The Greenback party evolved into the Greenback Labor party. While grassroots support for the Greenback party was initially stronger among Illinois farmers than workers, the labor component of the party eventually grew, and the party's platform shifted in response to the increased importance of labor concerns.[39]

The industrial conflict of the late 1870s challenged the free labor and equal rights traditions. Nationally, Republicans narrowed their belief in a free labor society, becoming less aggressive in their pursuit of civil rights for the South and more assertive in protecting economic gains (even at the expense of economic opportunity) in the North. For labor, the challenge was to preserve a belief in a common producers' interest despite evidence of conflict between workers and bosses. Socialism, an ideology of class antagonism, first became significant in Illinois labor circles in the late 1870s. Opposite this development was the rise of Red-baiting tactics by Republicans, such as those employed by the Honest Money League against Marcus Pomeroy (see fn 42 and proceeding text). Illinois's political leaders responded to the strikes by praising the use of government force against the strikers and denouncing them as un-American, thus placing them outside the "imagined community" of the nation. When the railroad strike came to Chicago in July, 1877, it was met by federal troops ordered in by President Hayes at the request of Governor Cullom. Eighteen strikers were killed in the ensuing battle. After it was over, the headlines in the Chicago *Inter-Ocean* (a Republican paper) rejoiced, "Red Rabble Routed." Greenbackism, which drew from both the equal rights and free labor traditions, was harmed by these developments.[40]

39. Stephen Freedman, "Organizing the Workers in a Steel Company Town: The Union Movement in Joliet, Illinois, 1870–1920," *Journal of the Illinois State Historical Society*, v.79, n.1 (Spring 1986): 5–7; Unger, *Greenback Era*, p.305.

40. For my analysis of the fading of the free labor and equal rights traditions, I am indebted to Eric Foner, *Reconstruction*, chap. 11; and Montgomery, *Beyond Equality*, pp. 444–447. See also Philip S. Foner, *The Great Labor Uprising of 1877* (New York: Monad Press, 1977), pp. 139–156. On the rise of labor radicalism, see Dorothy Culp, "The Radical Labor Movement, 1873–1895," *Papers in Illinois History and Transactions for the Year 1937* (Springfield: Illinois State Historical Society, 1938), pp. 92–99. The term "imagined community" comes from Benedict R. Anderson, *Imagined Communities: Reflections on the Origin and Spread of Nationalism* (London : Verso, 1983).

Silver and the reestablishment of regular party dominance

Leaders of both parties became harsher in their assessments of the Greenback party once organized labor joined the fold. But by then the silver issue was taking hold of the public's imagination, offering a more bullionist alternative to greenbackism. Now, according to the *Chicago Tribune*,
it was the "Crime of '73" in which silver was demonetized that was an
"evil conspiracy against the welfare of the American people." The silver
issue quickly took on a sectional tone, as expressed by the *Illinois State
Register*, which supported the following resolution of the silver convention held in Springfield in 1878:

> We view with intense indignation the efforts now being made by the money-
> power of New York, and other cities of the East, to enforce public opinion
> in the West and South upon the question of silver remonetization . . . the peo-
> ple of this section of the Union will never be surrendered at the dictation of
> greedy capitalists and bondholders, let the consequences be what they may.

By the late 1870s, the major parties had recaptured the money issue by
supporting silver remonetization as a sectional issue. The Greenback party was isolated and demonized as a classist organization. As in North
Carolina, party loyalty was maintained, particularly to the benefit of
the Republicans, by invoking sectional geographical interests over class
interests.[41]

The Illinois Greenback party was also hurt by the controversy over
Marcus "Brick" Pomeroy. Pomeroy was a former Copperhead editor who
returned from New York to the Midwest in the 1870s. From his press in
Chicago, Pomeroy put out two greenback newspapers, *Pomeroy's
Democrat* and *The Great Campaign*. His writings were marked by denunciation, anti-Semitism, slander, and threats of violence. Through the
newspapers, he promoted greenback clubs all over the Midwest. To his
detractors, Pomeroy was an irresponsible provocateur. Opponents of
greenbackism, such as the Honest Money League of the Northwest, took
Pomeroy's writings as evidence of the revolutionary and communistic nature of the movement. In 1878, the League published *Extracts: From the
Communistic, Inflammatory and Treasonable Documents Circulated by
the National Greenback Party*, which consisted entirely of excerpts from
Pomeroy's writings, along with editorial comment. Despite Pomeroy's repudiation by the party that year, many Midwesterners still supported him.
At his last Greenback appearance – before the Union Greenback Labor
convention (a splinter group from the regular Greenback party) in 1880

---

41. Quoted in Bogart and Thompson, *The Industrial State*, pp. 126 and 127, respectively.

– Pomeroy came to the podium with a banner of a greenback dollar superimposed on an American flag with a bayonet running through it. Although the split was healed by the National Greenback Labor convention in June 1880, many greenback sympathizers were repulsed by Pomeroy's presence in the late 1870s, and the larger public was estranged from the greenback cause.[42]

Changes in the party system and political debates of the late 1870s contributed to the decline of greenbackism. The Republican party solidified its hold on Illinois politics. The Republicans became the party of patriotism, financial responsibility, and property. Meanwhile, while the strikes of 1877 created a short-term upsurge in greenback sentiment among laborers, these industrial conflicts began to reshape the terms of class identity. The notion of a society divided between producers and nonproducers was slowly being replaced by the idea of a society divided between the working-class and the business class. The struggle between the greenbackers and the corporate liberals, between a regional economy with community control and economic autonomy on one side and a centralized economy with large-scale production and less individual autonomy on the other, was already tilting in favor of centralization.

The Greenback party in Illinois represented the culmination of more than a decade of agitation among farmers and labor reformers for antimonopolism and financial reform. Farmers, with their long tradition of Jacksonian politics and anti-bank campaigns, led the movement that gave birth to the Greenback party in the mid-1870s. Although many agrarians were reluctant to forfeit their faith in hard money, farmers eventually accepted the greenback philosophy, which articulated their disdain for banks, their desire to resist the advance of corporate liberalism, and their faith in the equal rights tradition. The transformation of agrarian radicalism into greenbackism in Illinois was assisted by labor reformers, who had been convinced of the greenback philosophy since the late 1860s. Although the labor reformers were demobilized in the mid-1870s and provided little assistance in the organization of the Greenback party, there was a resurgence in labor participation with the strikes of 1877. While these strikes provided a short-term boon to the greenback movement, they

42. Frank Klement, "'Brick' Pomeroy: Copperhead and Curmudgeon," *Wisconsin Magazine of History*, v. 35 (1951); and *The Great Campaign* and *Pomeroy's Democrat*, with letters from around the country for an indication of the papers' wide circulation. *The Great Campaign*, August 15 and 23, 1876; Honest Money League of the Northwest, *Extracts: From the Communistic, Inflammatory and Treasonable Documents Circulated by the National Greenback Party* (Chicago: Honest Money League of the Northwest, 1878); Richard M. Doolen, "Brick Pomeroy and the Greenback Clubs," *Journal of the Illinois State Historical Society*, v. 65, n. 4 (Winter 1972): 434–450.

also inaugurated a transformation in the social categories of industrial society, away from producerism toward class-based identities. Eventually,
the labor reform movement was replaced by labor radicalism. This change
inspired the Republicans to move further along the path of economic and
political conservatism. Illinois moved from a fairly competitive two-par-
ty system to one in which the Republicans were dominant. With Republican dominance intact and specie resumption successfully accomplished,
greenbackism declined. In this battle, the farm-labor alliance failed in its
efforts to maintain a system in which economic development remained
competitive, and equal economic and political rights were preserved. In
time, Illinois moved further toward a political geographical alignment
that favored a centralized industrial nation.[43]

III. Massachusetts: An early labor reform state

Massachusetts was situated at the political and economic core of the
country. The state was thoroughly Republican, economically wealthy, and
financially well-endowed. In the financial debate, Massachusetts' political leaders could generally be counted on to articulate a financially orthodox position. They promoted the gold standard and defended the NBS.
Yet even in this New England citadel of financial conservatism there was
support for greenbackism. Indeed, the labor movement there was distinguished by the nature and depth of its commitment to financial reform.
Further, one of the nation's leading Republican greenbackers was Massachusetts Congressman (and later governor) Benjamin F. Butler. The existence of financial reformism in this core state suggests that political geographical interests were not fully coherent or hegemonic even there.

In the early nineteenth century, Massachusetts shifted from an agrarian to a manufacturing economy with the aid of a well-integrated network
of financial institutions. The textile and banking businesses grew up together, often linked by kinship structures that eased the flow of funds between the two. At this earlier stage, manufacturing was done by small and
medium-sized firms (for example, in machine tools, shoe production, and
textiles) that emphasized worker loyalty and skill. Most of these firms remained privately owned. Later in the century, industrial growth shifted
further west, as new and larger firms in steel, iron, coal, and agricultural

---

43. Roy V. Scott, *The Agrarian Movement in Illinois, 1880–1896*, Illinois Studies in the Social Sciences, vol. 52 (Urbana: University of Illinois Press, 1962), pp. 15–16; John R.
Commons, et. al., *History of Labour in the United States*, vol. II (New York: Macmillan Co., 1936), pp. 356–394; and, Alfred W. Newcombe, "Alson J. Streeter – An
Agrarian Liberal," *Journal of the Illinois State Historical Society*, v. 38, n. 4 (December
1945): 433.

machinery emerged, putting less emphasis on skills and affording workers less control over the production process. Massachusetts then became a capital exporter, helping to fund railroads and farm mortgages outside the state. As the regional economy and its relationship to the national economy shifted, so too did class relations. The distance between the financial class and the working class widened, and was exacerbated by the cultural differences that emerged between Irish immigrants and Yankee elites.[44]

There was no shortage of financial resources in postwar Massachusetts. In congressional debates, Massachusetts and New England were often held up in contrast to the South and West as examples of financial abundance. The state had long had a strong banking system, and it eagerly converted to the NBS during the war. In a debate over the sectional distribution of national bank currency at the end of the 1860s, Alabama Representative William Warner did not find it "fair that Massachusetts and other states should have privileges which we do not enjoy," and compared his own state's 35 cents per capita circulation to Massachusetts' 35 dollars per capita circulation. In number of banks, capitalization per bank, and circulation per capita, the state and region were national leaders in financial resources. It comes as no surprise that the state's political representatives sought to preserve the state's financial position, and fought against measures designed to hurt creditors or otherwise alter the financial relationships between states or regions. The interest of financiers and traders rather than producers dominated in Massachusetts politics.[45]

The Republican party dominated state politics. But though thoroughly Republican and committed to financial conservatism, among its members were prominent financial reformers. Benjamin F. Butler was an ongoing source of controversy in the Republican party nationally and within the state. Despite his military record and commitment to the Radical agenda in Congress, Butler alienated many of the state's Republican leaders with his popular political style and positions on economic issues. Butler, a former Jacksonian Democrat and admirer of Pennsylvania economist Hen-

---

44. On the early relationship between the textile and banking industries in Massachusetts, see Naomi Lamoreaux, "Banks, Kinship and Economic Development: The New England Case," *Journal of Economic History*, 46 (1986): 649–667. On Massachusetts' changing economic position and its role as a capital exporter, see John Lauritz Larson, *Bonds of Enterprise: John Murray Forbes and Western Development in America's Railway Age* (Cambridge, MA: Harvard University Press, 1984); John A. James, *Money and Capital Markets in Postbellum America* (Princeton: Princeton University Press, 1978), table 22, p. 145; and Jack Tager, "Massachusetts and the Age of Economic Revolution," in *Massachusetts in the Gilded Age*, Jack Tager and John W. Ifkovic, eds. (Amherst: University of Massachusetts Press, 1985), pp. 3–28.

45. Seip, *The South Returns*, p.177, and chap. 6 passim.

ry Carey, had long been a proponent of financial reform. His writings and speeches suggest that his financial views were producerist, that he was sympathetic to labor, and that he supported the equal rights tradition. Butler also advocated women's suffrage and Irish nationalism. To the Yankee elites within the party, Butler's agenda and political approach smacked of demagoguery and class radicalism. Rather than awaiting the call of the people, Butler unabashedly sought their political support through rigorous campaigns and patronage networks. Regular party leaders organized to stop Butler in his bid for reelection to Congress in 1868.[46]

The effort failed. Richard Henry Dana was a gentleman politician, unprepared for the rough and tumble of a political campaign against Butler. Although Dana received support from the county of Essex's manufacturing and financial interests, Butler was the champion of the middle and working classes. Voters were persuaded by Butler's charge that Dana was an elitist and outsider. Finance was another important election issue. Dana criticized Butler's proposal to repay federal bonds in greenbacks as "a fraud and national dishonor," adding that repayment in gold was not "a moral question, but a question of religion." Constituents were evidently unconvinced. As one Dana supporter wrote in dismay, "Eastern Massachusetts is more thoroughly debauched on the great financial – which is the great moral – question of the day than any other Republican region." The final tally was 66 percent for Butler, 9 percent for Dana, and 25 percent for Lord, the regular Democratic candidate, with upper-income areas giving the strongest vote for Dana, and the working-class districts of Lynn most heavily supporting Butler. Financial reformism was linked to class politics in Massachusetts.[47]

The labor reform movement

The following year, labor greenbackism emerged on the state's political scene. In 1869, the Knights of Saint Crispin (KOSC), a shoemakers union, sought incorporation from the General Court in order to promote cooperative production. Cooperation represented an attempt to remain eco-

---

46. Howard P. Nash, *Stormy Petrel: The Life and Times of Benjamin F. Butler, 1818–1893* (Rutherford: Fairleigh Dickinson University Press, 1969), chaps. 19–21; Robert S. Holzman, *Stormy Ben Butler* (NY: Macmillan, 1954), chaps. 15–18; Unger, *Greenback Era*, pp. 85–86; Richard H. Abbott, "Massachusetts: Maintaining Hegemony," in *Radical Republicans in the North: State Politics During Reconstruction*, James C. Mohr, ed. (Baltimore: Johns Hopkins University Press, 1976), pp. 1–25.

47. Samuel Shapiro, "Aristocracy, Mud and Vituperation: The Butler-Dana Campaign in Essex County in 1868," *New England Quarterly*, v. 31, n. 3 (September 1958): 347–348; and Samuel Shapiro, *Richard Henry Dana, Jr., 1815–1882* (Lansing, MI: Michigan State University Press, 1961), p. 231; and Montgomery, *Beyond Equality*, p. 368.

nomically viable in an increasingly industrialized productive system while maintaining shop floor autonomy and avoiding the coercion of wage employment. Difficulties in securing credit for cooperatives led to an interest in financial reform. The KOSC's request was denied by the legislature's Republican majority. In response to the legislature's denial of a charter for the cooperatives, union members joined other labor reformers in calling for independent political activity to promote cooperation and financial reform.[48]

The New England Labor Reform League (NELRL), which included many KOSC members, led the movement toward independent political action. At its convention in 1869, President Ezra H. Heywood called "Free contracts, free money, free markets, free transit, and free land" the "living issues to be tested at the ballot box." Of these, "the central question of honest money" was what united the league. Its cause was that of all producers; "it fights the battle of the manufacturer, of the merchant, of the farmer, of legitimate enterprise in all its manifold relations." Placing the movement historically, Heywood stated its effort was "at once a return to the past, and effort toward the future," which "hastens the day when men will have neither the power nor the wish to own more than they earn." Producerism offered the means for a creative democratic response to the challenge of economic change.[49]

This was classic financial antimonopolism. Yet there were distinctive elements of Massachusetts labor greenbackism as well. Borrowing from the libertarian anarchist philosophy of Josiah Warren, and the proposals for mutual banking of French philosopher Pierre Joseph Proudhon, labor intellectuals Ezra Heywood, William B. Greene, and Edward Linton crafted financial theories premised on ideas of unregulated and nonmonopolized money, and credit based on physical wealth and supplied at cost. For these New Englanders, freedom (as in "free banking" or "free money") implied the complete absence of governmental oversight, so that *any* citizen could issue money (which would function, therefore, as promissory notes) or set up a bank. For other greenbackers, freedom implied equal regulatory conditions for banks (that is, general incorporation laws as opposed to chartering) or direct government control over the money supply. Yet, ultimately, the Massachusetts labor reformers were neither Proudhonists nor libertarian anarchists. Like other greenbackers, they continued to rely on the democratic process to achieve their ends.[50]

48. Commons et al., *History of Labour*, vol. II, pp. 76–79.
49. *Workingmen's Advocate*, June 12, 1869.
50. On the association of Massachusetts labor reformers with anarchism and Proudhon, see Joseph Dorfman, *The Economic Mind in American Civilization*, volume III, 1865–1918 (NY: The Viking Press, 1949), pp. 35–42; Charles A. Madison, "Benjamin Tucker: Individualist and Anarchist," *New England Quarterly*, v. 16, n. 3 (September

In the fall of 1869, the Massachusetts Labor Reform party was formed. The party's platform affirmed the equal rights tradition, called for the extension of the incorporation rights to labor organizations, and advocated both the eight-hour day and financial reform. The new party did well, receiving 10 percent of the statewide vote for governor in 1869, 16 percent in 1870, and 10 percent in 1871. Chairman S. P. Cummings attributed the party's quick success to its financial planks. In 1870, the party ran Wendell Phillips for governor. Phillips, the famous abolitionist and longtime labor sympathizer, was also endorsed by the Prohibition party. It was around this time that Phillips' labor reform views became more developed. In a speech on the labor movement in 1872, Phillips suggested his familiarity with Kelloggism and his commitment to producerism.

> I say, let the debts of the country be paid, abolish the banks, and let the government lend every Illinois farmer (if he wants it), who is now borrowing money at ten per cent, money on the half-value of his land at three per cent. The same policy that gave a million acres to the Pacific Railroad, because it was a great national effort, will allow of our lending Chicago twenty millions of money, at three per cent, to rebuild it.

Elsewhere, Phillips commented that it was the money power or money monopoly that had debauched England and now threatened American democracy. Thus, money was seen as a broad political issue, in which farmers, workers, and democratic citizens shared a common interest. The early 1870s labor reform movement in Massachusetts was one of the most nationally significant.[51]

The Labor Reform party declined after a devastating strike crippled the KOSC, and economic improvement diminished interest in financial reform. But as important as either of these factors was the inability of the

1943): 444–446, 449; Haynes, *Third Party*, pp. 92–93; Edward D. Linton, *Specific Payments Better Than Specie Payments: The Question of Money Divested of Verbiage and Technicalities* (Boston, 1876); E. H. Heywood, *Hard Cash* (Princeton, MA: Cooperative Publishing Co., 1874); and William B. Greene, *Mutual Banking: Showing the Radical Deficiencies of the Present Circulating Medium, and the Advantages of a Free Currency* (Boston: New England Labor Reform League, 1870). For the disputes between the eight-hour advocates and the financial reformers, see Commons et al., *History*, vol. II, pp.138–143; and Workingmen's Institute of Boston Notebook, Massachusetts Historical Society, January 19, 1869, June 29, 1869, July 6, 1869, and August 31, 1869.

51. Wendell Phillips, *Speeches, Lectures and Letters*, second series (Boston: Lee and Shepard Pub., 1891), pp. 176 and 157; Dorfman, *Economic Mind*, vol. III, p. 16; *The American Annual Cyclopaedia and Register of Important Events for the Year 1869*, vol. 9 (New York: D. Appleton and Co., 1872), pp. 416–417; *The American Annual Cyclopaedia and Register of Important Events for the Year 1870*, vol. 10 (New York: D. Appleton and Co., 1872), pp. 474 and 477; Haynes,*Third Party*, pp. 93–102; and Commons et al., *History*, v. II, p. 141.

labor reformers to mount more than a protest vote against Republican domination. Massachusetts was a preeminent Republican state. Party loyalty found constant reinforcement in the waving of the "bloody shirt," the meetings of the Grand Army of the Republic (a veterans' organization that was a virtual adjunct of the GOP), and the benefits secured for veterans by elected Republican officials. This lesson on the strength of Republican hegemony was one that would be learned again by the Liberal Republicans in 1872. Although Massachusetts voters were beginning to dissent from Republican dominance on economic issues, party loyalty still held firm in the election booth.[52]

As in Illinois, the Liberal Republican movement in Massachusetts fomented a partial realignment. While the Liberal Republican party itself was short-lived, its association with the Democrats in the 1872 election was of lasting consequence. After the election of 1872, the Democratic party was strengthened by the addition of many respectable former Republicans such as Francis Bird. The willingness of former abolitionists to join the Democrats also signalled their declining faith in popular democracy. To them, the growth of patronage networks and inclusion of class-conscious Irish immigrants belied the ideal of a selfless and virtuous citizenry. These former antislavery men turned against government activism in the South as well as the North, turning instead to education and the natural laws of the market to restore social harmony. In the aftermath of this liberal rebellion, the stalwart wing of the Republican party was strengthened against the Radicals.[53]

Economically, many of the Liberal Republicans were committed to tariff reduction and orthodox financial policies. Thus, men such as Samuel Bowles (editor of the *Springfield Republican*), Edward Atkinson (Massachusetts businessman, statistician, and hard-money crusader), and David Wells (Connecticut economist and hard-money advocate) all aligned themselves with the Liberal cause. When the national Liberal Republican convention nominated Horace Greeley, supporters such as Atkinson left

52. On the GAR in Republican politics, see Stuart Charles McConnell, *Glorious Contentment: The Grand Army of the Republic, 1865–1900* (Chapel Hill: University of North Carolina Press, 1992); Mary R. Dearing, *Veterans in Politics: The Story of the G.A.R.* (Baton Rouge: University of Louisiana Press, 1952); and Theda Skocpol, *Protecting Soldiers and Mothers: The Political Origins of Social Policy in the United States* (Cambridge: Belknap Press, 1992), esp. chap. 2. Because of party loyalty, Dale Baum argues, voters preferred to stay home rather than vote against their party on election day. See Baum, *The Civil War Party System: The Case of Massachusetts, 1848–1876* (Chapel Hill: University of North Carolina Press, 1984), pp. 112 and 173.
53. Francis Bird founded the famous "Bird Club" in the 1850s, from which many important Radical Republicans came. Abbott, "Massachusetts," pp. 1–25. My reading of the Liberal Republicans is indebted to Eric Foner, *Reconstruction*, chap. 10.

the movement. Greeley was a protectionist who was ambiguous in his financial politics. Over the years he had flirted with various financial reform measures. Although many liberals reluctantly returned to the Republican fold after 1872, they remained strong opponents of financial reform. Atkinson wrote to representative Henry Dawes on a financial matter in the early 1870s,

> It seems to me that there never was a time when courageous resistance to false measures was more needed . . . I am one of those who cannot forbear denouncing a fraud if I see it, and I consider the continued use of bad money without any attempt to make it good, a most infamous fraud. When the masses realize the cheat, as they surely will, there will be no forgiveness for any man, however true he may have been, if he has failed to resist the clamor of knaves and fools, like [Benjamin] Butler and [Rep. William] Kelley.

Like so many liberals, Atkinson saw the financial issue in terms of moral rights and wrongs. His tolerance for his opponents was quite low, while for the masses he hoped for the eventual dawning of enlightened views. These same men went to Washington in 1874 to lobby President Grant to veto the Inflation Bill. After 1872, both parties were increasingly dominated by financial conservatives.[54]

Though the Democrats gained little from their brief union with the national Liberal Republicans in 1872, the depression and local political issues worked in favor of the Democrats in 1874. Locally, distress over prohibition contributed to the anti-Republican backlash, as voters rejected the temperance stance of Governor Talbot and his party. Nationally, the depression resurrected criticism of Republican economic policies. With the panic of 1873, concerns about monetary deflation and the NBS reemerged. Discontent over the corrupt practices of the Grant administration and the ill effects of patronage practices both nationally and locally, aggravated the situation. A Democratic governor and several Democratic representatives – Butler was among those defeated in his reelection bid – were elected.[55]

54. Atkinson is quoted in Harold Francis Williamson, *Edward Atkinson: The Biography of an American Liberal, 1827–1905* (Boston: Old Corner Bookstore, 1934), p. 94. Greeley's tariff position is well known. See Ross, *Liberal Republican*, p. 94. On finance, Greeley was an early advocate of Edward Kellogg, but later supported quick specie resumption. See Unger, *Greenback Era*, pp. 117 ff; Robert P. Sharkey, *Money, Class, and Party: An Economic Study of the Civil War and Reconstruction* (Baltimore: Johns Hopkins University Press, 1959), p. 168; and Destler, *American Radicalism*, p. 62. Sharkey also discusses Atkinson's early role as a hard-money advocate, p. 162, while Unger chronicles the effort of the New England delegation in 1874, pp. 236–241.

55. On changing political attitudes about finance and banking, see Chapter 3. On the Republican backlash in Massachusetts, see Baum, *Civil War Party System*, pp. 181–195; and Charles Blank, "The Waning of Radicalism: Massachusetts Republicans and Re-

Benjamin Butler and the Greenback party

In 1876, the Greenback party also began organizing in Massachusetts. It faced a mighty task. The academic, business, and journalistic communities favored financial conservatism, while the state's working classes were politically disorganized and under the leadership of Brahmin elites within both the Democratic and Republican parties. Benjamin Butler and Wendell Phillips were the only major political figures to openly advocate greenbackism, and Butler was regarded as a maverick. Wendell Phillips headed the party's first electoral slate in 1877. Its platform called for repeal of the Resumption Act and a government-controlled legal tender currency. The convention results were endorsed by the Labor Reform and Workingmen's parties. But in 1877, with Butler still superficially attached to the Republican party and labor activism only slowly awakening, the Greenbackers did poorly.[56]

All of that changed in 1878. At a speech in Maine that August, Butler anounced, " I have left the old parties. I belonged to the democratic party until it attempted to destroy the Union, and was with the republican party until it deserted its founders the laboring-men. The capitalists now hold the republican party bound hand and foot." Now, financial antimonopolists and labor reformers from various partisan camps had a viable candidate available for an independent campaign. Labor activism grew again after the strike wave of 1877. The economy experienced a new downturn in the late 1870s. Further, the decade-long battle over the monetary standard was destined to be resolved with the resumption of the gold standard on January 1, 1879. Both nationally and within Massachusetts, the 1878 election provided a significant test of the public's sentiment on monetary and other reform efforts.[57]

During the early months of 1878, citizens wrote to Butler expressing support for financial reform. Others wanted to know more about greenbackism. Many complained about the biased nature of the press.

construction Issues in the Early 1870s" (unpub. PhD diss., Brandeis University, 1972), chap. 6, and Richard E. Welch, Jr., *George Frisbie Hoar and the Half-Breed Republicans* (Cambridge, MA: Harvard University Press, 1971), pp. 2–3, 45–48.

56. On Massachusetts conservatism see Unger, *Greenback Era*, pp. 326, 334 and 337. Labor was disorganized with the decline of the Labor Reform party and the disintegration of the KOSC in the early 1870s. The Irish working class was politically active under the leadership of people like Patrick Collins, but the state party remained under Brahmin control. *Appleton's Annual Cyclopaedia and Register of Important Events of the Year 1877*, vol. 17 (NY: D. Appleton and Co., 1883), pp. 488–489, 492; Alan Dawley, *Class and Community: The Industrial Revolution in Lynn* (Cambridge, MA: Harvard University Press, 1976), pp. 197–203.

57. Butler speech quoted in George Lowell Austin, *History of Massachusetts* (Boston: B. B. Russell, 1884), p.573.

I have desired to write you before this to let you know that you are not with-out friends among the people as the General Press does not fairly represent the real sentiment of a large portion of the community on the financial question, and the evidence of the complicity of the *Press* with the *Banks* is very noticeable [sic].

State residents were becoming increasingly interested in the financial question. D. M. Cross wrote that after reading works by Henry Carey, William Kelley, and Benjamin Butler,

I confess myself utterly surprised at the rapidity & clearness with which my views are changing on this question – I supposed I understood the question fairly well & was a bullionist because I so fully knew the history of the inflated currency of the past. I see now that the trouble with them was that they were *not money*, only *promises to pay* coined money, which was not in existence.

For Cross and others, the argument for a government-regulated currency with full legal tender status was convincing.[58]

Labor agitation swelled the ranks of the greenback movement. In May and June, workers called on Butler to accept the Greenback nomination for governor. H. H. Dwinell saw his support for Butler and greenbackism as another step in his commitment to labor reform. "I have been a Labor Reformer from the start. I voted for Chamberlain and Phillips . . . I was well acquainted with S. P. Cummings . . . I hope you will take the nomination as I think you can be elected." For others, the connection between labor and financial reform was a new revelation. James Tullis wrote about a meeting where he spoke on financial reform. Although the "subject is not generally understood by workingmen," by the end of this meeting the audience was "advocating paper money, receivable, not payable, as the only true money . . . " By the time that Denis Kearney arrived from California in August to advocate his own controversial brand of labor greenbackism, the audience of workers at Fanueil Hall in Boston who received him were primed for his message.[59]

58. H. to Butler, February 16, 1878; and D. M. Cross to Butler, March 30, 1878, Benjamin F. Butler Papers, Library of Congress, Manuscript Division. Cross's comments refer to the argument by financial reformers that greenbacks were deprived of value by their lack of full legal tender status (they could not be used for custom house receipts or for the interest on government bonds). This accounted for the discrepancy in the value of greenbacks and gold.
59. Michael Muhan to Butler, May 30, 1878; H. H. Dwinell to Butler, July 6, 1878; and James Tullis to Butler, March 9, 1878, all in Benjamin F. Butler Papers, Library of Congress, Manuscript Division. On Kearney's visit, see *Appleton's Annual Cyclopaedia and Register of Important Events of the Year 1878*, vol. 18 (NY: D. Appleton and Co., 1883), p. 530. On the controversy surrounding Kearney, see M. D. Downing to Butler, August 1878, Benjamin F. Butler Papers, Library of Congress, Manuscript Division; and Haynes, *Third Parties*, p. 145–146.

Late that summer, Butler announced his willingness to be drafted for the gubernatorial race. His supporters put together a petition that was eventually signed by over 50,000 voters, whereupon Butler declared his candidacy. While stressing his commitment to equal rights, Butler refrained from stating his positions on national issues in hopes of obtaining both the Greenback and Democratic nominations. The Greenback nomination was readily forthcoming. The party platform included a call for a state's labor bureau, opposition to the convict lease system, and increased emphasis on tax reform, an important local issue. The demand for an interconvertible bond system was dropped. These alterations reflected the changes occurring in the Greenback party nationally as well, with added emphasis on labor issues and depression concerns, and the declining significance of Kelloggism.[60]

Other Massachusetts political leaders found their own hard-money sentiments honed by Butler's candidacy. Senator George Frisbie Hoar, one of Butler's longtime opponents, came to regard the 1878 election as a crucial test on the financial issue, and "felt obliged to spur the Massachusetts Republicans to a major effort against the Greenback heresy." There was much educational work that needed to be done on the issue. While Hoar's financial constituents were committed to the gold standard, less certainty was expressed among the laborers and manufacturers who wrote to the Senator. At a major speech at the Worcester Mechanics Hall in September, Hoar offered the classic orthodox position on the value of money:

> We take gold and silver for money because they are the things which in their nature vary in value least, but we do not make or change value by law.

True money contained intrinsic value, while government-created paper money (or fiat currency) was a false standard of little worth. It was Hoar's sense of natural value and the natural economy (along with his support for the Republicans and disgust for Butler) that motivated his opposition to greenbackism.[61]

After some questionable machinations, the Butler forces also secured the Democratic nomination, leaving the ticket strongly placed to compete against Republican candidate Thomas Talbot in November. It was a bitter campaign. The Republicans referred to the Butler coalition as "Repudiationists, Greenbackers, and Communists." According to one biographer, "Nearly 1,000,000 pages of anti-Butler, hard-money literature was circulated by the Republicans." Butler lost the race 55 percent to 45 per-

60. *Appleton's Annual 1878*, vol. 18, p. 530–534.
61. Welch, *George Frisbie Hoar*, pp. 84–86, quote on p. 86.

cent – 134,725 votes to 109,435 votes. The fusionists won 17 General Court seats. Several of the congressional races where fusion candidates ran were quite close. In the Sixth District, Republican George Loring beat Democratic Greenbacker F. E. M. Boynton by 113 votes out of a total of 23,223 votes cast. Ultimately, the Republicans won in all but one district. Still, the Greenbackers were pleased to be counted as a significant electoral force in Massachusetts.[62]

Butler ran again in 1879 as the standard bearer for both the Democrats and the Greenbackers. By now the state Greenback platform had shifted toward a critique of the NBS, and a general indictment of the ill effects of the money power on American government and the economy. Butler's race was a virtual repeat of the previous year's contest. He narrowly lost to the Republican candidate, this time John D. Long, by a vote of 122,751 to 109,149 (with John Q. Adams, Jr. receiving 9,989 votes for the conservative Democrats). In the General Court races, Republican representation remained nearly the same, with 32 senate seats and 185 house seats (compared with 1878, when they won 34 senate seats and 185 house seats) and the Democrats increased their representation slightly at the expense of the Greenbackers. The Democrats obtained 8 senate seats and 52 house seats (compared with 1878, when they won 4 senate seats and 40 house seats), while the Greenbackers declined to 3 house seats from the previous year's 2 senate seats and 15 house seats.[63]

The Greenback party persisted into the 1880s in Massachusetts, after becoming an insignificant political force nationally. In contrast to Illinois, where greenbackism peaked before the National Greenback party was organized, or North Carolina, where greenbackism congealed into an electoral force only for the 1878 election, the Greenbackers in Massachusetts continued to compete after the national party faded. In 1882, Butler finally won the gubernatorial contest as the candidate of the Greenback and Democratic parties. Writing to an associate that year he stated, "I believe all thoughtful men are Greenbackers, and that the people will rise up en masse at any attempt to destroy the greenback." In 1884, Butler ran for president as standard bearer for the Greenback and Antimonopoly parties, and received 175,000 votes nationwide. The immediate economic burdens of war devastation, price deflation, and transportation monopolies did not have the same impact in the Northeast as they did in the South and West. Further, the prevalence of orthodox liberal economic under-

---

62. Nash, *Stormy Petrel*, pp. 272–273. *Appleton's Annual 1878*, vol. 18, p. 537.
63. *Appleton's Annual Cyclopaedia and Register of Important Events of the Year 1879* (NY: D. Appleton and Co., 1884), vol. 19, p. 63; Nash, *Stormy Petrel*, p. 275.

standings among academics, the press, and the political elites slowed the development of greenback thinking among producers in Massachusetts. But once such thinking finally did develop, greenbackism remained an important factor in Massachusetts politics well into the 1880s.[64]

While greenbackism was slow in coming to orthodox New England, and never succeeded in displacing Republican dominance, it was nonetheless a significant party movement in Massachusetts in the late 1870s and early 1880s. The ingredients for greenbackism were available in republicanism and free labor ideology, and in the precedent of a strong labor reform movement in the early 1870s. Ironically, republicanism provided the starting point for both the labor reformers and their orthodox liberal opponents in Massachusetts. Labor reformers drew from American republicanism in combining producerism with antimonopolism to form a critique of industrial concentration that focused on the financial system. Opposing them were the Radical Republicans of the Civil War era who moved toward orthodox liberalism out of disappointment with democracy and the desire to replace partisanship with market discipline. Neither of these developments found much room for expression within the Republican party, which was left as the bastion of probusiness partisans and nonideological party machinists. Yet the political geography of national party dominance, the state's position within the economic core, and Civil War loyalties made the Grand Old Party the regular victor in state elections.

When the rumblings of economic depression and political dissent appeared in the late 1870s, Benjamin F. Butler provided the focal point for greenback education among many Massachusetts voters. Butler was a popular political figure around whom the tensions of class difference often surfaced. His departure from the Republican party in 1878 modified the popular association of war loyalty with the Republican party, and allowed space for a more economically oriented politics. With his emphasis on equal rights, Butler served as a counterpoint to the Brahmins. These elites (for example, Charles Francis Adams, Jr., Edward Atkinson, and John Murray Forbes) were part of the state's investment class, which favored the building of a national economy under Northeastern dominance and strongly opposed greenbackism. But for the workers and manufacturers being threatened by newer and larger industrial sites further west, this was not the case. For them, economic and political control meant re-

64. Butler quoted in Holzman, *Stormy Ben Butler*, p. 225–231; Nash, *Stormy Petrel,* chaps. 21 and 22.

sistance to the growth of the "money power." This made for a subtle, complex political geography of class, regionalism, and nationalism.[65]

IV. Greenbackism and American political development in the 1870s

At the beginning of this chapter, I argued that to understand the relevance of greenbackism to American development, it is necessary to use a more integrated approach, which examines the interaction of different geographical levels in politics, and the coincidence of political and economic development. From the cases presented here, several important conclusions about greenbackism can be offered. First, the political geography of institutions and identities sharply affected the expression and viability of greenbackism. Second, the politics of money contributed to changing notions of class during the early rise of corporate capitalism. Third, greenbackism was both a politically motivated understanding of economic change and a politically designed program for economic development. Finally, the demise of greenbackism elucidates the role of the political system of the late nineteenth century in the rise of corporate liberalism.

Political geography

The relevance of political geography is most obvious in the case of North Carolina. The issues raised by greenbackism in North Carolina were funnelled into state and sectional concerns in the arena of national politics. For instance, arguments about the lack of available credit and the limitations of the NBS were used to promote a revival of the state banking system in Southern states and to criticize the economic dominance of the North over the old Confederacy. But locally, national political issues were used to tame greenbackism, to keep it within the domain of the Democratic party, and to prevent the emergence of a more class-skewed greenback analysis. This was done by arguing for the relevance of sectional concerns in financial matters and against the more class-based analysis offered by the Republicans as working to the advantage of the "party of the Union." Politically, the presentation of greenbackism as a sectional issue was used by the Democrats to gain advantage over the Republicans as the agents of Northern financial speculators and rapacious creditors.

65. On the Brahmin vision, see Larson, *Bonds of Enterprise* on Forbes; Tager, "Massachusetts," pp. 3–28 on the changing regional economy and class divisions; James Livingston, *The Origins of the Federal Reserve System* (Ithaca, NY: Cornell University Press, 1986), pp. 35–38, 95–96 , on Atkinson; and Gerald Berk, "Corporations and Politics: American Railroads, 1870–1916" (unpub. PhD dissertation, MIT, 1987) on Adams.

As championed by the North Carolina Democrats, greenbackism was limited theoretically as a sectional rather than a class issue and organizationally as a matter for the "party of the fathers" rather than for the Republican or Greenback parties.

Generally, the intersection of different geographical levels was strategically relevant for the advocates of financial reform in ways that were detrimental to their cause. Thus, the political geography of parties and sectional identities helps to explain why the broad sympathy for greenback principles in the South never gave rise to a strong greenback movement there. Similarly, in Illinois, the demands of the national party system worked to subvert the discussion of financial issues, particularly for Republicans. The national hegemony of the Republicans placed a premium on cross-sectional unity, which constrained the emergence of Republican greenbackism in the Midwest and limited the movement's overall success in that region. In each instance, local, sectional, and national politics all shaped the course and outcome of greenbackism.

The financial question and class politics

The rejuvenation of the Greenback Labor party in the wake of the 1877 strikes in Illinois typifies the way in which money politics affected class politics in this period. By highlighting the role of financial institutions in economic development, greenbackism gave continued relevance to producerist categories in the industrializing era. Drawing from republican ideas about community, Greenbackers were able to gather a broad coalition of farmers, laborers, and businessmen around the banner of economic independence, an ideal being threatened by the advance of large-scale industrialism. It comes as little surprise then that entire towns came to the aid of strikers in the late 1870s, for they shared a common interest in decentralized, regionally based economic development that would afford continued community control. Even where this idea of community was most significantly challenged, as in Chicago, where self-conscious capitalist and middle (professional) classes were emerging, European ideas of working-class radicalism promoted by the new socialist organizations had to contend with these very American ideas about democracy and economic autonomy.

The political economy of greenbackism

Ultimately, it is not beneficial to consider greenbackism separately as a political movement or an economic program, for the political and economic aspects of greenbackism are inexorably intertwined. Political beliefs about equal rights and the role of independent citizens in maintaining the republic is what motivated the greenback critique of the financial system. Elite control of the financial system violated the equal rights principle by setting up a special class of citizens who received exclusive privileges in the form of favorable legislation from the government. Thus, there was the regular complaint against the nontaxing of government bonds, and of the use of a "two-class" monetary system, with paper currency for the common citizens and gold for the bankers and bondholders. More disturbing to the greenbackers, however, was the impact that the financial system would have on democracy. The depression of the 1870s was viewed as the result of a monetary contraction designed to bring the country back to the gold standard, and the short-term sufferings of unemployed workers and impoverished farmers were regarded as a foretaste of the disempowerment that would be suffered by producers in an economy dominated by a nonproductive financial class. Such economic subjugation would be matched both directly and indirectly by the political corruption of the state, in the first instance through the influence on government of the wealthy, and in the second, by the undermining of the previously autonomous and vigilant citizenry.

Not only was the greenback critique politically motivated, but the greenback solution in correcting the course of economic development was politically framed. Many of the features of the greenback program – its critique of the gold standard, its understanding of the institutional reasons for credit differentials in different areas of the country, its arguments for a flexible currency controlled and created by the government, and so forth – are now accepted by most economists. But because the greenbackers linked their prescriptions to a particular social and political setting, which in this period were linked to mechanisms designed to preserve political and economic democracy, they implied different outcomes than they would when these same reforms were taken up by economists and corporate capitalists decades later. It is in this sense that schemes such as the interconvertible bond plan become significant, not merely as a short-term corrective to the problem of an inflexible currency standard, but as a democratic way of maintaining a currency that grows with the population and production, and thereby maintaining a democratic lever in directing the course of economic change.

The political system and the emergence of corporate liberalism

The role of the American political system in promoting corporate liberalism was one of frustrating the possibilities for its alternative, greenbackism. The organization of political institutions and identities made the task of constructing an enduring national coalition of producers seeking financial reform more difficult. The party system was typically organized, it seems, around everything but clear financial policy choices, including class, racial, ethnic, state power, and geographic issues. The regulatory structure of the federal government generally favored the organization of a centralized industrial economy. True, the Greenback party was poorly organized. It entered as a late arrival to the political debates over finance in the 1870s, and so had less influence on those debates. Strategic errors and a lack of resources further hindered the party's progress. By the time many of the difficulties were overcome, the nation had successfully returned to the gold standard, and the depression and deflationary conditions of the 1870s were lessening. The greenbackers had missed their moment. But the problems of timing and strategy only compounded the larger institutional constraints of the American political system in defeating greenbackism.

Antimonopolist efforts at financial reform did not die with the fading of the Greenback party. Through the Union Laborites, the KOL, the Populists, and the Progressives, the effort continued through the establishment of the Federal Reserve System in 1913 and beyond. Despite the constraints they faced, financial antimonopolists continued to hope and work for an alternative to corporate liberalism.

5

The battle of the standards:
The financial debate
of the 1890s

The Wicked Witch . . . looked down at Dorothy's feet, and seeing the Silver
Shoes, began to tremble with fear, for she knew what a powerful charm belonged to them. At first the Witch was tempted to run away from Dorothy;
but she happened to look in the child's eyes and saw how simple the soul behind them was, and that the little girl did not know of the wonderful power
the Silver Shoes gave her.

The Wonderful Wizard of Oz

In the midst of industrial strife, third-party activism, and economic depression, the dominant political issue of the 1890s was the battle of the
monetary standards. As they had done two decades earlier during the
greenback conflict, editors, intellectuals, labor leaders, agrarians, businessmen, and politicians turned their thoughts and their pens to the problem of finance. Several events contributed to this focus. In 1893, the nation experienced its third banking panic since the end of the Civil War. In
response to the ensuing depression and drain on the Treasury's gold fund,
the president called for the repeal of the Sherman Silver Purchase Act. That
act had mediated between the demands of financial conservatives and reformers and had quelled persistent rumors about the "Crime of '73" when
silver was demonetized under dubious legislative circumstances. The repeal of the Silver Purchase Act renewed conflict over the monetary standard. The debate over finance was at once a cultural, political, and economic debate. The issues encompassed within this debate ranged from
sectional relations to government corruption to the balance of payments.[1]

The advocates of gold mixed a wide range of themes in their writings
and speeches. For them, gold represented moral responsibility, national
greatness, and international alignment with other great nations. Silver

1. On the early history of the silver issue, see Allen Weinstein, *Prelude to Populism: Origins
of the Silver Issue, 1867–1878* (New Haven: Yale University Press, 1970.)

was the money of Western radicalism, national autarky, and popular threats to property rights. Failure to maintain a gold standard risked exposure to the dangers of wild inflation and a loss of protection for responsible savers and investors. These market liberals did not accept the idea that gold unfairly disadvantaged any class of people. Rather, gold produced investor confidence and steady economic growth. As the standard of international exchange, gold also brought America into the community of civilized and prosperous nations.

For financial reformers, the power of gold was the power of Eastern finance. It was the power of the city over the country, the industrialist over the farmer, the Northeast over the South and West, and the speculator over the common man. Economically, gold was a monometallic standard that made America vulnerable to international economic forces. It contributed to the rigidity of the financial system, the frequency of panics, and the concentration of financial control within certain sectors of the economy. The shortage of gold contracted the money supply. This raised prices and increased the cost of debt. By restoring silver, reformers hoped that economic balance and opportunity would be restored and the government reclaimed. Silver symbolized resistance to the growth of corporate capitalism.

This chapter identifies and analyzes the competing programs in the financial debate. In previous scholarship, more attention has been given to the views of the financial conservatives than to those of the financial reformers. The lack of attention to the antimonopolist position grows out of presumptions about the process of political development in the late nineteenth-century. Those who see political positions as determined by economic circumstances identify the Populists with responses to industrialization and their opponents with economic advance. The material presented here reveals that these positions within the financial debate have been discounted, overcredited, or mischaracterized. The financial reform and financial conservative positions were complex, interesting, and deeply politically imbued.[2]

I present three themes in this chapter. First, I establish that there were two general positions in the financial debate. Financial conservatives supported the gold standard and the National Banking System (NBS) and sought to limit or eliminate public regulation of finance. Financial reformers opposed the establishment of a monometallic gold standard, fa-

2. See Chapter 1 on the role of presumptions about development in the historiography on greenbackism and Populism. James Livingston, *The Origins of the Federal Reserve System: Money, Class and Corporate Capitalism, 1890–1913* (Ithaca, NY: Cornell University Press, 1986) provides an excellent account of the financial conservatism, particularly in chaps. 3 and 4.

vored monetary expansion, and sought greater government involvement in financial regulation. Second, I argue with the aid of secondary sources that these two positions offered both intellectually serious and economically sensible views on finance. Finally, I set the financial debate in the context of broader contests over sectionalism, class, and history. The money debate was both a conflict over competing plans for economic development and a wider contest over differing visions of democracy, the market, and the role of government.

The terms of the debate changed from the 1870s to the 1890s. Financial conservatives held a political advantage after the defeat of greenbackism. Elements of the greenback program had lost their intellectual currency. Many financial reformers shifted to advocating a bullion-based monetary standard. Further, the monetary standard debate eclipsed discussion of the credit system and capital markets. Yet the dire economic and political conditions of the 1890s gave rise to intellectual creativity as well, as seen in the Populists' subtreasury plan that would have simultaneously solved the agricultural credit problem and improved the monetary system. While the defeat of greenbackism narrowed the analysis of many financial reformers, antimonopolism still inspired intellectual innovation among the Populists.

Two economic events propelled the monetary debates of the 1890s. First was the panic of 1893 and subsequent depression of 1893–1897. The second involved fluctuations in the international economy. The immediate causes of the panic were believed to be monetary, and the proposed remedies were monetary as well. Gold advocates argued that the provisions of the silver purchase legislation debased the currency and caused concern over the continued viability of the gold standard. Declining confidence resulted in disinvestment and gold hoarding. The Cleveland administration responded by suspending silver purchasing and buying gold. Its aim was to defend the gold standard, even at the cost of contraction and increased national debt. Financial reformers argued that the gold standard made the American economy vulnerable to the whims of speculators and the perturbations of international trade, and that it provided an insufficient currency base. It was this, they argued, and not silver purchases, that led to panics. Their remedy was to expand from a monometallic standard (gold) to a bimetallic standard (gold and silver). Gold advocates believed that gold provided the only stable and internationally acceptable monetary basis, while their critics contended that bimetallism was both more stable and less deflationary.[3]

3. The monetary system of the 1890s was a complex mixture of gold and silver coinage, gold and silver certificates, government legal tender notes, and national bank notes. The standard measure of value for all of these was the gold dollar. Every other type of dollar was redeemable in gold bullion.

International economic conditions affected the American monetary position in four ways. First, silver was demonetized in several countries, including Germany and India, in the 1870s and 1880s. This increased the importance of gold internationally. Second, the United States was a debtor nation, which increased pressure on the country's gold holdings since gold was the international medium of exchange. Third was the international gold contraction. This put monetary strain on gold standard countries and caused English banks to call in foreign debts. Finally, there was the international economic crisis of the early 1890s, marked by the collapse of the Baring investment house in England, bankruptcies in Argentina, and depression in Australia. So, while international trade moved toward gold, gold standard nations suffered from contraction and depression. For the United States, moving toward silver would be risky, potentially isolating, and possibly disastrous. But remaining on gold meant certain further deflation and depression.[4]

Gold advocates and financial reformers emphasized different elements of the situation in their arguments. Gold supporters focused on the movement away from silver internationally and the risks entailed in promoting silver in the United States. They argued that silver contributed to monetary instability and could not create new wealth or diminish the national debt. Bimetallists stressed the international monetary depression and the power of England to affect the world gold market as reasons for avoiding gold monometallism. If silver coinage isolated the United States, then this would contribute to national economic independence. Neither the financial reformers nor the financial conservatives fully responded to the problems of international trade and monetary flows in the 1890s.

The late nineteenth century was an era of tremendous expansion in the U. S. banking industry. Between 1882 and 1892, the total number of national banks, state banks, and trust companies more than doubled from 2,973 to 7,147. After another decade of growth, the total rose to 10,349. Much of this expansion occurred in the South and West, areas previously lacking in adequate credit and currency facilities. As new banks sprung up in outlying areas, the interest rate differentials between regions began to decline.[5]

Despite these improvements in the banking system, problems remained.

4. On international monetary trends, see Milton Friedman and Anna Jacobsen Schwartz, *A Monetary History of the United States, 1867–1960* (Princeton: Princeton University Press, 1963), chap. 3. On the international crisis of the 1890s, see also Peter Gourevitch, *Politics in Hard Times: Comparative Responses to International Economic Crises* (Ithaca: Cornell University Press, 1986).

5. Fritz Redlich, *The Molding of American Banking: Man and Ideas* (NY: Johnson Reprint Co., 1968), part II, p. 178.

First, even though regional interest rates were beginning to converge, substantial differentials remained and continued to affect the cost of credit. Second, national bank notes were declining in volume because of the price of the federal bonds on which the notes were based. The NBS notes were highly inelastic, and their rigidity contributed to the danger of financial panics. Third, the banking system still did not address the credit needs of agriculture, leaving this largely to mortgage companies in the West and merchant creditors in the South. Finally, the late nineteenth-century banking system continued to concentrate funds in New York where it spurred the securities market, contributing to corporate concentration in industry. While the banking system was spare and exploitative in agricultural regions, it also excessively stimulated corporate securities and made the national economy vulnerable to panics.

The inadequacy of agricultural credit inspired efforts by Populists, Grangers, and other agrarian activists to reform the financial system. Initial efforts to pool resources through cooperative enterprises afforded little escape from the debt cycle that hampered farmers and held many Southerners in virtual peonage. Reformers then sought to expand the role of the government in currency management (currency being the major means of credit in many rural areas) or to establish small, publicly sponsored postal savings banks. Financial conservatives defended the NBS. For farmers they suggested self-help in the form of crop diversification, improved savings, and so on. Few financial conservatives were concerned with improving agricultural credit.

Instead, they were attentive to the continuing problem of panics and currency inelasticity. The panic of 1893 again demonstrated that an insufficient and inelastic currency was vulnerable to the stringency caused by annual crop movements. The volume of national bank notes declined by one-half between 1882 and 1891. These notes were issued against government bonds whose high price made note issuance unprofitable. Further, the slow bureaucratic process of note issuance and retirement meant that the monetary volume changed slowly in response to changes in demand. In the 1890s, financial conservatives proposed an asset-based bank currency system. They also sought to establish branch banking. Bankers wanted to exclude the government from banking and currency management. They believed that bankers understood the intricacies of currency and credit and were best equipped to provide efficient capital and credit flows. Neither the asset currency nor branch banking measures came to pass. But after the defeat of antimonopolism, bankers were more willing to consider reform measures.[6]

6. Bruce W. Hetherington, "Bank Entry and Low Issue of National Bank Notes: A Re-examination," *Journal of Economic History,* 50 (1990): 669–675.

The industrial securities market also developed in the 1890s. Earlier, textile and coal securities were regularly offered, and railroad securities had a well-developed market. But industrial securities were considered too risky until the passage of the Sherman Antitrust Act (1890) and the New Jersey general incorporation law (1889) encouraged the formation of corporations and investment financing. When the new industrial securities outperformed railroad securities in the depression, finance capital shifted. The leading investment houses moved from railroad, government, and textile issues to underwriting industrial securities. The demand for investment opportunities contributed to the great merger movement.[7]

Antimonopolists were concerned with the concentration of savings in New York through the NBS, and the use of call loan funds for investment in securities. Agrarian reformers often spoke about the unfairness of high interest rates, which they attributed to the "money power" – a financial monopoly identified as the NBS, English financiers, and bondholders. Some antimonopolists linked local disinvestment to corporate concentration. Generally, reformers sensed that Wall Street's control over finance impoverished producers while profiting a few Northeasterners. Reformers recognized that economic change had a differential impact on various groups in the population.

Financial conservatives were more optimistic. They saw the creation of economic winners and losers as examples of market efficiency. Conservatives contended that government regulation interfered with necessary economic adjustments. Even the panic was viewed as a natural purging process, while "freedom" in investment and contract was regarded as essential to civility, prosperity, and democracy. The charge that the financial system was institutionally biased was refuted by financial conservatives. Interest and investment rate differentials were taken as reflections of differences in risk and profitability. Thus, capital markets were believed to play a neutral role in the growth and concentration of industry versus agriculture.

The rest of this chapter elaborates further on the issues presented here. It is divided into six sections. Sections I and II discuss the views of the financial conservatives. Section I reviews the position of the gold standard advocates in the monetary debate. Section II considers the financial conservatives' position in the disputes over capital and credit markets. Sections III and IV discuss the views of the financial reformers. Section III considers the opponents of the gold standard, including both bimetallists

---

7. Thomas R. Navin and Marian V. Sears, "The Rise of a Market for Industrial Securities, 1887–1902," *Business History Review*, 29 (1955): 105–138; Gene Smiley, "The Expansion of the New York Securities Market at the Turn of the Century," *Business History Review*, 55 (1981): 75–85; and Naomi R. Lamoreaux, *The Great Merger Movement in American Business, 1895–1904* (Cambridge: Cambridge University Press, 1985).

and fiat currency analysts. Section IV presents the financial reform position on capital and credit markets. Turning to the secondary literature, Section V reviews the findings of economic historians in evaluating the financial debate, particularly concerning credit and capital markets. Section VI concludes with summaries of the philosophies of the financial conservatives and financial reformers and considers the relevance of their intellectual conflict to American political development.

I. Financial conservatism's defense of the gold standard

In the silver movement, financial conservatives saw the threat of greenbackism revived. Once again, the stability of the monetary standard was threatened. Again, the threat came from a popular political movement seeking currency inflation and public control over the money supply. But this time, few financial reformers promoted a fiat currency alternative. The work of establishing the intellectual legitimacy of a gold standard was already partially completed. After the defeat of greenbackism, the public generally accepted the need for a bullion-based monetary standard. Once gold was secured and financial issues were depoliticized, then conservatives could work to reform capital markets and the banking system. But in the middle 1890s, all efforts were turned to saving the gold standard.

Discussion of the financial conservatives' position in the monetary debate is organized into four topics. First, gold advocates criticized the use of silver. They contended that silver was an inferior metal, artificially promoted by the government, which left the economy vulnerable to financial crises. Second, financial conservatives expounded on the advantages of gold, an internationally recognized standard that set the American economy on a firm basis. Third, gold advocates attributed price declines to overproduction rather than monetary restriction. Fourth, there was the broader politics of money. The monetary debate incorporated a wide range of issues concerning social change and economic development. The gold standard position combined classical liberal economics with arguments designed to protect the position and autonomy of Northern financial elites.

The critique of silver

Financial conservatives could not treat silver the way they had treated greenbacks – as the heretical invention of political radicals. Rather, these specie advocates recognized that silver was legitimate money, but said it was bad for the American economy. Five points were included in the critique of silver. First, silver remonetization was seen as an artificial attempt to create values, thereby avoiding the laws of supply and demand. Second, gold advocates contended that silver made for a poor standard since it had depreciated greatly over the 1880s and 1890s. Third, they predicted that free silver coinage would result in economic crisis, producing disinvestment, financial contraction, hoarding, and bankruptcy. Fourth, they argued that silver bimetallism was impossible. Silver remonetization would drive out gold and create silver monometallism instead. Fifth, silver inflation would promote financial dishonesty, harm savers and investors, and encourage speculators and debtors. Gold men advocated that the economic well-being of the country was at stake in blocking silver remonetization.

Midwestern manufacturer A. B. Stickney argued that monetary value was determined by the laws of supply and demand. "This is the natural law of value . . . Let those who are tempted to believe that the free coinage of all silver into legal tender dollars and the issuance of paper money by the government will produce abundance and prosperity, remember the fact, that, although congress may declare they are legal tender yet Nature will refuse to accept them in exchange for her stores." Free silver, like paper money, was a false attempt to create value.[8]

How could silver be distinguished from gold? What made silver false money and gold true money? Edward Atkinson suggested Cernuschi's fire test. "It is by the ordeal of fire that money may be tried. The coins which, being melted down, retain the entire value for which they were legal tender before they were melted down, are good money. Those which do not retain it are not good money." This medieval procedure of a trial by fire would determine the true essence of money, separate from its inscrutable surface form where its value was declared by legal inscription. Since the value of silver bullion had fallen below its coined standard, it would fail this ordeal by fire. Its value, like that of paper currency, would be shown to be false or lacking.[9]

Historical trends worked against silver money. As William Everett argued:

> It has been said correctly to-day and on previous days that some nations are on a gold basis, that others are on a silver basis, and that others are endeavoring to keep up bimetallism. Be it so. But what has been the historic tendency? What is the road on which nations have generally advanced? Have they not generally been going in the direction of gold? Have they not shown what they regard as the better way by abandoning silver after they had used it?

8. A. B. Stickney, *The Economic Problems Involved in the Presidential Election of 1896* (Chicago, 1896), pp. 2–5.
9. Henri Cernuschi is quoted in Edward Atkinson, *Forced Loans: Greenbacks, Sherman Notes and Silver Certificates* (Boston, 1895), p. 3.

Monetary conservatives contended that history and the market showed gold to be the only logical path for prosperity and development.[10]

Both the financial conservatives and financial reformers recognized that silver had depreciated. Rather than acknowledge the effect of demonetization on silver's value, gold advocates focused instead on the problems of overproduction. As Representative Samuel McCall argued before Congress,

> Now, Mr. Speaker, notwithstanding the reduced demand for silver, caused by the demonetization of 1873, you will find that, in the face of that decreasing demand, the product of silver has constantly increased, and to-day the annual output of that metal is nearly 250 percent greater than it was in 1873. It has gone up so much that today silver can hardly be ranked among the precious metals . . .

An oversupply of bullion, rather than actions by the government, had depressed the price of silver.[11]

Silver remonetization, gold advocates believed, would be economically disastrous. William Cole suggested that free silver

> . . . would give a new meaning to the word 'dollar' in all contracts, and would make their value so uncertain that our credit currency, which is of vastly more importance than our specie or paper, would suffer an immediate and severe contraction, precipitating bankruptcies, shut-downs, and general business stagnation, with consequent distress among those dependent upon day wages . . .

Another essayist estimated that under a silver standard it would take a generation to "get back the full volume of our currency and our bank credits." Conservatives predicted that silver remonetization would contract rather than expand the money supply.[12]

Most financial reformers promoted a bimetallic standard. Under such a system, every American dollar would be worth a specific amount of gold or silver bullion, payable on demand. Silver bimetallists would set the relationship between the silver and gold bullion in dollars at sixteen to one. But at the time, the market value of silver and gold bullion was nearly thirty-two to one. Under Gresham's law ("cheaper money drives out dearer money"), since fifty cents worth of silver bullion would buy a legal dollar's worth of goods, silver would be preferred and remain in circulation

10. William Everett, *Repeal of the Sherman Act* (Washington, D.C.: Government Printing Office, August 18, 1893), p. 11.
11. Samuel W. McCall, *Stop the Purchase of Silver Bullion* (Washington, 1893), p. 4.
12. William Morse Cole, *When Coinage of Silver is Free* (Boston: Mathews Pub. Co., 1896), p. 26; and Merchant, *Silver: Points for Senator Butler to Answer* (Charlotte: Charlotte Observer, 1895), p. 11.

and gold would be hoarded or exported. Bimetallism at sixteen to one would have resulted in a monometallic silver standard.

While favoring bimetallism on a gold standard basis, George Hoar argued that silver bimetallism would fail.

> Otherwise it seems to me clear that our gold will take its departure, and we shall be left in that most wretched of conditions, a nation with a single monometallic standard composed of an inferior metal, constantly fluctuating and rapidly degenerating – a condition from which every wealthy commercial nation in the world, now including India, has escaped.

Silver monometallism would decrease circulation and prompt other nations to dump silver on the U.S. market. Further, gold advocates charged that silver miners would reap windfall profits from the sale of silver bullion to the Treasury at sixteen to one.[13]

John Dewitt Warner observed that the possibility of silver monometallism exposed divisions within the silver movement. Silver inflationists (for example, debt-ridden farmers) would not benefit from free silver coinage (minting all available silver bullion at sixteen to one) if it produced monometallism and contraction. Under a higher exchange rate (thirty-two to one), specie parity might be achieved and farmers would profit from currency inflation and rising prices. But mine owners would lose their windfall profits. The belief that free silver coinage at sixteen to one could be maintained on a bimetallic basis obscured deep differences within the silver coalition.[14]

Although gold advocates warned against the possibility of contraction, they also feared the success of silver inflation. Inflation would hurt small savers and pensioners. As one campaign booklet stated, "There are 2,000,000 of voters who have deposited gold standard money in National and State banks. They do not want a change of standards to cheap silver, whereby one-half of their deposits would be destroyed and lost to them." The supporters of free silver were "the men who do not want to pay their debts or for the property they bought except in money only worth 50 cents on the dollar of the kind of money they borrowed." While honest savers would be harmed, dishonest debtors and speculators would profit from silver inflation.[15]

Gold advocates consistently criticized silver as an unstable, artificially

13. George F. Hoar, *Gold and Silver* (Washington, 1893), p. 15. Also see George Roberts, *Bimetallism in France* (Chicago, 1895), which concludes that two-standard bimetallism was costly and ultimately unsuccessful.
14. John Dewitt Warner, *The Silver Question* (Concord, MA, 1891), pp. 28–30.
15. Henry L. Beach, compiler, *The Chicago Tribune Discussion of the Financial Issue of the Campaign of 1896* (Chicago, 1896), pp. 21–22.

created standard which would economically isolate the United States. They were less consistent in their projections on whether silver would cause contraction or inflation and between advocacy of limited bimetallism versus gold monometallism. Yet they were united in regarding silver as a threat to values and likely to precipitate a crisis.

The case for gold

According to supporters, gold was everything that silver was not – natural, stable, internationally acceptable, domestically sufficient without being inflationary, and capable of supporting economic growth and prosperity. Even bimetallism was possible with a gold standard, provided that it insured the ultimate sanctity of gold. Further, gold standard supporters extolled the metal's harmonious influence on relationships between social groups.

The National (Gold) Democrats proclaimed that "The experience of mankind has shown that, by reason of its natural qualities, gold is the necessary money of the large affairs of commerce and business, while silver is conveniently adapted to minor transactions . . ." In this secondary role, there was a place for silver. "Thus, the largest possible employment of both metals would be gained, with a value universally accepted throughout the world . . . " Edward Atkinson agreed that "money made of gold is good money; money made of silver is bad money . . . money derives its monetary power from the estimation in which the substance of which it is made is held by the community. I am speaking now of absolute money . . . " Mankind recognized the superior value bestowed on gold by nature, making it the appropriate basis for the national and international monetary systems.[16]

Government-made money stood in conflict with nature's creation of true monetary value. The "law can in no way influence the value of the dollar . . . In determining the weight and fineness of the gold dollar the government is not fixing the standard of payment, but merely saving the contracting parties the trouble of weighing and testing the gold in each special case," wrote Professor John Cummings. A dollar's value came from the bullion within it and not the government stamp affixed to it.[17]

16. National Democratic Committee, *Campaign Textbook of the National Democratic Committee, 1896* (Chicago, 1896), p. 7; and, Edward Atkinson, *The Money of the Nation: Shall it be Good or Bad?* (NY, 1896), pp. 584–585.
17. John Cummings, *Monetary Standards* (Reprint from the *Journal of Political Economy*, June 1894), pp. 350–351.

Financial conservatives promoted gold as stable and sufficient to the needs of the economy. As Republican Curtis Guild stated:

> There is more gold, not less, than there was in 1873. There is more money in circulation, not less, than there was in 1873. The fall in the price of grain and cotton is due to no appreciation of gold . . .

Similarly, the Gold Democrats asserted that "gold has not appreciated. The demand has been fully met and more than met by the supply." Compared with silver, the value of gold had remained steady. Fluctuations in commodity prices were unrelated to the price of gold.[18]

Stability made gold the honest money of contracts. Changing the standard would violate those contracts. "The gold standard is the existing standard in this country, and it should require some very potent reason to justify us in changing that standard to some other." Representative McCall asserted that gold's stability was evidenced by its relation to wages. "I submit that the most nearly correct unit of value you can get is the unit of human labor, which is the unit of production, and as measured in that, gold has been the most stable." Even the labor theory of value was used to justify the gold standard.[19]

Gold was also the money of international commerce. One Southern banker claimed that the international credibility of gold would promote development in peripheral regions.

> We want the confidence of people all over the world – want their brains and enterprise and money to aid in developing these resources . . . Give the country safe financial legislation and within ten years the idle accumulation of money of the East and other countries will come to us by the hundreds of millions. But give us free coinage of silver and we shall invite the ridicule and contempt of the civilized world.

Southerners should regard gold as a guarantee of entry into the community of wealthy, commercial states and nations.[20]

Some gold standard advocates claimed that they favored bimetallism:

> I have been, ever since I was old enough to have an opinion on the subject,

18. Curtis Guild, Jr., *The Issues of 1896* (Boston: Republican Club of Massachusetts, 1896), p. 5; and National Democratic Party, *Public Notification Ceremonies* (Chicago, 1896), p. 7.
19. McCall, *Stop the Purchase*, p. 6.
20. Edward Atkinson, *The Use and Abuse of Legal Tender Acts* (Boston: Damrell and Upham, Pub., 1895), p. 9; Beach, *Chicago Tribune*, p. 2; National Democratic Party, *Public Notification*, p.6.; Horace White, "Coin's Financial Fool," *Sound Money*, 2 (May 1895): 18–19; and W. B. Mitchell, *Dollars, or, What? A Little Common Sense Applied to Silver as Money* (Chattanooga, TN: Times Print, 1895), p. 11.

a bimetallist . . . But it has been the bimetallism of Alexander Hamilton, of Washington and his Cabinet, of the framers of the Constitution . . . It always recognized and took for granted that the money standard of the world's dealings must be settled by the usage of commercial nations. It recognized also that if there were a change in the relative value of the two metals the more valuable metal must, in the end, prevail.

Gold bimetallism was a de facto gold standard. Gold's superiority was historically evident, and in all likelihood, permanent. When subsidiary silver coinage or silver notes threatened gold, as it did under the silver purchase legislation, this was too much bimetallism. Maintaining gold was the first priority of financial conservatives.[21]

Gold inspired confidence in the broader monetary system. It was a secure basis for paper currency and banking deposits. Financial confidence depended on the banks' ability to offer prompt redemption in gold. In a gold-based system, banks would adjust their circulation according to the profits of note demand and the costs of note redemption. The market would determine currency volume. "Beyond everything else, it is essential to remove from the control of Congress the power of increasing and decreasing the volume of our paper money." With gold, a confident public would demand less cash and hoard fewer coins.[22]

Unlike silver, gold promoted social harmony. Writing about the monetary provisions of the 1896 Democratic platform, Curtis Guild exclaimed, "They were appeals to envy, to prejudice, to class and sectional hate." Such appeals must be fought by "explain[ing] the mutuality of interests in modern industrial society." A Baltimore editor agreed. "Thus it is that the industrial fabric of modern society ties us all together – we are children of one household – and what injures one injures another. Nobody is exempt from the risks. The few very rich who can live without work suffer in their incomes when the poorest suffer in their wages." Measures that assured prosperity were a benefit to all.[23]

Social harmony was evident in the commitment of gold advocates to national development. William Everett explained, "No state rejoices in that [Columbian] exhibit more than Massachusetts does, and she is proud of it, because she remembers that when Chicago sank in the flames, she assisted the starving citizens with immediate aid; and when Chicago began to arise from the ashes, her capital helped that glorious city to revive . . . " Likewise, New York national bankers were motivated to assist

21. Hoar, *Gold and Silver*, p. 9.
22. Charles C. Jackson, "Why Legal Tender Notes Must Go," *Sound Currency*, 3 (December 1895): 6. Also see S. A. Green, *A Family Likeness* (Boston: New England Tariff Reform League, 1896), p. 2.
23. Guild, *Issues*, p.7; Democratic Committee, *Campaign Textbook*, p. 81.

the country during the financial panic. Banker W.B. Mitchell wrote, "It has been claimed that the banks 'combined' to raid the Treasury and bring on the panic of 1893." But, on the contrary, "To stay the general disaster at the time, the New York banks imperiled their own safety by loaning money to banks in every part of the Union. I doubt whether there would have been a dozen banks with open doors in Tennessee if aid from the New York 'gold bugs' had been refused . . . " In comments directed at other sections, Northeastern financial conservatives combined pleas for cooperation with demands for gratitude.[24]

Gold standard advocates believed they had the best interests of the nation at heart. Their difficulty lay in convincing the general public that their views were correct. The authors of pro-gold pamphlets were men of means interested in public affairs. Often, they were deeply distrustful of the political process, but they nevertheless recognized the importance of public opinion. Their case for the merits of gold reflected their belief in the need for currency stability and the benefits of the market, a desire for increased American participation in the international community, and a faith that economic prosperity would benefit all Americans.

Prices

Declining prices inspired many farmers and businessmen to seek monetary reform. Economic and political historians see the long-term price decline of the late nineteenth-century as a motivating force behind the agrarian and silver movements. Although questions about real changes in incomes and the cost of living persist, the perception of lost income was significant, and the position of debtors (especially farmers in the South and West) was clearly difficult. Further, monetary contraction contributed to persistent panics and depressions, causing many to question national financial policy.

Financial conservatives contested the notion that gold appreciation had produced a decline in prices or that the decline was a problem. They argued that gold had actually declined in value over several decades, so it could not be held accountable for lower commodity prices. Or they minimized the effect of gold appreciation by noting high wage rates or the strong price of farm goods. Many contended that the price decline was caused by improvements in production. Further, orthodox liberals accepted the fact that price fluctuations were part of the natural pattern of economic growth.

Edward Atkinson and Charles C. Jackson addressed the price question

24. Everett, *Repeal*, p. 7; Mitchell, *Dollars, or, What?*, p. 75.

in their pamphlets, *The Precious Metals – Appreciation or Depreciation?* and *Has Gold Appreciated?* In the first, Atkinson put the price decline in historical perspective. Considering the previous half century, he concluded that "gold and silver had both depreciated in respect to commodities, and that both had lost a part of their purchasing power in varying proportion." Jackson concurred. "We have, then, since 1850, a great increase in the annual product of gold, a much lower cost of gold measured by the effort needed to acquire a given amount of it." While conceding that there was a declining supply of gold bullion, Jackson attributed this to its abundant use in the arts. The reasoning here is fairly contorted. It uses wages as a measure of effort, suggests that increased bullion supply affects its demand for art but not for coinage, and ignores the market price of gold entirely. Yet, such arguments enabled political speakers to declare that "gold has not appreciated."[25]

Gold advocates argued that both farmers and laborers benefitted from recent price trends. Atkinson wrote that "with respect to what the farmer sells it [the gold dollar] has depreciated; he can get more of it for his crops than he could a few years since. With respect to what the farmer buys, however, it has appreciated about fifty per cent., because he can buy a great deal more of what he wants with every dollar of gold which he has secured by the sale of his crops." Evidence suggests that Atkinson was right about the relative price position of farmers. But he did not account for the cost of credit or for the relative position of farmers in the South and West compared with those in other regions.[26]

Since industrial wages were more downwardly inelastic than commodity prices, the standard of living for workers rose while industrial profits declined. Industrialists regarded this as a problem, but in the monetary debate, financial conservatives cited high wages in support of the gold standard. Under gold, "the average rate of wages has, from decade to decade, steadily advanced, and this advance has been accompanied by an increase in their purchasing power." In contrast, silver "would raise prices, but in some industries earlier than others, and it would raise most prices earlier than it raised wages, and hence a good proportion of the

25. Edward Atkinson, *The Precious Metals – Appreciation or Depreciation?* (Boston, 1895), p. 7; Charles C. Jackson, *Has Gold Appreciated?* (New York: Reform Club Sound Currency Committee, 1895), p. 9; and National Democratic Party, *Public Notification*, p. 7.

26. Atkinson, *Money of the Nation*, p. 595. On the debate over the relative economic position of farmers, see Anne Mayhew, "A Reappraisal of Causes of Farm Protest in the United States, 1870–1900," *Journal of Economic History*, 32 (1972): 464–475; Roger L. Ransom and Richard Sutch, "Debt Peonage in the Cotton South After the Civil War," *Journal of Economic History*, 32 (1972): 641–667; and James Stock, "Real Estate Mortgages, Foreclosures and Midwestern Agrarian Unrest, 1865–1920," *Journal of Economic History*, 44 (1983): 89–105.

people would be forced to pay higher prices long before they received higher incomes." The gold standard helped workers to maintain their wage gains, while silver risked price and wage instability.[27]

Many financial conservatives attributed lower commodity prices to improved technology and productivity. Given such changes as "improvements in industrial processes," "centralization of industries and the accompanying division of labor," and "the introduction of such forces as electricity," changes in the monetary standard took on new meaning. If the monetary standard fell as commodities fell, gold men argued that this would provide an "unearned increment" to debtors. Money ought to remain fixed while production and commodity costs changed.[28]

Finally, conservatives were resigned about panics and depressions. Downturns often resulted from the natural cycles of expansion and contraction that accompanied economic development. Some saw such cycles as beneficial. After the boom of the early 1870s, "Finally the bubble 'busted.' . . . Those who had been prudent could settle, and those who had been imprudent could not." During busts, the economy purged itself from previous overexpansion. Given the importance of business cycles, conservatives argued against judging the monetary system by short-term price variations.[29]

Gold standard supporters had difficulty in accounting for the decline in prices. Improved productivity affected some prices, but did not account for the general price fall. Although the relative commodity price position of farmers had improved, the price of farm credit had not. Further, the appeal to workers that gold protected high wages was somewhat suspect given the ongoing efforts of pro-gold business leaders to lower wages. Perhaps this merely confirms the importance of gold to financial conservatives. Rather than accepting inflation, they pursued other solutions to the profit shortfall, such as consolidation. Gold was regarded as fundamental, despite the difficulties associated with contraction.

The politics of gold

The financial conservatives' discussions of exchange rates, price trends, and monetary movements was embedded in a broader dialogue about history, politics, sectionalism, and nationalism. Understanding the impact of

27. Democratic Committee, *Campaign Textbook*, p. 1.67; Cole, *When Coinage*, p. 26; and Beach, *Chicago Tribune*, p. 7. James Livingston discusses the high-wage issue as an impetus for class unity among industrial and financial elites in the late nineteenth century. See Livingston, *Origins of the Federal Reserve System*, chap. 2.
28. Cummings, *Monetary Standards*, pp. 354, 359, and 364. See also McCall, *Stop the Purchase*, p. 6.
29. Stickney, *Economic Problems*, pp. 77–78.

the sound money campaign requires that this broader discussion be explained. The gold advocates' politics of money can be discussed under four topics – historical lessons from the 1870s, the role of government, the political character of groups involved in the monetary debate, and the international politics of silver and gold. These larger messages were an essential part of the ideas being communicated by the gold forces.

Gold advocates refuted the financial reformers' account of the "Crime of '73." According to silverites, 1873 was the year that silver was covertly demonetized by Congress. A small clause in the larger mint act was supposedly inserted under the direction of British interests (represented by Ernest Seyd) in collusion with American bondholders. Horace White ridiculed this account.

> The law was not passed surreptitiously, or secretly, or without due consideration. Some of the hottest silver men were members of Congress at that time and voted for it . . . The silver dollar was an obsolete coin . . . worth two cents more than the gold dollar. Nobody could then anticipate that it would ever be worth less than the gold dollar.

Similarly, John Dewitt Warner attested to the innocence of silver demonetization.

> For forty years silver had been out of circulation, the few dollars which had been coined during that time having been promptly melted or laid aside as curiosities; and in 1873 no one either expected that silver would become cheaper, or suggested that the government dictate the rate at which its citizens estimate one metal in terms of another.

Conservatives believed that financial reformers were projecting history backward onto the events of 1873. Since the standard silver dollar was then worth more than gold, these men argued, demonetization was not intended to avoid currency inflation. Rather, demonetization legally recognized the de facto reality that silver was no longer in circulation.[30]

While rejecting the "Crime of '73," gold advocates drew a different lesson from the monetary politics of the 1870s. As E. S. Lacey, the president of the Bankers' Club of Chicago, said:

> While they [greenbacks] may have served a good purpose in preserving the Union, their issue has served to propagate an error and mislead public opin-

---

30. White is quoted in Weinstein, *Prelude to Populism*, p. 11. See also, J. D. Warner, *Silver Question*, p. 22. As for the historical merits of the "Crime of '73", Allen Weinstein has found that anticipation of a drop in the price of silver bullion, augmented by desire for a single gold standard, motivated government officials to pursue demonetization. Weinstein, *Prelude to Populism*, chap. 1. Also see Walter T. K. Nugent, *Money and American Society, 1865–1880* (New York: Free Press, 1968), pp. 65–171.

ion, so far as the currency question is concerned . . . Many have come to believe that the Government can by its fiat, create money, and that it ought to
so create all that the business of the country demands.

Yet Lacey overestimated the political legacy of greenbacks. The greenback
period did not create substantial ongoing support for irredeemable paper
currency. Although some feared that the paper currency "heresy" would become popular again, most conservatives dismissed this view. "Putting aside
the paper money cranks," began one essayist before launching into a critique of bimetallism. For gold advocates, the Greenback Era set a dangerous
precedent for government intervention in financial matters. But it also
demonstrated the effectiveness of campaigns against "financial heresies."[31]

Financial conservatives condemned the role of the government and the
voters in managing the monetary system. "In one respect, the condition
of the United States is peculiar. We settle our financial policy in accordance with the popular vote. The great mercantile nations of the world,
in fact, and commonly in form, refer such things to experts." A.B. Stickney criticized the role of the President in monetary matters.

> One half of this enormous capital of the present value of more than five bil-
> lions of gold dollars depends entirely upon the United States redeeming its
> paper promises and silver coinage in gold. And whether it will continue to
> redeem such promises in gold dollars is entirely within the discretion of one
> man, the president . . . Can there be any greater crime committed by congress
> than to put it in the power of a president to commit such a wrong, or to place
> before its voters the possibility of making such a terrible mistake . . . ?

Political control by a single official over the power of redemption was
dangerous. Financial conservatives sought to insulate monetary policy
from popular pressures and political regulation.[32]

Although they preached social harmony, gold advocates willingly attacked and villified their opponents. They pitted debtors against creditors,
Southerners and Westerners against Northerners, and agrarians against
other producers. In the 1896 campaign, numerous charges of political
radicalism were levelled against free coinage proponents, who were la-
belled as a threat to the money supply and the political system.

At a time when partisan language was often quite extravagant, the free
silver position of the Democratic ticket provoked vitriolic speeches on the
part of Republicans. Curtis Guild was unrestrained.

---

31. The Bankers' Club of Chicago, *Bank Currency and the Baltimore Plan* (Chicago:
Horstein Bros., 1895); and Atkinson, *Use and Abuse*, p. 5.
32. Hoar, *Gold and Silver*, p. 4; and Stickney, *Economic Problems*, pp. 83–84. See also Jackson, *Why Legal Tender*, p. 5, for his condemnation of "the recklessness and ignorance
of Congress, and of the public by which Congress is necessarily ruled."

The declarations at [the Democratic convention in] Chicago of what [socialist] Henry George and [anarchist] Johann Most hail as the foundation of a new party do not stop with free silver . . . Free silver alone does not, of course, mean anarchy; but a government without an army or navy, or supreme court, or fixed tenure of public service, or national banks, or power to borrow money or suppress riots is no government at all . . . It was no mere coincidence that his [Bryan's] chief supporter in Massachusetts offered to vote down the Christian religion, if need be . . . Though we fight not with bullets, but with ballots, we nevertheless face to-day the issue that the young republic of France faced in '71 . . . They have hoisted the red rag of the Commune. We fight for the Stars and Stripes.

For Guild, the (primarily Republican) opponents of free silver represented a strong federal government and preservation of the union. In contrast, the free silverites were in league with labor radicalism of various stripes, including anarchism and socialism. Further, the Bryan Democrats represented class rather than producer interests. Finally, Guild's message was saturated with images of the un-American nature of the free silver Democrats. McKinley and the Republicans defended the Stars and Stripes against the red bannered, atheistic revolutionaries of the Paris Commune. The Republican campaign also claimed the visual mantle of patriotism in making the American flag the symbol of their ticket. Republicans sought to characterize the free silver Democrats not as the champions of Jefferson, Jackson, and producerism, but as the descendants of Confederate disloyalists and the proponents of un-American labor radicalism.[33]

The Gold Democrats were no more merciful.

But now . . . there springs up against and amongst us another [Democratic] party, professedly built up on sectionalism, professedly and urgently insisting that one special interest in this country, that of the greedy silver miner, shall be built up at the expense of every other citizen in this land . . . [The Democrats' platform is] in reality the illegitimate offspring of Republican protectionism and fiatism and Populistic communism, repudiation and anarchism . . .

Among conservative Democrats, the official Democratic ticket of 1896 was portrayed as a new entry, not seen before in national elections. These "new" Democrats pandered to special interests, and combined the worst of Republicanism with Populism. Like the Republicans before them, the Bryan Democrats were a threat to the social order of the South. Given a choice between this misbegotten hybrid and the reformed Republicans, the latter were preferable.[34]

33. Guild, *Issues of 1896*, pp. 6–8.
34. National Democratic Party, *Public Notification*, pp. 15–16.

Gold advocates sought to reconstruct the notion of a money power. "That vague, greatly abused and little understood thing, the 'money power,' is a mightier force than even the Populists think it is. It is the PEOPLE – the millions of intelligent, thrifty and prudent people who have put aside the accumulations of their industry." Referring to Illinois Governor John Peter Altgeld's attack on the Republicans as the party of "Gold and Greed," the *Chicago Tribune* replied, "They [workers] deposited gold, or equally valuable money, and they want gold or equally good money back. Altgeld may call that 'greed,' but the two million of wage-worker depositors call it insisting on their rights." The "money power" was the productive wealth of the whole society.[35]

Under the threat of silver remonetization, the gold men invoked class and sectional unity. "We must look forward to many fights against the inflationists of the South and West. It is of the utmost importance that our business men should stand firmly together in opposition to everything that tends toward affecting the value of standard money." Speaking of elite bimetallism, the writer warned of a return to greenbackism. "If our educated men say it is right to reduce the value of standard money, we cannot fight successfully against issues of legal tender government paper." Elite and sectional conformity was demanded in the financial debate.[36]

Still more direct was Edward Atkinson's call for a capital strike against the proponents of silver.

> If States send representatives of bad money to Congress, the only safe rule is to stop not only the credit of the State, but of every customer that you have in it . . . Such a decision to deny credit . . . may seem to be a severe decision, yet it is a perfectly legitimate one . . . [when] the people of that State hold that creditors possess no rights which the law is bound to respect. Where that principle is found, the people are not fit to be trusted.

Social harmony, it seems, was to be found through compliance with the wishes of gold standard advocates.[37]

Finally, there was the international politics of money. Some gold advocates offered racist characterizations of silver countries, with their "peons," "coolies," and "rancheros." Poverty, the degradation of labor, and the lack of "civilized" standards in Latin and Asian countries were taken as evidence of silver's inferiority. As Representative William Everett asked, "China, the Argentine Republic, Peru – are those the nations which we wish to make our models?" The great "civilized" and commercial

35. Mitchell, *Dollars, or, What?*, p. 61; Beach, *Chicago Tribune*, p. 21.
36. Jackson, *Has Gold Appreciated?*, pp. 14–15.
37. Atkinson, *Money of the Nation*, pp. 596–597.

powers of Europe were gold-based. Gold was the money of human progress.[38]

In sum, gold was "honest money" and "sound currency." As George Hoar said, "A sound currency is to the affairs of this life what a pure religion and a sound system of morals are to the affairs of the spiritual life." Gold was moral money that went along with thrift, savings, and economic progress through honest labor. Unlike an inflated currency, gold did not lend itself to speculation, unearned increments, and lazy debt accumulation. It was a standard beyond the reach of demagogues, self-interested mine owners, or politically motivated representatives. Silver was the money of radicals and atheists who sought an easy way out. Silver would group the United States with impoverished, pagan nations such as China. Good morals required good money, and the only true money was gold.[39]

Gold and human progress

In their critique of silver, advocacy of gold, explanation of price trends, and broader politics of money, financial conservatives presented the role of the monetary system in economic and political development. They advanced liberal market ideals to justify a monetary system that was then squeezing the economies of most Western nations, but that avoided the uncertainties and isolation associated with a shift toward silver. The temporary difficulties faced by different social groups in the depression of the 1890s were regarded as an unfortunate part of the process of economic growth. They argued that the downturn was exacerbated by political interference. Depoliticization was the key to advancing the financial conservative system, which brought growth and prosperity to all.

II. Financial conservatism's defense of the NBS

Supplying commercial banking services, agricultural credit, and industrial investment were the major functions of the capital and credit markets of the 1890s. The most debated issue in banking circles concerned the role of the NBS. While bankers and their allies were careful to defend that system, they also recognized the need for change. With increased competition from state and private banks, national bankers called for less federal regulation, a shift from bond-based to asset-based currency, and permission to institute branch banking. Problems with agricultural cred-

---

38. National Democratic Party, *Public Notification*, p. 6; Everett, *Repeal*, p. 11; see also Beach, *Chicago Tribune*, p. 2.
39. Hoar, *Gold and Silver*, p. 5.

it and industrial investment received less attention. On agriculture, financial conservatives justified credit cost differentials and lectured farmers on the need for improved business methods. With industrial investment, there was some concern over the desirability of increased local investment, but little attention was given to the effects of bankers' deposits on industrial development patterns.

Commercial banking and the NBS

The depression of the 1890s renewed interest in reforming the NBS. The growth of state and private banks created a diversity of interests within the banking community and put greater competitive pressure on the members of the NBS. But because the antibanking tradition in American politics was still relevant, internal criticisms of the NBS were muted and the system was defended to the public. The reform debate among bankers and financial conservatives would not come to completion until the economic crisis of the 1930s.

Four issues were involved in the debate over banking reform. The first concerned the role of the NBS versus that of the state banks. Dispute centered on whether the 10 percent tax on state bank note issues ought to be abolished. The second issue involved the currency of the NBS. Many bankers proposed shifting from bond-based to asset-based currency to increase profitability and elasticity. The third issue concerned the role of the government. Financial conservatives agreed that federal authorities should be excluded from the banking business. Finally, there was the controversy over branch banking. These proposals, while recognizing some of the problems of the commercial banking system, sought to maintain banker control over that system.

Southern bankers advocated repealing the 10 percent tax on state bank notes. W.A. Blair, the president of the North Carolina Bankers' Association, argued that the old state banking system had merits.

> In North Carolina the old state banks were not bad and assisted greatly in developing the country and in furnishing the needed capital. In 1856, for instance, the bank circulation per capita was over ten times what it is today, and the banking capital per capita was nearly three times what it is now.

The state banking system had not recovered to its pre-Civil War level. Blair proposed extending the right of note issue to nonmembers of the NBS. Tennessee banker W.B. Mitchell agreed that "A State bank, with equal capital and deposits, can make more money than a National bank." Given the inadequacies of the NBS, Southern bankers called for revitalization of the state banking system. Divisions between Southern and

Northern bankers, and large and small bankers, became more prominent as the threat of antimonopolism receded.[40]

Some northerners were sympathetic to this proposal. New York Mugwump Alfred L. Ripley argued that "the privilege of note issue should not be made a monopoly" and that "a safe and elastic currency may and should be furnished by the banks, with safeguards along lines laid down." Others disagreed. "Whatever may be my views of the deficiencies of our present national banking system as compared to a proper one, the present system is immeasurably superior to any possible system that can be provided by the 44 separate states." The writer recalled the days of "wildcat" banking before the Civil War, and thought that any possible return to such financial anarchy would be disastrous. Northerners were divided on the question of abolishing the 10 percent tax, but agreed on the desirability of a national system of banking.[41]

Many economic conservatives hoped to reform the currency system of the NBS. There were two problems with the bond-based currency. First, the high price of the federal bonds needed for currency collateral made national bank notes unprofitable. Many banks issued only the minimum number of notes legally required. Second, the currency system was inelastic. The process of issuing new notes or retiring old ones was cumbersome and time-consuming. As an alternative, financial conservatives supported the Baltimore plan for asset-based currency (see fn 43 and the preceding text).

There was some contention over the elasticity question. Economist J. Laurence Laughlin told an audience:

> It seems to me, too, that the question of elasticity in connection with the bank notes is much exaggerated . . . we have to-day a medium of exchange in the form of deposits and checks coming through the clearing houses, by which to-day ninety-five per cent of our transactions are performed. This is an elastic medium.

But banker James Forgan disagreed. "The weakness of our present currency system is that there is no fluctuation in its volume, and therefore no elasticity in it . . . What we lack is, therefore, a circulating medium of ample volume, that will flow into the channels of commerce, do its work, then naturally retire by being presented for redemption." Financial con-

---

40. W. A. Blair, *Banks of Issue* (North Carolina, 1898), p. 6; Mitchell, *Dollars, or, What?*, pp. 74–75.
41. Alfred L. Ripley, *Currency and State Banks* (NY: Reform Club Sound Currency Committee, 1895), pp. 10 and 13; and J. H. Walker, *No Repeal of 10 Per Cent State Bank Tax* (Massachusetts, 1894), p. 21.

servatives desired a currency system that would respond quickly to the changing demands of the economy.[42]

The Baltimore Plan would allow for note issuance on up to 75 percent of a bank's unimpaired capital. The assets on which notes were based would be highly liquid commercial bills. The banks would be held responsible for redeeming the notes in "legal tender money." This plan would make it easier to obtain new notes or retire the old, and other requirements provided incentives for adjusting a bank's currency volume. An asset system would make "the whole capital of the banks available for business purposes, and the profit on the circulation in excess of [the government's tax of] one per cent. would be quite sufficient to induce the creation of a volume of bank-note currency which would automatically adjust itself to the conditions of business year by year . . . " This system would have improved circulation with minimal government regulation. But it did not address the cyclical problems associated with the crop cycle and the pyramid reserve structure (PRS).[43]

Financial conservatives sought to reduce the role of the government in finance. "Our troubles come from issuing as currency Government notes direct to the public and thereby forcing the Treasury to try to perform the functions of a bank of issue, without giving it the assets and powers of such a bank." The Treasury Department's apparent mismanagement of currency matters led conservatives to call for nongovernmental solutions. Gold Democrat John Palmer agreed, reminding voters of the noble Democratic tradition that "entirely divorced the government from banking and currency issues." James Forgan was more direct. "I am emphatically of the opinion that the whole financial system of the country should be taken out of the realm of politics." He favored the establishment of a nonpartisan commission of financial experts (including bankers) to study the financial system and recommend reforms.[44]

Branch banking would help national banks to compete with state and private banks. "Were branch banking permissible, the number of banks would decrease through the amalgamation of banks in the principal cen-

42. Bankers' Club, *Bank Currency*, pp. 9–10 and 18.
43. Edward Atkinson, *The Banking Principle* (NY: Reform Club Sound Currency Committee, 1895), p. 12. See Forgan's speech to the Bankers' Club, *Bank Currency*, pp. 16–17 for a summary of the Baltimore Plan.
44. Jackson, *Why Legal Tender*, p. 4; National Democratic Party, *Public Notification*, p. 10; and Bankers' Club, *Bank Currency* , p. 25. Richard Bensel makes a similar point about financial conservatives view of the Treasury Department in *Yankee Leviathan: The Origins of Central State Authority in America, 1859–1877* (Cambridge: Cambridge University Press, 1990), chap. 4.

ters with others in smaller cities and towns, to the great advantage of remote sections, which would be better served with banking facilities than
now, and money would be quoted at practically the same rates in all
places." Branch banking would bring the range and efficiency of services
of large banks to small communities, and equalize the cost of credit between sections. However, branch banking might lead to concentration in
the commercial banking industry. This was the proposal's chief political
liability.[45]

Financial conservatives sought to liberalize banking regulation to improve profits and performance. Although hesitant to return to the old
state banking system, many were willing to have state banks issue currency under national regulation. To reform the NBS, they proposed a shift
from bond-based to asset-based currency, which would be more profitable
and elastic. Further, financial conservatives wanted the government to
stop performing banking functions. Finally, members of the NBS wished
to establish branch banking, which would improve banking services in
small communities. Bankers and their allies recognized the need for reform, but sought to control its implementation.

Agricultural credit

Financial conservatives gave little attention to the shortage and expense
of agricultural credit. They favored the extension of banking services to
small communities through branch banking. They also supported the use
of agricultural commercial paper for credit. Yet they firmly opposed mortgage lending by commercial banks. Nor did conservatives favor legaliz-
ing postal savings banks, which would have served rural, agricultural
communities. Most financial elites were uninterested in or unaware of the
financial problems faced by farmers.

Opposition to mortgage lending appears repeatedly in the proposals for
asset-based currency. "The law prohibits discount banks taking real estate security, not because it has any objection to that as a final payment,
but because these funds must be kept 'quick' and are especially devoted
to handling your crops." Another wrote that mortgages limited the liquid-
ity of bank assets. "Bank notes secured by a deposit of bonds or mortgages require that the capital of the bank which might otherwise be used
for discounting business paper shall have been invested in such bonds,
thus limiting the ability of the bank to discount commercial paper by the
amount of capital thus invested." These men were referring to the "real
bills doctrine," which held that banks must keep their capital liquid

45. Bankers' Club, *Bank Currency*, p. 24.

through the extension of short-term loans to meet the demands of commerce. This doctrine underlay the commercial banking system's bias against providing agricultural credit, since land was the farmer's greatest asset.[46]

But commercial loans issued against crops were considered quite reliable.

> This consumption of food cannot stop, even in the hardest of times . . . hence it follows that bank notes issued and circulated in farming districts . . . may or must be sure of prompt redemption if due care is exercised in granting such credits. The very prompt payment of this class of paper was very noticeable during the recent panic.

Crop-based credit was issued to farmers only during the harvest season. During the spring and fall when money was scarce and seeds and supplies were needed, such loans were not available.[47]

The Populists proposed postal savings banks to address the banking needs of farm communities. Under this plan, post offices would receive deposits, provide interest on these accounts, and offer small loans. This was not intended as a solution to the agricultural credit problem. Rather it was meant to provide rural residents with some measure of financial autonomy and experience with banking. Nonetheless, commercial bankers feared any further competition.[48]

Competition forced conservatives to consider extending banking services to small, agricultural communities. Proposals such as the subtreasury plan or postal savings banks were resisted, while the establishment of branch banking and the use of crop credit was championed. Commercial bankers were dedicated to maintaining the prohibition on mortgage lending. Only modifications that did not violate the established principles of commercial banking or threaten bankers' control over banking services were deemed acceptable. Fundamentally, financial conservatives were unwilling to develop mechanisms to meet the need for agricultural credit.

Industrial investment

By the late nineteenth century, the cyclical pattern of growth and crisis seemed deeply entrenched. Many financial conservatives accepted this as

---

46. J. H. Walker, *No Repeal*, p. 9; and Atkinson, *Banking Principle*, p. 5. See also John A. James, *Money and Capital Markets in Postbellum America* (Princeton: Princeton University Press, 1978), pp. 59–62, on the real bills doctrine.
47. Atkinson, *Banking Principle*, p. 5.
48. James H. Hamilton, *The Relation of Postal Savings Banks to Commercial Banks* (Philadelphia: American Academy of Political and Social Sciences, March 22, 1898): 44–53.

natural. Others blamed monetary instability for producing sharp economic downturns. Some called for a flexible bank currency. But few noted the effects of accumulated reserves in New York. Under the NBS, country banks sent a portion of their reserve funds to correspondent accounts
in the New York City national banks. These funds fuelled the call loan
market and the growing industrial securities market. They may also have
raised the cost of credit in outlying areas, deprived many regions of local
investment funds, and contributed to the tendency for panics to occur during the harvest season.[49]

Financial conservatives suggested improvements for the use of local investment funds. One proposal would allow local banks complete use of
their capital for loans and currency. Another would change note redemption provisions to encourage money to return to its place of issuance. Under the NBS's bond-based currency system, "more currency is taken out
of the community than is brought into it." J. H. Walker acknowledged
that "Under present conditions the [national] bank has no inducement to
favor the farmer or small operator who want currency to the man who
wants drafts on New York." He proposed a bill. "Under the system of H.R.
171 it [money] will be forced away from New York where it now congests,
back into the section of the country where it was issued." While seeking
to improve local fund circulation, financial conservatives were reluctant to
address the broader impact of financial concentration in New York.[50]

After the depression of 1893, financial conservatives focused on reforming the NBS, establishing an asset-based currency system, and creating branch banking. But they failed to address the problem of agricultural credit or the effects of the PRS, which biased investment decisions and
contributed to the likelihood of panics. These silences were understand-
able. In a climate where most Americans were suspicious of the bankers
and antimonopolists were still active, financial elites were reluctant to engage in public discussions. Instead, they hoped to neutralize the financial
debate and remove it from the political realm.

III. Monetary reform: Bimetallism, greenbackism, and opposition to the gold standard

The financial reform coalition was broader and shallower than it had been
in the 1870s. It included committed greenbackers and narrow silver inflationists. Greater attention was given to the monetary question than to
related issues concerning banking and capital markets. Yet from this di-

---

49. See also Chapter 3 and Section IV of this chapter.
50. J. H. Walker, *No Repeal*, pp. 12–13. See also Blair, *Banks of Issue*, p. 4.

versity can be discerned a more general commitment to increased government involvement in financial regulation, a belief in the political nature of economic structures, and an effort to increase economic opportunity for financially underserved communities. Further, the development and advocacy of the subtreasury plan showed innovation and depth of analysis that was comparable with the best greenback efforts. Although the historical legacy of the 1870s diminished the financial reform movement of the 1890s, within Populism there remained a vibrant financial antimonopolist tradition.

Critics of the gold standard included advocates of silver remonetization and financial antimonopolists who advocated a fiat currency system. Most silverites were bimetallists who supported full monetary status for both standards. Conservative silverites were committed to securing an international agreement before launching bimetallism in the United States. Others focused on securing the benefits of silver remonetization, even if gold were driven out of circulation. In general, silverites supported an increase in government-issued legal tender notes. The Populists advocated both free silver and the subtreasury plan under which farmers would obtain greenbacks on crop or land mortgages. Radical financial reformers retained a greenback opposition to all specie-based currency. The antigold movement generally agreed on its support for silver remonetization and an expanded role for government-issued legal tender currency.

Four issues were prominent in the pro-silver analysis. First, silverites criticized the gold standard. They argued that it caused contraction, depression, a concentration of economic power, and international dependence. Second, reformers promoted monetary alternatives, including free silver, bimetallism, and fiat paper currency. Third, reformers argued that the price decline resulted from monetary contraction and silver demonetization. Finally, there was the broader politics of money, which involved issues of social and political identity. Where appropriate, distinctions are made between the different tendencies within the financial reform movement.

The critique of gold

Financial reformers believed that gold was economically detrimental and politically dangerous. It provided an insufficient monetary base, caused contraction, depressed prices, and encouraged panics and depressions. Gold monometallism was particularly unstable. Politically, gold contributed to the creation of a two-class society and afforded financiers undue influence over economic development. The government was weakened and corrupted by its dependence on gold dealers. Finally, silver advocates argued that America was losing its national independence. As a debtor nation, America's economy was suppressed by gold. The trend toward gold increased competition over scarce bullion, leaving gold nations caught in an international depression.

The monetary problem was summarized by Populist leader Leonidas Polk. "Scarcity of money means high-priced money . . . The high priced dollar lessens the price of labor products . . . " This was the result of "the wicked financial system of our government," a system which had made agriculture "the helpless victim of the rapacious greed and tyrannical power of gold." He concluded that "our currency has been contracted to a volume totally inadequate to the demands of legitimate business of the country with the natural and inevitable result – high priced money and low priced products." Contraction created high-priced money that depressed the position of producers.[51]

Some argued that all specie-based systems were deficient. Populist author K. L. Armstrong explained that specie-based systems were deficient because they failed to provide a sufficient basis for the credit system, fostered panics, encouraged speculation, and relied on a bullion supply that was being overwhelmed by international economic growth. Armstrong was a "middle-of-the-road" Populist who remained close to greenbackism and rejected all specie-based currency systems.[52]

Others contended that the problem was gold monometallism.

> I do not believe that the ability of our people to feed and clothe themselves should be made to depend upon the possession in this country of the scarcest article in the world . . . To place ourselves upon an exclusively gold basis will be, it seems to me, recklessness building on a shifting sand foundation, upon which there can be no continuance of prosperity.

Because it was specie and subject to variations in availability, gold was unstable. Because it was gold, the most sought-after precious metal in the world, it was likely to fall short of demand, leading to contraction and depression.[53]

Gold demand rose after silver was demonetized. According to the American Bimetallic Union,

> The demonetization of silver in 1873 enormously increased the demand for gold, enhancing its purchasing power and lowering all prices measured by that standard . . . Such fall of prices has destroyed the profits of legitimate industry, injuring the producer for the benefit of the nonproducer, increasing the burden of the debtor and swelling the gains of the creditor, paralyz-

51. Leonidas L. Polk, *The Protest of the Farmer* (Washington, 1891), pp. 7–11.
52. K. L. Armstrong, *The Little Statesman: A Middle of the Road Manual for American Voters* (Chicago, 1895), p. 157.
53. Anonymous, *Light on the Silver Coinage Question* (Chicago, 1893), p. 16.

ing the productive energies of the American people, relegating to idleness vast numbers of willing workers . . .

Silver demonetization exacerbated the economic problems associated with gold.[54]

Gold was socially and politically harmful as well. Agrarian leader Lewis Parsons argued that currency contraction made "the rich, richer and the poor, poorer." According to A. J. Streeter, gold standard laws were "class laws, enacted in the interest of the creditor and money loaning classes . . . " By narrowing the monetary base to gold and national bank notes, bankers gained control of the nation's currency supply, becoming virtual money monopolists.[55]

Indeed, it seemed that the "money power" had already secured the cooperation of the federal government at the expense of democracy. In the crisis of 1893, the government could have paid out silver for its coin notes, but "the Secretaries of the Treasury, by giving the holders of these notes the right to demand gold have made it possible for gold speculators to get gold from the Treasury of the United States easier than from any other source . . . " The Treasury decided to pay out gold on all federal obligations. At a time when the government held a great deal of silver, and its gold bullion was growing short, this was an expensive commitment not required by law.[56]

Reformers claimed that this policy was economically unsensible and politically biased. Senator Marion Butler called on the administration to meet its obligations in silver, thereby "doing what any patriot would do in exercising the option of the government in paying our coin obligations." Otherwise, the government acted "as if they were agents for the gold combine instead of the trusted servants of the people." Further, when the president replenished the Treasury's gold supply with Wall Street bond deals, accusations of corruption increased.

They are both [the Democrats and Republicans] in favor of bonds, more bonds! More bonds! They are both for piling up the debt of the nation to be paid by future generations; they are both for contracting the currency to the curse of the present generation.

According to financial reformers, Northeastern financiers were corrupting both major parties.[57]

---

54. American Bimetallic Union, *Proceedings of the Bimetallic Conference* (Washington, January 1896), pp. 6–7.
55. *Proceedings of the First National Silver Convention* (St. Louis, November 1889), pp. 37 and 268.
56. A. J. Warner, *Opening Address, Delivered Before the Silver Convention in Chicago, August 1, 1893* (Washington: Geo. R. Gray, 1893), p. 4
57. Marion Butler, *To Stop Further Issuance of Bonds* (Washington, 1896), pp. 4, 10, and 11.

International bimetallists were also critical of the nation's reliance on gold. Francis A. Walker (president of M.I.T.) and Brooks Adams (of the famous New England political family) were prominent international bimetallists. In Adams's writings, he notes that the value of gold rose after 1873. This appreciation was compounded by the repeal of the Sherman Act and the closure of India's mints to silver in 1893. Consequently, there was a widespread currency contraction in gold standard nations. "Under such circumstances, the suffering could not have been otherwise than severe." Agriculture was particularly hard hit. "It is perfectly evident that this process cannot go on without producing the direst misery to the debtor, culminating in certain bankruptcy . . . the disease which is devouring the world is an appreciating debt, and if this be true it is a disease which does not admit of local remedy." The remedy, according to Adams, was through a bimetallic agreement.[58]

In his writings, Walker focused on the defects that would be corrected under an international bimetallic system. "The history of the precious metals is a story of highly spasmodic and intermittent production." The irregularity of monometallism would be partially corrected by the counterbalancing effects of two specie standards. Gold alone was insufficient to the demands of international trade. As a result, "the great commercial countries have been brought and kept in an unceasing contest for gold during the past twenty, ten and five years . . . " Competing for gold was especially difficult for debtor nations such as the United States.[59]

There was also a nationalist argument against gold. As the American Bimetallic Union proclaimed in 1896, "[we are] in favor of a distinctively American financial system." The country's monetary standard could not "be safely submitted to the decision of foreign governments, or be made to depend on what other governments may do or may not do." America's debtor status connoted dependence on Britain. "In payment of annual dues to other countries we must compete with . . . Argentine, with Egypt, with India, with all the colonies of Great Britain . . . " Silver would put the United States on equal terms with other nongold countries, providing for national autonomy.[60]

Financial reformers opposed gold because of its effects on the domestic economy, the American social and political structure, and international monetary relations. They argued that gold was bad for the economy as a whole and that it hurt particular classes (producers and debtors)

---

58. Brooks Adams, *The Gold Standard: An Historical Study* (Boston, 1894), pp. 25–33.
59. Francis A. Walker, *Bimetallism: A Tract for the Times* (Boston, 1894), pp. 6–7.
60. American Bimetallic Union, *Proceedings*, p. 5; *The American Bimetallic Party: A New Political Organization* (Washington, 1895), pp. 5–6.

more than others. They also believed that gold made the nation vulnerable to the vagaries of international trade and mining discoveries and that it was too narrow a financial base on which to support a thriving economy.

The monetary alternatives

Reformers proposed several alternatives to the gold standard. The majority supported silver remonetization. They also sought an increased role for government-issued legal tender currency, sometimes to the exclusion of any specie-based money, but more often in conjunction with silver and gold-based currency. The three major monetary alternatives advocated were free silver, bimetallism, and fiat paper currency. Each alternative was intended to expand the monetary base and stabilize the economy.

"Free silver" referred to a policy under which United States mints would accept for purchase and coinage any silver bullion offered at the stated rate of 412 1/2 grains per dollar. The only limit on silver coinage would be set by the market rate and supply of silver bullion. Over time, the market rate for silver would rise as its supply dwindled. Eventually, silver and gold would reach parity at sixteen to one bullion amounts per dollar.

Under this policy, silver would probably have become the dominant monetary standard, inflating the value of the dollar and increasing the volume of currency. That was exactly what many silver advocates hoped for: "We favor this proposition because it will increase the volume of currency in circulation and contribute not only to make better prices for the products of labor, but to break the power which the bankers now have to control the currency." Silver inflation would expand the economy and raise prices.[61]

Silver, like gold, was seen as natural money. "Silver and gold are nature's money, and their uses as such are plainly shown in the Holy Scriptures. From the beginning until the present time their use has been maintained, and the Constitution of the U. S. forbids the use of any other metals." Silver had legal and religious legitimacy. Silver's use as a subsidiary coin under the Bland and Sherman Acts was evidence for the viability of bimetallism. As of 1889, $340 million silver dollars were "in circulation either in kind or through the medium of Silver Certificates. Not one of them I think has ever failed to have the same purchasing power as a Gold Dollar." Given silver's previous history as a specie standard, and

---

61. Armstrong, *Little Statesman*, p. 72. Walker saw de facto monometallism under silver as a workable part of a bimetallic standard. See F. A. Walker, *Bimetallism*, pp. 12–21.

its presence in the monetary system of the 1890s, silverites contended that full remonetization was practical.[62]

Silver had the benefits of specie currency without the faults of gold. It would not require any new bonded debt to maintain its presence in circulation. "It stands confessed that the gold standard can only be upheld by so depleting our paper currency as to force the prices of our products below the European and even below the Asian level . . . " Silver standard nations had no difficulty maintaining their currency in the international system.[63]

Silver was nationalist currency.

> The man who favors the British gold standard is at heart opposed to every principle enunciated in the Declaration of Independence. He is unAmerican; he stands for trusts, combines and monopolies, and for everything that is dangerous to American prosperity and American liberty . . . [while those who support free silver] stand for the true democracy of Thomas Jefferson and the republicanism of Abraham Lincoln . . .

Gold was the currency of British domination, while silver was the coinage of national autonomy. Silver was consistent with American political principles, such as democracy and republicanism, while gold was the standard of monopoly, and was therefore un-American. Such views drew many Populists to the silver cause.[64]

Some reformers perceived the call for international bimetallism as a political diversion.

> I call your attention to the fact that some of the very people who are in this convention today and who tell us that we ought to declare in favor of international bimetallism – thereby declaring that the gold standard is wrong and that the principle of bimetallism is better – these very people four months ago were open and avowed advocates of the gold standard, and were then telling us that we could not legislate the two metals together, even with the aid of all the world.

Although they favored parity at sixteen to one, silver monometallism was also acceptable. As the Bimetallic Conference of 1895 stated, "but should gold for any reason temporarily go to a premium, it will nonetheless operate on prices generally, and certainly a premium on gold here would, like a fall in the gold price of silver to silver using countries, inure on every

62. William H. Oliver, *An Address to the National Silver Convention at Saint Louis* (Newbern, N.C., date unknown), pp. 2 and 10.
63. American Bimetallic Union, *Proceedings*, p. 8.
64. Butler, *Stop*, pp. 26–27.

side to the advantage of the United States." Indeed, a silver-based monetary system could be advantageous in international trade.[65]

Others asserted that bimetallism was possible under free silver. Brooks Adams and Frances Walker focused their discursive energies on this issue. There were many plans for assuring a workable bimetallic system. The most common proposal involved an international agreement setting the parity rate between silver and gold and guaranteeing each nation's acceptance of all bullion for mintage. Another proposed removing the legal barriers to the use of silver coinage, thereby releasing the demand for silver and raising its value. Finally, there was Adams' proposal to remonetize silver and dump gold on the world market, thereby raising the value of the first and lowering the price of the second.[66]

Plans for an international bimetallist agreement had circulated since the 1870s, when failure to reach such an agreement caused many European nations to close their mints to silver and adopt the gold standard. In the 1890s, Francis Walker was optimistic that the international gold depression made an agreement more likely. The key was England.

> A selfish, shallow, supercilious gold monometallism is intrenched today in the London banking interest and in the London city press, but tomorrow it may be driven from even this refuge . . . Changing conditions like these have for the first time created a reasonable hope that England may yet take the lead in restoring silver to its true place in the commerce and exchanges of the world.

Were the great citadel of the exclusive gold standard to fall, then the trend toward bimetallism would be assured.[67]

While asserting the natural status of silver money, bimetallists also believed that legal status affected monetary value. Political discrimination against silver contributed to its devaluation. Gold had many legal and institutional advantages. Economist John Thompson reviewed them in 1889. The first advantage "consists in the discrimination made at the United States Mints, in receiving gold bullion for free coinage, and not receiving silver bullion in the same manner." Second came bank clearing house practices. "Notwithstanding the law which prevents a national bank from belonging to a Clearing House Association at which 'silver cer-

---

65. William Jennings Bryan, "Cross of Gold Speech," in George Brown Tindall, ed., *A Populist Reader: Selections from the Works of American Populist Leaders* (Gloucester, MA: Peter Smith, 1976), p. 209; and *American Bimetallic Party*, p. 6.
66. On Adams' proposal, see Brooks Adams, *Address of Brooks Adams* (Quincy, MA, July 1896), p. 7.
67. F. A. Walker, *Bimetallism*, pp. 23–24.

tificates are not received in payment of balances,' by tacit consent, or un-
written social law – as it might be called – the banks of the clearing houses as a matter of fact seldom or never offer silver certificates in payment
of balances." In their internal practices, the banks had declared silver an
unwelcome currency. The third and most serious discrimination against
silver involved the Treasury's gold reserve. There were no laws from which
to conclude "that there has ever been any contract to redeem the legal tender notes in anything except the current coin of the United States, whether
gold or silver." The Treasury always paid out gold when it could have paid
out silver or gold. These political and institutional discriminations against
silver were thought to contribute to its drop in value.[68]

Free coinage alone would not restore parity (at sixteen to one) between
silver and gold. "Therefore if we pass a free coinage bill here today gold
and silver can not come to parity . . . unless the secretary of the treasury
and the president will observe and carry out the letter and spirit of the
law." Silver and gold would come into balance "provided that there are
no other laws, or conditions created by law, to artificially disturb this parity." This argument combines an acknowledgment of the role of institutions in affecting values, while retaining some notion of a natural economy in which bullion has intrinsic value. The sophistication of greenbackism
was sometimes interspersed with the naivete of bullionism.[69]

Some financial reformers advocated a purely paper currency standard.
Among Populists, those experienced in cooperative enterprises and independent politics were often more prepared to break from the accepted traditions of partisanship and bullionism. Others focused on electoral victories and currency expansion. This division was captured by the People's
party platform, which simultaneously advocated free silver and the subtreasury plan. The former offered an element of immediate relief, while
the latter promised a broad reorientation of the financial system and its
role in economic development. In this plan for democratically issued and
backed fiat currency, the antimonopoly tradition in financial reform continued.

The Populists' subtreasury plan originated with Dr. Charles Macune,
an agrarian organizer and intellectual leader from Texas. The plan, as presented at the St. Louis convention in 1889, sought to reduce "the power
of money to oppress." The plan report argued that the monetary system
was inelastic and unresponsive to the demands of the annual harvest season. Further, inadequate currency strained the nation's financial system,
providing profits to bankers, but suppressing prices and reducing income

68. *First National Silver Convention*, pp. 178–181.
69. Butler, *Stop*, p. 11.

for farmers. The solution to these problems lay in a flexible currency standard that expanded and contracted according to the demands of the crop cycle.[70]

The subtreasury proposal contained two major features, including a warehouse storage plan and a currency issuance plan, the latter being of immediate interest. According to the proposal, greenbacks would be issued against crops held in government warehouses for storage. The currency issued would be worth up to 80 percent of the certified value of the farmer's crop, and interest of 1 percent would be due on this currency until the crop was sold and the certificate redeemed within twelve months of its storage date.

This proposal solved several problems at once. In one stroke, the agricultural credit shortage would end. The plan also established an elastic currency standard that expanded and contracted along with the economy. Further, this system would alleviate the effects of crop cycle, by spreading crop sales over several months rather than concentrating them in the fall. The regional distribution of currency would be broadened, particularly to the South and West, areas often starved for money under the NBS. Finally, there were the social effects of the subtreasury system. By bypassing the role of specie holders and national banks, the Populists strengthened the role of the government relative to that of financial elites. This was an antimonopolist monetary system that would maintain equal economic opportunity between farmers and industrialists, between outlying regions and the Northeast, and between producers and nonproducers. Productive wealth would translate into monetary power, and the currency system would be democratized.[71]

70. For a discussion of the subtreasury plan, see Lawrence Goodwyn, *Democratic Promise: The Populist Moment in America* (NY: Oxford University Press, 1976), Appendix A and B. In economist William Yohe's evaluation of the subtreasury plan (Appendix B), he states "The mechanism for making land and commodity loans was a very subtle one, which simultaneously would have contended with the problems of financing cooperatives, the seasonal volatility of basic commodity prices, the scarcity of banking offices in rural areas, the lack of a 'lender of last resort' for agriculture, inefficient storage and cross shipping, the downward stickiness of prices paid by farmers vis-a-vis prices received for crops, and the effects of the secular deflation on the price burdens, all of which, in a far less comprehensive fashion, were the objects of legislation in the next five decades" (p.580). The major problem which Yohe attributes to the plan was the potential for inflation.

71. "Report of the Committee on the Monetary System," in Tindall, *A Populist Reader*, pp. 80–87. Money would be democratized in two senses. First, the distribution of money into the economy would occur through the farm community. Thus money would be available at a local level, in poor, rural communities. Second, a fiat currency standard under government control meant that the nation would be run in the interest of the public. The gold standard allowed money to remain under the control of a few wealthy bankers.

These were the alternatives offered by the critics of a monometallic gold standard. Free silverites sought to remonetize silver at the rate of sixteen to one. This would inflate the currency, raise prices, and end depression and monetary instability. Conservative silverites sought an international bimetallic agreement to assure the continued circulation of gold and silver. This would improve trade and lessen the monetary shocks that troubled the international system. Finally, there were the antimonopolists who supported the subtreasury proposal. These latter-day greenbackers looked beyond the problems of contraction and price decline to the broader issues of economic development. Proponents of all three alternatives hoped to end contraction and stabilize the economy.

Prices

Prices were an important impetus to the political rebellions of the late nineteenth-century. While there was no simple translation between economic conditions and political action, the members of the sound money, silver, and Populist movements responded to material events such as bankruptcy, unemployment, and foreclosure. Financial reformers asserted that prices declined as a result of monetary trends such as the demonetization of silver and the rising value of gold. They rejected the claim that prices fell because of overproduction, arguing that the economy suffered from underconsumption instead. Declining prices increased the level of farm debt, creating more bankruptcies and mortgage failures, and raising unemployment. They proposed expanding the monetary supply to ensure prosperity.[72]

Reformers discussed both domestic and international aspects of the monetarily induced price fall. Domestically, "The demonetization of silver in 1873 enormously increased the demand for gold, enhancing its purchasing power and lowering all prices measured by that standard . . . " International demonetization of silver had the same effect. There was "a new scramble for gold" creating "a veritable 'monetary warfare,'" in which more countries competed for scarce bullion. Domestic and international monetary policies combined to depress prices.[73]

72. Other factors affecting political action include the political culture through which citizens interpreted the events of their daily lives, the political opportunities available within the larger structures of politics, and the contingent nature of historical moments which added a temporal element to the determination of winners and losers.

73. American Bimetallic Union, *Proceedings*, pp. 6–7; A. J. Warner, *Opening Address*, p. 12; and *American Bimetallic Party*, p. 5. See also N. A. Dunning, *The Power of Money to Oppress and the Volume of the Currency* (Washington, 1891), in which he argues that there has been a decline in the per capita circulation of money, which in turn has led to a high level of business failures. Although the accuracy of his findings is uncertain, it nonetheless affirms that the Populists were aware of the role of bank note circulation and other monetary instruments in the money supply.

The Populists refuted the argument that overproduction lowered prices.

> Others high in authority tell us that the meager return for the products of our labor is due to "over production," . . . He forgets that there are 3,000,000 tramps in this country and 5,000,000 human beings living in a state of semi-starvation. There can be no over production so long as the cry for bread from a single child in the land is heard. It is not over production, but it is under consumption – a want of a just and equitable distribution of the products of labor.

The demand for goods would rise with a better income distribution. This maldistribution of income, like low prices, resulted from the monetary system's tendency to concentrate wealth. The monetary system was the root cause of the nation's economic woes.[74]

Farmers were debtors. During a contraction, "agricultural prices are the most sensitive," making farmers especially vulnerable to monetary shifts. Eventually, all producers were affected. As Catherine Bergan of the Woman's National Industrial League of America explained, "By that infamous act [silver demonetization], the farm industrial workers of our country are deprived of the just reward of their toil, and . . . their inability to purchase the products of the manufacturing classes has caused great depression in the trade . . . " Contraction and declining prices dampened the prosperity and livelihood of the entire economy starting with the agricultural sector.[75]

The remedy was obvious. "All history shows that prosperity accompanies an abundance of gold and silver money; that industry is quickened, enterprise stimulated, production encouraged, wealth increased and civilization advanced . . . " History showed that when "the gold and silver of the West, pouring in a steady stream on the East for forty years, vitalized every form of business there, steadied and upheld the credit of the nation through the great war and made resumption possible . . . " Silver remonetization would expand the currency and raise prices.[76]

Financial reformers blamed the price deflation on monetary contraction. Their analysis is supported by Milton Friedman and Anna Schwartz, who explain in *A Monetary History of the United States, 1867–1960* that the period between 1879 and 1897 was one of international deflation for nations on the gold standard. During the 1890s, both the United States money supply and the net national product declined. While silver had little direct effect on the money stock, it contributed to monetary uncertainty and gold flight. The authors argue that the United States could have

---

74. Polk, *Protest*, p. 10.
75. Polk, *Protest*, p. 12; Adams, *Gold Standard*, p. 27; Dunning, *Power of Money*, p. 3; and *Proceedings of the First National*, p. 52.
76. A. J. Warner, *Opening Address*, p. 13; and *Proceedings of the First National*, p. xiv.

abandoned the gold standard and embraced silver, thereby creating greater exchange flexibility and avoiding the international gold depression and price deflation. While bimetallism may have been unattainable, the financial reformers' desire to raise prices and stabilize the economy was potentially realizable.[77]

The politics of financial reform

For the financial antimonopolists, the politics of the money involved issues of sectionalism, nationalism, class, and democracy. Reformers had their own sense of history, which provided lessons for the conflicts of the 1890s. There were villians and heroes in their political narrative. The villians constituted the "money power" – bankers and bondsmen, often portrayed as British or Jewish. The heroes were the producers – honest laborers and hard-working farmers. The antimonopolist map of America was sectionally divided between the wealthy, domineering Northeast and the struggling South and West. Reformers were also alarmed by the changing class structure in which the upper and lower classes grew at the expense of independent producers. Finally, financial antimonopolists called on the political ideals of Jefferson, Jackson, and Lincoln in their effort to preserve American republicanism.

Agrarian radicalism is often presented as rife with racism, anti-Semitism, xenophobia, and conspiracy thinking. These elements were present and played a role in the monetary debates. For instance, one Southerner contended that during the war, "It was too plain that while legal tender money was being transported [in war ships] one thousand miles to be locked up . . . at the same time the New York National Banks, assisted by the Government, were sending thousands of dollars of non-legal tender money all over the country." Thus the federal government robbed the South at the behest of the "money power." For this man and others like him, the realities of economic discrimination were explained by personal greed or evil, rather than by the institutional structures that biased the financial system.[78]

The "Crime of '73" was often invoked in connecting the British to American financial elites. According to popular myth, a representative of the British financial elite, Ernest Seyd, came to the United States with $500,000 to influence legislators to demonetize silver. As Sarah Emery wrote, "Judge Kelly . . . saw the original draft of the bill for demonetiza-

---

77. Friedman and Schwartz, *Monetary History*, chap. 3.
78. Also see Richard Hofstadter on the agrarian myth and anti-Semitism in *The Age of Reform: From Bryan to F.D.R.* (New York: Vintage Books, 1955). Oliver, *An Address*, p. 11.

tion of silver, and it was in Ernest Seyd's own handwriting." She asked rhetorically, "Do you ask for evidence that this [American] people were deliberately robbed by a band of men at the head of our government, who were in league with the money power of Europe?" Other conspiracy stories also highlighted the role of the British. Ironically, according to Allen Weinstein, Seyd (a British mintage expert) actually helped to prevent the total demonetization of silver.[79]

There are also references to the Jewishness of New York or British bankers. A.J. Warner denounced journalists as men who "slander everything American and extol everything that is British or Semitic in finance." Bankers were called "Shylocks." Ignatius Donnelly and the author of *Coin Harvey* characterized financial elites as Jewish, and expounded on the role of the Rothschilds in controlling British finance. Richard Hofstadter quotes Populist lecturer Mary Lease as stating that Grover Cleveland was "the agent of Jewish bankers and British gold." The Populists frequently exploited anti-Semitic stereotypes in their complaints against financiers.[80]

British, Jewish, Northeastern; these were the identities associated with the "money power". Such prejudices do not displace the seriousness of the Populist financial program, or the realities of economic suffering among farmers and workers during the depression. Rather than using these revelations of anti-Semitism and nationalism to dismiss the financial reform effort, these characterizations provide clues about the nature of social divisions and social relations in American politics at this time.

Financial reformers sought to overcome Civil War divisions by uniting the South and West against the Northeast. L. L. Polk exclaimed "Force bills, 'bloody shirts,' the cry of 'negro supremacy in the South,' and of 'rebels' in the North, will lose all the power of their baleful charm in the presence of these great, overshadowing questions [those addressed in the Populist platform]." Sectional prejudices worked in the interest of the political and economic elites. Bryan asserted that the money issue was essential to sectional relations.

> The money question is the great question which divides the Northeast from the rest of the country . . . The gold standard appreciates the value of mon-

---

79. Emery, "Demonetization," pp. 54 and 58. On Seyd's role, see Weinstein, *Prelude*, pp. 23–24.
80. A. J. Warner, *Opening Address*, p. 16; Hofstadter, *The Age of Reform*, pp. 77–82, on Populist anti-Semitism. Hofstadter is correct in pointing out the continuity in anti-Semitic rhetoric between the Greenbackers and the Populists. It should also be noted that financial conservatives were often inclined to use anti-Semitic references. Like racism, it seems, anti-Semitism was a pervasive part of American political culture in the late nineteenth century.

ey, and since the Northeastern states own a great deal of capital and loan money to other parts of the country they secure what might be called the unearned increment . . . The people in the South and West are, relatively speaking, debtors, and as the purchasing power of the dollar increases they feel their pecuniary burdens become heavier.

K.L. Armstrong concluded that "These constant drains of wealth from the producing States into the nine States called the wealth district are the cause of the new sectionalism in American politics." The sectionalism of slavery was being replaced with the sectionalism of money.[81]

Not everyone agreed that sectionalism was the proper division in the battle of the monetary standards. Some exclaimed the role of class instead. One Midwesterner wrote,

> You farmers are deceived when you believe your oppressors are far away off in Wall Street, in Chicago, St. Louis, and the manufacturers off in the East . . . No, they are right among you . . . [They are] All those who do not create any wealth, and in any way become of service to the wealth creators, such as the interest gatherers, bankers and brokers, most lawyers, speculators, operators on change, etc.

The question was not one of location but of economic position. The true social division was between the producers and the nonproducers.[82]

Financial reformers were concerned with the social consequences of economic development under the gold standard. By concentrating wealth, the gold economy contributed to the decline of independent producers. This was what Bryan meant when he spoke of "the masses versus the classes." The masses were the majority of economically independent Americans, while the classes were the very wealthy and very poor. According to A.M. Waddell, both organized capitalists and organized labor radicals threatened "the great body of fair-minded, conservative, and intelligent citizens . . . " Polk, too, worried that "the rapid absorption of the small farms and the rapid expansion of the large landed estates portends the due approach of the crucial era of republican form of Government." The social changes wrought by economic concentration had negative political consequences.[83]

81. Polk, *Protest*, pp. 21–22; Bryan, quoted in Armstrong, *Little Statesman*, p. 93; and Armstrong, *Little Statesman*, p. 96.
82. *The Farmers' Voice*, November 9, 1889, p. 4. Another article in this issue goes so far as to assign specific numbers to the class of producers versus nonproducers. The latter were a mere "25,000 banded monopolists" seeking to dominate the producers, "67,000,000 of their good fellows." *The Farmers' Voice*, November 9, 1889, p. 9.
83. A. D. Waddell, *Some Public Dangers* (Enfield, N. C., 1894), p. 10; and Leonidas L. Polk, *Agricultural Depression. Its Causes – The Remedy* (Raleigh: Edwards and Broughton, Printers and Binders, 1890), p. 21.

Under a gold standard system the republic itself was threatened.

So delusive has been the idea of safety under a republican form of government, so forgetful the people that eternal vigilance is the price of liberty, and so crafty and successful the tyrant, whether in the garb of a republican or disguised as a democrat, that we can no longer boast of this as the home of liberty . . . aristocracy has appeared in a new form. It is not now taxation through the tax-gatherer only, to support royalty; but it is taxation in all the various forms, which monopolies are able to impose through their control of the currency.

The old threat to the American republic – aristocracy – now appeared in a new guise as a monied monopoly. Within society, the threat appeared as a changing class structure. The very rich and very poor were "classes which in all ages have proven themselves to be the weakest defenders of civil liberty." Politically, the threat came from wealth's control over the government itself. As Donnelly's famous preamble to the Populist platform states, "Corruption dominates the ballot box, the Legislatures, the Congress, and touches even the ermine of the bench." The loss of liberty would be halted only through democratic renewal, which would assure the nation of a monetary policy set in the interest of the whole people.[84]

The money issue was the slate on which other social and political beliefs were written. Fears and prejudices were vented in xenophobia, anti-Semitism and the perception of conspiracies. Geographically, reformers sought to erase the lines of Civil War memory and draw in new distinctions between the money-holding Northeast and the productive, debtor sections of the South and West. Within sections, antimonopolists feared that producers were being displaced by a class-based society dominated by the rich and poor. Finally, there were concerns over the survival of the republic itself, threatened by the corrupting influence of wealth on society and the government. Money was the key to a larger process of social and economic change, changes that financial reformers sought to redirect for the sake of democracy and national unity.

Like the gold advocates, financial reformers offered a broad understanding of the monetary system and its role in economic and political development. They criticized the gold standard system for producing contraction, depression, and international dependence. They proposed monetary alternatives such as free silver, international bimetallism, or the sub-treasury plan. They believed that these alternatives would expand the currency and stabilize the economy. Reformers argued that declining prices were caused by monetary factors and required a monetary remedy.

84. Westrup, *Financial Problem*, pp. 15–16; Polk, *Agricultural Depression*, p. 21; and "The Omaha Platform, July 1892," in Tindall, ed., *Populist Reader*, p. 90.

Finally, all of this was situated within broader views on nationalism, sectionalism, class, and democracy. Antimonopolists sought to prevent the emergence of a financial conservative society in which the few held power over the many, and to preserve a nation in which economic opportunity was available to all and political power was held by each.

IV. The financial reformers' critique of the banking system

Financial reformers were critical of the NBS and the agricultural credit system. The Populists responded negatively to the early development of the commodity and securities markets. They regarded the commodity futures market as legalized price manipulations that benefitted speculators at the expense of producers. More generally, reformers contended that financial concentration was promoting the development of corporate capitalism at the expense of agriculture. Although their analyses were often incomplete or misdirected, financial reformers offered the beginnings of a critique of the financial sector's role in the emerging corporate economy.

Commercial banking and the NBS

Many reformers believed that the NBS should be abolished. The three main arguments against the NBS concerned the 10 percent tax against state bank notes, which limited banking services in many areas, the real estate lending prohibition, which biased the NBS against agricultural lending, and the tendency of NBS currency to displace greenbacks and silver from the monetary system. There were also minor criticisms about the role of bonds in the NBS, the practice of issuing loans beyond circulation, and so forth. As an alternative, reformers proposed establishing postal savings banks. The reformers' analysis of commercial banking and the NBS was deeply indebted to the views of the earlier greenbackers.

According to A. B. Waddell, the NBS constituted a special interest that distorted government policy.

> And who ever dared to suggest the degradation and destruction of one of the money metals of the Constitutions, until after the government had gone into partnership with money lenders, and had deprived the States of their power to establish banks of issue? . . . And, when, before this system was adopted, were valuable farm lands and other real estate useless as security for bank loans?

For many Southern representatives, the NBS was a Civil War product of the North. The NBS interfered with the rights of the states and disregarded the Constitution. National bankers sought to further their self-interest by limiting the money supply. Finally, the NBS was antifarmer – it did not accept land as security for credit. This message brought together Democratic ideology and Southern political identity with an appeal to debtors. The concentration of financial wealth and the bias against agriculture both favored Northeastern over Southern interests.[85]

In an address before the Farmers' Alliance, L. L. Polk added two further complaints.

> Organized capital demanded that Congress should degrade and destroy our legal-tender currency and establish in lieu thereof national banks of issue, which should be based alone on interest-bearing government bonds . . . In 1880 we had 2,090 national banks with a circulation of $317,000,000 and yet their loans and discounts amounted to $1,041,000,000 . . . On what principle of equity or safety can individual or corporate credit be thus substituted for money?

According to Polk, bond-based bank currency increased the federal debt and contributed to the power and profits of the bankers. The banks obtained these bonds cheaply, at a direct cost to the public. Public resources were being used for private gain. But Polk failed to consider the role of bank capital in his assessment that the banks exceeded their resources in making loans and discounts. The analysis suggests a mixture of political astuteness, some solid economic reasoning, and fallacious economic understanding. This was typical of the Populists' views on credit and capital.[86]

A postal savings bank system (which lacked a PRS) was proposed as a safer alternative. "The bank failures of 1893 made many advocates of the postal savings banks. Such banks would make panics impossible." Some preferred postal savings banks to the subtreasury plan, stating that "we favor the distribution of money through the sub-treasury, or a better system. Our opponents think there is a better system, and I think so, too . . . I believe that the Omaha convention thought so when it put a declaration in the platform favoring government postal banks." The plan's appeal lay in its public rather than private character, its accessibility to small savers, and its social and economic neutrality.[87]

Financial reformers were critical of the NBS. They argued that it was biased against rural agricultural areas, increased the power of the financial elite, benefitted from public resources, and corrupted government policy in monetary matters. Further, the NBS was fostered at the expense of state banks, which had been an important source of banking services

---

85. Waddell, *Some Public Dangers*, p. 9.
86. Leonidas L. Polk, *To the Supreme Council of the National Farmers and Industrial Union* (1891), pp. 3–4.
87. Armstrong, *Little Statesman*, pp. 73 and 91.

in the antebellum South. The Populists proposed a postal savings bank system, which would reduce the likelihood of panics and decrease manipulations of the financial system. Reformers sought a commercial banking system that was responsive to the needs of the entire citizenry and neutral in its effect on economic opportunities.

Agricultural credit

Barred from assistance by the national banks, farmers in the West and South turned to mortgage companies and store merchants. These sources of credit were also problematic. Mortgage companies provided Eastern funds to Western farmers at high rates of interest. During monetary contractions, these debts were difficult to meet, and many lost their farms. The dearth of banks and currency gave rise to the Southern crop lien system, which reduced white and black farmers to a state of debt peonage. The subtreasury plan was an attempt to solve the credit problem by offering loans against crops or land at a low rate of interest.

William Peffer, the Populist Senator from Kansas, discussed the mortgage debt problem. He compared farmers to railroad businessmen. "The farmers, while not being reputed as good managers, and while being rated as thriftless, wasteful and extravagant . . . can show on the tax rolls of their respective counties an amount quite as large as that [of their assessed mortgage value]." Farm debts were not excessive, "the farmers' debts are not greater than the assessed valuation of their property, while their shrewder and more competent competitors in business – the railroad managers – have in some way fastened upon their roads debts in proportion vastly beyond that which rests upon the farmers." Relative to railroad managers, farmers were conservative and civic-minded in their business practices.[88]

Debt was a problem for other reasons. According to the 1890 census report, the rate of mortgage debt nationally and in Kansas was quite high.

> Farmers find that difficulties in the way of payment of their debts are increasing from year to year, that it is growing constantly harder to meet their obligations . . . unless lower rates of interest can be obtained, one half of our farmers will be renters within the next ten years, and . . . [eventually] the occupied lands of the country will be owned almost wholly by a few comparatively wealthy men.

Currency contraction and high interest rates raised the cost of debt. Consequently, the independent farmers were rapidly becoming farm tenants. The solution lay in lowering the cost of credit.[89]

88. William Alfred Peffer, "The Debt Burden," in Tindall, ed., *A Populist Reader*, p. 40.
89. Peffer, "Debt Burden," pp. 40–41.

The crop lien system was notorious. Store credit was provided by local Southern merchants who ran tabs on farmers' purchases until harvest time. When the crop came in and accounts were settled, many farmers failed to pay out their store debt. The store merchant obtained title to the farmer's next harvest and the debt cycle continued through another year. Reverend Charles H. Otken of Mississippi described the consequences.

> The business system prevailing with such hurtful and dangerous tendencies in the Southern states is enslaving the people, and, by its insidious opera-tions, concentrating productive wealth in the hands of the few. It reduces a large body of people to a state of beggary, fosters a discontented spirit, checks consumption, produces recklessness on the part of the consumer, places a dis-count on honesty, and converts commerce into a vast pawning shop where farmers pledge their lands for hominy and bacon upon ruinous terms . . .

Store merchants were local monopolists who charged up to twice the rate for credit goods as they did for cash goods. When 50–75 percent of the farmers failed to pay off their debts, they lost control of their crops and often their land. This vicious system made financial reform the leading concern of many Southern farmers.[90]

The Populists expended much time and energy trying to solve the agri-cultural credit problem. The subtreasury plan was developed after the fail-ure of cooperative ventures. This proposal would have extended govern-ment credit to farmers on the security of their crops or land. Proponents of the plan cited the NBS as an example of government involvement in credit operations. "Is it paternalism for the Government to issue to the farmers of the country money on short time at 1 per cent. on evidences of wealth, when for a quarter of a century it has been issuing money to the banks at 1 per cent. on evidences of indebtedness?" Under the subtrea-sury plan, banks would no longer issue paper currency. The proposal would both eliminate the negative influences of the NBS and resolve the agricultural credit problem.[91]

Neither the mortgages supplied to farmers in the West nor the store credit offered to farmers in the South provided them with low-cost cred-it. Instead, high-priced mortgage loans and crop liens made farmers vulnerable to the economic downturns and poor crop seasons. Unable to meet their obligations, many lost title to their crops and land. The subtreasury system would have provided reliable credit at low rates. As a publicly operated system, it would also have avoided the tendency

90. Charles H. Otken, "The Credit System," in Tindall, ed., *A Populist Reader*, pp. 42–51.
91. Lawrence Goodwyn, *The Populist Moment: A Short History of the Agrarian Revolt in America* (Oxford: Oxford University Press, 1978), pp. 90–93, 109–113; and Polk, *Agri-cultural Depression*, p. 27.

toward economic exploitation present in practices such as the crop lien system.

Industrial investment and commodity markets

Although many financial reformers suspected the link between financial concentration and the growth of the financial conservative economy, few clearly understood it. The Populists' proposal to ban commodity futures trading exhibited limited economic insight. Only Henry Carey Baird, the nephew and intellectual heir of greenback economist Henry Carey, demonstrated a clear grasp of the role of the PRS in industrial investment. Antimonopolist analysis weakened in the 1890s, as the increasing realities of corporate growth and the growing legitimacy of financial conservative ideology overpowered the intellectual imaginations of disheartened reformers.

In 1890, the Populists asked Congress to "pass such laws as shall effectually prevent the dealing in futures of all agricultural and mechanical productions." The campaign to prohibit futures trading was nearly successful. The Hatch Bill, which would have imposed a 10 percent tax on futures trading, passed both houses of Congress in 1893. When the bill failed to go to conference, commodity market regulation was put aside until the early twentieth century. Criticism of futures trading was explained in a letter to *The Farmers' Voice* in 1889.

> . . . just before the new crop was in the grain, gamblers took oats enough out of *"Their Warehouses"* and dumped them on the market at a decline each day until they had *"bear-ed"* the market price . . . and we see the curious spectacle of the farmer who raised the oats, being so poor that his must sell his oats to brokers, like a tramp does his coat to get money with which to buy a meal, and instead of the legitimate demand for oats being supplied from the graineries of the grower, it is supplied from the warehouses of speculators, who rob both the producer and consumer of the oats.

Futures trading was speculation. Big traders manipulated sales to lower the price of crops at harvest time and then raised them for increased profits from the millers. Farmers, burdened by debt and in need of immediate cash, were unable to hold their crops until the price rose. As a result, the profits from production fell to the speculators.[92]

The possibility of a well-functioning trading market that improved prices, stabilized exchanges, and even helped to solve the credit problem was not foreseen by most farmers. They saw economically weak farmers

92. "The Ocala Platform, December 1890," in Tindall, *A Populist Reader*, p. 88; and *The Farmers' Voice*, November 9, 1889, p. 4.

exploited by strong traders. Had their debt constraints been different (improving their ability to bargain with traders), they might have reconsidered. Philosophically, agrarians interpreted economic manipulations by abusive commodity traders as reason to condemn rather than reform the entire system. Most likely their attitude toward the stock market would have been similar.[93]

But for one financial reformer, the role of capital markets was quite clear. In 1892, Henry Carey Baird discussed the PRS and its relation to the call loan market.

> The manner in which the counting of balances due by reserve agents as part of the reserve of national banks, becomes vicious, is not merely that it places at the control of banks in New York City large sums of money by means of which to foster speculation, but because it tends to aggravate the natural flow of money from those places where money is scarce to those where money is plenty . . . On very high authority it is learned that this money is loaned to Wall street nominally "on call" . . . throughout the country it [call lending of bankers' balances] aggravates every period of financial disturbance arising out of the overtrading of banks.

Here then was the relationship of the commercial banking system to the incidence of financial panics, the deprivation of funds from outlying areas and their concentration in New York, and the rise of speculative investment on the stock exchange. Financial concentration not only deprived rural areas of needed credit, but created a supply-side push of investment funds on the stock market. Economic historians have concluded that this supply push gave impetus to the merger movement. Except for Baird, few participants on either side of the financial debate clearly saw these connections.[94]

More generally, financial reformers suspected an association between financial and industrial concentration. The Populists believed that a biased financial system favored industry over agriculture. Yet the details of this process were poorly understood. Populist analysis of commodity futures trading recognized the potential problems involved, but failed to offer workable alternatives. The older antimonopolist analysis of the connection between commercial banking and securities investment pointed to the problems of the PRS and the call loan market. But this level of greenback analysis was beyond the reach of most reformers in the 1890s. Financial reformers formulated elements of a broader critique of cred-

---

93. Cedric B. Cowing, *Populists, Plungers and Progressives: A Social History of Stock and Commodity Speculation, 1890–1936* (Princeton: Princeton University Press, 1965), pp. 3–24.

94. Henry Carey Baird, *Banks and Banking* (Chicago, 1892), pp. 2–3.

it and capital markets. The NBS was attacked for its neglect of the needs of rural, agricultural communities, its contribution to financial concentration, and its nurturance of political corruption. The available farm credit alternatives – Western mortgage companies and Southern store merchants – were criticized as deficient and exploitative. To remedy the lack of credit and establish a banking structure that provided equal economic opportunities to all citizens, financial reformers proposed the creation of postal savings banks and a subtreasury system. Reform analysis was weakest on the subject of commodity markets and industrial investment. While some suspected a link between financial and corporate concentration, few retained the older antimonopolist insights into the nature of this connection. At the moment when the economy was turning in the direction of financial conservatism, the analysis that criticized this trend and suggested an alternative was fragmented.

V. Academic findings

Economic historians and social scientists have found merit and deficiency in the accounts of both the financial reformers and the financial conservatives. Most scholars conclude that interest rate differentials and the slow integration of regional capital markets owed much to constraints imposed by the institutional structure of the NBS. The issue of agricultural credit and the economic conditions that may have fostered the agrarian revolt has remain contentious. Whether the high mortgage rates in the West were determined by risk or noneconomic factors is uncertain. However, the damaging consequences of the crop lien system are well documented. Finally, there is interesting recent work on the links between financial concentration and the growth of corporate capitalism.[95]

Commercial banking

The availability of credit and other commercial banking services was sharply affected by the structure of the NBS. That is the conclusion drawn by Richard E. Sylla in *The American Capital Market, 1846–1914* and John A. James in *Money and Capital Markets in Postbellum America.* They argue that institutional constraints, such as the mortgage lending prohibition, capital and reserve requirements, and the tax on state bank note issues, concentrated banking services in the Northeast and raised interest rates in the South and West. Rural national banks often held a mo-

95. Much of this discussion builds on the analysis provided in Chapter 3.

nopolistic advantage. Further, the NBS funnelled funds to New York City, making the financial system more vulnerable to panics. While some studies have challenged aspects of these findings, the overall conclusions have been substantiated.[96]

The growth in state and private banks improved the commercial banking system, moving the nation toward greater capital market integration and lessening regional interest rate differentials. Competition promoted responsiveness to rural needs. Some national banks even provided mortgage loans to farmers, despite legal prohibitions. However, the competitive advantages of the state and private banks often derived from the absence of regulatory supervision. New banks became involved in speculative behavior, to the ultimate disadvantage of their customers. Further, country banks of all types were reluctant to forgo their monopolistic advantages, and resisted the advent of branch banking. Ironically, country bankers used the language of antimonopolism to criticize branch banking and protect their local monopoly positions. Branch banking might have lowered interest rates in rural areas.[97]

Several studies partially validate the views of both the financial reformers and financial conservatives. Reformers were probably correct in arguing that the NBS was regionally biased, that the South and West were deprived of sufficient financial resources, and that their interest rates were unusually high. Further, wealth was being concentrated in the Northeast. Finally, there is evidence that monopolistic control in banking mattered, as in the case of country banks. Perhaps the greatest credence which these

---

96. Richard E. Sylla, *The American Capital Market, 1846–1914: A Study of the Effects of Public Policy on Economic Development* (New York: Arno Press, 1975); James, *Money and Capital;* William Clark and Charlie Turner, "International Trade and the Evolution of the American Capital Market, 1888–1911," *Journal of Economic History,* 45 (1985): 405–410; John A. James, "A Note on Interest Paid on New York Bankers Balances in the Postbellum Period," *Business History Review,* 50 (1976): 198–202; Richard H. Keehn, "Federal Bank Policy, Bank Market Structure, and Bank Performance: Wisconsin, 1863–1914," *Business History Review,* 48 (1974): 1–27; Richard Keehn, "Market Power and Bank Lending: Some Evidence from Wisconsin, 1870–1900," *Journal of Economic History,* 40 (1980): 45–52; Richard Sylla, "Federal Policy, Banking Market Structure, and Capital; Mobilization in the United States, 1863–1913," *Journal of Economic History,* 29 (1969): 657–686; John J. Binder and David T. Brown, "Bank Rates of Return and Entry Restrictions, 1869–1914," *Journal of Economic History,* 51 (1991): 47–66; and Eugene Nelson White, "The Political Economy of Banking Regulation, 1864–1933," *Journal of Economic History,* 42 (1982): 33–42. For a general history of commercial banking, also see Paul B. Trescott, *Financing American Enterprise: The Story of Commercial Banking* (NY: Harper and Row, 1963); and Redlich, *Molding,* part II, chaps. 18–21.

97. Sylla, *American Capital Market,* pp. 113–115; James, *Money and Capital,* pp. 27–43 and 91; and E. White, "Political Economy," p. 35.

findings offer to financial antimonopolism is the most general. The role of politics and institutions in creating economic winners and losers is clear in the history of the banking system.

But there are other points on which the appraisal of the financial conservatives was stronger. New York bankers were not monopolists. There was no Wall Street "money power." Information on loan rates and other financial services shows that the New York banking community was quite competitive. It was the country bankers who were local monopolists, not the city bankers. The historical record provides no evidence of collusive activities by individuals seeking control of the national economy. Instead, institutions shaped outcomes that favored some groups and regions over others. Finally, the proposal for branch banking would probably have aided rural communities, just as its proponents believed. The most questionable aspect of the financial conservatives' outlook was their belief in market fairness.

Agricultural credit

There is a market argument to be made about the price of Western farm mortgages. Recent literature suggests that risk factors contributed to the higher interest rates on Western farm mortgages. Yet the history of the Southern crop lien system defies economic logic. The Southern social structure and the absence of banking services gave rise to a system that hampered production, innovation, and the development of regional self-sufficiency. While the economic complaints of Western farmers have been discounted, the deficiency of agricultural credit until the early twentieth century has been validated.[98]

Western farm mortgages ran at substantially higher interest rates than

98. For general treatments, see Allan G. Bogue, *Money at Interest: the Farm Mortgage on the Middle Border* (Lincoln: University of Nebraska Press, 1955); Roger L. Ransom and Richard Sutch, *One Kind of Freedom: The Economic Consequences of Emancipation* (Cambridge: Cambridge University Press, 1977); and Fred A. Shannon, *The Farmer's Last Frontier: Agriculture, 1860–1897*, volume V, *The Economic History of the United States* (Armonk, NY: M. E. Sharpe, Inc., 1945). Also see Allan G. Bogue, "The Administrative and Policy Problems of the J. B. Watkins Land Mortgage Company, 1873–1894," *Business History Review*, 27 (1953): 26–57; Richard H. Keehn and Gene Smiley, "Mortgage Lending by National Banks," *Business History Review*, 51 (1977): 474–491; Glenn H. Miller, "The Hawkes Papers: A Case Study of a Kansas Mortgage Brokerage Business, 1871–1888," *Business History Review*, 32 (1958): 293–310; and Kenneth Snowden, "Mortgage Rates and American Capital Market Development in the Late Nineteenth Century," *Journal of Economic History*, 47 (1987): 671–691; and Barry Eichengreen, "Agricultural Mortgages in the Populist Era: Reply to Snowden," *Journal of Economic History*, 47 (1987): 757–761.

those in the East. Further, Eastern and foreign investment funds were supplied to Western mortgage companies. Politically, these facts were timber for the fire of agrarian rebellion, but economically the evaluation may be different. In a debate between Kenneth Snowden and Barry Eichengreen in the *Journal of Economic History* in 1987, the authors agree that the mortgage differentials are substantially accounted for by economic risk factors, and that the industry was competitive. However, Snowden argues that other nonrisk factors, such as the role of financial intermediaries and the segmentation of capital markets, also contributed. The debate remains unsettled. What has been established is that Western farmers were debtors to Eastern loaners, their interest rates were high relative to rates in the Northeast, and while economic factors predominated, institutional factors may have played a role.[99]

The work of Ransom and Sutch establishes three major points about agricultural credit practices in the cotton belt. First, NBS restrictions prevented many communities from reestablishing commercial banking during Reconstruction. Second, local monopoly merchants filled the void left by banks. The crop lien system was inefficient, and charged rates that ranged from 50–110 percent. Third, the crop lien system prevented the development of food self-sufficiency, since merchants commanded debtor farmers to raise only cotton. The South's capacity to feed itself declined and tenancy rates rose. In the South, the absence of banking facilities or mortgage lending fostered a system of "debt peonage."[100]

Evaluation of the agricultural credit debate differs by region. For the West, economic risk factors and competitive mortgage provisions offered relatively fair economic opportunities. But in the South, the absence of commercial banking services and the abuses of merchant monopolists severely hampered economic development. The provision of low-cost funds to farmers could have substantially increased financial autonomy.

Investment and securities markets

The relationship between capital markets and industrial investment has been examined by several scholars. Margaret Myers establishes the connection of the commercial banking structure to the growth of stock market funds through the New York call loan market. Thomas Navin and Marian Sears establish the effects of the new industrial securities market on the merger movement. Further, studies of investment in outlying re-

---

99. Snowden, "Mortgage Rates," pp. 671–691; and Eichengreen, "Agricultural Mortgages," pp. 757–761.
100. Ransom and Sutch, "Debt Peonage," pp. 641–667.

gions show that fund deprivation affected regional development. The links that financial reformers suspected between capital market integration, industrial investment, and economic development were valid.[101]

In their seminal article, Navin and Sears specify the linkage between the industrial securities market and the industrial concentrations in the period 1887–1902. During the 1890s, the effect of New Jersey's new general incorporation law and the Sherman Antitrust Act made incorporation more attractive. The depression of the 1890s and overcapacity in railroads shifted interest from railroad securities to the new industrial securities. As investment funds grew, large investment houses facilitated the completion of the great corporate mergers.[102]

This history is well established. Of interest here is the effect that the institutional structure of finance had on investment. Studies suggest that the merger movement was not motivated merely by technological advances or economies of scale, but was also driven by investment demand. According to Gene Smiley, financial intermediaries changed their asset mixes in response to the depression of the 1890s. Local loans declined, and more funds were placed in bankers' balances. This created greater demand for industrial securities, encouraging the issuance of new securities and feeding the merger wave. This account implicates the commercial banking system in several ways: The NBS structure contributed to the panics that led to the shift toward bankers's balances; local monopoly control by

101. Kerry A. Odell, *Capital Mobilization and Regional Financial Markets: The Pacific Coast States, 1850–1920* (NY: Garland Pub., 1992); Naomi Lamoreaux, "Banks, Kinship and Economic Development: The New England Case," *Journal of Economic History*, 46 (1986): 649–667; Vincent P. Carosso, *Investment Banking in America: A History* (Cambridge, MA: Harvard University Press, 1970); Margaret Myers, *The New York Money Market*, volume 1, Origins and Development (New York: Columbia University Press, 1931); James T. Campen and Anne Mayhew, "The National Banking System and Southern Economic Growth: Evidence from One Southern City, 1870–1900," *Journal of Economic History*, 48(1988): 127–137; David L. Carlton and Peter A. Coclanis, "Capital Mobilization and Southern Industry, 1880–1905: The Case of the Carolina Piedmont," *Journal of Economic History*, 49 (1989): 73–94; John A. James, "Structural Change in American Manufacturing," *Journal of Economic History*, 43 (1983): 433–459; Navin and Sears, "Rise of a Market," pp. 105–138; Anthony Patrick O'Brien, "Factory Size, Economies of Scale, and the Great Merger Movement of 1898–1902," *Journal of Economic History*, 48 (1988): 639–649: Kerry A. Odell, "The Integration of Regional and Interregional Capital Markets: Evidence from the Pacific Coast, 1883–1913," *Journal of Economic History*, 49 (1989): 297–310; Gene Smiley, "Banking Structure and the National Capital Market, 1869–1914," and Marie E. Sushka and W. Brian Barrett, "Banking Structure and the National Capital Market, 1869–1914: A Reply," *Journal of Economic History*, 45 (1985): 653–665; and Smiley, "Expansion," pp. 75–85.

102. Navin and Sears, "Rise of a Market," pp. 105–138; Carosso, *Investment Banking*, pp. 29–50; Myers, *New York Money Market*, vol. I, chaps. 12–14.

banks accommodated such a practice; and the PRS was the link through which funds flowed from outlying regions into New York, there to be used for call loans. By the 1890s, roughly one-half of the funds loaned by New York banks were placed on the call loan market. This giant drain of resources into one city created an investment push that funded industrial concentration.[103]

The plethora of funds in New York was mirrored by the scarcity of resources in outlying areas. Just as the agricultural credit structure dampened innovation in Southern agriculture, the absence of investment funds hindered development in Southern industry. There is some debate over the rate and nature of regional capital markets integration. One Southern case study finds that local banks supplied ample investment for economic development. But most studies suggest that opportunity for industrial development was hindered by the financial structure. This is the conclusion that David Carlton and Peter Coclanis reach in their examination of the Carolina Piedmont, where they found that the difficulties of obtaining local investment funds restricted growth and innovation in textiles and furniture. In interesting countercases, Kerry Odell and Naomi Lamoreaux discuss the development of well-integrated regional capital markets in the Pacific region in the late nineteenth century, and in New England in the early nineteenth century. Such integration was precisely what the South lacked. Southern banks sent their funds to New York instead of recycling them locally. These findings affirm the view of reformers that the financial structure favored the development of one region (the Northeast) over others (especially the South).[104]

Investment patterns in the late nineteenth century were neither neutral nor natural. Regionally, funds were centered in the Northeast and used for investments there and in the upper Midwest. The pattern of investment contributed to geographical and corporate concentration. The merger wave was fueled by the excess of funds in the New York money market. What this all suggests is that the antimonopolists were right. Financial concentration skewed economic opportunities in favor of some regions and groups, and contributed to the rise of a concentrated corporate economy.

Economic historians have found some validity in the views of both fi-

103. James, "Structural Change," pp. 449–451; O'Brien, "Factory Size," pp. 639–649; and Smiley, "Expansion," pp. 75–85.
104. The argument over capital market integration appears in the exchange between Smiley, "Banking Structure," and Sushka and Barrett, "Banking Structure" (both in *Journal of Economic History*, 45: 653–665). Also see Campen and Mayhew, "National Banking System," pp. 127–137, Carlton and Coclanis, "Capital Mobilization," pp. 73–94; Odell, "Integration," pp. 297–310; and Lamoreaux, "Banks, Kinship."

nancial reformers and financial conservatives. The commercial banking system was regionally and economically biased against the interests of the South, the West, and farmers. But it was not controlled by a money monopoly in New York. Deficiencies in agricultural credit harmed the South, where the crop lien system limited food self-sufficiency and contributed to expanding tenancy rates. But in the West, mortgage credit was competitive, and rates were determined primarily by economic risk factors. Most significantly, studies on investment find that there was a funnelling of funds to New York that deprived outlying areas of investment opportunities and contributed to corporate concentration.

VI. The victory of financial conservatism

The 1890s was the decisive decade in the long battle for political and intellectual hegemony between financial conservatives and financial antimonopolists. In this contest over the future direction of the American political economy, each side marshalled its arguments and gathered its forces for a showdown over control of the financial system. Both groups regarded money and banking as keys to the development of the economy and the society. For financial conservatives, the gold standard, the NBS, and an unrestricted market economy provided the basis for economic growth and international leadership. Gold advocates were orthodox liberals engaged in a public campaign to limit political control over economic change. Financial reformers saw the gold standard and the NBS as biased against equal economic opportunity for all. Only through democratic vigilance could the financial system be maintained as a neutral arbiter of economic competition, and only through fair competition could a republic of independent citizens be preserved. These were the programs the two groups fought over in the 1890s. Each side understood that these economic programs had broad political implications.

This contest was not evenly matched. Previous battles helped set the terms for this new confrontation. After the defeat of the greenbackers, financial reform views lost some of their legitimacy. By the Populist era, fewer citizens would consider proposals for a fiat monetary standard. A fiat system would have regulated the monetary supply to fit larger patterns of productive growth, and made the economy more resistant to panics and depressions. Not until the early twentieth century would these matters come up for reconsideration. Fewer still could competently discuss the connection between financial concentration and industrial growth. Though they sensed the link between financial concentration and industrial capitalism, the 1890s financial reformers failed to persuade the public. The erosion of the historical memory of financial reformers was politically determined. As antimonopolism became more fragmented, financial conservatism became more unified and coherent.

By the close of the century, the financial conservatives were victorious. They won the political match with the election of 1896. They won the economic contest in the booming expansion and merger movement that occurred after 1897. The struggle over regulation continued into the early twentieth century. Most importantly, the conservatives won the intellectual conflict with the ascendancy of orthodox liberal understandings of economic development that have lasted to this day. This victory was not inherent in either the superior nature of their economic analysis or in the inevitable historical emergence of a corporate economy. Both the financial conservatives and the financial reformers presented reasonable, coherent programs for regulating the monetary and banking systems. The role that such regulation would have played in economic development is evident in the historical connections between the commercial banking structure and the growth of corporate concentration. Their differences, and the reason for the financial conservatives' victory, were political. Having gained control over the government and (eventually) over the regulatory structures, financial conservatives implemented their world view and explained the outcome as the inevitable result of natural forces. The telling of history belonged to the victor.

6

Populism and the politics of finance in North Carolina, Illinois, and Massachusetts in the 1890s

"Can't you give me brains?" asked the Scarecrow. "You don't need them. You are learning something every day. A baby has brains, but it doesn't know much. Experience is the only thing that brings knowledge, and the longer you are on the earth, the more experience you are sure to get."
The Wonderful Wizard of Oz

The Populists and their allies spoke of themselves as participants in a revolution. It was a revolution against party dominance and against the power of money. Like their ancestors in the American Revolution, the rebels of the 1890s were not radical firebrands but conservatives seeking to restore the democratic promise of American life. Their greatest enemy was not Wall Street's financial elites, but the prejudices that divided them one from another – divisions of North against South, white against black, farmer against laborer, Democrat against Republican, Protestant against Catholic. That history has recorded Populism as a Southern, white, Protestant movement is testimony to the effectiveness of those divisions. But the effort was larger than this. It was an effort to unite producers of all persuasions in pursuit of an antimonopolist alternative. The failure of that effort contributed to the rise of a corporate capitalist economy and a narrowed democracy.

The subject of this chapter is the political geography and historical contingency of the regime shift of the 1890s. The three state cases first explored in Chapter 4 are returned to here. These cases show how political actors attempted to construct alignments of local, sectional, and national interests. I argue that preexisting political geographical alignments distorted the contest between financial reformers and financial conservatives to the disadvantage of reformers. These alignments, which were largely based in the party system, prevented a clear contest between the antimonopolists of the South and West and the financial conservatives of the Northeast. Historically, the timing of this contest mattered both in terms of the temporal order of events and the historical narratives used to frame political alternatives. For instance, the Illinois Populist alliance was unable to build on the state's great farmer-labor tradition, since the labor upheavals of the 1886–94 period left many labor activists alienated. In Massachusetts, narratives on the 1870s financial conflict emboldened financial conservatives and delegitimized the antimonopolist alternative. This chapter explores the contextual constraints faced by the antimonopolists and corporate liberals and their strategic responses to those circumstances.

These three state cases provide regionally diverse examples of the politics of finance. North Carolina had a strong Populist movement that was electorally successful in fusion with the Republicans. But contradictory claims about the relationship between local and national Populist politics hurt the farmers' movement and limited its antimonopolist thrust. The Illinois Populist party had a mixed agrarian and labor base. Within the movement there were competing attempts to construct alliances around various class, party, and geographical interests. Eventually, the Republican party's Northern, pro-industrial alignment succeeded in defeating the reformers. In Massachusetts, there was less interest in financial reform. Competition occurred primarily between the orthodox liberal Democrats and stalwart Republicans. Across these cases, the combination of contextual constraints and strategic choices ultimately favored the corporate liberals.

The Populists pressed their political challenge at a moment of both historical opportunity and historical constraints. The Civil War party system, which had organized politics since the 1850s, finally ended in the 1890s. Tensions over economic change that had surfaced and faded several times over previous decades succeeded in provoking a political realignment. But the realignment that resulted was not made by the antimonopolist challengers. Historical legacies from past contests shaped this moment of change. The labor upheavals of the 1880s and early 1890s left agrarian radicals without a partner for their producers' coalition. Institutionally, economic regulatory structures favoring large-scale production were already in operation and changing the terms of competition between classes and sections. Culturally, the opponents of financial reform constructed historical narratives to help make the antimonopolist alternative unimaginable. In all of these ways and more, history shaped the political opportunities implicit in the financial contest of the 1890s.

The remainder of this chapter is organized into four sections. Section I analyzes financial politics in North Carolina, where the political geography of sectionalism constrained an otherwise vibrant Populist alternative. Section II returns to Illinois, where the state's farmer-labor tradition continued with a labor-led Populist coalition. This case exemplifies the potential and the problems of such coalitions, which faced Red-baiting and political disorganization in the wake of the labor upheavals of the late 1880s and early 1890s. Section III considers the financial debate in Massachusetts, where orthodox liberalism dominated and free silver was considered a political heresy. Section IV returns to the main theoretical themes on the roles of political geography and historical contingency in 1890s financial politics.

I. North Carolina: An emerging "New South" state

In the early twentieth century, North Carolina was celebrated for its economic dynamism and commitment to education. It was a premier New South state. Yet beneath these achievements lay repressive institutions and practices that were established in the late nineteenth century. By 1900, North Carolina was a one-party state with low rates of political participation, racial rule, and an absence of unions. The founding of these hierarchical institutions did not go unchallenged. Indeed, the Knights of Labor (KOL), black Republican political activists, and the Populist party all tried in the 1880s and 1890s to create a more democratic social order. They failed, and their failure occurred within the context of a political contest between antimonopolism and financial conservatism.

After Reconstruction, the Democratic party was the dominant force in North Carolina politics. Yet there was strong party competition. Although a minority, the Republicans took a substantial vote share in state elections. Beginning in 1888, the Farmers' Alliance also competed for political recognition. Farmers established the People's party in 1892 and joined the Republicans in sweeping the Democrats out of power in the mid-1890s. But divisions within the coalition, Populist losses nationally, and renewed campaigning for white supremacy led to the reassertion of Democratic dominance in 1898.

There were challenges to North Carolina's "New South" economy as well. New South advocates hailed the appearance of small farming and industry in their state. But doubters criticized the agricultural credit shortage and the oppressed position of laborers and tenants. The agricultural economy was mostly devoted to cotton and tobacco, cash crops for which there was a developed market. Although the need for crop diversity and food self-sufficiency was acknowledged, attempts to diversify were limited. Without economic autonomy, farmers could not choose which crops to grow. Further, conditions in the state's major industries – textiles and tobacco products – were notoriously oppressive. The old plantation sys-

tem characterized the development of social relations in industrial production. The tobacco industry was racially integrated, but textiles was
not. Neither offered much beyond subsistence to their workers. The KOL
and the Farmers' Alliance tried to alter these forms of economic organization by changing the position of the producers.[1]

In the late 1880s, the KOL briefly flourished. The Knights organized
some farm laborers, and the wage workers and craftsmen in larger cities.
When they formed their state assembly in 1886, their organization was
open to producers of all races and either sex. That year, the KOL entered
into partisan politics in affiliation with the Republicans. State Master
Workman John Nichols ran as an independent in the fourth Congressional district. Nichols (a longtime Republican) ran on a platform advocating government regulation to improve the plight of workers, both rural and urban. Local slates were organized in six cities. Nichols was
victorious, as were the labor independents in two cities. The results signalled the possibility for cooperation across racial groups and between
farmers and workers.[2]

But cooperation did not last long. Once the Farmers' Alliance was
formed in 1887, the Knights' role in organizing farmers ended. While
workers needed farmers to be politically effective in state politics, the
farmers were not inclined to assist them. In the legislative session of 1887,
agrarian representatives were as often enemies as allies in efforts to establish a labor bureau, legislate a ten-hour day, and require prompt payment of wages. Urban Republicans proved more reliable partners. Race
added a further complication. In 1888, the KOL's white membership declined as its black membership grew. One white member complained that
"Nigger and Knight have become synonymous terms." Many white farmers were angered by the organization of black farm hands. When Nichols

1. On the New South, see C. Vann Woodward's classic, *Origins of the New South,
1877–1913* (Baton Rouge: Louisiana State University Press, 1951), and more recently,
Gavin Wright, *The Political Economy of the Cotton South: Households, Markets and
Wealth in the Nineteenth Century* (NY: Norton, 1978); Dwight B. Billings, Jr. *Planters
and the Making of a "New South": Class, Politics and Development in North Carolina,
1865–1900* (Chapel Hill: University of North Carolina Press, 1979); and Philip J. Wood,
Southern Capitalism: The Political Economy of North Carolina, 1880–1980 (Durham:
Duke University Press, 1986).
2. For a general account of labor organizing in North Carolina, see Harley E. Jolley, "The
Labor Movement in North Carolina, 1880–1922," *North Carolina Historical Review,*
30 (1953): 354–375. Also see Melton McLaurin, "The Knights of Labor in North Carolina," *North Carolina Historical Review,* 49 (1972): 298–315; and Leon Fink, *Workingmen's Democracy: The Knights of Labor and American Politics* (Urbana: University
of Illinois Press, 1983), pp. 28–29.

ran for reelection, he was denounced by Farmers' Alliance leader L. L. Polk. Nichols lost the contest. Shortly after, the Knights' state newspaper folded.[3]

The rise and decline of the Knights in North Carolina is consistent with the larger pattern of expansion, political activity, and contraction the national KOL experienced. There were also important differences. The KOL was never as strong in North Carolina as it was nationally. The state was agricultural, and had an aggressive anti-union tradition. Race and party politics also affected the fate of the Knights. Their association with the Republicans and black citizens harmed their public image with the majority white Democrats. Finally, as Melton McLaurin notes, agrarian politics shifted. The victories of 1886 suggested that farmer-labor cooperation was possible. Yet the events of 1887 and beyond indicated more conflict than cooperation between farmers and workers. Before the 1890s, the Farmers' Alliance gave little attention to the concerns of producers more generally. Then its movement became national. Farmers in North Carolina expanded their political horizons and renewed their support for the labor movement. Considerations from a broader geographical arena changed the farmers' calculation of their political interests. While the Knights struggled to gain a base in the mid- and late-1880s, farmers pursued separate political goals.[4]

The Farmers' Alliance

When the Farmers' Alliance was formed, its priority was economic cooperation. Purchasing and marketing cooperatives were organized by both the State Alliance and suballiances, which reached to every county by 1891. The success of these endeavors contributed to the phenomenal early expansion of the Alliance. But the experiments were not broad enough and could not be sustained. Because they required cash participation, the cooperatives did not reach the poorest farmers. Monetary and credit problems undermined both state and local efforts. As historian Robert McMath comments:

> [The] plethora of local projects weakened attempts by state leaders to coordinate business activities and, more importantly, diffused the meager capital available to support them . . . Students of Alliance cooperatives have attributed their critical undercapitalization to rural poverty, poor management,

3. McLaurin, "Knights of Labor," pp. 305–307, 313. Ambivalent relations between white and black agrarians in North Carolina lasted throughout the history of the Farmer's Alliance. See Robert C. McMath, Jr., "Southern White Farmers and the Organization of Black Farm Workers: A North Carolina Document," *Labor History*, 18 (1977): 115–119.
4. McLaurin, "The Knights of Labor," p. 314.

and opposition from financial institutions. All of these contributed to their demise, but the lack of control by the state Alliance and the resulting diffusion of resources . . . suggest another reason for their failure.

Their experiences with cooperatives gave Alliancemen a glimmer of economic autonomy and demonstrated the continued burdens imposed by capital and credit shortages.[5]

In 1888, the Alliance asserted its political strength by putting forward president S. B. Alexander for the gubernatorial nomination at the Democratic convention. His bid was unsuccessful, although in first-round convention voting he obtained a respectable 245 votes against the victor's 374 votes. Many regular Democrats were angered by Alexander's bid. They suspected L. L. Polk, editor of the *Progressive Farmer,* of promoting Alexander's candidacy. But Alliance leaders, who represented some 400 farmers' clubs, thought they deserved some political influence. As the strength of the Farmers' Alliance became more apparent, the direction of Democratic politics was bound to change or the farmers would become dissatisfied.[6]

These tensions became pronounced in 1890. That year, Senator Zebulon B. Vance and Polk engaged in an intense battle over the subtreasury plan. At Polk's request, Vance submitted a subtreasury bill in Congress. But after submitting the bill, Vance concluded that he could not support it. In the subsequent furor, newspapers and citizens around the state offered competing views on the merits of the proposal, and the worthiness of Vance and Polk. The conflict threatened the political careers of both men. This incident reveals a great deal about the nature of party loyalty, the commitment to Populist ideals, and the impetus behind the agrarian crusade in North Carolina.[7]

As Lawrence Goodwyn has written, the subtreasury plan was an essential part of the transition from the Farmers' Alliance to Populism. The plan addressed broad problems of credit and monetary instability. It was an antimonopolist measure in the tradition of Edward Kellogg and the

5. Lala Carr Steelman, "The Role of Elias Carr in the North Carolina Farmers' Alliance," *North Carolina Historical Review,* 57 (1980): 133–158; and Robert C. McMath, Jr., "Agrarian Protest at the Forks of the Creek: Three Subordinate Farmers' Alliances in North Carolina," *North Carolina Historical Review,* 51 (1974): 41–63.
6. *Appleton's Annual Cyclopaedia and Register of Important Events of the Year 1888,* vol. 28 (New York: D. Appleton and Co, 1889), p. 619; James L. Hunt, "The Making of a Populist: Marion Butler, 1863–1895," Part I, *North Carolina Historical Review,* 62 (1985): 74.
7. Also see Alan B. Bromberg, "'The Worst Muddle ever Seen in North Carolina Politics': The Farmers' Alliance, the Subtreasury and Zeb Vance," *North Carolina Historical Review,* 56 (1979): 19–40.

Greenback party. While the ultimate viability of this proposal is debated, it provided an educational tool that focused producers on the role of the financial system in economic development. The proposal separated reformers with a mild commitment to improving the lot of farmers from antimonopolists who sought to restructure the economy in favor of small-scale, regionally based production.[8]

When this division was made in North Carolina, Zeb Vance found himself on the side of reformers. Recognizing this, farmers began to question their loyalty to him and his party. One wrote from Mount Olive to explain why so many Alliancemen supported the subtreasury.

> They ask it not only as an act of Justice to them, but in behalf of the life and Salvation of the Country . . . The financial policy of the Government . . . [results in] directly building up, strengthening, and empowering huge Corporations, Trusts, and Syndicates, to crush out the life blood and living of the masses, in the interests of the few . . .

This farmer argued that the nation was moving toward a corporate economy and a divided society. The subtreasury plan would alter that course and assure the economic opportunity necessary for the middle-class farming community to survive.[9]

Others were more urgent, and warned the Senator of the consequences should the bill not pass.

> Our nation is on the verge of a revolution . . . The farmers are very much in earnest about [having] the sub treasury bill or something of its nature made into law . . . we are watching every move made by Congress in regard to these oppressive laws to the laboring classes, and will hold each one responsible for what he does . . .

Most farmers admired and supported Vance. But they were concerned about his accountability. Farmers called on the North Carolina delegation to demonstrate its commitment to the proposals of the Farmers' Alliance.[10]

Some handled the difficulties of divided loyalties by offering Vance a way out of the quandary. One farmer wrote:

> In the present contingency, between *yourself* as *U. S. S.* [Senator] and the *Farmers Alliance of No. Ca.* on the *"Sub. Treasury Bill"* . . . I would suggest

8. On the political role of the subtreasury plan, see Lawrence Goodwyn, *Democratic Promise: The Populist Moment in America* (New York: Oxford University Press, 1976), chap. 8.
9. James F. Olivin to Vance, May 28, 1890, Zebulon B. Vance Papers, Southern History Collection (SHC).
10. William M. Blalock to Vance, May 20, 1890, Vance Papers, SHC.

as a remedy, to reconcile the support of our order . . . to yourself . . . that you frame a bill embodieing [sic] the main principles as aimed at, by us, in the "sub. treas. bill," to meet your ideas of "constitutionality and practicability" . . .

Or, as another writer put it more succinctly, "I think it is your duty as our representative to find out some means to support the sub-treasury bill . . . " Given the general conservatism of the state Democratic party, Alliancemen were reluctant to abandon Vance, a traditional agrarian progressive. Many still sought to reconcile their standing as Alliancemen with their position as loyal Democrats.[11]

Others began to question that loyalty. A resident from Chapanoke expressed "surprise and disappointment" in Vance.

> I am but an humble tenant farmer . . . You say the Democratic party favors the repeal of all unjust legislation of which we complain. My Dear Sir, we have been voting with the Democratic party for the past quarter of a century looking for the relief promised from year to year by our party leaders and find none. We feel, Sir, that we have been deceived and we have become dissatisfied with those who make promises only to be broken and have become impatient & we have allied ourselves together . . . to secure . . . just & equal laws for the protection of all classes.

For this farmer, the Alliance had become a political alternative to the Democratic party. From there, it was but another step to the formation of a third party.[12]

Rather than remain satisfied with the politics of race-baiting and Confederate loyalty, farmers began to demand greater attention to economic issues. Having learned from the cooperative endeavors and the subtreasury controversy about the importance of the credit and currency systems, they were dissatisfied with mild reform measures and pressed for a more thorough restructuring of the financial system. When their representatives were slow to respond, many questioned their support for the party. Nonetheless, white farmers in North Carolina were deeply attached to the party. Alliancemen struggled with the choice of suppressing dissent and remaining loyal Democrats, or becoming Populists.

Departure from the Democratic fold

Over the next two years, some Alliancemen left the party to join the Populists, while others left the Alliance to remain with the party. In 1891,

11. Abbott L. Swinson to Vance, August 21, 1890, Vance papers, SHC; and E. C. Beddington to Vance, September 1, 1890, Vance Papers, SHC.
12. W. A. Nanbold (?) to Vance, July 14, 1890, Vance Papers, SHC.

Marion Butler replaced Elias Carr as the head of the State Alliance. Carr had ably led the farmers while Alliance loyalty and Democratic loyalty were still conjoined. When the Populist party was formed in 1892, the Democrats moved to stave off defections by nominating Carr for governor. But the Alliance under Butler was less willing to compromise. Faced with these difficult choices, distraught by the ongoing agricultural depression, and disappointed by the meager gains made through cooperation, some Alliance members departed and others became Populists.[13]

The man who symbolized the transition to political independence was Leonidas Polk. Despite his conflicts with Vance, Polk still retained his membership in the Democratic party. But by the St. Louis convention in February 1892, Polk was ready to join the new People's party. Many saw Polk as the Populists' best hope for breaking the Democrats' solid hold on the South. This was the view of H. H. Boyce, the New England reform editor from *The Arena*. Southerners were even more conscious of the task which the Populists faced. One Allianceman wrote:

> I have been a Democrat for 35 years, I have believed that through it only, could the liberties of the country be preserved. But of late years I have found that it is under the lion's paw . . . I repeat that the Alliance will suffer if you attempt to hold them any longer . . . I fully understand what this means, it means the destruction of the Democratic party in the South . . . she ought to die the death of a traitor . . . Yes I firmly believe that, as things now stand in the South, the Alliance or the Democratic party (as now controlled) must go down . . .

Many agrarian activists now believed that the survival of the Alliance and its principles required abandoning the Democrats and joining the People's party.[14]

The Democrats' response to the threat of Populist defection was twofold. They promoted their sectional interests within the national party, and worked to discipline or exclude party rebels locally. The North Carolina delegation opposed the renomination of Grover Cleveland, favoring Adlai Stevenson, an Illinois bimetallist, instead. The party also sup-

13. On Carr, Butler, and Alliance politics in the early 1890s, see L. C. Steelman, "Role of Elias Carr," pp. 135–158; Hunt, "Making," Part II, pp. 179–202, and Joseph F. Steelman, "The Progressive Era in North Carolina, 1884–1917" (unpub. dissertation, University of North Carolina at Chapel Hill, 1955), pp. 20–36.

14. John D. Hicks, *The Populist Revolt: A History of the Farmers' Alliance and the People's Party* (Lincoln: University of Nebraska Press, 1961), chap. 8. H. H. Boyce to Polk, April 13, 1892, Leonidas Lafayette Polk Papers, Southern History Collection; and Marion Cannon to Polk, April 1892, L. L. Polk Papers, SHC. The "lion" referred to in this quote represents England.

ported free silver and criticized the gold interests of the Northeast. Locally, they excluded independents such as Marion Butler, and limited Alliance influence except in the gubernatorial nomination. Elias Carr's candidacy was a highly visible reward for a loyal Democrat and farmers' representative. By playing symbols over substance and sectional issues over internal, class-oriented issues, the Democrats retained control of state politics in 1892.[15]

By year's end, the Farmers' Alliance had finally split from the Democratic party. There were now three parties competing in local, state, and national elections. But political independence was costly. The Democrats controlled the General Assembly and the Governor's house. Populists locally and nationally were faced by questions of strategy. Leonidas L. Polk died suddenly in June 1892, shortly before the Populist convention at which he was widely expected to be nominated for President. His departure diminished hopes for success through an independent third-party strategy. Meanwhile, Marion Butler, now head of the State Alliance and the state Populist party, was a rising star in the National Farmers' Alliance and Industrial Union. Butler pushed the Populists toward fusion.

The path toward fusion began with the split among Democrats over the monetary issue. Vance led the faction opposed to President Cleveland's repeal of the Sherman Silver Purchase Act, while Senator Matthew Ransom supported the President. Both men were respected party leaders whose differences were revealed on an issue that pitted section against party. The conflict made the Democrats vulnerable. By the beginning of 1895, both Vance and Ransom were gone. Vance had died, and Ransom was replaced by the new senator.[16]

Some Democrats sought to recover the support of dissident farmers. Senator Thomas Jarvis, appointed by Governor Carr to replace Vance, promoted free silver. He was friendly to other Alliance demands as well. But party conservatives resisted rapprochement. Instead, they stressed racial purity and electoral exclusion. Eventually, these approaches were combined. Nationally, North Carolina Democrats supported silver, banking reform, and the candidacy of William Jennings Bryan in 1896. Locally, they sought to reinforce white elite dominance through electoral re-

15. Ronnie W. Faulkner, "North Carolina Democrats and Silver Fusion Politics, 1892–1896," *North Carolina Historical Review*, 59 (1982): 230–234; Hunt, "Making," Part II, pp. 193–202; and Joseph Steelman, "Vicissitudes of Republican Party Politics: The Campaign of 1892 in North Carolina," *North Carolina Historical Review*, 43 (1966): 430–442.
16. Faulkner, "North Carolina Democrats," pp. 230–251.

striction, white supremacy campaigns, and Red-baiting. Once perfected, this two-tiered strategy would prove effective.[17]

The Republicans were also divided. During the elections of 1892 and 1894, the party was split over race and money. John J. Mott's faction hoped to "purify" the party by excluding blacks. Mott was from the eastern region where the black population was greatest. His group (including Daniel L. Russell and J. C. L. Harris) supported free silver as well. The other faction, led by John Baxter Eaves, supported black rights and the gold standard. The Mott faction was more Southern and local in its outlook, while the Eaves faction was more national. For the Republicans, creating a workable political geography in which their local and national positions did not conflict was difficult.[18]

The party debated whether to run a slate in 1892. Eastern Republicans were opposed, for fear of promoting black candidates and officeholders. When a ticket was finally fielded, the Mott faction looked to the Populists to solidify an all-white, anti-Democratic coalition. Daniel L. Russell explained:

> White Republicans of Eastern North Carolina will not support the negro revenue ticket which Eaves and his gang have put up in order to save the Democratic party. We will support the People's ticket and it looks like thousands of colored men will follow us . . . The gang who control the Republican machine want to drive all white men out of the party in the negro belt.

Russell believed that the nomination of black candidates would assure a Democratic victory and even urged black voters to support an alternative all-white ticket.[19]

Fusion and electoral victory for the Populists

By 1894, fusion appealed to both the Populists and the lily-white Republicans. They had a common desire to end Democratic rule. Populist participation in the fusion campaign owed much to the leadership of Marion Butler. As the *Daily Charlotte Observer* commented, "Mr. Marion Butler comes nearer to being an absolute boss than any man North Carolina has ever known." Butler saw fusion as a way of breaking the Democrats' hold on state politics and initiating a realignment of the party system. The new party alignment would pit progressives against conservatives. At the Populist convention in August, delegates were persuaded by

18. J. Steelman, "Vicissitudes," pp. 430–442.
19. Russell is quoted in J. Steelman, "Vicissitudes" p. 440.

these views and gave their executive committee authority to work out the details.[20]

Democrats and some dissenting Populists rebuked the fusionists. They portrayed fusion as a means to promote Butler's personal ambitions. Indeed, the fusion pact included a commitment to elect Butler to the U.S. Senate. Dissenters also charged that fusion was a betrayal of party principles. The Populists deleted the subtreasury plan and the call for government ownership of the railroads to increase the party's appeal. A third criticism concerned the role of political expediency in selecting candidates. William Kitchin, a conservative, demagogic figure with a questionable commitment to the People's party platform, was especially controversial. Finally, fusion was branded as the product of undemocratic, backroom bargaining by party leaders. All of these charges were muted by the ticket's electoral victory in November.[21]

The election results were spectacular. In the General Assembly, 9 Democrats, 15 Republicans, and 26 Populists were elected to the Senate, while in the House, 46 Democrats, 36 Republicans, 33 Populists, and 1 Prohibitionist were elected. The new Congressional delegation included 3 Republicans, 4 Populists, and 3 Democrats. Populist William H. Worth (former Alliance business agent) won the state treasurer's race. The legislature selected two new U.S. Senators, including Republican Jeter Pritchard (a pro-silver fusionist) chosen to complete Vance's term, and Marion Butler, who replaced Matthew Ransom. The Democrats blamed their losses on disaffection with Grover Cleveland and the gold standard.[22]

Fusion produced quick results for the Populist party in 1894. But they were not lasting. When the new legislature convened in early 1895, there were troubling signs. The Populists' electoral victory was due to vote trad-

---

20. Joseph F. Steelman, "Republican Party Strategists and the Issue of Fusion with Populists in North Carolina, 1893–1894," *North Carolina Historical Review,* 47 (1970): 244–269; Hunt, "Making," Part III, pp. 326–336. The comment from the *Daily Charlotte Observer* is quoted in Hunt, "Making," Part III, p. 333. See also Josephus Daniels, *Editor in Politics* (Chapel Hill: University of North Carolina Press, 1941), pp. 120–125.
21. Hunt, "Making," Part III, pp. 333–339; Larry H. Ingle, "A Southern Democrat at Large: William Hodge Kitchin and the Populist Party," *North Carolina Historical Review,* 45 (1968): 178–194; and J. Steelman, "Republican Party Strategists," pp. 255–263.
22. The election results for the General Assembly are taken from *Appleton's Annual Cyclopaedia and Register of Important Events of the Year 1894* (New York: D. Appleton and Co., 1895), p. 553. Joseph Steelman, from whom I took the congressional results, offers slightly different results for the Assembly. He found that 41 Republicans, 32 Populists, and 47 Democrats had been elected in the House, and 17 Republicans, 25 Populists, and 8 Democrats in the Senate. See J. Steelman, "Republican Party Strategists," p. 269. On the Democrats' assessment, see Daniels, *Editor in Politics,* p. 124.

ing with the Republicans, rather than expanded support among former Alliancemen. Further, by joining forces with the lily-white wing of the Republicans, the Populists legitimated racial exclusion. Four years later, that same tactic was used against the Republicans and the Populists. After the 1894 election, there was a sense that the Populist party had lost its political mission. State candidates were elected and an independent, committed Senator was sent to Congress. Yet the party's platform was narrowed and its autonomy compromised. After their painful departure from the Democratic fold in the early 1890s, many farmers were confused by these adjustments, and drifted from the Populist standard. The compromises made to achieve short-term success soon undermined the Populists.[23]

After 1894, North Carolina Populists advocated fusion at the national level as well. Many Populists gravitated to the silver cause as a means of uniting national reform forces on a common platform. The state silver convention of 1895 was viewed as a first step in the coming reform crusade. The convention was primarily a Populist gathering. Although the Democrats were largely pro-silver, their resentment of the Populists and fear of deeper reform measures prevented cooperation. Among the Republicans, it was the reverse. The party was split on the monetary issue but eager to continue the coalition arrangement that provided it with access to state power. Only for the Populists was silver both a matter of conviction and party advancement. When the convention gathered, 27 Democrats, 8 Republicans, and 235 Populists were present. The Democrats tried to limit the convention's actions to an endorsement of free silver, but the Populists promoted other monetary reform measures as well. Afterward, the Democratic *Raleigh News and Observer* denounced the Populists as adherents to "fiat money, socialism, Coxeyism, Pefferism, and other 'isms' . . . " Silver unity was prevented by partisan division.[24]

The 1896 fusion arrangements were complex. This time, the Populists allied with the Democrats nationally and the Republicans locally. The Republicans responded to the Democratic contention that the previous legislature was an example of pro-black governing by nominating white supremacist Daniel Russell for governor. Divisions on race, monetary matters, and party affiliation caused confusion among both Republican and Populist voters. Although they won a narrow electoral victory, the fusionists did so at great cost to their party organizations.

23. Marion Butler was an outspoken and committed Senator. However, he often spoke of placing issues above party in a way that suggested he never really understood the significance of the Populists' break from the major parties and their role as an independent third party. See, for instance, Marion Butler, *To Stop the Further Issuance of Bonds* (Washington, D.C., 1896).
24. Faulkner, "North Carolina Democrats," pp. 242–245.

Black Republicans were uncertain about what to do in the election. Most felt that Russell could not be trusted. They recalled his 1888 statement that "The negroes of the South are largely savages . . . they are no more fit to govern than are their brethren in African swamps . . . " More recently, in accepting the gubernatorial nomination, Russell attempted reconciliation.

> I entertain a sentiment of deep gratitude to the negroes . . . I stand for negroes' rights and liberties. I sucked at the breast of a negroe woman. I judge from the adult development, that the milk must have been nutritious and plentiful.

In this extraordinary passage, the adult white supremacist expressed goodwill to the black community by recalling his infant pleasure at the breast of a black nursemaid. Despite their misgivings, many black Republicans believed that fusion was necessary. James H. Young, editor of Raleigh's black newspaper, the *Gazette,* warned, "If the Democrats get hold of the legislature, they will pass an election law that will virtually and practically disenfranchise a large majority of voters . . . " Though many blacks eventually voted for Russell, they did so more for fear of the Democrats than enthusiasm for the Republicans.[25]

Populists were also uncertain about how to vote. During the previous election, many of them supported fusion out of opposition to Democratic rule. But now, party leaders were bargaining with both Democrats and Republicans. The Republicans were distrusted because of their association with the gold standard nationally. The Democrats remained suspect given their history of local elite rule and indifference to farmers. Many wondered whether their hard-learned lessons about Democratic corruption were now in error. Others feared fusion with state Republicans would aid McKinley nationally. Marion Butler's papers are full of letters questioning or condemning fusion. For Southern Populists, the political geography of fusion stood in a contradictory and confounding relationship to the effort to break free from the regular party system.

As W. B. Osbourne wrote from Huntersville, NC, "I have been voting the Democratic ticket for over 40 years and the Populist ticket for 4 years and for the first time in my life politics are so muddled that I do not know

---

25. Jeffrey J. Crow, "'Fusion, Confusion and Negroism': Schisms among Negro Republicans in the North Carolina Election of 1896," *North Carolina Historical Review,* 53 (1976): 364–384. The quotes appear on pages 365–366, 375, and 382, respectively. As one might imagine, a psychoanalytical perspective on Russell's confession would have done little to reassure his black listeners. As Freud and Lacan both suggest, the pleasure of the breast is connected to the infant's sense of omnipotence, while the eventual denial of the breast produces anger and alienation.

how to vote to get what I want." Others, such as L. M. Neal of Yancyville, were distraught and angry.

> How can we afford to vote for any goldbug who is opposed to Populist principle? . . . I find that our leaders in this state are for the spoils before principle and the people are not going to follow them . . . we cannot afford to lose this time for if the gold standard is fastened upon our people this time our liberty [is] gone and nothing but revolution will satisfy the people . . .

Farmers were often unable to make Butler's clean separation between local and national politics, and were bothered by the contradiction of working with both the Republicans and the Democrats.[26]

National leaders were also dismayed. N. A. Dunning and Thomas Watson wrote that in acceding to the Bryan-Sewall Democratic ticket, the party was betraying its principles. Marvin Warren of Chicago reminded Butler that "the main difference between Populists and the silver democracy is, that the Democracy by their platform hold to the coin redemption of paper money, and the Populists do not." Watson carried the critique further.

> For eight years, we reformers who have organized the People's Party have been denouncing the National Banking System. How then can we support Sewall, the National Banker? . . . When Populist state leaders openly avow the policy of selling the national ticket and the national principles in return for the local spoils, he who runs may read the doom of Populism. Its mission as a regenerator of the National political body is ended.

Watson was campaigning not to win one election, but to change the political system.[27]

Afterward, Butler sought to justify the fusionist strategy. Although Watson was the party's vice-presidential nominee in 1896, William Jennings Bryan (endorsed as the presidential candidate) already had another running mate on the Democratic ticket. This left the Populists in the difficult position of supporting Watson (the Populist) and Bryan (the Democrat). The party's National Executive Committee (headed by Butler) responded by campaigning for Bryan and ignoring Watson. Many committed Populists accused the committee of betrayal. Butler wrote a long essay, dated December 1896, responding to these charges.

26. W. B. Osbourne to Butler, October 5, 1896, Marion Butler Papers, Southern History Collection. L. M. Neal to Butler, September 24, 1896, Butler Papers, SHC. The personal gain theme was reported by one Populist who wrote to Butler about a rumor that Butler had accepted a payment of $1.5 million for selling out the Populists. See John D. Meares to Butler, September 17, 1896, Butler papers, SHC.

27. Marvin Warren to All Populists, December 2, 1896, Butler Papers, SHC. Thomas Watson to Butler, October 28, 1896, Butler Papers, SHC.

. . . every man with common sense knows that this [an effort to support a Bryan-Watson ticket] would have killed our party and given the Democratic politicians a chance to . . . put themselves forward as the leaders of the true reform forces . . . When [Watson] says that a straight People's party ticket would have been elected . . . he shows that his judgment is weak and dangerously unreliable . . . So great was his [Watson's] distress that he preferred to see M'Kinley elected, and the yoke of the gold standard forced on the necks of suffering humanity for four more years than to see Bryan elected and relief come to the masses . . . Watson's course, as everyone knew, was the most effective way to help M'Kinley and the gold ring.

Besides the bitterness and sensitivity it expresses, this passage also reveals a man who firmly believed his actions were the only way of advancing the cause of reform. Butler did not regard his various political bargains as compromises. He was able to deliver scathing denunciations of the major parties on one day and make bargains with them the next. Butler felt that his own clarity about his principles and motivations ought to be sufficient for the party as a whole. But for many it was not.[28]

After the election, in which Russell won and Bryan lost, both the national and state Populist parties declined. Fewer Populists and more Republicans were elected to the General Assembly. Once seated, the coalition partners failed to cooperate and the Populists bickered amongst themselves. Governor Russell tried to promote progressive economic policies, but his efforts were generally thwarted. Only the Democrats showed greater coherence after the election. Under the leadership of Furnifold Simmons, the Democrats directed a white supremacy campaign in 1898. While the fusion government of 1894 was one of possibilities, that of 1896 was an anomaly that seemed to be a lame duck when it began. The attempt to change politics through fusion had failed. In North Carolina, the elections of 1894 and 1896 were deviations rather than a realignment.

The consolidation of Democratic conservatism

North Carolina's New South was not the one that the KOL, Populists, or the state's blacks had fought for. Rather, this New South was a white man's South, a South where economic and social elites still dominated, and in which the opportunities for small farmers and workers were narrowed. Like the South of old, this was one in which racial and political loyalties were of paramount importance. North Carolina's new regime was not determined in 1860 or even 1880. The era after Reconstruction was a time of political possibility, when participation was high and sub-

28. "Some Facts the Public Should Know," December 1896, Butler Papers, SHC.

stantial alternatives were offered. The failure of these alternatives was a matter of political struggle rather than historical destiny.

The possibilities offered by the Populists and Knights were both political and economic. They sought to change the economy by changing the political system and expanding the role of producers in the democratic process. Both groups were drawn into politics after finding that the distribution of economic opportunities was affected by government actions that favored nonproducers. When they found little satisfaction from the regular parties, these reformers struck out on a course of independent political action. In state and national legislatures, they sought to guarantee prompt paychecks, reduce the length of the workday, limit the rate of interest, regulate the behavior of transportation and warehousing monopolists, and establish the subtreasury plan, all in order to assure economic autonomy for North Carolina's producers.

At first, the North Carolina Populists seemed successful in their transition from an agrarian cooperative organization to an independent political party. In alliance with Republicans, they broke through Democratic rule in the mid-1890s. This was a substantial achievement. But the transition from the Farmers' Alliance to Populism was problematic. The failure of Alliance cooperatives and the trauma of departure from the Democratic party weakened the new People's party. The party might have broadened and expanded on the lessons learned in the struggle over the subtreasury plan. But under Marion Butler, the strategic choices made after 1892 led them down a different path – fusion – acceding to a system in which racial division and partisan loyalty triumphed over programmatic politics. They narrowed their platform and made myriad political bargains, instead of continuing educational and cooperative work. The electoral victories of 1894 and 1896 failed to realign politics.

The burden of the fusion strategy revolved around the Populists' relationship with the Democratic party. Alliance with the Democrats was contrary to what the Populists had tried to do in the South. The Democrats had maintained their political dominance with race-baiting and party loyalty. These powerful cultural ideals constrained voters who otherwise sympathized with the goals of the Farmers' Alliance and the Populists. In the transition to a third-party standard, many would-be Populists were held to the Democratic fold by reminders of the party's association with the Confederacy, resistance to Northern rule during Reconstruction, and support for white supremacy. Pursuing fusion meant ignoring the distinction between reform and restructuring made during the dispute over the subtreasury plan. It also meant forgetting the cultural norms used to hold voter loyalty and create a Southern political identity. Marion Butler envisioned a segmented political geography, in which local and national alliances were separated. Instead, the existing geographical alignments of the party system undermined the Populists both locally and nationally.

The intersection of state, sectional, and national arenas mattered for the political fortunes of each party. The Democrats used representations of sectional interests within the national arena to support financial reform as a "Southern" issue, while suppressing local calls for economic reform with pleas for partisan loyalty and white supremacy. Republicans did the opposite, stressing their local interest in overthrowing Democratic rule in coalition with the Populists over national concerns where the two groups were often at odds. The Populists attempted to carry the juxtaposition furthest in their 1896 fusion arrangements that joined them with Republicans at the state level and Democrats at the national level. The evidently contradictory nature of these arrangements undermined support for the party. Each party attempted to construct a political geography that would undermine its opponents and promote its own claims with voters. The Democrats used well-established cultural norms and institutional arrangements regarding geographical interests and identities most successfully.

Race played an important and complex role in the politics of the 1880s and 1890s. The Democrats were the quickest to use racist rhetoric for political purposes. The Republicans were the best defenders of civil rights in the state legislature. The Populists vacillated between racial conservatism and progressivism. White leaders varied between expressions of hostility and pleas for cooperation with blacks. While there was never widespread racial enlightenment, only in the latter 1890s did the racist hysteria associated with the disenfranchisement campaigns reach maturity. Whether a racially moderate regime could have survived attacks by white supremacists is difficult to say. But examples of racial cooperation and the fluidity in public attitudes suggest that a stronger Populist movement, clear in its commitment to economic and racial cooperation, might have weathered the storm.[29]

The Populists, and before them the KOL, failed in their attempts to challenge the establishment of a conservative New South in North Carolina. It was a failure caused by the internal strategic choices within the party that favored short-term political victory over long-term political change, by a political culture in which race and partisanship were available for building a conformitarian ideology against such challenges, and by a political geography which benefitted groups most clearly able to align

---

29. C. Vann Woodward's classic, *The Strange Career of Jim Crow*, third rev. edition (NY: Oxford University Press, 1974), makes a similar point about this shift from a period of racial possibility to one of racist rigidity, which he connects to the Democrats strategy to defeat the Populists.

local, sectional, and national interests. As a result, North Carolina continued to be controlled by white elites who excluded both poor whites and blacks from politics and who retained control over an agricultural and industrial economy built on high levels of labor exploitation.

II. Illinois and the labor-Populist alliance

When the World Columbian Exposition was held in Chicago in 1893, it provided an occasion for reflection on American historical development and the dawning of "modernity." Wealth, technological advance, class harmony, and governmental efficency were among the futures prophesized by the speeches and exhibits on Chicago's Midway. Frederick Jackson Turner brought the themes of geography and development together in his lecture on "The Significance of the Frontier in American History." While Turner's "frontier thesis" celebrated the economic and social advance associated with industrialization, it also bemoaned the loss of an older, simpler America. Illinois politics in 1890s involved conflicts over development and geography, not just between capitalists and workers or East and West, but more deeply over competing notions of political geography and historical development. Eventually, it was Turner's vision – a romantic melancholy for a simpler society doomed by historical progress and a celebration of industrial modernity – that came to dominate political understandings in Illinois.[30]

The Republicans dominated Illinois politics during most of the 1880s and 1890s. But Democrats and third-party groups contributed to the state's volatile, competitive party system. Both major parties had difficulty with their Eastern-dominated national party organizations. Attention to Western and class concerns came primarily from third parties and political independents. In 1886 and 1887, labor reformers formed the United Labor party. In 1890, farm groups organized slates calling for regulation of the transportation, finance, and warehousing industries. By then, the Democrats, who were breaking with the national party mandates, were in the ascendance. They controlled one or both branches of state government through 1896. It was at the peak of this surge by Populists and progressive Democrats that the Republicans regained political control. The voters retreated from depression, class conflict, and political radicalism to promises of social peace and economic prosperity.

Economically and geographically, Illinois was centrally positioned. In-

---

30. Richard Slotkin, *Gunfighter Nation: The Myth of the Frontier in Twentienth Century America* (NY: Harper Perennial, 1992), chap. 2; and Frederick Jackson Turner, *The Frontier in American Life* (NY: Holt, Rhinehart and Winston, 1962).

dustrial production was linked to the state's central status in the agricultural heartland – distilling, meatpacking, farm machinery, and cereal production were all important industries. Illinois was also at the center of industrial strife in the United States. Both the Haymarket Riot of 1886 and the Pullman strike of 1894 were watershed moments for changing class relations. The state's farmers were ambivalent about their partisan affiliations and class allegiances. Sometimes, agrarians and workers coalesced in movements to alter the course of industrial development, as with the Populist alliance of the mid-1890s. But just as often, farmers and laborers were unable to agree on the proper path to development, and this failure was followed by losses at the polls. As the American economy moved toward increasing integration, Illinois, and particularly Chicago, became a crucial link between East and West, and between agriculture and industry.

The state's growing economic status was accompanied by expansion of the financial sector. The Chicago Board of Trade was the major market for the trading of agricultural commodities nationally. While the Board had the potential to regularize the grain trade, thereby stabilizing prices and expanding credit, it was also subject to speculative abuse. Agrarians opposed futures trading in the early 1890s. The banks were another target of criticism. Chicago eclipsed Philadelphia, and was nearing Boston as the most important financial center after New York. Powerful Chicago bankers, such as Lyman Gage, J. R. Walsh, and James B. Forgan, supported the gold standard during the financial debate. The growth of finance capitalism supplied both a target of political criticism and a source of political power in Illinois.[31]

Labor reform

This period of contest over economic and political development began with the Haymarket riot and the formation of the United Labor party in 1886. The story of the Haymarket affair is well known. Six policemen died when a bomb was thrown during an anarchist protest meeting on May 4, 1886. Middle and upper-class citizens around the country were horrified. In the ensuing Red scare, many labor leaders (including KOL Grandmaster Terence Powderly) withheld their support or openly denounced anarchism and the anarchists who organized the event at which

31. Jonathan Lurie, *The Chicago Board of Trade, 1859–1905: The Dynamics of Self-Regulation* (Urbana: University of Illinois Press, 1979), especially chap. 5. Fritz Redlich, *The Molding of American Banking: Men and Ideas*, Part II (NY: Johnson Reprint Co., 1968).

the bomb was thrown. Yet the evident injustice of the trial and executions later that year left workers alienated and angered. Belief in equal rights dwindled as working men and women looked cynically on a government acting in the apparent interest of capitalists. Doubts about the fairness of the political process and the neutrality of the state crystallized in hostility toward the major parties, prompting the decision to form a separate labor party.[32]

Class lines hardened after Haymarket. The Illinois state legislature passed two anti-labor laws – the Merritt Conspiracy Act and the Cole Anti-Boycott Act. In September, labor activists met to draw up a platform and select a slate for the new United Labor party. The platform called for land reform, tax reform, the establishment of the eight-hour day, and the prohibition of convict labor and private detective agencies. The new party elected seven state assemblymen and one state senator. The ticket fell sixty-four votes short of winning a congressional race as well. Haymarket helped to reactivate independent labor politics.[33]

After unsuccessfully trying to preempt or absorb the new party, Chicago Democrats turned to the Republicans to establish a solid front against the United Laborites. Rival organizations, such as the Cook County Labor League (under the auspices of the Republicans) and another United Labor party (led by William Gleason, a Democratic party loyalist) were established. Regular politicians employed antiradical rhetoric to delegitimize the laborites. Under this broad assault, the party fared poorly. The spring 1887 election was won by John Roche, who was jointly supported by the Democrats and Republicans. The United Labor party demonstrated the potential for a labor vote. But it also showed the vulnerability of working-class parties to the coordinated assaults of the regular parties and corrupt unionists.[34]

Just as the United Labor party declined, efforts to form a farm-labor alliance were rekindled. Reform editors and farm organizers responded favorably to the United Labor party, and discussions began about joining forces around a producerist agenda. In 1888, the Union Labor party was

32. Accounts of the Haymarket incident can be found in Commons et al., *History of Labour*, vol. II, pp. 392–394; P. Foner, *History of the Labor*, vol. II; and Ray Ginger, *Altgeld's America: The Lincoln Ideal Versus Changing Realities* (NY: New Viewpoints, 1973), pp. 35–60.
33. Ralph William Scharnau, "Thomas J. Morgan and the United Labor Party of Chicago," *Illinois State Historical Society Journal*, 66(1973): 41–61.
34. On the "labor skates" (corrupt unionists) see Chester M. Destler, "The People's Party in Illinois, 1888–1896: A Phase of the Populist Revolt" (unpub. dissertation, University of Chicago, 1932), pp. 93–94, and Destler, *American Radicalism, 1865–1901: Essays and Documents* (New London, CT: Connecticut College, 1946), p. 164.

formed. The party's presidential nominee was Illinois greenbacker Alson J. Streeter. Its platform called for a national monetary system that provided currency at low interest through land loans. Other planks called for a prohibition on government bonds, reduction of the national debt, free coinage of silver and gold, the use of legal tender greenbacks, and the establishment of a postal savings bank system. There was also a demand for public ownership of "the means of communication and transportation." In accordance with the views of the KOL and other progressive reform groups, the party endorsed women's suffrage and equal pay for equal work. The platform concluded that "the paramount issues to be solved . . . are the abolition of usury, monopoly and the trusts." Although the labor planks did not go far enough for many union organizers, they suggested the direction that the Illinois labor-farmer alliance would go in emphasizing antimonopolism and accepting moderate socialism.[35]

Despite the poor showing of the Union Labor party in the 1888 elections, the trend toward agrarian electoral activism continued. There were five major farmer organizations in Illinois by the end of the 1880s, including the Northern Alliance, the Farmers Mutual Benefit Association, the Grange, the Patrons of Industry, and the Southern Alliance. These organizations joined with other reform organizations to establish the Farmers' and Laborers' Conference in May 1890. The new alliance was committed to participating in political action. The convention avoided the issue of political autonomy by leaving it to local groups to decide whether to endorse a major party candidate, seek the nomination of a farmers' candidate within one of the major parties, or support an independent instead. In the General Assembly races, three independents and seventeen fusion candidates were elected. All together, the coalition was represented by twenty-eight out of 204 officials in the new state legislature.[36]

35. Illinois held a state convention that preceded the national Union Labor convention. Among those involved in the party's establishment were A. J. Streeter, B. S. Heath of the *Chicago Express,* and S. F. Norton of the *Chicago Sentinel,* all previously associated with greenbackism. Initially, Charles Dixon and Benjamin Goodhue of the Illinois KOL were also involved, but withdrew complaining that the new party was "simply the old Greenback party disguised by a new name." See Destler, "People's Party," pp. 47–48 and 92–93; and Alfred W. Newcombe, "Alson J. Streeter – An Agrarian Liberal," *Journal of the Illinois State Historical Society,* 39 (March 1946): 70–71. The names United Labor and Union Labor were used by various local labor parties around the country. Newcombe, "Alson J. Streeter," pp. 70–75. The platform quotes appear on p. 73.

36. Roy V. Scott, *The Agrarian Movement in Illinois, 1880–1896* (Urbana: University of Illinois Press, 1962), chaps. 2 and 3, pp. 90–101. Destler, "People's Party," pp. 55–62. On membership levels, as of about 1890, the FMBA had 43,175, the Grange had over 11,000, and the NFA had some 7,000. The other two organizations were smaller.

Agrarian reform and the resurgence of the Democrats

The farmers' gains reflected larger changes in state party politics. After the Civil War, the Republicans usually controlled the state government. Beginning in 1890, the Democrats controlled the legislature and many of the state's executive offices. Traditionally associated with the agrarianism in southern Illinois, the party benefitted from local grievances and from farmer dissatisfaction with Republican tariff and monetary policy. In urban areas, working-class and immigrant groups were also Democrats. The Democrats were well placed to forge an alliance based on producerism and the new industrial politics.[37]

The availability of the Democrats complicated the politics of Populism. After the 1890 election, the General Assembly was scheduled to elect a new U.S. Senator. Since the number of Democrats and Republicans were split almost evenly at 101 to 100, the three independent agrarians held the balance of power in the contest. These men supported A. J. Streeter, the longtime agrarian antimonopolist. But after dozens of votes and weeks of pressure, two of the three independents switched to John Palmer, the candidate of the Democrats. This outcome had major consequences for agrarian politics in the coming years.

Many farmers responded cynically to the election of Palmer. Palmer was a conservative Democrat and business lawyer who represented the Illinois Central Railroad. In 1896, Palmer would lead the conservative defection from the Democratic party to form the National (Gold) Democrats. Farmers felt betrayed by the independents who (reportedly in exchange for monetary favors) voted for the Democratic nominee. Agrarians were disillusioned by these corrupt machinations. The state's farm organizations declined in response to these events.[38]

The Senate election also elevated Herman Taubeneck as an uncompromising agrarian champion. Taubeneck was the third independent, who never gave up his support for Streeter. Prior to 1890, Taubeneck dabbled in agrarian politics and worked with the Republican party. Of the three independents, he was the least well known. Following the Senate race, the young legislator became a popular figure. In 1892, Taubeneck was selected as national chairman of the People's party. As chairman, he promoted fusion between the Populists and the silverites, and later supported the candidacy of William Jennings Bryan. Ironically, Taubeneck's

37. On the shifts in Illinois politics from the 1870s through the 1890s, see John H. Keiser, *Building for the Centuries: Illinois, 1865 to 1898* (Urbana: University of Illinois Press, 1977), chap. 3.
38. The 1891 Senate election is covered in Scott, *The Agrarian Movement*, pp. 103–117; Destler, "People's Party," pp. 63–71; and Newcombe, "Alson J. Streeter," pp. 78–88.

autonomy in 1890 promoted an inexperienced politician who later forfeited the independence of the People's party.[39]

After the Senate race, some farmers withdrew from independent politics entirely. Others sought to establish a third party to provide the support and organization needed for independent electoral efforts, and eventually joined in the creation of the People's party at the St. Louis
convention held in February 1892. At first, the Illinois People's party suffered from several problems. Economically, many farmers were either too
poor (tenancy rates were rising) or too rich (farmers engaged in specialized agriculture were more immune to depression) to be inclined toward
Populism. Corn and southern wheat farmers were more likely to be politically available. After the disorganization that followed the 1891 Senate race, farmers were left without grassroots activism or extensive experience in economic cooperation. It was left to the movement's intellectual
leaders to carry the agrarian reform tradition forward. Further, the Populists were competing with the Democrats, who were increasingly dominated by progressive leaders like John Peter Altgeld. The People's party of
Illinois was born into a difficult political context.

John Peter Altgeld was elected governor in 1892. Although he quickly
became a nationally known progressive Democrat, Altgeld began his public career in a fairly ordinary fashion. The former Cook county judge ran
an assertive, door-to-door campaign. The state Democratic platform that
year was mild and noncontroversial – it supported sound money, bimetallism, and Grover Cleveland. Other statewide candidates were progressives. The nominee for Lt. Governor, Joseph B. Gill, was associated with
labor reform. The candidate for congressman-at-large, John C. Black, was
the lawyer who defended the Haymarket men. The extent of the new governor's political radicalism was only revealed once in office. Democratic
success gave continued relevance to reform politics among farmers and
workers in Illinois.[40]

Reformers were attracted to Altgeld's "outspoken denunciation of monopolies, corruption and the 'invisible government' of the trusts." Few
voted for the Populist ticket. People's party candidates received only 2.5
percent of the vote in the 1892 election. Afterward, agrarian reformers
were receptive to overtures from urban labor reformers. The Chicago

39. On Taubeneck, see Scott, *Agrarian Movement*, pp. 112–117; Destler, "People's Party,"
    pp. 72–77; Hicks, *Populist Revolt*, pp. 216, 229, 271, 319, 326, 344, and 359.
    Lawrence Goodwyn, *The Populist Moment: A Short History of the Agrarian Revolt in
    America* (Oxford: Oxford University Press, 1978), pp. 237–249 and 254–255, discuss-
    es Taubeneck's belated realization that fusion was a costly strategy for the Populists.
40. *Appleton's Annual Cyclopaedia and Register of Important Events of the Year 1892* (NY:
    D. Appleton and Co., 1893), p. 343.

KOL had already organized the Cook County branch of the People's party as a counterweight to the Citizen's Alliance, a corrupt organization controlled by labor boss William C. Pomeroy. With the onset of the depression and the expression of diverse strands of labor reformism at the Columbian Exposition in 1893, labor interest in an alliance with the agrarians was growing.[41]

National labor organizations were also showing a renewed interest in politics. The American Federation of Labor (AF of L) endorsed Thomas Morgan's political program at its annual convention in 1893. Morgan was a Chicago socialist who advocated the creation of a third party with a broad labor program:

> The eleven planks of the programme demanded: compulsory education; the initiative; a legal eight-hour work-day; governmental inspection of mines and workshops; abolition of the sweating system; employers' liability laws; abolition of the contract system upon public work; municipal ownership of electric light, gas, street railway, and water systems; the nationalisation of telegraphs, telephones, railroads, and mines; "the collective ownership by the people of all means of production and distribution"; and the referendum upon all legislation.

American laborers were inspired by the British, who had just founded a labor party. Even conservative leaders such as Samuel Gompers and Peter McGuire were willing to consider political action during these eventful years. Many state federations of labor (including Illinois') also endorsed Morgan's plan. While dissent soon emerged over plank 10 (the "collective ownership" plank), labor at this juncture was ready to engage in political action.[42]

The labor-Populist alliance

By 1894, the Illinois labor-Populist alliance was ready. Agrarians and laborites had made overtures to one another for years; their national organizations were pursuing common concerns, the country's dismal economy provoked political unrest, and the national political parties seemed locked in irrelevant debates and outmoded responses. After a series of conventions and meetings, the diverse strands of the reform movement were brought together behind Populism. It was a coalition in which labor dominated and the socialists were intregal members. This was the party's

41. Destler, "People's Party," pp. 84 and 99–100. See also Dennis B. Downey, "The Congress on Labor at the 1893 World's Columbian Exposition," *Illinois State Historical Journal*, 76 (1983): 131–138.
42. Commons et al., *History of Labour*, vol II, pp. 509–512.

strength, for it meant that Populism was relevant to an urban, industrializing society. Producerism and antimonopolism combined with socialism in a critique of corporate capitalism. But it was also the movement's weakness, for the differences between farmers and laborers, immigrants and natives, and socialists and nonsocialists created centrifugal forces that would pull the coalition apart.[43]

Two important conventions were held in Springfield during the late spring and summer of 1894. The first was the official People's party state convention held in May. The convention endorsed the national party's Omaha platform and nominated state candidates. The next convention was the industrial conference held in July. About this conference, state federation president M. H. Madden wrote, "The conference will be attended by possibly two hundred delegates . . . They will be more representative in character than ever gathered together in the world. The trades unionist . . . Populist . . . Knight of Labor . . . single-taxer . . . socialist . . . [and] silverite . . . [will] be in evidence. Thus you can see all the schools of thought save the philosophy of greed will be under the canopy of Labor." The excitement of the meeting was heightened by the Pullman strike, which raged in Chicago as delegates gathered in Springfield. After an embittered debate, the convention narrowly rejected "plank 10," and it seemed that the labor socialists were likely to withdraw. Then Henry Lloyd brokered a compromise that pledged the delegates "to the principle of the collective ownership by the people of all such means of production and distribution as the people elect to operate for the commonwealth." Labor activists committed themselves to actively support the Populist ticket. With this, the labor-Populist alliance was complete.[44]

The Pullman strike was a watershed event both nationally and locally. Locally, the strike increased social and political divisions and raised the level of political desperation among workers. Class relations were strained, the Democrats were divided by the Altgeld and Cleveland feud, and conflicts between the American Railway Union (ARU) and the AF of L fractured labor unity. For some, these events clarified the need to radically democratize the political system. For others, the strikes reinforced

43. The history of the labor-Populist coalition has been written by Chester McArthur Destler. Destler is the only scholar I know of who fully credits the significance of the antimonopolist tradition in the late nineteenth century. See *American Radicalism, 1865–1901;* his dissertation, "People's Party," and his biography of Lloyd, *Henry Demarest Lloyd and the Empire of Reform* (Philadelphia: University of Pennsylvania Press, 1963).
44. M. H. Madden to Henry Demarest Lloyd, June 27, 1894, Henry Demarest Lloyd Papers, State Historical Society of Wisconsin. Destler, "People's Party," pp. 115–117, 120–126.

their belief that politics was a game they could not win. Workers divided between supporting Populism and retreating to business unionism.[45]

Labor activists supporting the Populists in Chicago faced many challenges. The regular parties opposed them, and used Red-baiting tactics to hold their labor adherents in line. Divisions within the reform movement kept erupting, turning Henry Demarest Lloyd, Clarence Darrow, and Willis Abbott (among others) into continuous peacemakers. There was even a false third party fielded under the Populist label by labor boss William Pomeroy. Despite all of this, enthusiasm for the party was evident in long parades and crowded auditoriums where national and state reformers such as Eugene Debs (leader of the Pullman strike), Ignatius Donnelly, Lyman Trumbull, and Darrow were loudly cheered. The improvement in the party's vote that year came mostly from Cook County.[46]

The Populist campaign was weak outside Chicago. The party was short on money and organization. The agrarian movement was still marred by the political debacle of the 1891 Senate contest. Nor had the cooperative movement ever taken root. When the Southern Farmers' Alliance tried to organize an aggressive membership drive, it was attacked by competing farm organizations. Farmers were often suspicious of the party's connection to laborites and socialists. The greatest statewide efforts came from the pens of reform editors. Only the urban wing of the Populist party ever developed into a true reform movement.[47]

The Republicans did well in the 1894 election. They took twenty of twenty-two Congressional seats (indeed, after contesting the two Democratic seats, these were given to Republicans as well), and won the elections for State Treasurer and Supervisor of Public Instruction in landslide victories. The causes of this political turnover were both national and local. The depression and President Cleveland's handling of the Sherman Silver Purchase Act repeal hurt the Democrats. Labor strife and Governor

45. Nick Salvatore, *Eugene V. Debs: Citizen and Socialist* (Urbana: University of Illinois Press, 1982), chap. 5. The Spring Valley strike of that spring also contributed to labor's discouraged state. Lorin Lee Cary, "Adolph Germer and the 1890s Depression," *Illinois State Historical Journal*, 68 (1975): 337–340.
46. Destler, "People's Party," chap. 6; Henry Demarest Lloyd to the editor of the *Chicago Times*, October 14, 1894, and rally flier, November 3, 1894, Lloyd Papers, SHSW; and Salvatore, *Eugene V. Debs*, pp. 147–149. Destler's chapter discusses some of the divisions among labor groups that emerged at the Cook County convention on August 18.
47. Besides Destler's dissertation, see Scott, *Agrarian Movement*, pp. 125–136. Destler suggests that most of the Populist vote in 1894 came from Cook County, and that the increase in votes from downstate (approximately 26,000 rather than 20,000 votes) was mainly due to the votes received in coal mining towns. See Destler, "People's Party," pp. 166–167.

Altgeld's increasingly visible radicalism (he pardoned the remaining Haymarket defendants and opposed the use of federal troops during the Pullman strike) were also factors. Conservative Democrats withdrew their active support from the ticket. In the Treasurer's election, the Republicans received 463,264 votes, the Democrats 317,611 votes, and the Populists 58,330 votes (approximately 7 percent of the total). The trend toward Republican dominance and the failure of the Democrats or Populists to construct a successful producers' coalition were evident.[48]

Afterward, the Democrats and Populists went through a period of reflection and evaluation. Lloyd, Darrow, and Morgan were uncertain about the possibilities for democratic politics or the viability of the Populist coalition. Morgan wrote to Lloyd wondering whether he should bother to attend a state party meeting in Springfield, given "the poverty of the State Machinery of the party . . . " Darrow's letter, written shortly after the ARU men were convicted, was more pessimistic.

> The people are dead. Can anything be done to resuscitate them before liberty is dead[?] I am very much discouraged at the prospect. I can not join the other side but what can be done?
>
> I am also in a quandary about the People's Party. I might be willing to join a socialist party, but I am not willing to help run another socialist movement under the guise of "the people's party." We must take some stand or drop out all together.

Darrow's discouraging fight for democratic renewal under the Populist banner left him politically disillusioned and in search of alternatives.[49]

But Lloyd was not ready to give up on Populism. He responded to Darrow with critical realism and faith in democratic possibility.

> My dear Darrow: The conviction of the ARU men I have expected from the beginning. Our judges register the ruling opinion, as judges always do . . . The radicalism of the fanatics of wealth fills me with hope. They are likely to do for us what the South did for the North in 1861. . . . The course of the socialists in Chicago deserves sympathetic attention . . . the Chicago Social-

48. Charles A. Church, *History of the Republican Party in Illinois, 1854–1912* (Rockford, IL: Wilson Bros., 1912), pp. 175–177; Green B. Raum, *History of Illinois Republicanism* (Chicago: Rollins Pub. Co., 1900), chap. 30; *Prominent Democrats of Illinois* (Chicago: Democrat Publishing Co., 1899), pp. 61, 96–99; *Appleton's Annual 1894*, pp. 362–363; and Horace Samuel Merrill, *Bourbon Democracy of the Middle West, 1865–1896* (Seattle: University of Washington Press, 1967), pp. 233–238, 245–246.

49. Thomas J. Morgan to H. D. Lloyd, November 13, 1894, and Clarence Darrow to H. D. Lloyd, November 22, 1894, Lloyd Papers, SHSW. On similar transitions from Populism to socialism in Illinois, see Allen M. Ruff, "Socialist Publishing in Illinois: Charles H. Kerr and Company of Chicago, 1886–1928," *Illinois Historical Journal*, 79 (1986): 21–22.

ists gave up their political identity, and went in with all their might for the success of the People's Party . . . The People's Party platform is socialistic, as all democratic doctrine is . . . What we ought to have at once is a conference of the most active reformers from all over the country to try to bring about this cooperation of all. But if we begin to read each other out of the ranks for differences of opinion we are lost.

Despite recent events, Lloyd continued to view the Springfield industrial conference and the course of the Chicago socialists as models for united action. In his writings about monopoly in *Wealth Against Common-wealth*, in his efforts to unite agrarians, labor radicals, and liberal reformers behind Populism, and in his desperate attempt to save the national party from merger with the Democrats and the silver movement in 1896, Lloyd represented the best and most promising elements of the American antimonopolist tradition.[50]

The Altgeld wing of the Democratic party gave up its connections to the national party to promote state and sectional concerns. It sought to create a new political geographical alignment in which the East no longer dominated. The Illinois governor blamed Cleveland for the party's electoral losses. By highlighting financial and labor issues, Altgeld hoped to make his differences with the Clevelandites apparent, and to rebuild the party with progressive support. The Illinois Silver Convention was organized under the auspices of the state Democratic party in June 1895. William Jennings Bryan was among the speakers. The 1076 delegates committed themselves to free silver, regardless of the national party's position. Local gold Democrats, such as John Palmer and John R. Walsh, were infuriated, and actively organized against Altgeld. Silver became an issue around which intraparty squabbles and competing political geographies found their expression.[51]

Meanwhile, the Populists divided over the role of socialists within the party. Chicago leaders sought to extend the socialist-Populist alliance, by clarifying the terms on which the alliance was based, and working to expand the coalition nationally. The Radical Club was formed, and among its members were Lloyd, Darrow, Morgan, and Abbott. Henry Vincent used the *Chicago Searchlight* to articulate the terms of socialist-Populist unity. Elsewhere, conservative trade unionists and agrarians tried to purge the socialists from their ranks. Downstate farm leaders such as A. L. Maxwell and H. S. Taylor gained control of the state organization. They excluded the socialists and denied the legitimacy of the Chicago Populist

50. H. D. Lloyd to Clarence Darrow, November 23, 1894, Lloyd Papers, SHSW.
51. Harvey Wish, "John Peter Altgeld and the Background of the Campaign of 1896," *Mississippi Valley Historical Review*, 24 (1937–38): 506–510.

committee. This division ran parallel to the split between the middle-of-the road and fusion factions nationally. Lloyd and Taubeneck were active in both disputes, the former as a middle-of-the-road radical and the latter as an antisocialist fusionist.[52]

The fight against silver fusion accompanied the effort to maintain the labor-Populist alliance. The first battle against fusion went the way of the Illinois radicals. Along with other middle-of-the-roaders, they halted an attempt by Taubeneck and James Weaver to delete the more progressive planks (including the subtreasury plan) from the Omaha platform. But the fight was costly. With open hostilities between the state organization and the Chicago socialists, energy was diverted from the spring 1895 Chicago mayoral election. Bayard Holmes, the Populist candidate, received less than ten percent of the votes received by the winning candidate, Republican George B. Swift. Over the next year and a half, the radical Populists fought in vain to maintain a broad progressive coalition. Instead, as the Democrats, Populists, and silver Republicans bargained, squabbled and vacillated, the regular Republicans assured the voters that social peace and economic prosperity lay with them.[53]

In the end, even Lloyd lost faith, though he continued to give his best effort to the cause. There was still some spirit of optimism in September 1895, when Lloyd advised Morgan to stay with the party. Morgan agreed, but not for long. He and other socialists broke from the Populists in the spring of 1896 to form the Socialist Trade and Labor Alliance. The new organization was Morgan's "answer to the attacks of the Pomeranian forces." It was also an expression of his lost faith in Populism. He criticized

> the antisocialist attitude of the official element of the P. Party of this state & county and the timid apologetic policy of the "radical" element of that party in this city who while praising the honesty and seeking the support of the Socialist element deem it most unwise to have it known that that element is active within it.

Morgan's evident bitterness at his mistreatment by Populist colleagues ended his participation in the alliance. While many laborites remained with the Populists through the fall elections, Morgan was not among them.[54]

---

52. Destler, "People's Party," chap. 7.
53. See Paul Van der Voort to H. D. Lloyd, January 1895, and Henry Winn to H. D. Lloyd, February 14, 1895, Lloyd papers, SHSW, on the St. Louis meeting. See Destler, "People's Party," pp. 182–187, on the Holmes campaign and intraparty squabbles.
54. Thomas Morgan to H. D. Lloyd, June 15, 1896, Lloyd Papers, SHSW. See also Paul Ehmann to H. D. Lloyd, July 3, 1896, Lloyd Papers, SHSW, who argues that the working-class socialists can no longer cooperate with the middle-class Populists.

By July, Lloyd's outlook had also darkened. In a letter to Bayard Holmes, he analyzed the political situation.

> I do not believe that "free silver" is a step as Coxey has said recently, except to be a step backward. The men in the management of the P.P. who are specially and bitterly and traiterously opposed to the real issues now before the public are the ones who have fanned this free silver backfire. All the . . . monopolists could ask nothing better than that the dangerous—to them—sentiment among the people be beguiled into believing that the principal cause of their woes was that the privilege of the silver owners to compel the people to accept their product as legal tender had been taken away . . . As to gathering . . . at St. Louis, I don't believe that that scene of ruin, confusion and defeat will be the place and time to organize a really radical party.

Despite his sense that the People's party was doomed by its leaders' commitment to free silver, Lloyd went to St. Louis and fought for a ticket led by Debs that might unite farmers and laborers against monopolists. But Debs was unavailable, and there were no other national figures strong enough to lead the antimonopolist forces.[55]

Other Populists expressed similar discouragement and resolve. Before the Democratic convention, R. I. Grimes expressed his sense of the historic moment before them.

> There are times . . . when a single move changes for good or bad the history of a nation. It is at such moments that true intelligence is displayed . . . We will disorganize the Dem party and out of the wreck we shall obtain all that is worth saving. We will produce a natural alignment of the masses against the classes . . . I have no thought that we will win an office but I do feel sure that the movement will come out of this coming struggle better, stronger, and more compact than it was before.

To many, it seemed that clearly drawing the lines of conflict was the greatest difficulty. They were aware that a moment of possibility was before them. But that moment was clouded by old partisan ties, ideological divisions, and bad strategic choices. Still, radicals continued to push for a real political contest between the "classes and the masses."[56]

---

55. H. D. Lloyd to Bayard Holmes, July 13, 1896, Lloyd Papers, SHSW. Earlier in the year, Lloyd was in touch with other radical Populists nationally concerning a plan to take the fight against fusion and for a broader alliance to the convention. See, for instance, H. R. Legate to H. D. Lloyd, May 13, 1896, and Florence Kelley to H. D. Lloyd, June 18, 1896, Lloyd Papers, SHSW. On Lloyd's attempt to have Debs nominated and Debs' refusal, see Nick Salvatore, *Eugene V. Debs*, pp. 156–161.

56. R. I. Grimes to H. D. Lloyd, July 6, 1896, Lloyd Papers. After fusion did occur at both the national and state levels, a "middle-of-the-road" party was formed, and fielded several candidates in the state elections, including Lloyd for Lt. Governor. Eventually, so as not to threaten Altgeld's chances in the gubernatorial race, Lloyd withdrew. See

John Peter Altgeld found himself in much the same position. Despite signs that his reelection effort was doomed, he ran an aggressive campaign on national issues. At the Democratic national convention, Altgeld succeeded in partially changing the geographical and class alignments within the party. The platform, which he wrote, was vocally pro-silver and pro-labor. It brought the party back toward producerism. This was the document on which Bryan stood as the party's presidential candidate. This platform made Altgeld the focus of attacks by gold Democrats and corporate Republicans. He was soundly defeated by conservative Republican John R. Tanner in the gubernatorial race. The Republican sweep was nearly complete, and with it a moment of democratic possibility was lost.[57]

Defeat of the antimonopolist tradition

The labor-Populist alliance was the last great expression of antimonopolist farmer-labor politics in Illinois. From the late 1860s until the late 1890s, Illinois was the most persistent site of efforts to redirect the course of economic change toward a decentralized, mixed agrarian-industrial economy. Monopolies and trusts got hostile treatment from Illinois citizens, whose attempts to regulate land, transportation, and finance were aimed at equalizing the terms of competition between small and large producers and retaining a degree of economic autonomy for wage workers. Agrarians and labor reformers did not obtain the cooperative commonwealth they sought in the 1880s and 1890s. Yet their effort left lasting marks on the liberal corporate polity that emerged instead.[58]

Because of its strong antimonopolist tradition and the economic position of the state (mixed agrarian-industrial, with a growing financial sector), Illinois in the 1890s was an intellectual hotbed for political programs that merged new radical programs such as socialism with older traditions such as producerism. The state of Alexander Campbell, Andrew Cameron, the *Workingmen's Advocate,* and the Illinois State Farmers' Association

A. B. Adair to Lloyd, August 20, 1896, Lloyd Papers, SHSW; *Appleton's Annual Cyclopaedia and Register of Important Events for the Year 1896* (NY: D. Appleton, 1897), p. 363; and Wish, "John Peter Altgeld": 380–381.

57. Under their fusion arrangements with the Democrats, the Populists won one congressional and three state legislative seats. Destler estimates their voting strength that year at approximately 40,000 votes out of a total of over 1 million. Destler, "People's Party," pp. 217–225. Other accounts of the election can be found in *Appleton's Annual 1896,* pp. 349–350; Wish, "John Peter Altgeld": 353–384; and John E. Pixton, Jr., "Charles G. Dawes and the McKinley Campaign," *Illinois State Historical Society Journal,* 48 (1955): 183–306.

58. Robert McGuire, "Economic Causes of Late Nineteenth Century Unrest: New Evidence," *Journal of Economic History,* 41 (1981): 835–852.

became the home of Thomas Morgan, Henry Vincent, the ARU, Henry Demarest Lloyd, and *Wealth Against Commonwealth*. Labor led the reform effort, after the "politics by fire" experiences of Haymarket and Pullman. Laboring men and women had tested the democratic political process and found it wanting. As class divisions became distinct and the opportunities for success under Populism beckoned, these reform leaders forged a creative blend of government ownership, financial regulation, and democratic reform, all aimed at the growing power of the corporate monopolists and their political clients. This mixture of greenback Populism and socialism provided the terms for the labor-Populist alliance. It was an intellectually promising formula that many reformers hoped to reproduce at the national level. But ultimately it was a formula that they failed to sustain in their own state.

The labor-Populist alliance had a strong political program backed by a weak political movement. Both the agrarian and labor wings of the movement were disorganized, rife with internal dissension, and vulnerable to external attacks. Labor suffered from bickering among different ideological groups, and was hampered by corrupt machine unionists (or "labor skates") and Red-baiting by anti-socialists. Farmers faced destructive competition among agrarian organizations, dissatisfying experiences with independent political action, and strong partisan loyalties which worked against third-party participation. Farmers and laborers, who were often of different ethnic and religious backgrounds, were suspicious of each other. But perhaps the most important factor that undermined grassroots participation in the Populist party was the reformist nature of the Democrats in the 1890s.

North Carolina's farmers were held to their party by strong cultural traditions often backed by violence and intimidation, not by opportunities for achieving political change. In Illinois, the cultural ties were looser and the society more heterogeneous, but the viability of regular politics was greater and more likely to attract reformers. This made strategic choices difficult. John Peter Altgeld brought many potential Populists with him into the Democratic party. As the governor vocalized his support for labor and antimonopolism, he found himself among other Western critics of the Cleveland administration, including Populists and Republicans. When he gathered these dissenting voices around the issue of silver, party dissidents and reformers followed his lead, culminating in the Chicago convention of July 1896. Yet Altgeld and other progressive Democrats failed to completely realign their party. This created confusion rather than clarity in the political choices offered in the election.

There were many ironies in this strategic formulation. Altgeld helped to draw a line down the middle of his party, between East and West, silver and gold. As the Altgeld Democrats articulated their interests in sectional terms, they pulled the national coalition apart and created a realignment in the party that favored Western interests. But in this realignment between East and West, the South remained stationary. Southern Democrats were content to articulate a reformist line within the national arena while they retained class and political control locally. So the real antimonopolist coalition was never created. The local price of this choice was the defeat of the Democratic coalition, from which the conservatives withdrew. Illinois Populists were caught between supporting the vaguely reformist silver Democrats (and their genuinely reformist governor) and holding onto a radically democratic, but failing, farm-labor coalition. Only the Republicans benefitted locally and nationally – as the anti-radical, pro-prosperity party – from the line that Altgeld helped to draw.

Illinois' Populists and other reformers knew they faced a historic moment during the political contests of the mid-1890s. But it was a moment beyond their grasp. The contest they hoped for – between the masses and the classes – never materialized. The coalition and program that briefly appeared at the Springfield industrial conference of 1894, which joined farmers and laborers in an attack on the corporate commonwealth, might have been a model for the Populist movement nationally, but was never clearly articulated in the state. For those who saw it, this was a tragedy that drove some to socialism and others out of politics altogether. For those who remained within the mainstream, the terms of political participation were narrowed, to local concerns and marginal reforms, and expectations of economic opportunity and autonomy were lessened. The twentieth century brought new contests between labor and capital. But with the close of 1890s, the dream of an antimonopolist cooperative commonwealth had faded.

III. Massachusetts: Home of liberal orthodoxy

Massachusetts was the ultimate, orthodox gold standard state. The Bay State provided many of the intellectuals, financiers, and manufacturers involved in the "sound money" campaign. This commitment to conservative finance, which was shared by most of the state's citizens, was based partially on their economic position and largely on principles. Even though Massachusetts businesses were somewhat disadvantaged by the rise of mass production and the concentration of commercial and financial operations in New York, the state's political elite still identified themselves with the Northeast. Signs of disaffection with the course of economic development appeared mostly in the tariff reform debate. There was also a reform movement of laborers and middle-class intellectuals, who supported Fabian socialism, labor Populism, and the KOL. But this political current was limited by machine politics and liberal orthodoxy. The debate between antimonopolism and corporate liberalism was a one-sided conversation by the 1890s. This state illuminates the workings of corporate liberal politics.

The party system of Massachusetts was dominated by the Republicans – the party of social conservatism, business interests, and Yankee respectability. But the Democrats were a stronger and more important party than they had been at any time since the Civil War. This revitalization began during the 1884 presidential campaign. Liberal reformers (the Mugwumps) rejected the Republicans to support Grover Cleveland. Further, after the departure of Benjamin Butler, the weakened Democratic party organization was easily remolded by these well-funded social elites. This "new" Democratic party was an odd hybrid of righteous advocates for civil service and tariff reform and Irish bosses who managed the votes of Boston's working-class wards. The Democrats' political strength peaked in 1890 with the election of William E. Russell as governor and seven Democrats (out of twelve seats) to the Congress. But as the divisions in the national party over financial and other sectional issues became apparent, the Massachusetts Democrats suffered.

The "sound money" campaign

Orthodox liberalism went beyond the bounds of party in Massachusetts. It was a movement, which in the 1880s identified itself as "Mugwump," and in the 1890s was associated with the "Sound Money" campaign. While the Mugwumps were closely aligned with the Cleveland Democrats, the Sound Money men were a bipartisan coalition forged to protect the gold standard. The senior figures in the Sound Money campaign were veterans from the antigreenback era. Some were motivated by economic interests. Others acted on the basis of sectional identity or political ideology. The views of these liberal elites were nearly hegemonic in the mid-1890s (though some international bimetallists remained within the ranks of the socially acceptable), when to support free silver was to be accused of "financial heresy."[59]

59. Prominent bimetallists included Frances Walker, president of MIT, and Brooks Adams, of the famous Adams family. On the connection between the antigreenback campaign of the 1870s and the sound money campaign of the 1890s, see Richard E. Welch, Jr., *George Frisbie Hoar and the Half-Breed Republicans* (Cambridge: Harvard University Press, 1971), pp. 83–88, 172–176, and 196–197; Harold Francis Williamson, *Edward Atkinson: The Biography of an American Liberal, 1827–1905* (Cambridge: Riverside Press, 1934), p. 94, 158–161, and 206–212; Geoffrey Blodgett, *The Gentle Reformers: Massachusetts Democrats in the Cleveland Era* (Cambridge: Harvard University Press,

In 1890, a free silver bill was offered in Congress. This provided the starting point for the Massachusetts Sound Money campaign. Coming shortly after the passage of the Sherman Silver Purchase Act, this new silver legislation seemed but another step toward a debased monetary system. In January 1891, Edward Atkinson wrote to Grover Cleveland:

> I know what action will be taken for those who have carried Massachusetts on the tariff issue for the Democratic party. They look upon the tariff as *second* in importance to the maintenance of a sound currency, and they will not support a party which commits itself at the present time to the free coinage of silver.

After the free silver legislation passed the Senate, Massachusetts businessmen organized a protest rally at Fanueil Hall. They then sent a delegation of academics and businessmen to Washington to testify before Congress. Their statements, which focused on the instability and economic damage caused by monetary meddling, were published as a pamphlet for the gold forces. The silver bill was subsequently stopped in the House of Representatives, and the Massachusetts Sound Money campaign began with a success.[60]

Next, the Sound Money campaign sought to repeal the Sherman Silver Purchase Act. Both Republicans and Democrats favored repeal. There were disagreements about who was to blame for the nation's financial woes and about the timing of the effort, but all were committed to repeal itself. The Democrats had assaulted the Republican party's Sherman Act since it passed in 1890. A 1892 Mugwump election tract stated:

> We know that both parties contain friends of silver, and that members of both are entitled to credit for the recent defeat of a free silver bill, but the Democratic opponents of free silver fought for their faith, and triumphed in 1892, while the Republican opponents of this dangerous heresy voted for the [Silver Purchase] Act of 1890.

Republicans argued that the Sherman Act was better than either the Bland-Allison Act, which it replaced, or the free silver bill offered as an alternative. Both parties competed for the mantle of "most conservative" on the money issue, and the state's congressional delegation voted over-

1966), chap. 2. See also Edward Atkinson's account of the fight against the Inflation Bill (in which he played a leading role) and its relevance to the politics of the 1890s in a letter to E. D. Meier, July 23, 1895, Edward Atkinson Papers, Massachusetts Historical Society.

60. Quoted in Blodgett, *Gentle Reformers*, pp. 178–179. The Fanueil Hall meeting is discussed in Williamson, *Edward Atkinson*, p. 158. The pamphlet appears as *Gold and Silver: Statements of a Committee of Boston Businessmen, Before the Committee on Coinage, Weights and Measures*, January 28, 1891.

whelmingly for repeal. Massachusetts bankers also expressed their support for the financial policies of President Cleveland. Bay State politics were consistent with those of other New England states in opposing the movement toward a silver standard.[61]

As the Sound Money campaign broadened, Massachusetts bankers and businessmen volunteered funds to purchase newspapers in silver areas. *Sound Currency,* the publication of the New York Reform Club (to which many Boston reformers contributed), began publication in 1893. Charles C. Jackson organized a call for "sound money" people to urge their "Southern and Western correspondents" (particularly "Business men, boards of trade and similar organizations") to support the President's financial policies. From late 1893 until 1895, the movement gathered strength as gold standard men wrote pamphlets, gave speeches, and collected funds. These Northeastern conservatives sought to shore up a political geographical alignment in which local political positions coincided with the dominant national position (of Cleveland Democrats or McKinley Republicans) on questions of finance.[62]

The Massachusetts Reform Club created a Sound Money Committee in August 1896. A Business Mens' Non-partisan Sound Money League in Boston helped to oppose the Bryan campaign. The league was probably an adjunct to the Republican party, although Cleveland supporters such as Atkinson were listed as prominent members. But partisanship was not the main point. Atkinson's correspondence from this period is filled with letters from allies agonizing over whether to support McKinley or the National (Gold) Democrats. In the end, many of them (Atkinson included) did a bit of both. They all opposed William Jennings Bryan. Free silver was seen as a threat to well-ordered democracy. For Moorfield Storey and Winslow Warren, it was a campaign against "socialism" and the "overthrow of the Republic." Massachusetts political and economic elites were united in their opposition to Bryan and silver.[63]

61. *To the Voters of Massachusetts* (Boston, 1892), p. 8; Young Men's Democratic Club of Massachusetts, *Position of the Massachusetts Democrats in the Silver Question* (Boston, 1891); Welch, *George Frisbie Hoar,* pp. 173–176; and Blodgett, *Gentle Reformers,* pp. 187–191.

62. Moses Williams to Edward Atkinson, April 24, 1893, Atkinson Papers, MHS; A. Lawrence Lowell et al. to "Dear Sir," January 4, 1893, Atkinson Papers, MHS; and Charles C. Jackson to Edward Atkinson, March 3, 1896, Atkinson Papers, MHS. A piece by Charles C. Jackson appears in volume III, number 2, of *Sound Currency,* dated December 15, 1895. Since the journal was published semimonthly, volume I, number 1, probably appeared on December 1, 1893.

63. Massachusetts Reform Club to Edward Atkinson, August 8, 1896; J. R. Leeson to Edward Atkinson, August 24, 1896; Edward S. Bragg to Edward Atkinson, August 1, 1896; Arthur Lyman to Edward Atkinson, August 8, 1896; Joseph H. Walker to Ed-

The Sound Money campaign was concerned with more than mere money. For orthodox liberals, the financial issue involved the proper role of government in a democratic society. According to historian Geoffrey Blodgett, these liberals combined a faith in laissez-fairism (drawn from Adam Smith, John Stuart Mill, Herbert Spencer, and William Graham Sumner) with belief in social harmony. "They had been taught, as one of them recalled, 'to hold the balance between the powerful and the lowly, the rich and the poor, as the first principle of humane authority.'" Harvard economist and gold advocate F. W. Taussig discussed his cohorts' liberal philosophy in a biography of Edward Atkinson.

> Edward Atkinson belonged to the generation which, in the last quarter of the nineteenth century, maintained the unqualified liberal faith . . . These men stood for the belief in competition and the devotion to liberty that characterized their English predecessors and contemporaries . . . .
>   'Fiat money' was to be got out of the way, and the specie standard, abandoned during the Civil War, to be restored. When the agitation for free coinage set in, it was treated as merely another form of the cheap-money heresy . . . The gold standard was the corner-stone of the creed . . .

For its advocates, gold stood for a balanced, liberal political economy. Silver was regarded as antimarket and antiliberty.[64]

The reformers: Nationalists, Populists, Knights, and silverites

Although small in number, there were also radical reformers in the 1890s who supported the state's tiny Populist party, participated in National (Bellamy socialist) clubs, or were members of the KOL. They were allied with the state's labor movement. Their views were articulated by various radical reform journals, the most prominent of which was the *Arena*, edited by Benjamin O. Flower. Flower and his journal were involved in the Populist and Debsian socialist movements nationally. The reform movement in Massachusetts combined middle-class socialism with working-class producerism.

After being devastated by depression and antilabor actions in the 1870s, organized labor in Massachusetts began to recover in the 1880s. The large labor organizations of this decade included the KOL, trade unions, and city labor councils. Labor strength grew to 25,000 union

ward Atkinson, September 23, 1896; and A. B. Farquhar to Edward Atkinson, October 19, 1896, all in Atkinson Papers, MHS. Storey and Warren are quoted in Blodgett, *Gentle Reformers*, p. 224.
64. Geoffrey Blodgett, "The Mind of the Boston Mugwump," *Mississippi Valley Historical Review*, 48 (1961/62): 628–629; and Williamson, *Edward Atkinson*, pp. xiii-xiv.

members in Boston in 1886, the year that the Democratic party placed Frank K. Foster, a Knight, former greenbacker, and Benjamin Butler supporter, on the ticket as the nominee for Lieutenant Governor. Foster's strong showing (he ran 5,000 votes ahead of gubernatorial candidate John Andrew) came in a year of independent labor politics both nationally and locally. Heightened political awareness was also generated by the Eighthour Day campaign.[65]

Just as the Knights peaked in Massachusetts in the mid-1880s, the Nationalist movement began. This movement grew out of public enthusiasm for Edward Bellamy's *Looking Backward,* a novel about a utopian socialist future. Bellamy was a Massachusetts native. His book captured the interest of many Americans distressed by the harsh effects of industrial development. Some of Bellamy's Boston followers founded the Nationalist movement, which preached municipal socialism. Begun in the late 1880s, Nationalism grew to include eleven clubs in the Bay State. Members were typically middle-class men and women. In Massachusetts, Nationalism was closely aligned with the Populist movement.[66]

By 1893, the *Arena* was one of the major reform publications in the Northeast, and published articles such as "The Menace of Plutocracy" and "Pure Democracy Versus Government Favoritism." During the mid-1890s, the journal drew ever closer to the Populists' political economy analysis and the central role which they assigned to the financial system. The election of 1896 was covered as "The Unconditional Battle of the Wealth Creators of the Republic Against the Bank of England." Despite the *Arena's* allegiance to the Bryan campaign and the silver movement, reformist views in Massachusetts on finance remained underdeveloped. One observer wrote to Henry Demarest Lloyd in 1895, "Theologically Boston is advanced enough. Every Bostonian I meet is an out and out heretic in religion, but so narrow in economics . . . ! His cant about an 'honest dollar' is downright fatiguing." While the intellectual material for the development of an antimonopolist movement in Boston may have been present, it did not take root. The state's conservative elite dominat-

65. Alexander Keyssar, *Out of Work: The First Century of Unemployment in Massachusetts* (Cambridge: Cambridge University Press, 1986), pp. 178–179, 191–202; Jama Lazerow, "'The Workingman's Hour': The 1886 Labor Uprising in Boston," *Labor History,* 21 (1980): 201; and Blodgett, *Gentle Reformers,* p. 65. Lazerow also discusses the narrowing of earlier labor ideologies to the more materially focused pursuits of the eight-hour campaign in the mid-1880s. See Lazerow, "'The Workingman's Hour,'" pp. 208–213.
66. Henry F. Bedford, *Socialism and the Workers in Massachusetts, 1886–1912* (Amherst: University of Massachusetts Press, 1966), pp. 12–21.

ed public discourse on the monetary matters, leaving most citizens with solidly conservative views on finance. Having lost the campaign both intellectually and electorally, Flower was fired from his post as editor in late November 1896.[67]

Formed in 1891, the Populist party was established at a gathering of Grangers, Knights, Nationalists, Christian Socialists, and Greenbackers. Some trade unions were also affiliated. The agrarian element of the party was overwhelmed by the labor and middle-class reform elements. The party was largely an adjunct to the Nationalist movement and, for some labor leaders, a stop on the route to socialism. The small party had several strong leaders – such as Sylvester Baxter, Henry Legate, Henry Winn, and Harry Lloyd – who contributed to the reform movement nationally, often steering a course between the single-issue fusionists (such as Populist chairman Taubeneck), and the more radical greenback agrarians from Texas and Kansas.[68]

Over its six-year lifespan in the Bay State, the Populist party's greatest strength followed the onset of the depression in 1893. Before this economic downturn, the party ticket was headed by Major Henry Winn, a former Republican and respected businessman who advocated tax reform and appealed to farmers. Yet Winn was more popular in eastern industrial towns than in western farm centers. Beginning in 1893, the Nationalists were ascendant in the party and attention shifted to municipal socialism. In towns such as Haverhill, which had fielded independent labor candidates in the 1880s, the Populists absorbed the old labor reform element and succeeded in electing a coalition-backed mayor. Gradually, these labor reformers, such as shoemaker James Carey, left Populism and joined the Socialist Labor party. By the middle 1890s, the remaining Populist activists were either working on national matters (such as preserving the Omaha platform) or looking to the newly emergent silver element in the Massachusetts Democratic party. Although there were labor reformers,

67. Allen J. Matusow, "The Mind of B. O. Flower," *New England Quarterly*, 34 (1961): 492–509; *Prospectus of the Arena for 1896* in the Marion Butler Papers, SHC; and Ruff, "Socialist Publishing," p. 22. The quote appears in Bedford, *Socialism and the Workers*, p. 20.

68. Bedford, *Socialism and the Workers*, pp. 18–32. There are several letters from Massachusetts Populist leaders in the papers of Henry Demarest Lloyd. See, for instance, Henry Legate to Lloyd, December 19, 1894; Henry Winn to Lloyd, February 14, 1895; Sylvester Baxter to Lloyd, April 27, 1896; Henry Legate to Lloyd, May 13, 1896; Sylvester Baxter to Lloyd, May 27, 1896; and Sylvester Baxter to Lloyd, August 1, 1896, all in the Lloyd Papers, SHSW. On the vote share of the Populists between 1891 and 1896, see Bedford, *Socialism and the Workers*, appendix, pp. 289–290. At their height in 1894, the Populists obtained 9,037 votes statewide.

reform intellectuals, and socialists associated with Populism, the movement's potential as an electoral alternative was small.[69]

The silver faction of the Democratic party emerged when George Fred Williams, a former Mugwump and erstwhile gubernatorial candidate, declared his conversion to the movement in July 1896. Williams was influenced by Sylvester Baxter, the journalist, Nationalist, and former Populist with whom he had discussed political economy matters for several years. Financial reformism was an extension of Williams' anticorporate views. Nonetheless, the social stakes of this intellectual and political shift were high. As Williams said to reporters:

> In taking this step of supporting a silver Democrat, I realize that I am doomed politically in Massachusetts, and that I shall never be forgiven by men who claim to be Democrats. I realize also that these men can punish me socially and financially, but I invite the persecution with the conscientious feeling that I am doing right by voicing the sentiments of an outraged public.

Following the lead of this Yankee elite figure who had parted ways with the other Massachusetts Brahmins, men and women from the labor and reform movements rallied to the free silver cause.[70]

The initial news of Williams' conversion and Bryan's nomination created a surge of support for free silver. Williams was greeted on his return from the Chicago convention by an enthusiastic crowd of Butlerites, Nationalists, Populists, and trade unionists. As Frank Foster said in a welcoming speech, "Those of us who for nearly a quarter of a century have been protesting against the crucifixion of the laboring man on the cross of gold are only too glad the time has come when a great party organization preaches the same doctrine . . . " Other labor leaders, such as George McNeil, James Mellon, and Harry Lloyd, joined the Bryan-Williams campaign. Partially, this was habitual loyalty to the Democratic party. As had been the case in the Butler years, financial reformism was most effective when it was secured within the shelter of the Democratic party.[71]

The Irish community also showed some support for the reform cause. Under editor James J. Roche, *The Boston Pilot* (the city's leading Irish paper) started expressing a conservative antimonopolist position (since cor-

69. Henry Winn, *Position of the People's Party of Massachusetts as to Monopolies, Taxation, Money and the Liquor Question* (1892?); Henry Winn to Henry Demarest Lloyd, February 14, 1895, Lloyd Papers, SHSW; Bedford, *Socialism and the Workers*, pp. 18–32; and Blodgett, *Reformers*, p. 217.

70. Blodgett, *Gentle Reformers*, pp. 212–220. Williams is quoted on pp. 214–215. On the relative unity in elite opinion, see Atkinson's Papers from August to November, 1896, MHS. For one exception, see Robert Treat Paine to Edward Atkinson, April 27, 1895, and July 10, 1896, Atkinson Papers, MHS.

71. Blodgett, *Gentle Reformers*, pp. 220–230.

porate monopolies led to state ownership and expanded government). With the 1893 depression, the paper voiced stronger sympathy for the plight of workers. By 1896, Roche and the *Pilot* supported Bryan, though they retained doubts about the money issue. Indeed, after Bryan's second electoral defeat in 1900, Roche explained the outcome in an editorial entitled "Dollar Beats the Man." Bryan was too obsessed with silver. But the paper's commitment to the reform wing of the Democratic party remained strong through the mid-1890s.[72]

This surge in financial reform sentiment evaporated with the self-destruction of the George Fred Williams campaign and the defeat of William Jennings Bryan. Williams was a self-righteous politician with a political style that worked poorly among immigrants and laborers. Already faced with opposition from the gold Democrats and regular Republicans, Williams alienated the Boston Irish machine as well, further isolating the reform effort. Although the Irish ward bosses backed Williams as the regular party candidate, they did so with little enthusiasm. The brief moment when the workers went "Bryan mad and silver crazy" was lost as party schisms, movement disorganization, and liberal hegemony won the day. The liberal orthodoxy of the Bay State's elite became the liberal persuasion of the state at large.[73]

The political economy and political geography of financial conservatism

Massachusetts political elites had tense relations with the Southern and Western wings of their respective parties. The state's Cleveland Democrats preferred to lose control of the national party than to cede power to the West. They hoped to build a partnership with Southern elites who supported financial conservatism in exchange for assistance in economic development. When Southern Populists and silverites threatened this bargain, Northeastern Democrats in turn threatened economic blackmail. Their Republican counterparts did better, managing to retain both partisan power and economic advantage. Gold fit with the economic strategy of developing a partnership with the industrializing Midatlantic and Midwest regions. In each case, political geographical considerations were intricately involved with party positions on the money question.

There was a greater tendency among Democrats to identify with the

---

72. Roger Lane, "James Jeffrey Roche and the Boston *Pilot*," *New England Quarterly*, 33 (1960): 347–353.

73. Blodgett, *Gentle Reformers*, pp. 221–239. The quote appears in Bedford, *Socialism and the Workers*, p. 61.

South, with whom members of the state's social elite felt an economic and political connection. Former textile producer Edward Atkinson was a prominent Northern advisor to the "New Southerners." There was some sympathy for the plight of the Southern farmer as well. Several Boston financiers supported lifting the 10 percent tax on state bank notes to release financial resources in that region. When the "silver craze" began to spread in the old Confederacy, Mugwumps vacillated between warning their Southern allies ("This craze for cheap money is more dangerous to the South than to almost any other section") and expressing a sense of betrayal ("the people of Mississippi . . . [do not] deserve credit"). After the campaign, men such as Arthur Lyman believed that Southerners were being punished for their heretical monetary views and would continue to suffer until they reformed.[74]

Western financial radicals were treated as dangerous fanatics who deserved no sympathy. Atkinson trivialized Western political concerns. He wrote about the Pullman strike that "these labor troubles are only a little irritation on the edges – not serious." A. B. Farquhar also wrote, "We here cannot appreciate or understand the intense bitterness and excitement prevailing in the Western states." After the Chicago convention, Illinois' governor, John Peter Altgeld, was called an "alien" and "anarchist" by his Eastern Gold Democratic opponents. Altgeld (a German immigrant) symbolized the dangerous foreign influence spreading through the Democratic party. When forced to choose a political path in 1896, elite Democrats repudiated these Western radicals in favor of either the Republicans, whom they found odious on tariff matters, or the Gold Democrats, who were politically appealing but unlikely to be electorally effective.[75]

The Massachusetts Republicans were in an easier position. The interests of the party's national leaders coincided with those of state leaders on finance and tariff matters. There were some difficulties in the early 1890s, when the presence of new Western silver states threatened an internal party division. The compromise required to avoid party factionalism – the Sherman Silver Purchase Act – provided the Democrats with an issue. When the national factional disputes shifted to Democratic terrain in 1893 with the repeal of the Sherman Act, the Republicans were able to join the Sound Money campaign without threatening their party position. Although the state was somewhat divided on tariff matters, Republican

---

74. Edward Atkinson to R. H. Edmonds, April 16, 1894; A. B. Farquhar to Edward Atkinson, November 27, 1896; and Arthur Lyman to Edward Atkinson, December 3, 1896, all in the Atkinson Papers, MHS.

75. A. B. Farquhar to Edward Atkinson, November 19, 1896; and Edward Atkinson to Mrs. Atkinson, July 25, 1894, both in Atkinson Papers, MHS. On some of the reaction to Altgeld and the Chicago platform, see Wish, "John Peter Altgeld": 362 and 367–368.

support for a high tariff was consistent with their promanufacturing out-look. Under the banner of William McKinley – the "Advance Agent of Prosperity" – the Republicans brought together financial conservatism with an East-West coalition based on industrialism. In 1893, they recap-tured control of the state government, which they retained well into the twentieth century.[76]

The changing character of Massachusetts' economy was slow to affect the state's position in the monetary debate. As national markets grew, and transportation and finance became more centered in New York, Massa-chusetts was eclipsed as a leading port and banking center. Further, al-though the Bay State had been an early entrant in the industrial revolu-tion – by the 1890s, it had long since ceased to be a primarily agricultural state – industrialism there revolved around small and medium-sized firms in textiles, shoe production, machine tooling, and the like. While some firms and sectors continued to thrive in the late nineteenth century, oth-ers were made vulnerable by the organization of large-scale corporate manufacturing in the Midatlantic and upper Midwest regions, and cheap labor competition in the South. Some business leaders turned outward, expanding their connections to European rather than domestic markets, a move predicated on the need for lower tariffs. Consistent with their lib-eral creed, their political allegiance to England, and their economic desire for foreign markets, Massachusetts Mugwumps took up the tariff reform banner.[77]

The politics of money remains more complex from an economic per-spective. There was no shortage of banks or capital in Massachusetts. In-deed, while Boston may have fallen behind New York, it was still a ma-jor investment center. The state's representatives tended to identify with the interest of creditors. While still a Mugwump in 1892, George Fred Williams defended the Eastern creditors of his state as "relatively poor people." But in a private memo, he was more frank. "We could not car-

76. Welch, *George Frisbie Hoar*, chaps. 6 and 7; Michael Hennessy, *Four Decades of Mass-achusetts Politics, 1890–1935* (Freeport, NY: Books for Libraries Press, reprinted 1971), pp. 1–40; Richard Harmond, "Troubles of Massachusetts Republicans During the 1880s," *Mid-America*, 56(1974): 85–99; and Young Men's Democratic Club, *Position*, pp. 4–5, in which they criticize the Republicans for supporting the Sherman Silver Pur-chase Act.

77. John Winthrop Hammond, "Twentieth Century Manufactures," *Commonwealth His-tory of Massachusetts*, Albert Bushnell Hart, ed., vol. 5 (New York: The State History Co., 1930), pp. 370–398. Two of Massachusetts' biggest industries from the late nine-teenth century – shoemaking and textiles – came under competitive pressures from oth-er regions in the early twentieth century. In these cases, pressure was due not to large-scale manufacturing efficiency, but to the low wage, transportation cost, and resource proximity advantages of the South.

ry one Congressional district with free silver . . . The business community and the prominent contributors to our campaign funds would not justify a vote against [sound money]." In the longer term, there were reasons
for Massachusetts to be concerned about the growth of large-scale manufacturing to its west. Such concerns moved some labor leaders to advocate financial reform. Yet, with prominent regional identities on the side
of Eastern creditors, and liberal understandings supportive of the gold
standard, few followed the labor reformers' lead toward financial antimonopolism.[78]

By the 1890s, the labor reform tradition that inspired greenbackers in
Massachusetts two decades earlier had dimmed. The assault against fiat
money in the 1870s set the stage for the organized effort against silver in
the 1890s. In the place of antimonopolism was an orthodox liberal culture that emanated from the universities, the political parties, and the
business councils. Citizens from the Bay State both reflected and shaped
the conservative financial sentiment of the Northeast. By ideological persuasion, sectional identity, and economic interest they stood firmly behind
the gold standard. The weakness of Populism and financial reformism was
determined by the structure of politics in Massachusetts, the changing nature of class relations, poor strategic management, and the geographical
and cultural distance of New England labor men from the Populist epi-
center. While both labor groups and liberal elites interpreted economic
conditions as supporting financial conservatism, there were reasons to
doubt the benefits of national economic development for Massachusetts.

Political geography affected both the strategies selected by the state's
political parties and the ways that different social groups interpreted their
economic interests. For the Democrats, their position as leaders of the national party was forfeited in order to protect their sectional position on
monetary matters. When Western Democrats gained control of the party
and repudiated the policies of Grover Cleveland, the Mugwumps joined
the opposition. This was done even at the expense of local party control.
For a few years, the party was run by financial reformers and local party
machinists. Gold Democrats who had been the party's major patrons then

78. The quotes from Williams appear in Blodgett, *Gentle Reformers,* pp. 181 and 184. The
argument here is that Massachusetts was losing out in the construction of the national
large-scale manufacturing system. The corporate reorganizations of the turn of the century obtained some assistance from Massachusetts banks, but were primarily funded
and directed by New York. Once these reorganized systems were in place, Massachusetts began to be, like the South, at a competitive disadvantage. To see how such nationalism eclipsed regionalism in railroads, see Berk, "Constituting Corporations and
Markets: Railroads in the Gilded Age," *Studies in American Political Development,* vol.
4 (1990): 130–168.

contributed to its demise. The Republicans were able to coordinate local, sectional, and national political interests in a coalition with Western industrialists on a protariff, gold standard platform. This political geographical alignment provided lasting success to the Republicans. For both parties, sectional position was of primary importance, and support for the gold standard was nearly unanimous. Differences in the party identifications with other sections, and their relations to the national organizations, affected the strength and strategies of the parties locally.

Superficially, it is easy to explain the weakness of Populism in Massachusetts. It was an industrial state with few farmers and plentiful financial resources. The Northeastern immigrant workers were culturally, geographically, and economically different from the core Populists of the Western plains and the Southern cotton fields. Yet two factors complicate this picture – the presence of labor Populism in Minnesota, Illinois, and elsewhere, and the earlier history of labor reformism and greenbackism in Massachusetts. The economy and culture did not preclude the possibility of an antimonopolist alternative. In the early twentieth century, Edward Filene and Louis Brandeis assisted Bay State labor organizations in experiments in industrial cooperation under a vision of "regulated competition." But in the 1890s such creative responses were deadened by the political strength of local party machines and the cultural strength of liberal orthodoxy. A few imaginative labor and intellectual leaders such as Frank Foster, Harry Lloyd, Sylvester Baxter, and B. O. Flower tried to do more. But they failed to penetrate the atmosphere of financial conservatism.[79]

IV. Conclusion

The conflict between the "masses and the classes" was never clearly contested. In each of these states, there was a political battle fought in which the financial issue was central. When the conflicts concluded, politics was not the same. In North Carolina, after an interlude of Populist-Republican rule, the Democrats would assert hegemonic control of state politics, driving blacks and many former Populists out of the political system. Likewise, in Illinois and Massachusetts, a period of political possibility was followed by an era of Republican dominance. These changes helped to validate the emergence of corporate liberalism and narrow the realm of democratic choice. Yet these changes were made in a complex political context in which the ability to choose was itself contested and constrained

79. On Brandeis and Filene, see Philippa Strum, *Louis D. Brandeis: Justice for the People* (Cambridge: Harvard University Press, 1984), chaps. 7 and 10.

by the structure of the party system, dominant political geographical alignments, and the effects of historical contingency.

There are four theoretical points around which this conclusion is organized. First, this chapter has employed a notion of political geography to understand the political opportunities offered by the organization of state, section, and nation in political culture and institutions. Second, the chapter argues that the competition between political programs and ideologies involved efforts to develop cultural hegemony in support of political ends. Third, the chapter contends that the course of economic development consisted of struggles over the determination of economic interests. Finally, political development is presented as historically contingent. Influences from previous political battles, opportunities inherent in particular critical moments, and consequences for future politics and historical understandings all affected the course of development.

The political geography of Populism

One classic way of interpreting the Populist revolt is as an economically motivated conflict between the industrial core and the agrarian periphery. Divergent interests related to national economic policies such as the tariff and the monetary standard bring sectional groups into conflict with each other. This view seems consistent with the variations in Populist strength in the three state cases examined, with agrarian North Carolina as the strongest, mixed agrarian-industrial Illinois as weaker, and industrial Massachusetts as the weakest Populist state. Broadening the traditional sectional explanation, we might add that party leadership gave regional coherence to the demands of different economic groups. Thus the Democrats expressed the concerns of the agrarian South and some of the agrarian-extractive elements of the West, while the Republicans represented the concerns of the industrial North and Midwest. Some have argued that economically based and politically encoded sectional differences were a motivating force behind the Populist revolt and the political realignment of 1896.[80]

However, this chapter and the one before it suggest a different way of understanding political geography. Geographical concerns are neither clearly determined by economic interests, nor clearly represented by the parties. Rather, parties and political coalitions helped construct geographical interests, using competing racial, class, and partisan identities

---

80. The position I am critiquing here is consistent with Richard Bensel's argument in *Sectionalism and American Political Development: 1880–1980* (Madison: University of Wisconsin Press, 1984).

in so doing. Established parties and cultural norms may express one set of political geographical alignments, while political challengers attempt to construct new alignments.

There are many examples of this process. North Carolina Democrats posed economic issues in terms of a North-South divide, repressing the class dimensions of the financial question and reinforcing Southern Democratic solidarity with racist appeals. The Massachusetts Mugwumps betrayed their loyalty to the national Democratic party in 1896 in order to maintain financial conservatism within the state. For challengers, the construction of new political geographical alignments was more difficult, as John Peter Altgeld discovered when he helped to realign the national Democratic party toward Western interests but was ousted in his own state, and Marion Butler learned when he sought to mix different partisan alignments at the state and national levels, only to be accused of betrayal by both local and national Populists.

The structure of political geography formed an important strategic terrain on which the financial question was fought.

The political culture of monetary politics

The winners in these three states succeeded not just electorally, but also at the level of political culture. The Populists and their allies attempted to offer a different means of interpreting economic and political life. It was an interpretation grounded in prior political traditions such as republicanism and equal rights, and characterized by the experiments of farmers and workers as they cooperated for self-improvement. But this interpretation, which led them to participate in politics, diagnose the problems of the nation, and offer distinct remedies, failed under the assault of other cultural outlooks. In North Carolina, the competing outlook was racism and sectionally based partisan loyalty. In Massachusetts it was orthodox liberalism. And in Illinois it was a combination of antiradicalism, industrial progressivism, and the distortions of the free silver campaign. In each case, a clear contest between the political programs of antimonopolism and corporate liberalism was submerged beneath competing demands for group loyalty. Afterward, the losing alternative lost again in the annals of history where it was framed through the eyes of the victors.

The politics of economic interest

Economically, Populism is also often seen as a movement inspired by declining prices, mortgage burdens, and drought that plagued regions of farmer unrest. More profoundly, some scholars suggest, as farmers were absorbed into a national market system through transportation and financial markets, they responded with attempts to preserve the realities of simple market life. The history of these states raises several problems with this interpretation. First, Populism was not merely a farmers' movement. Indeed, in Illinois the movement was labor-led and the Populist platform was mixed with socialism. Second, Populism was neither backward-looking nor merely concerned with immediate economic gains. The goals of Populism went beyond mere inflation. Populists sought to redirect the course of economic development in order to preserve economic opportunity for all citizens. In North Carolina, the core struggle in the Populist movement was over the subtreasury plan. Third, Populist politics and Populist economics were inseparable, as the struggles in these various states make clear. Democracy was a term that applied to both the government and the economic system. Should democracy be lacking in either realm, then the other was surely threatened. For instance, Henry Demarest Lloyd fought for a clear political contest between antimonopolism and corporate liberalism. For him, the decline of the movement and the rise of the silver issue were interrelated events. Fourth, and finally, Populism was not an isolated instance of reaction to economic troubles, but part of a long history of farm-labor politics. Populism was part of the ongoing antimonopolist struggle over the direction which the nation would take both economically and politically.[81]

Instead of seeing Populism as a case of economic reaction, it should be seen as a part of the antimonopoly tradition that presented an alternative form of economic and political development in the late nineteenth century. In Illinois, antimonopolism was the basis for a political and economic program that would check the power of large corporations, reassert worker autonomy through measures such as the eight-hour day and government ownership of basic industries, and maintain competitive opportunity for farmers through regulation of the finance and transportation industries. This creative mixture of cooperation, socialism, and older-style antimonopolism would not halt industrialization, but would change its form. It would also assure a more mixed agrarian-industrial economy and would expand democracy by making the government more responsive to the needs of its citizens and the citizens more capable of democratic participation. There was nothing backward-looking or reactionary about this vision.

81. The notion of farmers as rooted in simple market capitalism is often based on C. B. Macpherson's *The Political Theory of Possessive Individualism: Hobbes to Locke* (Oxford: Oxford University Press Paperbacks, 1964). Bruce Palmer uses Macpherson in explaining Populism's ideology in *'Man Over Money': The Southern Populist Critique of American Capitalism* (Chapel Hill: University of North Carolina Press, 1980), pp. 12–13.

The historical contingency of Populism

Lastly, there is the question of history. Historical contingency shaped the past, present, and future of Populism's impact on American political development. Populism's fate was shaped by the contested legacy of greenbackism, the political withdrawals that appeared in the wake of defeated labor producerism, and the emergent structures of a centralized corporate economy. These pasts were part of the present in which Populism competed. The present also contained political and economic disruptions in the party system, industry, the international monetary system, and industrial labor relations. These disruptions culminated in regime shifts across several fronts, shifts the Populists helped to provoke but were unable to control. The ultimate nature of the regime that emerged was shaped by future events that legitimated and increased the significance of choices made during the 1890s. Those events included an influx of gold, which reinflated the monetary economy; the merger movement, which consolidated the corporate economy; the disenfranchisement of large segments of the nonelite South, which insured Democratic one-party rule; and the hegemony of the Republican party nationally, which assured the nation of the wisdom of industrial prosperity and business liberalism. Eighteen hundred and ninety-six was a critical moment in American politics. But its critical character was made by both past and future events and narratives that shaped this moment in U. S. history.

7

Money, history, and American political development

"All the other animals in the forest naturally expect me to be brave, for the Lion is everywhere thought to be the King of Beasts. I learned that if I roared very loudly every living thing was frightened and got out of my way . . . But whenever there is danger my heart begins to beat fast."

"But what about my courage?" asked the Lion, anxiously. "You have plenty of courage, I am sure," answered Oz. "All you need is confidence in yourself. There is no living thing that is not afraid when it faces danger. True courage is in facing danger when you are afraid, and that kind of courage you have in plenty."

The Wonderful Wizard of Oz

By the close of the nineteenth century, it seemed that Americans had chosen the road to "Oz." The antimonopolist alternative was defeated politically and economically. Voters trusted William McKinley's promises of industrial prosperity on the gold standard. That trust was rewarded when the world gold supply rose and monetary contraction finally stopped. Further, the assault of the hinterlands on Washington ended with the collapse of Populism, the rise in voter apathy, and Republican hegemony. In America, as in Oz, the rule of gold was secured, sectional divisions were retained, and political dissension dissipated.

The antimonopolist vision – in which equalized investment opportunities and a flexible monetary standard shifted economic development away from geographical and industrial concentration toward a regionally dispersed, mixed agrarian-industrial economy – was lost after the election of 1896. The farmers, workers, and small businessmen who joined the Greenback and Populist parties were committed. Yet they were discouraged by race-baiting, strike-breaking, and electoral manipulations. And they were distracted by the silver movement and their hopes for the electoral success of the fusion ticket of Bryan and Watson. After the defeat of Bryan and the Populists, the dominance of financial conservatism was secured. The reign of an orthodox financial system and its relation to the advent of a corporate liberal society have been anticipated rather than explained in this book. The emphasis in the past six chapters has been on the monetary debate, the antimonopolist alternative, and the role of history in political development.

Was the advent of financial conservatism inevitable? The argument throughout this book has been that it was not, and that the notion of historical inevitability is problematic. The antimonopolist alternative was politically indigenous, economically sensible, and historically persistent. The greenbackers and the Populists failed not because they lacked programmatic coherence or political appeal, but because of strategic errors, structural constraints, and the effects of historical timing and understandings. The cumulative effect of these elements was great, and the possibilities for antimonopolist success were slim. But the character of their failure provides an important lesson for American political development.

The significance of this historical tradition is the subject of this last chapter. The chapter is divided into three sections. In Section I, three topics are taken up. First, the findings of the previous chapters are reviewed. The continuity and coherence of the antimonopoly movement is considered in order to establish that there was an antimonopoly "tradition." Second is the antimonopoly program and its failure. While there were changes in the economic proposals of the antimonopolists over time, their plans were intelligent and appealing. Why did the antimonopolists fail? This crucial question is considered at length. The answer does much to assist us in understanding the dynamics of late nineteenth-century American political development. Third, the last topic of the first section is the character of antimonopolism's failure and its relationship to historical development. Given the structure of politics and economic power in this period, was it likely that the antimonopolists could have gained the political authority needed to implement their proposals? The chances for antimonopoly success were slim. Yet the legacy of the tradition shaped and characterized the political economy regime which emerged.

The other two sections move the discussion beyond the findings of the preceding chapters. Section II considers the Danish banking system, which aided in the development of a mixed agrarian-industrial economy in that country. The comparison substantiates claims about the intelligibility of the antimonopolist program and the viability of alternative paths of economic development. Section III carries the history of antimonopolism forward into the twentieth century. The design of the Federal Reserve System and the debates over the National Recovery Administration are two of the places where the effect of antimonopolism may be found. Although anti-

monopolism was decisively defeated in the 1890s, it continued to characterize debates over economic regulation well into the twentieth century.

I. Evaluating the antimonopoly tradition

Both the antimonopolists and financial conservatives associated money
with a broader social vision. The money debate became a place where other political conflicts over citizenship, nationalism, race, and gender were
aired. In previous chapters, I have argued that the efforts of farmers,
workers, and small businessmen to change the financial system were
about much more than a narrow desire for currency inflation. Rather,
these various social actors came together in a movement for an alternative development path. They sought to preserve economic opportunity
and to protect republican institutions from the corrupting influences of
economic concentration. Despite the diversity of the participants involved
in the antimonopolism and the time span covered by their organizations,
there was a common core to their beliefs, goals, and political identities. It
is these groups and their program for financial reform that constitute the
antimonopoly tradition.

The movement

From the National Labor Union to the Populists, dozens of farmer and
labor organizations were involved in the financial debate between 1865
and 1896. Many of these organizations were the largest of their type in
the nation. Often they participated in independent or third-party politics.
Their programs addressed common concerns and proposed common solutions. Yet rarely have these groups been treated as a coherent whole.
Their geographical diversity has made historians reluctant to group them,
as has the presumption that farmers and laborers are politically and economically distinct social categories. Such a presumption belies the self-cat-
egorizations made by antimonopolists who saw themselves as producers
with common interests and outlooks. By retrieving the writings that reveal these expressions of social identity, the previous chapters have un-
covered the connections and coherence among the various antimonopolist groups.

The state studies demonstrate the persistence and consistency of antimonopolism across groups, geographical domains, and decades. In the
Midwest, Northeast, and South, certain themes persisted, certain issues
continued to provoke agitation. Massachusetts laborers discussed the
shift from worker autonomy to wage servitude in terms of the growth of
financial power. Illinois farmers and workers alike spoke about credit in-

equalities and economic hardships brought about by the banking structure. North Carolina farmers objected to the control of Northeastern financiers over the money supply and the corrosive influence of financial
stringency on agrarian autonomy. The farmers joined groups, fought in
elections, then returned to their original partisan loyalties, only to come
forth again years later in a renewed effort to alter the course of economic and political development. Although the antimonopolists rarely mobilized into an effective national political force, they expressed persistent
political dissatisfaction with the course of economic change. They also offered a programmatic political alternative.

Antimonopolism's appeal among many farmers, workers, and their
business and middle-class reform allies exceeded their success in the
polling booth. Chapters 2, 4, and 6 discussed the various ways in which
the party system, political culture, and political geographical alignments
precluded direct competition between the antimonopolist and financial
conservative programs. Yet, the appeal becomes apparent in a closer examination of politics in the three state cases studied here. From the writings, speeches, and records of participants in labor conventions and
farmer organizations, articles in reform newspapers, debates among pamphleteers, and letters to political leaders it is apparent that the political
appeal of the antimonopolist program was strong – stronger than the
third-party voting record indicates.

The program

The coherence of the antimonopolist alternative is apparent in their political and economic program. The term "coherence" here refers to the
systematic, integrated nature of the antimonopolist analysis and proposed
solutions. Chapters 3 and 5 reviewed the financial programs of the greenbackers and the Populists, and it is here that the current argument is
grounded. The specifics of the antimonopolists' financial proposals
demonstrate a well-developed understanding of the monetary and banking systems as well as carefully formulated plans for effectively restructuring those systems. The proposals had flaws – some antimonopolist
schemes were impractical, some were highly inflationary, and a few were
narrowly conceived. But when these proposals are compared with those
put forward by the antimonopolists' hard-money opponents, they stand
up well under historical scrutiny. Developmentally, the antimonopolist
program changed over time. There was a loss of analytical breadth between the 1870s and the 1890s. Political defeat was followed by a decline
in the intellectual legitimacy of greenbackism, which narrowed the financial debate in subsequent decades. But with these factors in mind, the out-

standing impression the platforms and pamphlets of the antimonopolists convey is of intelligently argued, plausible proposals for financial reform. A similar evaluation may be offered of the political aspects of the anti-monopolist programs. The philosophy and language of antimonopolism has a strongly indigenous American feel. The language resonates with the language of republicanism, albeit altered by the changing conditions of an industrializing society. The philosophy drew from the equal rights tradition of the Jeffersonians and Jacksonians, with its emphasis on democratic solutions to political problems. There are contradictions as well, particularly regarding state power and social diversity, contentious subjects for the antimonopolists. Expressions of nationalism, racism, and xenophobia plagued both the antimonopolists and their opponents. In the intersections between money, class, race, and sectionalism, both sides put forth distinct visions regarding the social and political ordering of American society. Although the antimonopolist creed had its weaknesses and contradictions, it was generally a dynamic programmatic vision for the American future.

Money and finance were at the center of the antimonopolists' political economy analysis. They drew from the tradition in republican thinking that accentuated the role of money and financiers. Fear of the corrupting influences of bondsmen and increased state fiscal capacities led many Jeffersonians to oppose the Hamiltonian plan. Jacksonians made opposition to the Second Bank of the United States the crux of their critique of economic and political concentration. This earlier language and analysis was transformed by the post-Civil War antimonopolists, who ceased to oppose the use of legal tender paper currency while retaining their criticism of banks and financial concentration.

The antimonopolists also responded to contemporary economic events such as the panics of 1873 and 1893. The rhythms of the national economy in the late nineteenth century were strongly tied to the rhythms of the financial system, which was given to regular cycles of expansion and collapse, and an overall pattern of monetary and price deflation. Through both the heritage of an earlier political economy discourse and the realities of current economic conditions, the antimonopolists were drawn to develop a broad analysis of political and economic organization in which finance played a central role.

During the 1870s, the greenbackers exhibited a detailed grasp of economic issues. Greenbackers criticized the National Banking System (NBS) for its regional maldistribution of wealth and credit opportunities, its bias in favor of commercial and against agricultural lending, its privatization of monetary functions, and for the rigidity of the pyramid reserve structure (PRS), which raised lending rates, depleted funds from outlying regions, encouraged railroad overexpansion, and increased the likelihood of system-wide banking crises. The financial antimonopolists also sought to prevent a return to a specie-based currency standard. They correctly argued that return to the gold standard would involve price deflation and reliance on an inflexible monetary base that grew and fell according to the whims of nature rather than the needs of an expanding economy. As remedies, they proposed abolishing the NBS and establishing an inter-convertible bond scheme for automatic adjustments of the currency volume. This analysis was situated within broader concerns about the social and political effects of economic concentration. The views of the hard-money advocates were sometimes less specific about the role and problems of the financial system in the wider economy and polity.

By the 1890s, financial conservatism was more developed. Both groups had their intellectual strengths and weaknesses, and in some instances antimonopolist views still stood out for their analytical power. Political defeats for the greenbackers and their labor reform descendants in the 1880s helped to fragment the movement and delegitimize the antimonopolist analysis in the public consciousness. Historically, financial knowledge narrowed rather than progressed because of the politics of the financial debate. Meanwhile, the silver movement provided a new basis for criticizing the gold standard and the nation's deficient monetary base. But this was ground won at an intellectual expense, for it meant a loss of emphasis on the need for a flexible monetary standard managed by democratic means. Nor was the analysis of credit and capital markets as robust as it had been. The Populists' view of futures markets was short on critical understanding and long on condemnation.

Yet, the imagination and seriousness of the Populists' organic intellectuals (for example, Harry Tracy, Harry Skinner, Charles Macune, Annie Diggs, and Henry Demarest Lloyd) should not be underestimated. The subtreasury plan was an innovative, ambitious attempt to solve the agricultural credit problem, stabilize the monetary system, and equalize currency and credit opportunities among classes and regions. The plan had defects, and would likely have led to rapid inflation, but it was a prescient idea in many ways. The interconvertible bond segment of the plan continued earlier greenback efforts to provide an automatic stabilizer for the monetary system, in which market signals served to expand or contract the money supply according to the rate of economic growth. Further, the plan sought to regulate the tie of the monetary system to the agricultural economy, thereby redistributing financial resources in a geographically balanced manner and halting the cyclical shortfalls of the banking system. Even the bimetallists (including many Populists) were capable thinkers whose proposals might have aided the United States in avoiding the depression induced by a gold shortage. The subtreasury advocates went furthest with proposals which would have relieved short-term economic hardship and changed the long-term direction of economic development.

Less consideration was given to the problems of banking, commodities, and securities trading. The Populists continued the antimonopolist critique of the NBS. As alternatives, financial reformers variously proposed revitalizing the state banks, establishing a postal savings bank system, and expanding the financial functions of the federal government. Like the subtreasury plan, a publicly run banking system and public control of the money supply would correct the biased nature of the commercial banking system of the 1890s, replacing it with a more geographically and class-neutral system. Although their concerns over abuse within the commodity futures market were legitimate, agrarians showed little intellectual depth in their proposal to ban futures trading altogether. Similarly, the full implications of the PRS and its effect on industrial investment were not well understood. Populists sensed that the shortage of money and rigidity of the banks was responsible for financial panics, and that Wall Street was contributing to economic concentration, but the mechanisms through which this occurred remained obscure. Their instincts proved valid, however, as later writings on the operation of the call loan market, capital markets, and industrial investment have shown.

While the views of the Populists may have been shallower than those of their antimonopolist forebearers on some issues, they were broader on others. Despite their concerns about political corruption, the Populists also had a more positive view of the state and state action. Populists called for a revitalization of democracy and an increase in regulatory authority over land, money, and transportation. Many endorsed public ownership of utilities, railroads, and municipal services. To counter the concentration of economic and political power, antimonopolist reformers called for a more vigilant, active polity, one capable of enforcing just regulations for all citizens. The Populists' views on economic and political development were linked, and their theories of democracy and the state reflected both inherited political traditions and creative reformulations in response to economic change.

Although there were flaws and inconsistencies, these did not overwhelm the main lines of argument put forth by the greenbackers and Populists in the financial debate. They provided both a solid analysis of the deficiencies of the contemporary monetary and banking systems, and reasonable remedies for those problems. While some elements of the economic analysis of the greenbackers had been lost by the time of the Populists, these latter antimonopolists were more broad-ranging in their political and economic views, taking up matters which the greenbackers had neglected. Whether these proposals were practical in the context of late nineteenth-century America is another matter. The point here is to revive our understanding of the intelligence and appeal of the antimonopolist alternative.

Failure

Why the antimonopolists failed matters a great deal for our understanding of their significance for American political development. They failed not because of the inherent limits in American political culture – neither because of liberal narrowness nor racist proscriptions. Nor was the political structure an impenetrable barrier to the antimonopolist challenge. Not even the forces of industrial development were alone responsible. Rather, failure was a multifaceted phenomenon that belies deterministic accounts about the superiority and inevitability of corporate industrialism, the forces of bureaucratic modernization, and the encompassing rigidity of the liberal tradition. Instead, there was an intersection of institutional structures, strategic choices, and the effects of historical contingency that accounts for antimonopolism's demise. This argument validates the antimonopolist alternative despite its failure, and makes our understanding of political development more complex and contingent than it would otherwise be.

The institutional structures that hindered the antimonopolists were both economic and political. The party system figures largely in Chapters 2, 4, and 6 as a major constraint on the third-party labor and agrarian movements of the 1870s-1890s. Economic issues were often neutralized by national party organizations seeking to hold together diverse constituencies, while cultural loyalty issues, such as those related to race and region, were highlighted in efforts to rally electoral support. The basic structure of the state (for example, the courts, the Congress, and federalism) also made attempts to organize effective national coalitions around financial reform more difficult. Within the political realm, the financial debate was often stalemated, although the crucial battles were won by hard-money and national banking advocates.[1]

National economic institutions changed the economic system antimonopolists hoped to affect as the financial debate proceeded. When gold payments were resumed in 1879, the greenbackers were left without the issue around which they had organized. For both the greenbackers and

---

1. Stephen Skowronek, *Building a New American State: The Expansion of National Administrative Capacities, 1877–1920* (Cambridge: Cambridge University Press, 1982), and Samuel Huntington, *Political Order in Changing Societies* (New Haven: Yale University Press, 1968), chap. 2.

the Populists, although the national financial system provided a target for criticism, it was also an engine for industrial investment. As corporate capitalist development proceeded, the possibilities for constructing an antimonopolist economy diminished. Economically, liberal orthodoxy dominated in finance and investment.

There were bad strategic choices made as well. The North Carolina Populists chose to enter into a coalition with the Republicans at the expense of expanding and maintaining links with Farmers' Alliance members locally. The Greenbackers chose to nominate elderly Peter Cooper in 1876 although he had neither the energy nor the appeal to run a serious national campaign. Endorsing William Jennings Bryan was another mistake. Bryan was supported by the free silver movement and the unreformed Southern Democrats. Supporting Bryan meant abandoning hopes of real economic and political restructuring. The antimonopolists, a group suffused by passion and desperation, were vulnerable to the pleas of political charlatans and the promise of false symbols, such as silver. These pursuers of the cooperative commonwealth were often distracted from their goals and divided among themselves. Consistent will and clarity might have carried them further.

Political geographical alignments contributed to the political context in which the antimonopolists competed. The preexisting alignments represented in the party system, capital markets, and political culture were unfavorable for the antimonopolists nationally. They fought sectional divisions based on the old Confederacy-Union conflict, and tried instead to construct either a nationwide producer versus nonproducer demarcation, or a coalition of the South and West against the Northeast. In the 1890s, both local antimonopolist groups and some of their opponents were displaced by new geographical alignments. In Illinois, antimonopolists reclaimed a Western identity when they entered the Greenback party and separated themselves from the North versus South alignment of the Democratic and Republican parties. This was to be the first step toward joining a national coalition of producers from all regions of the country. The Massachusetts orthodox liberals of the 1890s forfeited their local political standing as Democrats in an attempt to preserve the conservative character of the national party. They failed, and eventually moved toward the Republicans, as part of an emerging alignment of interests under William McKinley. As the challengers to the more institutionally and culturally embedded alignments, the antimonopolists had the more difficult task of constructing new notions of political identity across geographical realms.

Cultural constraints intersected with institutional structures in several areas. The use of racist and regional identity pleas strengthened the Southern Democratic party against the challenge of the Populists. Similarly, both the party structure and political culture of Northern Republicans during the 1870s helped them to combat disaffection among soft money advocates. Chapters of the Grand Army of the Republic often operated as adjuncts to the Grand Old Party. Veterans' pensions undergirded the connections between Republican party membership and Northern, Union identity. But neither institutional structures nor cultural meanings were entirely fixed, which left room for strategic choices in claiming or countering different cultural identities for groups and organizations. As the often vitriolic language of the political pamphleteers attests, much effort was expended on just such attempts.

Political culture was an element in the broader regime shifts of the 1890s. There was the shift from the Civil War party system to the System of 1896. Although Civil War identities continued to dominate party politics in the 1870s and 1880s, issues related to economic development were churning beneath the surface, ready to emerge when the old modes of party organization were sufficiently weakened. During the mid-1870s, such a break almost occurred with the greenback crisis. In the mid-1890s, it finally did occur, partly due to the expression of an alternative vision of economic and political life by the antimonopolists. Yet, when the lines of party allegiance were redrawn, the sought-after confrontation between the antimonopolists and financial conservatives was blurred by a political geography that preferred older sectional solidarities.

More broadly, there was the regime shift to a new organization of government. This involved changes in the organization of the state bureaucracy, expansion of regulatory structures, the development of new beliefs about the role of the state and its relation to the economy, and the growth of new modes of political participation. This emergence of political "modernity" has not been deeply discussed in this book. These changes came largely after the events referred to here, during the Progressive era. The shape of these changes reflected the legacy of antimonopolism, though the substance of these changes was not antimonopolist in nature.[2]

Finally, there was the shift to mass production and the corporate form

2. Skowronek, *Building a New American State.* See Leonard White, *The Republican Era: A Study in Administrative History* (NY: Macmillan, 1958), on the changes in administrative governance in the late nineteenth century. For the institutional legacy of antimonopolism down through the 1930s, see Ellis Hawley, *The New Deal and the Problem of Monopoly* (Princeton: Princeton University Press, 1966); and Alan Brinkley, "The New Deal and the Idea of the State," *The Rise and Fall of the New Deal Order,* Steve Fraser and Gary Gerstle, eds. (Princeton: Princeton University Press, 1984). The relationship between party politics and changing modes of governance is a complex issue, as Richard L. McCormick argues in *The Party Period and Public Policy: American Politics from the Age of Jackson to the Progressive Era* (NY: Oxford University Press, 1986), pp. 19–20, 83–85.

of enterprise. This shift created both the crisis and the opportunity for the antimonopolist challenge, and its success represents a defeat of the antimonopolist vision. This involved both the change from an agrarian to a manufacturing economy, and to a particular type of manufacturing economy based on economies of scale and mass production. Antimonopolist economists such as Henry Carey favored a different type of manufacturing economy – more regionally centered and skill-based, with smaller production batches that fit the needs of the area's community. In such a system, a regional banking network that pooled and recycled local financial resources would have played a key role. Over the course of the decades discussed here, the legal and institutional structures undergirding a mass-production economy grew thicker and less mutable, making the advent of antimonopolism ever more difficult and less likely.

The regime crisis of the 1890s was a crisis of party, a crisis of state, and a crisis of the economy. None of these crises were entirely contained in the decade of the 1890s, nor was their resolution contained within this time span. The emergence of the new corporate, mass-production economy was long in the making, although the events of the 1890s further established this new economic regime. The change in the party system was the shift most closely contained within the decade. Even here, however, it was years before the outlines of the new system (one-party sectional rule, low voter participation, and national Republican dominance) were clearly apparent. The crisis of the state still lay largely ahead. Progressive-era state builders benefitted from the political space created by voter apathy in the wake of the election of 1896. But at all three levels, the period between 1865 and 1896 was a time of opportunity and choice which culminating in the decisive confrontations of the 1890s. By the end of the century, the path toward financial conservatism and corporate concentration was firmly chosen.

The effects of history on this reordering involved both chance and memory. By chance, the Populists gained momentum *after* the labor movement was broken and disorganized by the events of 1886–1894. A change in timing might have changed the coalitional possibilities. It was happenstance that led to new discoveries of gold *after* the election of 1896, ending the international monetary depression and legitimizing the Republican administration of William McKinley. The role of prior events on the 1890s depended on the memories offered of past occurrences. For the financial conservatives, greenbackism was a previous episode of irrational monetary politics in which the fiat currency heresy was defeated. For the antimonopolists, the Crime of '73 was an example of the money power's self-interested manipulations of the public good. The terms on which contemporary debates were argued depended on the participants' narrations of past histories. To imagine changes in the link of historical events may seem extreme, for it suggests that the significance of historical events depend on their temporal contexts. That is precisely the argument here – that temporal order and historical narration matter for political outcomes. Finally, current constructions of the greenbackers and the Populists as economic simpletons or agrarian reactionaries swimming against the stream of progress demonstrates the long-term nature of historical imagination in political development.

To understand the failure of the antimonopolists means to understand the time and place in which they fought. To say that many elements – structural and strategic, geographical, and temporal – contributed to the failure of the antimonopolists is not to say that their failure was overdetermined, but to suggest that their fate was contingent and contextual. The rise of financial conservativism was not a case of natural outcomes or historical destiny. The reality was murkier and more fluid. Just as there was no one great causal force determining this outcome, there was also no single missed opportunity for the antimonopolists, although the mid-1890s come the closest to such a critical moment. The battle between the antimonopolists and the financial conservatives was broadly based, occupying several different arenas of social life. The regime shift that settled this struggle came gradually (with fits and starts) and differentially to the various sectors of American society.

Political failure and historical contingency

We have considered the antimonopolist program and the reasons for its failure, but the question remains: what is the historical significance of the antimonopolist alternative? Given the distribution of power and resources in the United States, was antimonopolism merely the dream of a few idealists, or was it sufficiently popular and feasible to affect our understanding of American political development? Discussions of untried alternatives are necessarily speculative and imprecise. This exercise is not intended to constitute a Weberian counterfactual, since such an approach presumes a more linear and holistic view of history than the one that is offered here. In counterfactual reasoning, an ideal type of social system is constructed, then the facts of social reality are altered to show that such a system could emerge and function. Yet I would argue that no system of social organization is fully coherent or hegemonic – there is always the presence of less fully realized alternatives. Further, the intellectual exercise of setting an alternative system in motion and then watching to see how it runs underestimates the ability of actors and institutions to make adjustments over time. Thus, this exercise is intended to deepen our understanding of antimonopolism's failure rather than to argue for its potential success.[3]

The greenbackers and the Populists were part of a long line of farmer and labor movements with an antimonopolist agenda. During the three decades covered in this book, a consistent set of planks and philosophical tenets dominated the platforms and statements of the major agrarian and labor reform groups. The financial issue was stressed by the National Labor Union, the Labor Reform party, the Readjusters, the Greenback and Greenback Labor parties, the Grangers, the Agricultural Wheel, the Knights of Saint Crispin, the Union Labor party, the Antimonopolist party, the Knights of Labor (KOL), the National Farmers' Alliance, and the People's party, among others. The consistency of this effort justifies the characterization of antimonopolism as a tradition, and requires that this tradition be seriously considered in accounts of American politics. What is more, pamphlet sales (such as those for *Coin's Financial School*), newspaper coverage, and political campaigns indicate that antimonopoly sentiments were prevalent in many parts of the country – more prevalent than third-party vote tallies suggest. At the level of popular political sentiment, antimonopolism had substantial appeal.[4]

But the electoral system in which they competed was not a neutral arena permitting such straightforward choices between political alternatives. Rather, the party system distorted and constrained the expression of alternatives in ways that were highly unfavorable to the antimonopolists. This was an important barrier to antimonopoly political success that could not have easily been overcome. Yet two considerations should temper our estimation of this barrier. First, it is apparent that antimonopoly supporters were politically active on financial issues within the two major parties. So the electoral potential of antimonopolism was not confined to its success in various third parties. Second, as the 1890s demonstrated, the party system was not an immutable structure. As the scramble of alignments, potential alignments, and conventioneering from that period makes clear, the partisan structure that emerged in the mid-1890s was not the only possible realignment that could have occurred. Better strategic

---

3. Max Weber, *The Methodology of the Social Sciences* (New York: Free Press, 1949), pp. 164–88.
4. Pamphlet sales alone do not indicate that there was popular support for antimonopolism. Pamphlet purchasers may have been curious or concerned rather than favorable toward the views expressed there. But both silverites and gold advocates believed that works like *Coin's Financial School* were generating broad prosilver enthusiasm. See, for instance, James Barnes, *John G. Carlisle: Financial Statesman* (NY: Dodd, Mead & Co., 1931), p. 438; and Richard Hofstadter's introduction to William H. Harvey, *Coin's Financial School* (Cambridge, MA: Belknap Press, 1963), pp. 5–8.

choices might have helped to mold a party system in which the political choices between antimonopolism and financial conservativism were more clearly pitted.

The antimonopolists never had the opportunity to implement financial policies at the national level. The legislative contest over financial policy in the late nineteenth century was generally stalemated, though somewhat favorable to the financial conservatives. Despite repeated public assaults and admitted deficiencies, the NBS remained intact. Supporters feared that the NBS would be replaced by a system of financial chaos such as the one that existed before the Civil War. In the area of monetary policy, the national government swung back and forth over the 1870s, 1880s, and 1890s, vacillating between a firm commitment to the gold standard and a willingness to subsidize silver and allow for the circulation of greenbacks. However, the overall tenor of federal policy favored protection of the gold standard, a commitment that was formalized with passage of the Gold Standard Act of 1900. Not until the 1930s would the nation return to a legal tender paper currency system. The stalemate in financial policy suggests that there was some room for the construction of financial alternatives.

Other laws passed at the state and national level suggest the possibility for the regulatory alternatives as well. The Granger laws of the 1870s and the Interstate Commerce Act of the 1880s were intended to alter the market framework – shifting development away from economic concentration and geographic centralization. Even the Federal Reserve Act of the 1910s indicated the continued presence of antimonopolism in the design of regulatory statutes. Yet none of these legislative acts resulted in effective antimonopolist regulation. Their failure is attributable to the role of hostile federal courts, subversions by financial conservative administrators, and the passage of time during which the institutions and ideals of corporate liberalism became increasingly entrenched.[5]

There are several historical examples of alternative systems of financial regulation and industrial production One comes from Denmark, where the cooperative banking system supported cooperative production in agri-

5. The Federal Reserve System (FRS) was not truly an antimonopolist institution, even in design. But the continued importance of antimonopolist language and symbols did contribute to aspects of the FRS. Victoria Hattam argues for the important role of the courts in undermining the labor reform tradition in "Economic Visions and Political Strategies: American Labor and the State, 1865–1896," *Studies in American Political Development,* 4 (1990): 82–129. Gerald Berk has discussed the failure of the ICC and its effect on attempts to construct regionally integrated railroad networks. Gerald Berk, "Constituting Corporations and Markets: Railroads in Gilded Age Politics," *Studies in American Political Development,* 4 (1990): 130–168.

culture and industry. In the United States, the early nineteenth-century New England banking system and the late nineteenth-century Pacific regional banking system are both suggestive examples of the viability and consequences of regional bank networks. There are examples of regional production networks in other sectors as well, such as Philadelphia textiles and Midwestern railroads. However, most bankers and creditors in the late nineteenth century were tied to a centralized NBS that skewed economic development against regionalism and a mixed economy. Unable to secure adequate financial resources, many producers' cooperatives started by labor and agrarian groups in the nineteenth century failed. In these instances, the move toward a regionally integrated, relatively self-sufficient economy did not prove lasting. But these historical alternatives underscore the importance of financial structures to different modes of production.[6]

Were we to take a counterfactual approach but allow for political agency, then our ability to judge the historical potential of antimonopolism would weaken. With the implementation of the subtreasury plan, there might have been a greater equality of financial resources among regions and less threat of financial panics, since the monetary system would respond more readily to demand. Yet there might also have been substantial inflation. How would actors and institutions respond? Different responses were possible (a capital strike, an institutional adjustment that would lessen inflation, an attempt to further manage the money supply through creation of something like a Federal Reserve System [FRS], and so on) and we cannot know which would be taken. Thus, the potential success or failure of antimonopolism cannot be judged merely by its proposals. Our judgment about the significance of an alternative should be based instead on a nuanced reading of history. The use of comparative cases such as Denmark does not show that the antimonopolism could have succeeded here, but suggests that the antimonopolists were not foolish, irrational, or antimodern and thereby doomed to failure.

Antimonopolism was an imaginable but unlikely alternative in the late nineteenth century. Its proponents had a well-conceived program with broad political appeal. They faced substantial electoral barriers, although the structure of the party system was clearly mutable. The antimonopo-

6. Philip Scranton, *Proprietary Capitalism: The Textile Manufacture at Philadelphia, 1880–1885* (Cambridge: Cambridge University Press, 1983); and Kerry A. Odell, "The Integration of Regional and Interregional Capital Markets: Evidence from the Pacific Coast, 1883–1913," *Journal of Economic History,* 49 (1989): 297–310. Pennsylvania was the state of Henry Carey, who called for a regionally integrated economy, and was a prominent center of business-based greenbackism in the 1870s. The work on the San Francisco financial network is discussed in Chapter 6.

lists were excluded from policymaking, but room for securing regulatory alternatives was evidently present. Further, historical examples from the United States and elsewhere suggest the viability of alternative modes of production. In the United States, antimonopolism was the path that was not chosen. It grew out of American republicanism, was applicable within the nation's political institutions, and was consistent with the vibrant agrarian-industrial economy of the 1870s and 1880s. But it was an option that was never tried.

By escaping the confines of counterfactual reasoning, we move beyond the stark alternatives of inevitability or fully realizable alternative paths. Instead of arguing that antimonopolism could have been a historical success, this book calls for a reevaluation of how antimonopolism failed and what it meant. Such an approach should affect our thinking about the system that "won," the alternative that lost, and how history affects political development. This, then, is the crux of the argument – that historical development is contingent and layered. It is an argument for going beyond a historical imagination that sees only coherence, dominance, linearity, and inevitability. Indeed, the success of corporate capitalism and liberal pluralism in the twentieth century helped shape the modernist historical imagination that I have questioned.[7]

II. Banking and economic development in Denmark

The inheritors of the antimonopolist tradition in the early twentieth century still hoped to reform the financial system. By then, the potential consequences for economic development were differently arranged. Many Progressive-Era reformers looked to Denmark as their model, and advocated the development of small banks to meet the needs of farmers and small savers. Denmark had gone through an agricultural crisis associated with increased international competition and the onset of industrialization. The Danes responded by forming cooperative dairies, wholesale stores, bacon and fertilizer factories, and poultry packing stations. These cooperatives led to a successful shift from grain production to high-quality animal goods such as ham, bacon, and butter. Similarly, Denmark's industrial sector, which grew gradually over the late nineteenth and early twentieth centuries, emphasized skilled labor, market niche strategies, craft production, and extensive subcontracting. In both industry and agriculture, Denmark built a flexible, internationally oriented economy. The

---

7. I am grateful to the participants of a conference held at the University of Texas at Austin in April 1994 on "The Nation in Time: Crisis and Continuity in American Politics." That conference greatly helped me in my thinking about the role of history in political change.

financial sector developed in synchronization with this mixed agrarian-industrial economy.[8]

Three components of the Danish financial industry are of interest here. The first is the savings banks, begun in the early nineteenth century as a means of protecting and securing savings for workers and small-holders. The second is the cooperative commercial banks, particularly the great Andelsbanken. Finally, there are the mortgage credit associations, which market bonds to supply credit to farmers and homeowners. All three of these types of financial enterprises expanded during the late nineteenth century, when the transition to a mixed industrial-agrarian economy was taking place.

Until the early twentieth century, Denmark's savings bank industry was more significant than its commercial banking sector. Savings banks provided small traders, workers, and farmers with long-term loans. Although savings institutions specialized in meeting local needs, cooperation developed among savings banks and between savings and commercial banks. Sharing services and information, these banks benefitted from the financial networks formed in the early twentieth century. In contrast to the United States, Danish savings banks met the credit needs of local agrarian communities and assisted them in responding to the agricultural crisis of the 1870s and 1880s through specialization and increased export of animal products.[9]

From the first cooperative dairy established in West Jutland in 1882, the agricultural cooperative movement expanded until there were some 1000 dairy cooperatives in 1900. With the early appearance of cooperative purchasing societies (modeled after the English Rochdale plan), savings banks, and the Folk High Schools, Danish cultural life and institutional structures were well prepared for this large-scale experiment in cooperative production. The cooperatives allowed Danish farmers to standardize and guarantee the quality of the specialty goods, thus facilitating the nation's export strategy. As the cooperatives grew, their financial needs were supplied by the Danish Cooperative Bank (Andelsbanken), created in 1909. The Andelsbanken, which now deals mostly in

8. On Danish economic development generally, see Hans Christian Johansen, *The Danish Economy in the Twentieth Century* (London: Croom Helm, 1987); Peter J. Katzenstein, *Small States in World Markets: Industrial Policy in Europe* (Ithaca: Cornell University Press, 1985); Mogens Korst, *Industrial Life in Denmark: A Survey of Economic Development and Production* (Copenhagen: Det Danske Selskab, 1975); Anders Ølgaard, *The Danish Economy* (Brussels: Commission of the European Communities, 1980); and Royal Danish Ministry of Foreign Affairs, *Denmark* (Copenhagen: Royal Danish Ministry of Foreign Affairs, 1956).

9. On the history of the savings banks, see Korst, *Industrial Life*, pp. 159–162; and Royal Danish Ministry, *Denmark*, pp. 201–203.

foreign exchange and other export matters, made possible the continued operation of small, independent producers who are federated through the cooperative associations. This was similar to what American antimonopolists had sought – an institution that improves the supply and cost of credit to small producers by pooling risk and resources.[10]

Denmark's mortgage credit associations provide credit to property owners and establish new investment opportunities for the nation's capital markets. The associations are organizations of borrowers. Each borrower is issued bonds based on the assessed value of his or her property. The bonds are marketed on the Stock Exchange, where they have historically been considered secure and reliable because of the joint liability that covers their issuance. Instead of funding railroad and industrial securities (as with the funds pooled through the PRS of the NBS), Danish investors turned to fixed-rate mortgage association bonds. Early funds for industrial investment were raised through mortgage credit bonds. Building, plant, and housing construction expanded gradually with the growing national economy. Unlike the United States, where the connection between commercial banks and the capital market facilitated the merger movement, in Denmark the relationship between the mortgage credit associations and the expanding capital market encouraged the development of a heterogeneous agrarian-industrial economy.[11]

Denmark is not the only place where alternative financial structures were considered or attempted. Indeed, it appears that the Danes borrowed from the Germans, among others, in constructing their financial institutions. Yet the conditions under which the Danish system developed were particular. As Peter Katzenstein argues in his work on the small European social democracies, the position of these small national economies within the international system encouraged cooperation among social groups

10. The parallel I am drawing here, while fairly loose, is based on the idea that small producer networks are often organized with large infrastructural or other type organizational center points. Thus, in the alternative regional railway networks that Berk discusses, there was to be shared access to trunk lines between major cities. Or in the various European and American examples of craft-based manufacturing economies which Sabel and Zeitlin review, there are large corporations, family networks, or municipal service institutions that serve as center points for looser confederations of flexible producers. See Gerald Berk, "Constituting Corporations," 130–168; Charles Sabel and Jonathan Zeitlin, "Historical Alternatives to Mass Production: Politics, Markets and Technology in Nineteenth Century Industrialization," *Past & Present*, number 108 (August 1985): 176. On the Andelsbanken, see Korst, *Industrial Life*, p. 102.

11. Johansen, *Danish Economy*, pp. 4–5; Korst, *Industrial Life*, pp. 147–148, 162–164; and Royal Danish Ministry, *Denmark*, pp. 205. There is an obvious parallel between the mortgage credit associations and the Populists' subtreasury plan, which would also have generated capital and credit for the economy on the basis of land.

seeking flexible national responses to the changing global economy. The history and circumstances of American economic development were quite different. Yet, Denmark provides a valuable example of how alternatively arranged financial institutions supported the development of a successful mixed agricultural-industrial economy with many small and medium-sized producers.[12]

III. The legacy of antimonopolism

The exercise of discretionary control over the money supply was urged by some interests in the last quarter of the [nineteenth] century as a counter to the redistributive effects of deflation. These interests were, in fact, soundly defeated. Paradoxically, discretion in money matters was firmly entrenched about a quarter century later – to serve the interests of the victors in the earlier battle.[13]

There are two puzzles about the establishment of the Federal Reserve System in the 1910s. The first (ironic) puzzle is raised by John T. Woolley. Why did the financial conservatives, after politically defeating the financial reformers, then proceed to implement aspects of the antimonopolist program? The second puzzle is partly resolved by the answer to the first. It concerns the ongoing debate over who benefitted from the establishment of the FRS. Some scholars, including John Woolley and James Livingston, contend that the financial conservatives and large banking interests were victorious. Others, such as Elizabeth Sanders, argue that the Populists and their Southern and Western allies had the last word. These puzzles are resolved by remembering the politics of antimonopolism and the earlier battles over the financial system.[14]

12. Katzenstein, *Small States*. The suggestion about borrowing from the Germans is made in Korst, *Industrial Life*, p. 19.
13. John T. Woolley, *Monetary Politics: The Federal Reserve and the Politics of Monetary Policy* (Cambridge: Cambridge University Press, 1984), pp. 31–32.
14. The literature on the Federal Reserve System is broad and diverse, and my reading of it is quite selective. I am interested only in the political accounts of the system, and how these might be enriched by looking at the history of nineteenth-century antimonopolism. Such accounts include Woolley, *Monetary Politics;* Robert H. Wiebe, *Businessmen and Reform* (Elephant Paperbacks, 1989); Gabriel Kolko, *The Triumph of Conservatism* (NY: Free Press, 1963); Richard H. Timberlake, Jr., *The Origins of Central Banking in the United States* (Cambridge, MA: Harvard University Press, 1978); Milton Friedman and Anna Jacobsen Schwartz, *A Monetary History of the United States, 1867–1960* (Princeton: Princeton University Press, 1963); James Livingston, *The Origins of the Federal Reserve System: Money, Class, and Corporate Capitalism, 1890–1913* (Ithaca: Cornell University Press, 1986); Elizabeth Sanders, "Farmers and the State in the Progressive Era" (1989); and Robert Craig West, *Banking Reform and the Federal Reserve, 1863–1923* (Ithaca: Cornell University Press, 1977).

In the wake of the financial panic of 1893, bankers and their allies recognized the need for reforming the banking system. However, the issue was not pursued in the 1890s for several reasons. Preserving the gold standard and defeating William Jennings Bryan took priority over mending the banking system. Financial conservatives also feared provoking fresh attacks against the Wall Street "Money Power." Finally, there was concern that the antimonopolists, though defeated, were not yet banished from the political field. Discussions of banking reform might provide the Populists and their allies with an opportunity to redraw the reform package in the interests of country agrarians and laborites. Although there were initial forays into banking reform with the Baltimore Plan and the report of the Indianapolis Monetary Commission, the issue languished until the next financial crisis.[15]

That crisis came with the financial panic of 1907. By then, the nation had lived for a decade under Republican rule. William Jennings Bryan was preparing for his third unsuccessful run for the presidency in 1908, reflecting the disorganized and delegitimized status of the national Democratic party. Electoral participation was dropping to its post-Civil War low, to an average of 51.7 percent in presidential years and 35.2 percent in off-election years in the 1920s. This broad-based de facto (and, in the South, de jure) disenfranchisement meant that the challengers of the previous era were largely gone. Their goals and perspectives on how the economy should be organized were gone with them. Those left to fight over banking reform were the financiers and businessmen themselves, who split into various factions over currency standards, branch banking, and centralization. The factions agreed, however, on the need for improved elasticity and currency distribution, and on the desirability of banker rather than political control.[16]

There were three major groups of bankers weighing in on the reform proposals of the early twentieth century. The first group included large New York bankers, who were recognized as the center of power within the financial community. They were initially reluctant to consider any reform proposals, but then advocated a central bank with asset-based currency under the control of the banking community. The second group consisted of city bankers from other large financial areas such as Chicago. They were early advocates of reform, more open to a regional organization (also under the control of bankers), and interested in a broadly based form of asset currency. Finally, there were the country bankers from the West and

15. On this early history, see West, *Banking Reform*, and Timberlake, *Origins*, chap. 12.
16. The electoral statistics come from Walter Dean Burnham, "The Changing Shape of the American Political Universe," in *The Current Crisis in American Politics* (Oxford: Oxford University Press, 1982), p. 29.

the South. They feared dominance by the large city bankers as much as they did dominance by the government. These bankers opposed branch banking, favored regional organization, and believed that any asset-based currency must include short and long-term agricultural paper. Some members of this group thought that no reform was better than reforms that would increase the power of the Wall Street financial community.[17]

None of these factions advocated antimonopolist policies. The country bankers, while adept at using the language of antimonopolism to speak out against Wall Street, sought to protect their own local monopoly position, which allowed them to raise local interest rates while profiting from correspondent accounts held in large city bank vaults. Their funds were not recycled to the local communities, but were sent through the PRS to New York, where they funded the stock speculation that accompanied the merger movement. Yet the use of antimonopolist language was important. For while a real antimonopolist alternative was not to be found among the options being considered, residues of antimonopolist sentiment were used to shape this policy conflict. As a result, branch banking was prevented, and the central banking system created by the Federal Reserve Act was given the semblance of regionalism.[18]

Here lies the irony and complexity of banking reform in the 1910s. Financial and business leaders arrived at a consensus on the need for reform. It was a consensus delayed by the politics of finance in the late nineteenth century, and which involved many of the same proposals (federal regulation of the currency supply, regionalism, and greater flexibility in managing the currency volume) made by the antimonopolists years earlier. The terrain on which reform proposals were fought over in the 1910s was different from the political terrain of the 1890s. There was no organized antimonopolist opposition. The Populists and their allies were disenfranchised, alienated, and scattered. The possibility of a state regulatory program again became permissible among financial conservatives, who no longer feared that such a system would be run in the interest of their old adversaries. Changes in the national economy, with the growth of large corporations and the concentration of production and wealth in the Northeast and Middle West, made the antimonopolist vision anachronistic. Therefore, implementing elements of the antimonopolist program in financial reform no longer served antimonopolist ends. Currency elastic-

17. This division of bankers into various groups can be found in Woolley, *Monetary Politics*, p. 38; Kolko, *The Triumph of Conservatism: A Reinterpretation of American History* (Glencoe, IL, 1963), p. 149; and Wiebe, *Businessmen and Reform*, pp. 62–63.

18. For the importance of the antimonopolist language see Wiebe, *Businessmen and Reform*, pp. 63–64.

ity and improved distribution of credit served to stabilize a national corporate economy in which capital markets were already centralized.

Yet it may be argued that the Progressive surge of 1912, which brought the Democrats back into power, changed the politics of financial reform back toward an agrarian, if not antimonopolist, direction. Much has been made of the resistance offered by New York banking leaders to the Glass-Owen bill, and of President Woodrow Wilson's successful effort to ensure government control over the Federal Reserve Board. But it is important to place these events in the context of antimonopolism's legacy. There were few committed antimonopolists within the Wilson coalition. While expressions of antimonopolism were present among the Debsian socialists, the Brandeisian Democrats, and the La Follette wing of the Republican progressives, these groups did not coalesce or form a movement. Antimonopolism had ceased to be a national movement, and there was no organized alternative to financial conservatism in the debates over the Federal Reserve System.[19]

But there was another element of the antimonopolist legacy that remained important. This was the element in political culture that made superficial appeals to antimonopolism politically vibrant, whether they were made by the Democratic presidential candidate, the Pujo committee investigating investment banking in New York, or Southern and Western country bankers interested in protecting their local monopoly standing. Antimonopolism's absence as a political movement and its presence as a political language contributed to the ironies of financial reform during the Progressive Era.

Consequently, the historical accounts of the FRS remain contradictory. In the contest that preceded passage of the Federal Reserve Act, antimonopolism appears to have made a comeback and won control over the design of the new banking system. Further, the party that passed and implemented the Act was the Democratic party – the party of William Jennings Bryan and the financial reform movement of the 1890s. This Democratic party represented the South and some of the West, areas long known to be resistant to the domination of Northeastern financial interests. Yet, in the longer history of the movement toward banking reform, the large financiers emerge as the winners. As this book shows, they won

---

19. For more information on the antimonopolist legacy in the 1910s, see Gretchen Ritter, "Visions of a New Social Order: The Election of 1912" (unpublished, 1987), paper in possession of the author. Also see the first two chapters of Hawley, *The New Deal and the Problems of Monopoly*. For a contrasting interpretation, see Martin Sklar, *The Corporate Reconstruction of American Capitalism, 1890–1916* (Cambridge: Cambridge University Press, 1988).

before the battle over the Federal Reserve System took place. Financial conservatism won in a series of conflicts with the antimonopolists in the latter half of the nineteenth century.[20]

Echoes of antimonopolism appear not just in the history of the Federal Reserve System or in the overall decentralized structure of American banking, but also in the failure of the National Recovery Administration in the 1930s. Ellis Hawley writes that antimonopolism was invoked by the opponents of the NRA to legitimize their opposition to government-sponsored business cartels. The generation of regulated competition advocates that was powerful during the Wilson years still had a place within the Washington establishment when Roosevelt came to power. Although antimonopolism had ceased to have sufficient strength to positively affect federal economic regulation, it may have helped to undermine support for a more corporatist approach, leaving the NRA politically vulnerable. Similarly, Alan Brinkley suggests that the Justice Department in the late 1930s used antimonopolist language to justify its proconsumer policies. These echoes may appear to be faint, but they had a significant impact on the range of regulatory paradigms available to political actors in the early twentieth century.[21]

History and political change

This account of antimonopolism offers a lesson about the role of history in political change. The revival of the antimonopolist tradition demonstrates that there was a politically significant and economically reasonable alternative to the development of financial conservatism. Although the antimonopolists lost, the reason and way that they lost matters. Their loss was not destined or natural. It was not dictated by the anonymous forces of historical progress and economic modernity, as the modern, but differently structured, political economy of Denmark suggests. Rather, political choice, structural constraints, and historical contingency shaped the fate of the antimonopolists. This is not so much the story of what "might have been" had the Populists taken power, although the merits of

20. Recent expressions of this conflict over interpreting the FRS include Livingston, *Origins*, and Sanders, "Farmers and the State." By arguing that the prior defeat of antimonopolism was important, I am not saying that there was a capitalist conspiracy over the design of the FRS. My view differs from the latter position in two respects. First, both the antimonopolists and the financial conservatives were capitalists, though they advocated different forms of capitalism. Second, I argue that the political possibilities for economic regulation were narrowed by changes in the economy and the polity. Therefore, the question is not one of individual personalities, but of structural differences.

21. Hawley, *New Deal*, part I; and Brinkley, "New Deal."

their program are worth remembering. Rather, it is an account that seeks to overturn the historical narrative of what "must have been" – that the nation was on a singular track that brought it to this moment, despite the distractions of disgruntled farmers and rebellious workers. By realizing the complexity and weight of historical pasts, the lack of historical closure, and the importance of historical imagination, we reassert the role of choice and politics in lives past and present.

Appendix A

Financial terms used between the Civil War and 1896

Absolute money – Money that is said to have intrinsic worth – that is, specie-based currency.

Bimetallist – Advocate of a monetary system based on both a silver and gold standard.

Blackbacks – A popular term used for national bank notes, a form of currency issued by banks belonging to the National Banking System. Unlike the greenbacks, they were printed with black ink.

Crime of '73 – In a long monetary bill in 1873, the silver dollar was demonetized. During the 1880s and 1890s, many monetary reformers claimed that this legal change had been made at the behest of gold conspirators, including top government officials and British financial interests.

Fiat money – Term used by the critics of greenbacks to mean government currency that had no economic worth, but was regarded as money only because it was declared so by government fiat.

Free banking – 1. Banking system in which banks could be organized by general incorporation principles, with no limit as to the number of banks in the system or for the amount of notes issued for the system as a whole. 2. Some financial reformers used the term to signify banking done at cost for the mutual benefit of its members.

Free money – Money at cost – that is, money on which no interest is charged.

Free silver – Policy under which all silver bullion offered to the Treasury would be purchased and coined into dollars.

Goldbugs – Derisive term used for the supporters of the gold standard, particularly in the 1890s.

Greenbacks – Government currency issued under the Legal Tender Acts of the 1860s. Until 1879, the value of this currency was based on government authorization only. After that date, greenbacks were tied to the gold standard. The name refers to the green ink they were printed with.

Gresham's law – Principle that bad (or cheap) money will drive out good (or dear) money. Gold advocates invoked Gresham's law to support the view that gold would disappear under bimetallism.

Growing up to specie – Strategy employed in the 1870s for bringing greenbacks to par with gold coin in order to return to the gold standard. It involved freezing the amount of greenback currency in circulation, so that as the economy grew, the value of each greenback dollar would appreciate.

Honest money – Term used by financial conservatives for currency based on specie.

Interconvertible bond – Greenback proposal for automatically adjusting the currency volume through the use of 3.65 percent bonds that could be converted into or purchased by legal tender currency on demand.

Legal tender – Currency made payable for public and/or private debts by an act of law. Often used to refer to paper currency – in particular, greenbacks.

Money power, or money monopoly – Supposed financial elite in control of the banking and monetary system. Often considered synonymous with Wall Street.

Monometallism – Monetary system based on a single specie standard, usually gold.

National Banking System (NBS) – Created in 1863 by the National Bank Act for the purposes of establishing a uniform national currency and a market for federal bonds. National banks are private banks chartered under the requirements of this act.

Panic – Financial collapse created by a sudden increase in demand for currency and credit, thereby depleting the reserves of the banking system and causing the bankruptcy of some banks.

Pendleton Plan – Early set of greenback proposals that criticized the NBS and currency contraction and proposed more extensive use of greenbacks in place of national bank notes. It was developed by Ohio Democrat George Pendleton under the guidance of financial reformers Washington McLean and Hugh Jewett in 1868. It became part of the Democratic national platform that year. Also known as the Ohio Idea.

Pyramid Reserve Structure (PRS) – System by which the smaller banks keep a portion of their reserves in larger city banks, which in turn place a portion of their reserves in New York banks. The larger banks pay interest on the deposits of the smaller banks. This system, which was codified by the NBS, centralized financial resources in New York City and made the banking system vulnerable to panics.

Rag baby – Term used by critics to refer to greenback currency.

Redemption – Under a gold standard, paper currency may be legally exchanged or "redeemed" for gold coin, on demand of the holder.

Repudiation – Refers to the refusal to meet debt obligations. This term was used as an accusation against the greenbackers, that their refusal to return to a gold standard and make greenbacks redeemable in coin amounted to repudiation.

Resumption – Refers to the return to the gold standard in 1879.

Sixteen to one – Standard of exchange (by bullion weight) between silver and gold proposed by most bimetallists. During the mid-1890s, the market price of silver and gold bullion was thirty-two to one, prompting many gold standard advocates to claim that silver proponents were calling for a "50 cents dollar."

Sound currency – Used by the hard-money advocates to refer to metallically based currency. Also used occasionally by greenbackers to refer to legal tender paper currency.

Subtreasury plan – Populists' plan for saving the banking system, inflating the currency, ending the agricultural credit shortage, and making the monetary supply more flexible.

Suspension – Departure from the gold standard. National bank notes and greenbacks were operating under suspension from the early 1860s until 1879, so they were not customarily redeemable in gold coin during this period.

Appendix B

Major banking and currency legislation, 1860–1900

1862–63   **Legal Tender Acts**
Authorized the issuance of legal tender bills, or greenbacks, to help fund the Civil War for the Union.

1863   **National Bank Act**
Created the National Banking System (NBS) whereby banks meeting the specified requirements were chartered by the federal government, and provided for the issuance of national bank notes against the security of federal bonds held at the U.S. Treasury.

1870   **Act to Authorize Additional Bank Notes**
Raised the note issuance limit for the NBS by $54 million in an attempt to correct the maldistribution of notes between the various sections of the country.

1873   **Coinage Act of 1873 ("Crime of '73")**
Demonetized the silver dollar.

1874   **Inflation Bill Veto**
President Grant vetoed a bill that would have increased the currency in circulation.

1875   **Resumption Act**
Committed the nation to resume specie payments for legal tender notes as of January 1, 1879. Also lifted the note issuance ceiling on national bank notes, and provided for the retirement of legal tender notes down to $300 million in circulation.

Source: Herman E. Krooss, ed., *Documentary History of Banking and Currency in the United States,* vols. 2 & 3 (New York: Chelsea House Publishers, 1983).

1878   **Bland-Allison Act**
Provided for the purchase and coinage of silver bullion at a
rate of $2–4 million per month.

1890   **Sherman Silver Purchase Act**
Replaced the Bland-Allison Act and provided for the month-
ly purchase of 4.5 million ounces of silver.

1893   **Repeal of Sherman Silver Purchase Act**
With the depletion of the Treasury's gold reserve, President
Cleveland called for and obtained the repeal of this act.

1900   **Gold Standard Act**
Formalized the nation's commitment to a monetary standard
based on gold.

Appendix C

An antimonopolist reading of L. Frank Baum's The Wonderful Wizard of Oz

Dorothy – An all-American girl from the heartland, Kansas.

Toto – Her faithful dog.

The Tin Woodman – Under a spell by the Wicked Witch of the East (Eastern capitalism), this worker is turned from a man into a heartless machine.

The Scarecrow – A farmer who has lost faith in his own common sense.

The Cowardly Lion – Commonly identified as William Jennings Bryan: someone meant to be a leader who lacks sufficient courage and gets by with his loud roars (or oratory).

The Wicked Witch of the West – The land of the West appears to be a desert, and perhaps a mining region (there are goldsmiths – Baum lived for a time in South Dakota). This witch may be an evil mine owner, who rules through her gold cap.

The Wicked Witch of the East – Eastern capitalism. She ruled over the good people of the East, Munchkins, who were dressed in blue (the color of the Union).

The Wizard of Oz – Evidently the President. Stays invisible in his palace and rules through fear and illusion. Started in the West, indeed in Omaha, Nebraska, which may also suggest an association with Bryan.

The Emerald City – Washington, DC, where the people are less than friendly, the world is colored green (for money), and is at the center of the kingdom. All the people wear green glasses held on by gold bands (the rule of money is held together by the power of gold).

The Winkies – Yellow people, from the West, a yellow land. They are presented as docile and unintelligent. They are under the rule of the Wicked

Witch and are grateful to be liberated. May be a reference to Asian immigrants (Chinese miners and railroad workers).

The Good Witch of the North – The North, a land of forests, may mean the Upper Midwest, or the Old Northwest. (Baum was from Upstate New York.) She is a friend of the Munchkins, associated with the land of blue.

Glinda, the Good Witch of the South – Described as having red hair, a white dress and blue eyes, the colors of patriotism. Her people, who are also good and friendly, are dressed in red.

The Winged Monkeys – Probably American Indians. These were mischievous, free-living creatures of nature previously from the North, who were under the rule of the Wicked Witch of the West. They have a king.

The Munchkins – People of the East, previously dominated by a bad witch. Good, friendly people, dressed in blue (the color of the Union).

Hammer Heads – They occupy a hill that leads to the land of the South, and use their strong heads to keep travellers from getting there. These are perhaps hard-headed individuals who promote sectionalism or the isolation of the South.

The Wizard as a Head – How he is seen by Dorothy as someone too smart and intimidating to be challenged.

The Wizard as a Beautiful Woman – How he is seen by the Scarecrow, suggesting that agrarians are being seduced by deceitful politicians.

The Wizard as a Monster – How he appears to the Tin Woodman. For laborers, Washington represents oppression and aggression.

The Wizard as a Ball of Fire – How he appears to the Lion. Indeed, the Lion gets too close and is burned by him, perhaps an analogy to what happened to Bryan and other reformers when they sought to take on Washington.

The Yellow Brick Road – The road of gold leading to the Emerald City, or Washington.

The Silver Slippers – They are powerful, but their power remains unknown to their possessor, Dorothy. This suggests that common people sensed the power of silver and the monetary issue, but never understood it completely. (Or, that the power of silver was imaginary.) When Dorothy travels in the silver slippers down the yellow brick road, she symbolizes bimetallism.

Nine O'Clock, Four Minutes Past – Having slain the Witch of the West,

Dorothy and her band return to the Wizard, demanding their promised reward, and are admitted to see him at this time. This appears to be a reference to Coxey's army, which included many former veterans, who marched from the West to Washington in 1894, demanding their just reward. Like Dorothy and her friends, they were disappointed.

Seven Passages and Three Flights of Stairs – This is the path that Dorothy must take to reach her room within the Wizard's palace. It appears to be a reference to the Crime of '73, in which silver was demonetized.

Index

Abbott, Joseph, 118
Abbott, Willis, 234
Adams, Brooks, 182, 185
Age of Reform, The (Hofstader), 13
agriculture sector
  see also credit system; farmers
  commercial paper credit lines, 176
  credit needs of (1882–1902), 156
  credit practices, 202–3
  credit solution in Populist subtreasury
    plan, 187
Alexander, S.B., 118, 213
Altgeld, John Peter, 231, 234–6, 239–40,
  250
  attack on Republicans (1896), 171
  campaign (1896), 239
  progressive ideas of, 231, 236
  radicalism, 235
American Bimetallic Union
  on demonetization of silver, 180–1
  nationalism of, 182
  on silver monometallism, 184–5
American Federation of Labor (AF of L),
  54, 232
Anderson, Eric, 114
Anti-contraction Bill (1867), 42
antimonopolism
  after 1896 election, 258
  conceptions of history to analyze, 9–16
  Denmark, 273–6
  financial proposals, 261–2
  in Illinois, 256
  Illinois (post-Civil War era), 124, 127
  legacy of, 276–81
  of Populist subtreasury plan, 187, 263
  post-Civil War position, 4–8
  reading of *The Wonderful Wizard of Oz*,
    288–90
  tenets of, 2
  third parties of, 8, 33, 47–8, 55–8

antimonopolist parties. *see* Greenback
  party; People's (Populist) party
antimonopolists
  opposition to gold standard, 263
  opposition to National Banking System,
    262–3
  position on role of government, 105
Appleton, Nathaniel, 86
Arena, 245–6
Armstrong, K.L., 180, 192
Atkinson, Edward, 159, 162, 165–6, 171,
  243–5
  opposition to financial reform, 141–2
  position on free banking, 82

Baird, Henry Carey, 105, 198, 199
Baltimore Plan, 174–5
banking system
  see also banking systems, state-level;
    National Banking System (NBS)
  antimonopolist view of U.S., 6–7
  concentration of funds in New York,
    156–7
  conservative idea of free banking, 81–2
  debate over reform (1890s), 173
  Denmark, 273–6
  in depression (1893), 46
  early criticism of U.S., 3–4
  effect of NBS structure on, 200–201
  expansion (1882–1902), 155
  financial reformers' criticism of,
    194–200
  historical background, 66–73
  ideas related to (1870s), 63–4
  Illinois (post-Civil War era), 124–5, 130;
    125
  Illinois (pre-Civil War), 125
  Massachusetts (post-Civil War era),
    136–7
  National Banking Act (1863), 30

291